GUIDANCE AND COUNSELING IN GROUPS

McGRAW-HILL SERIES
IN EDUCATION

HAROLD BENJAMIN, *Consulting Editor-in-Chief*

ARNO A. BELLACK   *Teachers College, Columbia University*
CONSULTING EDITOR, CURRICULUM AND METHODS IN EDUCATION

HAROLD BENJAMIN   *Emeritus Professor of Education*
George Peabody College for Teachers
CONSULTING EDITOR, FOUNDATIONS IN EDUCATION

HARLAN HAGMAN   *Wayne State University*
CONSULTING EDITOR, ADMINISTRATION IN EDUCATION

NICHOLAS HOBBS   *George Peabody College for Teachers*
CONSULTING EDITOR, PSYCHOLOGY
AND HUMAN DEVELOPMENT IN EDUCATION

WALTER F. JOHNSON   *Michigan State University*
CONSULTING EDITOR, GUIDANCE, COUNSELING,
AND STUDENT PERSONNEL IN EDUCATION

GUIDANCE, COUNSELING, AND STUDENT PERSONNEL IN EDUCATION

WALTER F. JOHNSON, *Consulting Editor*

Bailard and Strang, *Parent-Teacher Conferences*

Bennett, *Guidance and Counseling in Groups*

Berdie, *Testing in Guidance and Counseling*

Bernhardt, *Discipline and Child Guidance*

Detjen and Detjen, *Elementary School Guidance*

Hoppock, *Occupational Information*

Johnson, Stefflre, and Edelfelt, *Pupil Personnel and Guidance Services*

Jones, *Principles of Guidance*

Stefflre, *Theories of Counseling*

Warters, *Techniques of Counseling*

Williamson, *Vocational Counseling*

laine

MARGARET E. BENNETT

Formerly, Director of Guidance and
Psychologist, Pasadena City Schools

GUIDANCE AND COUNSELING IN GROUPS

SECOND EDITION

McGRAW-HILL BOOK COMPANY, INC.

New York / San Francisco / Toronto / London

GUIDANCE AND COUNSELING IN GROUPS

III

PREFACE

This revision of *Guidance in Groups* is virtually a new book. Obviously, the title has been changed, and the entire organization of chapters has been revamped. A major portion of the content has been completely re-written and new chapters have been added. Bibliographies have been thoroughly revised.

The basic viewpoint with respect to group aspects of guidance and personnel work remains unchanged, but it has been expanded to include new developments in research and practice since the first edition was written about seven years ago.

The services with which this book deals are those of helping individuals (*a*) to understand themselves and others better; (*b*) to understand factors in their environment that influence their lives significantly; (*c*) to envisage the life goals for which they wish to strive; and (*d*) to achieve skill in self-direction in making choices, decisions, plans, and adjustments in har-mony with their growing knowledge of inner and outer forces in their lives, both in the present and the future.

It is assumed that the realization of these objectives involves many learnings, some of which can best be achieved in group situations; that others require individual counseling; and that there should be a con-tinuous reciprocal relationship between these two phases of guidance. This book deals with the group approaches through which this service is rendered.

Some of the sources of the group approach predate the counseling service; others have stemmed from it. The attempt has been made to trace some of these sources from their origins in order to sharpen our perspec-tives on present tasks by viewing them in the light of past developments and possible future trends. Pertinent research and descriptions of practices have been drawn upon not only from the educational field but also from the fields of sociology, psychology, and psychiatry.

This is not a how-to-do-it book nor a critique of research. The effort has been made to consider the *what, why, where,* and *how.* The *how* has not been dealt with by means of specific prescriptions as to methods. Varieties of techniques have been described. Research and experience have been drawn upon to provide background information for the various guidance areas that have been considered. It is assumed that a guidance leader will be creative in adapting techniques and information to each group and doubtless develop many new and novel approaches.

The *where* refers to both organization and personnel, and these vary considerably among educational institutions. A basic assumption throughout the book is that a total school staff is involved in a group guidance program with a definite plan for the distribution of functions on the basis of competencies. The competencies needed for group guidance are viewed in the light of professional standards for all phases of personnel work.

The new chapter on group counseling and the inclusion of *counseling* in the book title are responses to a rapidly developing phase of therapeutic group work. The writer has questioned the use of the term *group counseling* in recent years because of possible confusion of terminology in personnel work. However, having accidentally unearthed her own article published in 1928 dealing with "guidance and counseling in groups," it was decided to yield to the inevitable and accept the term graciously!

As with the first edition, there is a painful awareness of the limitations of the treatment of a subject that could be as broad and inclusive as life itself. However, the human need for the guidance service presses upon all of us in the personnel field and we require the courage to live with the uncertainties and break new ground as our understanding of life expands.

Appreciative acknowledgment is made to all authors and publishers who have given permission for the use of materials as indicated in the text, also to a multitude of students and innumerable professional co-workers who have shared their wisdom and encouraged experimentation over many years.

Margaret E. Bennett

CONTENTS

ix

PART THREE.
THE AREAS FOR GROUP GUIDANCE

Appendix   *383*

Self-descriptive Q-sort Statements of Trends of Group Members, 385. A Check List for Appraising a Secondary School Guidance Program, 387. Review Form: Occupational Literature According to NVGA Standards, 393. Problems in Vocational Planning, 395. Pasadena Pupil Judgment Test, 400. A Bibliography of Visual Aids, 404.

PART ONE

AN OVERVIEW

One psychologist (1) has expressed the conviction that this realm of choice is the peculiar heritage of counseling psychology; another (2) has written that research in the process of decision making is one of the two great research needs in the personnel field, the other being that of vocational development.

1 THE PLACE OF GROUP PROCEDURES IN GUIDANCE

Living within the complex, swiftly shifting currents of our modern culture requires a continuous succession of choices and decisions. Some of our choices are trivial and some are momentous in their influences upon our lives. Cumulatively, all decisions, big or little, play an important part in determining what we are becoming as individuals.

The choices and decisions we make and our ways of reacting to ourselves, to others, and to the vicissitudes of living are at any point in our lives the resultant of many interrelated factors. We rarely have available all the information that could help us to make the most intelligent judgments in formulating decisions. Usually we do not recognize all the inner motives that lead to these judgments. Often we do not control consciously the thought processes that lead to decisions. However, the more effectively we learn to marshal available pertinent facts, to understand our motives and drives, and to use sound problem-solving techniques in making choices and judgments, the more rational the control we can exercise in determining either what we do or how we react to the challenges of life. The development of this self-mastery and self-direction is a major goal of guidance. Our life goals and standards of value are products of this process and in turn serve as criteria in the choice of life activities.

Each stage of development in life presents all of us with many common problems, since there are common factors in our human nature and in our environment. On the other hand, individual and environmental differences cause many variations in the nature of problems or in the particular combinations of common problems faced by any person at a given time. Graduate students or experienced educators are as likely to have unsolved problems as are adolescents or children, and people in later maturity may have as many or more. Having problems is characteristic of living. One of the challenges of guidance, and of all education, is that of helping individuals to meet and solve problems and to develop skill in making choices and adjustments at each stage of development.

3

One psychologist (1)[1] has expressed the conviction that this realm of choice is the peculiar heritage of counseling psychology; another (2) has written that research in the process of decision making is one of the two great research needs in the personnel field, the other being that of vocational development.

THE GUIDANCE SERVICE

Words have been likened to little boats coming down from the past laden with all the meanings that have become attached to them. The word *guidance* has acquired a varied cargo of meanings over the years, *so* varied that some have suggested that a new term be found to subsume those services currently recognized as essential to the fullest self-development and self-realization of individuals in a democratic culture, and now also recognized as essential to the defense, maintenance, and improvement of our American way of life. Since an adequate substitute seems to be lacking, the word *guidance* is used herein to include all those services, whether on an individual or a group basis, that contribute to the individual's growing understanding of himself: his developing self-concepts, his attitudes, interests, and abilities, his physical, mental, and social maturity, and his personal and social needs for optimum development and achievement as a unique person and a democratic citizen. It includes services that help each individual, not only to gain self-understanding, but also to develop skill in self-direction: (*a*) in establishing suitable personal, educational, and vocational goals; (*b*) in planning desirable ways of pursuing these goals; and (*c*) in developing standards of value consistent with his life goals, so that he will be provided with criteria for the choice of experiences.

The person who has developed this skill in self-direction has inner resources for meeting the full range of life experiences. He might be described as an *integrating* person who can appropriate the values of each new experience and come to terms with inner and outer changes without a disintegrating loss of equilibrium.

Self-knowledge and self-direction are not static achievements that can result from a few interviews. They are dependent upon many types of learning and are lifelong quests. Guidance services should launch each individual soundly on these quests.

The preliminary report of the Commission on Guidance in American Schools, sponsored by the American Personnel and Guidance Association, contains the following summary statement as to why guidance in schools exists (3, p. 4):

---

[1] Parenthetic numbers refer to numbered references in chapter bibliographies.

Guidance services in our schools today are the direct outgrowth of the values of our American culture, namely, our concern for the individuality of each child and youth, our belief in freedom of choice, in individual self-realization, in planning for the future.

In a national and world culture that is accelerating its rate of change, the counselor's task is to: help young people set and maintain a personal pace that is adjusted to the changing pace in society; personalize the educational experience of the student; help the student find meaning in the present and to see relation between the present and the future. To accomplish these goals the counselor must develop an understanding of the persisting psychological needs of youth, needs that will be intensified by the rapid rate of social change. It is increasingly apparent that the counselor must understand the changing culture as well as the developing individual.

GROUP PROCEDURES IN GUIDANCE

In this book the term *group guidance* refers to any phase of a guidance or personnel program carried on with groups of individuals rather than between counselor and counselee or clinician and client in the face-to-face interview. It may include instruction in the classroom where the content is related to problems of self-appraisal, educational or vocational guidance, personal adjustment, and interpersonal relationships. It may embody a great variety of activities in the extracurriculum that relate to these same areas. It includes many types of informal play or discussion groups, which often serve the double purpose of studying individuals in their interaction with others as well as helping them to work through certain difficulties and achieve new levels of adjustment. This process may involve *unlearning* as one step toward new learning.

More intensive forms of group procedure, usually operating at deeper levels of the personality than those previously mentioned, are frequently called *group counseling* and *multiple counseling*. These terms are used with somewhat different connotations by various personnel workers, sometimes referring to groups with common problems and sometimes to those with heterogeneous problems. The most intensive form is called *group therapy*, which is now widely used in psychological and psychiatric practice for individuals with severe emotional handicaps. In this book methods commonly used in schools will be called *small-group counseling* and *therapeutic group counseling*.

Why have these group procedures developed? Many of the early efforts in education grew out of the realization of inadequacies of the traditional instructional program for meeting needs of students. For many years homeroom, orientation, and group-guidance programs have been aimed at assistance in adjusting to new school or college situations; improving study and learning methods; making new friends; improving social skills; learning to get along better with others; solving problems of growing up and establishing adult status; learning to appraise interests and abilities, and to make suitable educational and vocational plans; meeting frustrations wholesomely; and developing a workable philosophy of life values to furnish criteria for the choice of life experiences. What was often implicit and incidental in good teaching became explicit in organized instructional units or courses.

The new realization of youth needs was due in part to the increased emphasis on the individual fostered by personnel or guidance programs. These guidance programs have traversed several stages in the past three or four decades, and these changes have tended to bring the individual and the group approaches into closer relationship as to purposes and, increasingly, as to functions. These stages in the growth of personnel programs may be characterized roughly as (a) remedial, (b) preventive, and (c) developmental.

Some of the earliest guidance services were introduced to care for individuals with special problems, such as behavior difficulties, poor scholarship, or occupational maladjustment. These early efforts with special groups led to awareness of possibilities for helping to prevent maladjustments through services to all individuals. Here is where group approaches began to enter the picture, though much of the effort was carried on through expanded counseling services. This was the period when many counselors were "studying" and "advising" students and teachers were "instructing" them. The third or developmental stage, which has been gathering momentum for some time, is based upon the recognition that the total educational program, including the curriculum, the extracurriculum, and guidance, serves the purposes of helping individuals to learn and to mature. Within guidance this learning and maturing process relates to understanding of self, and self-direction in choosing experiences, planning ahead, and working out harmonious adjustments of plans in all phases of living.

The widespread use of the word *adjustment* by personnel workers has been challenged by some because of its supposed connotation of fitting the individual to the environment, or of changing one's purposes if the environment cannot be changed to fit the individual.

The word *maturation* has been suggested as a substitute for *adjustment*, with the assumption that mature or integrated people are not merely adjusted people, but those "who are intelligently about the work of ordering life and harmonizing it on an ever higher scale of human excellence" (4). It is difficult to see how any personnel worker could take issue with this definition of a mature and integrated person, but the Latin root of the word *adjustment* is defined in the dictionary as meaning "to bring into harmony with a general plan." In this sense of the word, it seems to express exactly what we are trying, through guidance, to help individuals to do in their lives. Therefore, we shall use the word as applying to a lifelong process carried on by maturing and integrating individuals (rather than mature and integrated), since ideally the process is never completed.

From the beginning, guidance services have been deeply involved in the question of adjustment, first of the few, but now of all. And this concern is presently directed not only toward prevention of academic, personal, and social difficulties, but toward the positive development of maturing and integrating individuals who can come to terms with life in the sense of finding or making personally satisfying and socially useful outlets for their potentialities and of recognizing and caring suitably for liabilities which everyone has in some degree. Obviously, these newer goals cannot be achieved through a few counseling interviews alone—nor without this counseling, we should add emphatically. Many phases of the group approach to guidance have developed in response to these new sights on the purposes of guidance and of all education.

Many of the traditional aspects of educational programs have taken on new meaning in the light of the newer objectives and have developed in new directions. Extracurricular activities provide innumerable life situations ideal for purposeful learning, and as these possibilities have been more fully envisaged, it has been suggested that the prefix *extra* should be left off or *co* substituted to indicate that these out-of-class activities are on a par with classroom activities in their educative functions.

Traditional subjects have likewise undergone change in the direction of more explicit applications of content to everyday problems of living. Core, general-education, and life-adjustment programs have incorporated many of the features of the specific group-guidance classes. And the group-guidance classes, where not absorbed into the other programs, have frequently taken on various new features more specifically related to the counseling services than were some of the earlier courses that were aimed, somewhat in shotgun fashion, at meeting numerous inadequacies in the older instructional program.

The present period of rapid technological development, ideological conflicts, widespread intercommunication within and among expanding national and world cultures, and the intensification of the defense program to preserve and improve our democratic culture is having significant impacts upon educational and guidance programs. The Commission on Guidance in American Schools anticipates that schools will focus more upon their major functions of intellectual growth while attempting to maintain a continued concern for social, vocational, and personal growth, and that some earlier guidance functions will be absorbed into the total school program of instruction and administration. On the other hand it is pointed out that an increased number of specialists in the area of personnel work will be needed to contribute to the individual's integration of school learnings with his growing understanding of himself, to relate school experience to out-of-school experience, to aid in planning for the future, and to relate present to possible future. One of the major functions of these specialists outlined in Wrenn's report is: "To use planned group situations as carefully as the interview is utilized in the development of improved student self-understanding and the facing of psychological realities" (3, p. 15). Group guidance appears to be coming into its own as an essential professional function in a modern personnel program.

THE PURPOSES OF GROUP GUIDANCE

The discussion here of purposes of group procedures in guidance is intended to apply to any of these group procedures, whether designated as guidance or not, if their functions include assistance to students in self-discovery, self-direction, and adjustment. The boundaries are naturally tenuous, since most subject areas contribute something to these objectives. Again, it should be borne in mind that purposes, techniques, and the relationship to counseling, rather than content, are basic criteria in classifying a group activity as guidance.

With these considerations in mind, the following outline of purposes of group procedures is suggested as covering most of the objectives of the various approaches.

1. To provide opportunities for learning essential for self-direction with respect to educational, vocational, and personal-social aspects of life through
    a. Assistance in orientation in new school situations and in the best use of school opportunities
    b. Group study of problems of interpersonal relationships and assistance in choice of group experiences in the school life that may modify both individual and group behavior in socially acceptable ways
    c. Group study of problems of growing up, establishing adult adjustments, and applying mental hygiene in living
    d. Group study and application of sound methods of self-appraisal of attitudes, interests, abilities, personality and character trends and traits, and personal-social adjustments

    e. Group study and application of efficiency methods in learning

    f. Group study about occupational life and problems of occupational adjustment and progress

    g. Assistance through groups in learning how to project suitable, long-range vocational plans

    h. Assistance through groups in learning how to project suitable, long-range educational plans

    i. Assistance in the development of discerning standards of value for making choices of experiences in various areas of living, and the developing of a growing philosophy of life

2. To provide opportunity for the therapeutic effects of group procedures through

    a. The perspectives gained from the study of common human problems

    b. The release of emotional tensions, increased insight into personality dynamics, and creative redirection of energy through group study of these common human problems in a permissive atmosphere

3. To achieve some of the objectives of guidance more economically—and some more effectively—than would be possible in a completely individualized approach

4. To implement individual counseling and render it more effective through background study of common aspects of problems and the reduction or elimination of many emotional barriers to the discussion of unique aspects of common human problems

To summarize: One of the most significant developments in the personnel or guidance point of view in recent years is the recognition that guidance is a *learning process,* for both the guidance worker and the individual, and that this learning for both parties occurs through both interviews and group procedures.

For years we talked and wrote glibly about self-knowledge, self-direction, and adjustment as guidance objectives, but proceeded to assume often that these goals would be reached in the course of a few interviews with a counselor and in incidental guidance throughout the entire educational program. We have been slow in the guidance field in analyzing all the various learnings that are essential for the achievement of our objectives, and in planning where and how the opportunities for these learnings shall be provided. Too often it was merely assumed that they were occurring, by some mysterious process, without considering the disparity between training time necessary for even an experienced teacher to learn how to be a good guidance worker and the time provided for immature students to learn and acquire skill in self-direction.

Learnings Essential for Self-direction

An inspection of the purposes of group procedures previously outlined will readily suggest a vast array of learning situations and types of information, skills, and attitudes that would be involved in these various situations. Some of these will be examined in later chapters dealing with orientation in new school situations, methods of learning to learn, questions of self-appraisal, personality development and interpersonal relationships, and of vocational and educational guidance. At this point we shall take a brief overview of some of the characteristics of these learnings that are especially essential if they are to contribute to power of self-direction.

1. *Learning to understand and face real problems.* In Chapter 3 we shall examine many problems and worries expressed by individuals of various ages through surveys and clinical studies. These concerns of individuals are excellent starting points for learning, but the search for causes of sensed difficulties is likely to lead into many devious bypaths. Counseling and clinical study have shown that expressed problems are not necessarily the real or basic ones. Often these have been lost from conscious awareness and are difficult to recover. A child who is angry in a particular situation may be taking out in that situation the results of other experiences, which he does not relate to the particular anger he is experiencing at the moment. The causes may even lie far back in his early training and be totally unknown to him. A young woman in a group-therapy class brought up the question of what she should do about her terrific sense of pressure in trying to keep many activities going—music, art, teaching, church and club work, and her home duties with husband and children. At the start she expressed the feeling that her strong ego drive was pushing her on in the many fields in which she had talent, but she admitted a sense of guilt over the possible neglect of home responsibilities. There are strong intimations that she may be escaping from some of her real problems through her present welter of activities, but her learning process has not yet brought her to the point where she can see these other possibilities.

It is sometimes painful to face our real problems. Skillful guidance or therapy is frequently needed to help in the process. But, when one learns that something can be done about them when they are understood, then learning to face and define real problems can become as interesting and challenging as learning the approach to a puzzle or the nature of a handicap in golf, tennis, or swimming.

2. *Learning the techniques of analyzing problems.* A normally well-adjusted person will enter into the succession of events in his life with

a fair degree of spontaneity and without conscious analysis of too many of the situations he meets with. However, because of the continuous change in ourselves and in life about us, no two of our life situations are ever exactly the same. Either we form rigid, and therefore often unsuitable, habits of reacting in these varied circumstances, or we learn to adapt our reactions to each unique event. Often, of course, our behavior may be partly suitable and partly unsuitable, and the results are then likely to be both satisfying and unsatisfying in various respects and to create new problems.

The more we can learn to analyze situations—a process that involves the recognition of our own needs, motives, and drives as well as those of others in a particular relationship and the reality demands of the environment upon both—the greater conscious control we can exercise over the part we play. Doubtless, this process can be mastered to the point where we are as free and spontaneous in living as in the performance of a skill such as dancing, driving a car, or playing a musical instrument. It is surely as important a technique as any of these others, but vastly more complex.

Most of our problems in living relate to interpersonal factors, even though some of our specific concerns may seem quite personal, such as appearance, success in an undertaking, or the desire to do or have something. Usually they involve considerations of one's relationships with others or of mutual welfare of oneself and others. Almost always there are multiple factors in any problem, and unless we can discover and understand these various factors, we cannot tackle solutions intelligently.

3. *Learning to use many sources of information in the study and solution of problems.* It has been said that any phase of life probed deeply enough will touch all phases of living. Life is not confined in compartments similar to our subjects in the curriculum. But every field of study makes its contributions to the understanding of life. To study a life-planning or adjustment problem soundly, one must draw upon information from many sources—subject areas in the curriculum, human experience past and present, both one's own and that of others. There will be gaps in the knowledge that is needed no matter how searching one's efforts have been. Here is a point in the guidance service where every teacher can make significant contributions by helping students to see the bearings of various fields of study on the understanding of human life and on its living.

A crucial step in group guidance is the learning to use knowledge in making choices, plans, and life adjustments. Knowledge will have no value in these processes unless it is related to the unique needs and circumstances of individuals. Acquiring knowledge and learning to make these adaptations can be achieved in part through group procedures, but counseling is needed to carry through on some of the adaptations of knowledge to individual needs. For example, groups can study profitably about the world of work, can learn about sound methods of self-appraisal, can take group tests, and proceed a fair distance in the compiling and organizing of data about self and proposed occupations. But a point is reached where implications of the data need to be studied individually with a trained counselor, who can help the person in both interpretation and applications in plans and action.

4. *Learning to understand and direct inner drives to action.* This is the most complicated aspect of learning, and one which is probably never fully achieved. Our drives are often conflicting and usually interrelated. Many are unrecognized results of earlier unconscious repressions, which are camouflaged even to ourselves by mechanisms of rationalization, projection, and all the devious ways of protecting our egos from facing derogatory or apprehensive considerations. Some of the activating unconscious repressions stemming from infancy and early childhood are so deeply imbedded in the personality and so thoroughly camouflaged that they cannot be uncovered without psychotherapeutic assistance.

Those who deal with the neurotic conflicts resulting from these repressions are increasingly urging that parents and teachers learn how to recognize difficulties in their early stages, how to prevent traumatic experiences that lead to repression, and how to teach children to recognize and deal with conflicts before they become serious.

5. *Learning to understand and get along with others.* Learning to understand self and others are reciprocal processes. Each helps the other. We can try to describe very simply what is a very complicated process by saying that each person is the result of what he started with, what has happened to him, and how he has reacted to his life experiences. It has been said that if we understood all these interacting forces in the life of an individual, we would never criticize him, because we would understand exactly why he acted as he did and would realize that his action was a natural result of the past. Of course, we can never reconstruct all the links in the chain of past events either for ourselves or others, but the search to understand as much as possible leads to objective acceptance of self and others rather than to critical and intolerant or overly euphemistic judgments.

This awareness of the operation of cause and effect in our lives clears the way for greater understanding of causal factors, the setting of goals, and more enlightened efforts to achieve the goals. Also, an accepting attitude toward others engendered by the attempt to understand them fosters good human relationships, which are a means to self-development and maturing for everyone.

6. *Learning to formulate long-range life plans.* The future is to a certain extent an unknown emergence. But one partial control that we have in this ongoing process is that of projecting plans on the basis of all we can learn about our potentialities, about trends and probable opportunities in the world about us, and realistic goals that can strike fire in our imagination, help to light the path ahead, and provide incentives for our efforts.

Guidance in this process is no simple task. The knowledge, attitudes, and skills required to project these plans soundly and realistically cannot be acquired incidentally or in a few brief interviews. They require co-operative, long-range efforts of the entire school personnel throughout the period of formal education and the concerted efforts of guidance workers at crucial points in the life span.

7. *Learning to establish a desirable balance between immediate and long-range goals.* Satisfying rewards of effort seem to be important for effective learning. The ability to strive for distant goals is an aspect of maturing, but it can become a meaningless habit or be lost through discouragement due to lack of adequate satisfactions along the way. Each teacher plans for intermediate satisfactions or rewards for learners. In the same way the individual who would direct his lifetime learning must know how to plan wisely for his intermediate satisfactions that help to give meaning to life as he moves toward the more distant goals.

8. *Developing criteria for the choice of experiences.* Choices of friends, of associates, and of activities in work, home, recreation, and civic affairs determine in large measure what life shall be. All the previous learnings that have been mentioned enter into these choices. The mature person has developed a system of values, or a life philosophy, which serves as a guide in the innumerable choices, little or big, that life presents. This system of values needs to be made articulate if it is to serve its purpose as a rational guide. An honest effort to formulate it will often help to reveal the conflicting motives that play upon it and thus lead to further self-discovery. Every phase of education should contribute to the development of significant life values, but somewhere and at expedient times there should be the opportunity to examine them with discernment and reformulate them in the light of new experience.

9. *Learning to move from knowledge and plans to action.* Erudition and beautiful plans may mean no more than an adolescent daydream unless they are translated into action and eventuate in better living. The applications of knowledge are the criteria in guidance of whether any functional learning has occurred. A pupil may decide to be more sociable, but he may need to learn to dance, or to improve his conversational skill, and if he fails to take this intermediate step, nothing is likely to happen with his original plan. Another pupil may decide that he needs to im-

prove his reading ability, but unless he formulates and carries out a remedial program, probably with much routine practice on difficulties, his planned reading improvement is not likely to occur. The habit of carrying through on suitable goals and plans is exceedingly important for self-direction.

10. *Learning to evaluate progress and reformulate goals and plans as the need is indicated.* Modifications in goals and plans are inevitable through life. Learning to appraise developing interests and new evidences of potentialities while in school and to readjust educational and vocational plans in harmony with new insights is excellent preparation for the continuous adjustment to inner and outer change in adult years. One aspect of this learning in school is to discriminate between ephemeral interests that may cause immature shifts in choices and plans and the more basic changes that have real significance for life planning. Evaluation of progress in every area of school experience should enter into this self-appraisal.

None of these learnings essential for self-direction can be acquired in a few simple lessons or in a few interviews. Most individuals will not acquire them incidentally except the hard way by trial, error, and much wasted effort. A well-planned program of opportunities for learning through group procedures and counseling suited to the needs of successive age levels is necessary if the guidance objective of effective self-direction is to be achieved. Important responsibilities of a group leader in guidance are (*a*) to use understanding of essential learnings in the cooperative planning with groups of ways to study and resolve problems of which they are aware; (*b*) to help them broaden and deepen their sights with respect to ramifications of immediate interests and needs; and (*c*) to guide them toward the recognition of other needs with which they are ready to cope.

THERAPEUTIC ASPECTS OF GROUP GUIDANCE

Guidance workers who have observed the lowered tension and reassurance of individuals who have become aware through group study that many others have worries and problems similar to theirs, and who have faced the increased demand for individual conferences when barriers to revealing these problems and securing help in solving them have thus been eliminated, need little proof through experimental research as to the therapeutic results of well-planned and skillfully conducted group discussions. Evidence is mounting through research, but the findings as to therapeutic outcomes vary greatly with the type of group experience provided and the measuring instruments used in the experiment. Two studies will be cited briefly in this overview chapter. Others will be considered in later chapters in relation to specific types of group services.

Caplan (5) compared outcomes for experimental and control groups of junior high school boys, grades 7 to 9, referred as unruly, antisocial, unteachable, or incorrigible. The group counseling was carried on weekly for a semester and interviews with their school counselors were available to both control and experimental boys. The Q technique was used to measure self and ideal-self concepts at the beginning and end of the experimental period. The data indicated nonrandom increases in the congruence of the self and ideal-self sorts for the experimental group but not for the control group. A significant decrease in the number of poor citizenship marks occurred in the experimental group and none had poorer records. No such significant decrease occurred in the total control group. The author comments that if a more integrated self-structure enables one to be less tense, less disturbed, and more accepting and understanding of others, it might be reasonably hoped that positive changes in behavior might also occur. The positive changes in citizenship marks within the experimental group would seem to support this hypothesis. The caution is added that the changes may have represented only temporary progress, but the conclusion is drawn that group counseling is a promising method for dealing with problems of adolescents and warrants serious consideration and further investigation.

Leino (6) compared the measured outcomes for college students in a twelve-week personal-adjustment course with those for an equated group in a psychology class. The methods in the adjustment course involved permissive, accepting, informal teaching and frequent use of camouflaged case studies. Among the limited outcomes of this course were increased staying power in college as compared with the psychology group, and some significant gains in maturity, independence, and emotional adequacy as measured, but these latter results were inconsistent for subgroups within the two experimental classes. No significant improvements were found in self-understanding and there was no consistent pattern for social adequacy. The author of the study commented that students would have liked to discuss more problems of real concern to them; also, that twelve weeks of study could not perhaps have had too significant effects upon lives that had been nineteen or twenty years in developing, and that suitability of measuring instruments should be considered in drawing conclusions about such a course.

ECONOMY AND EFFECTIVENESS OF GROUP PROCEDURES

The economy of assisting a small or a class-sized group, or even a larger group in some instances, with a common guidance problem, rather than dealing with all phases of the problem in separate individual interviews, would seem to need no proof or arguments, *provided* the service could be as effective for all using the group situation.

In the early days of group guidance in educational institutions, it was frequently assumed that much of the guidance carried on by counselors through interviews could be done through class groups. Slogans such as "Every teacher a guidance worker" appealed to administrators pressed with problems of stretching school budgets, and sometimes a sound counseling program was seriously curtailed or superseded by attempts at economy through so-called group counseling. When these efforts failed to achieve desired outcomes, the onus was often unjustly borne by the group procedures, which had merely been unsoundly applied by untrained personnel.

A crucial need is for thorough analysis of all the various aspects of guidance, together with experimental research to ascertain:

1. What phases can best be carried on in groups
2. What aspects require the individual interview
3. How these two procedures complement each other in the total guidance service

Research and practice have yielded significant, but as yet only partial, answers to these questions. One published research study that bears on them is that of Stone (7), who investigated the outcomes of a vocational-orientation course in the curriculum of the General College at the University of Minnesota. Both the experimental and control groups received vocational counseling, but members of the control group did not have the vocational-guidance course. Stone found that the combination of the vocational-orientation course and counseling resulted in more appropriate vocational choices in terms of abilities, aptitudes, and interests than did either service alone. The vocational-orientation course, by itself, without counseling, did not appear to be effective in offsetting poor choices by students, but it served as a preparation for counseling, and tended to reduce the amount of time needed to resolve educational and vocational problems. Also, significant favorable changes in social adjustment seemed to result from a combination of counseling and course instruction in vocational orientation.

An evaluation by the author (8) of an orientation course for eleventh-year and thirteenth-year students at a four-year junior college, using control groups with no orientation to compare with the experimental orientation groups, yielded significant differences in average scores on a battery of tests dealing with informational aspects of the program, and on quality of thinking with respect to reasons given for educational and vocational plans. Reasons for attending college had not changed. Comparison of orientation and nonorientation groups with respect to participation in student activities, leadership, and social adjustment, as measured by ratings over a two-year period, consistently favored the orientation group, but the differences were not statistically reliable. The tests of information developed for this evaluation were used later to study two orientation classes which were conducted as informal-discussion groups, without any organized plan of study and with no resource materials at their disposal. The average scores for these groups at the end of a semester were approximately the same as at the beginning. The information scores for the experimental group in the original study dealing with matters presented in lectures at the beginning of the semester under conditions somewhat comparable to Freshman Week programs did not show as large gains during the semester as did those dealing with problems studied more systematically with text and reference materials under the guidance of their counselors.

IMPLEMENTING INDIVIDUAL COUNSELING

Much of the research on interrelations of group and individual procedures has been directed to an evaluation of the group approach as preparation for the counseling interview. Richardson and Borow (9), who had taught the vocational-orientation course at the University of Minnesota, set up an experiment in which two groups of students with no previous vocational counseling were compared with respect to the effectiveness of their participation in interviews for vocational and educational counseling and their later ratings of the value of the interviews. The experimental group was prepared for the counseling through a lecture by the dean of the college and a group discussion led by an experienced counselor. Thus opportunity was afforded to consider the purposes of, and common misconceptions about, vocational counseling, the uses and limitations of psychological tests, and the appropriate roles of counselor and client. Each student in the control group merely received a letter from the dean of the college requesting that he make an appointment with a counselor to discuss educational and vocational plans. The same counselor served both groups without awareness of the group identity of each student.

The criteria used in the evaluation were: attitude-information tests containing items related to functions of the interview; a check list of possible interview complaints, and a rating of over-all value of the interview for the students; an estimate of the amount of client talk during the interview based on a simple count of the number of words spoken by each counselee; an estimate of the proportion of total talk contributed by each of the interview participants based on a client-counselor word-count ratio; and ratings of each client's interview behavior by three experienced counselors who read the typescripts of each of the seventy-six interviews.

The investigators concluded from the statistical comparisons of the two groups on these criteria that group orientation for counseling can potentially sharpen the client's conception of the counseling process and mold his verbal understanding of the roles of counselor, client, and tests in the vocational counseling interview. The control group registered more points of dissatisfaction with the interview than did the experimental group, but there was virtually no difference in the over-all value ratings of the two groups. The average experimental-group subject talked more than the average control-group subject. Ten out of fifteen ratings of the interviews by judges favored the experimental group; that is, the average experimental-group subject was rated as having exhibited the more effective interview behavior.

After reading this report, one is inclined to ask: If fifty minutes of group lecture and discussion can accomplish that much, what *could* be done through a more comprehensive, well-coordinated program of group and individual procedures?

Another intensive study of the influence of group orientation for counseling involved a comparison of two groups of students, one of which received an orientation period and a permissive counseling service; the other group had no orientation and was counseled in a traditional manner. The reactions of the counselees to the process were obtained by a third interviewer, and these interviews were analyzed in terms of the feeling tone of the clients, or positive statements about counseling and its effect. The individuals who had received the group orientation for the counseling expressed a more favorable evaluation on the feeling-tone criterion than did the others (10).

INTERRELATIONSHIPS OF GROUP AND INDIVIDUAL APPROACHES IN GUIDANCE

Years of trial-and-error methods and some sound experimentation and research have indicated that group and individual procedures in guidance are complementary aspects of a sound guidance program. Neither can fully take the place of the other, but each implements and supplements the other, rendering it more effective.

Basic factors common to both are that each procedure, properly used, involves learning on the part of both counselor and the counselee, and each may be therapeutic in its own way. The ways in which group and individual procedures implement each other are legion. A counselor who devotes full time to interviewing has very limited opportunities to observe his counselees in action in a group. Likewise, a full-time classroom teacher has limited opportunities to study personnel records of students and to conduct enough personal interviews to become well acquainted with the inner personality dynamics of students. The person who can combine both these functions with a given group of students is in an ideal position to understand their needs and develop a program adapted to these needs. This assumes that the worker has the training, insight, experience, and personal qualities to establish rapport either individually or in groups and really to understand and feel the dynamics of the personalities and the human relationships with which he is dealing. Thus endowed the guidance worker can bring to the classroom deep and rich understandings of members of the group. Through skillful group leadership he can help his students to become aware of their problems as common human problems, thus fostering knowledge about self and others—a learning aspect of group work—and helping to reduce tensions —one of the therapeutic aspects.

Most problems of adjustment or planning have individual facets which cannot be dealt with effectively in a group situation. However, with a background of successful group study, the counselor and counselee can approach these individual facets with economy of time and effort, and without the barriers of tensions due to embarrassment over supposed idiosyncrasies that have not been recognized as unique aspects of common human problems. New insights about students gained through interviews can, in turn, be used subtly to render group procedures more helpful. It is assumed that through both group and individual techniques the guidance worker holds in view as major objectives ultimate self-knowledge and self-direction on the part of those whom he serves. These objectives preclude or severely limit didactic teaching and prescriptive advice by the counselor, and emphasize purposeful learning and planning and wholesome release of emotional tensions on the part of the counselee.

COORDINATION OF GROUP GUIDANCE SERVICES

In school or college no one person or department can assume total responsibility for all the guidance services. All members of the school personnel make contributions, and each should understand clearly the nature and purpose of his guidance functions in relationship to the total guidance program. This cannot be mapped out definitively in the pages of a book, since functions will vary with the particular school organization and the total school program.

However, in any school, certain questions should be asked and carefully answered as the guidance program is planned and developed:

1. What aspects of group guidance can be carried on in classroom

situations by teachers and which require trained personnel workers? Suitable answers to this question require careful analyses of the total curriculum and the total guidance program and of requirements for effective conduct of each phase. This step leads to the next question and will, also, be a major concern throughout this book.

2. *Who* can do *what* aspects of guidance best? The answer to this question involves training, experience, competencies, interests, and personality of each member of the professional group, and the time and facilities available to each.

Many criteria have been set up for the requirements of those who perform guidance functions. There is no complete agreement on these standards, but there is increasing consensus on the broad outlines of requirements (see Chapter 7). Each professional staff faces the problem of appraisal of the qualifications of individual members as one approach to the question of who can do what best. Adequacies of staff members should be checked against job analyses of the various guidance services to answer the question.

This procedure is likely to uncover surprising resources within a school personnel. It may also prevent the placing of the responsibility for some of the most vital services to youths in the hands of individuals who may be willing, but who may also be thoroughly unprepared or unsuited. If the factors of time and of essential facilities such as private conference rooms, accessible personnel records, and instructional materials are likewise analyzed and appraised as to their availability, it is less likely that some workers will be asked, as it were, to make bricks without straw.

SOME COMMON MISCONCEPTIONS ABOUT GROUP GUIDANCE

1. *That group guidance, group process, and group dynamics are identical.* The burgeoning of interest and research in group dynamics has caused many to assume that effective group processes will automatically provide effective group guidance. Group processes that successfully involve individuals in active sharing of experiences with others are likely to result in increased understanding of self and others and in greater self-actualization and socialization. However, these outcomes are among the goals of the total educational program and may not contribute to specific guidance goals, except incidentally. Permissive, accepting, cohesive groups are essential factors in group guidance, but they are means to the achievement of guidance objectives, not ends in themselves. Group workers need to utilize these important means in programs aimed at guidance objectives for individuals.

2. *That the major purpose of group guidance is personal development.* This idea has been touched upon in the previous statement. Certainly the

fostering of self-realization is an essential aim of any guidance program, but this aim cannot be claimed exclusively by the personnel service. To do so would make guidance synonymous with all of education. The current trend is toward analysis of the specific functions of guidance in assisting individuals to choose long-range life goals, plan the steps whereby they progress toward these goals, and utilize their educational opportunities to the fullest extent. All educational opportunities through guidance and curriculum are thus partners in fostering self-development of persons.

3. *That group guidance is primarily an information service.* Information per se has little meaning except as it contributes to understanding of problems to be solved or decisions to be made. Some aspects of group guidance require more objective information than others. Life planning requires much educational, occupational, and social information as well as much self-knowledge but this information becomes significant only as it is related to thinking and decision making within this planning process. Understanding of self and the world is a lifelong process, but to be functional it must be integrated at each stage of development with some vital concerns of the person.

4. *That group guidance or counseling may be substituted for individual counseling.* This misconception which prevailed for many years needs little denial today, since experience and research have clearly demonstrated how each implements the other. The crucial need, as stated earlier, is for more evidence through research as to the areas in which each service can function most effectively and the ways in which services can best be coordinated.

5. *That group counseling is group therapy.* Interest in counseling in small groups has undoubtedly grown out of the widespread use of group therapy [2] by psychiatrists and psychologists in recent decades. However, it is as important to recognize the limits of school counselors in dealing with serious problems of maladjustment in group work as in individual counseling. The term *therapeutic group work* is a more suitable one to use within a personnel program, reserving the term *group therapy* for those who are trained and licensed or certified to serve those who are seriously handicapped according to medical classifications. This question will be considered more fully in Chapter 6.

6. *That any member of the school staff can carry on the group guidance function.* This idea has been applied for many years in the allocation of guidance functions to teachers in homerooms, social studies,

[2] Slavson is reputed to be responsible for introducing the term *group therapy* to meet criticisms regarding the use of the term *group psychotherapy* by other persons than psychiatrists or clinical psychologists. However, the term *therapy* has become practically synonymous with *psychotherapy* in professional literature.

English, and core classes. Doubtless the opprobrium directed to so-called *life-adjustment* classes, the recognition of the overwhelming administrative functions that have accumulated in homeroom programs, and the emphasis in the cold war period upon increased intellectualization of the educational program have helped to undermine this concept. Increased knowledge of the complexities of life planning and living in our rapidly changing technological world and the mounting threats to our way of life have produced increased awareness that guidance in human living may require as much training and skill as the mastery of our material environment. The Commission on Guidance in American Schools has recognized this fact in the recommendation that planned group situations must be used as carefully by trained personnel workers as the interview. No educator or personnel worker could question the important contributions to the guidance service that every teacher can make. The problem is that of a planned approach in which each staff member plays his appropriate role.

7. *That group guidance may stifle individuality and creativity.* This eventuality could readily happen if the group process were considered the end instead of the means in guidance. When the soundest self-actualization of the individual as a socialized member of a group is the objective of group guidance, this danger is minimized and the group process is used to serve individuals rather than to manipulate them to enhance the group. This is the basic tenet underlying our democratic way of life, and its skillful application in group guidance should contribute to the optimum benefit of both the individual and the group.

THE RAPID GROWTH OF GROUP GUIDANCE

Experimental research on various phases of group guidance is increasing, but it has not yet caught up with the rapid expansion in varieties of group procedures described in guidance literature. Some lag between practice and research is to be expected, and the amount of this lag in the area of group guidance is thoroughly understandable in view of the relative newness of the field.

Striking evidence of both the newness and the growth of group approaches in guidance is afforded by inspecting the amount of space devoted to research on group procedures in successive issues of the *Review of Educational Research* on guidance, counseling, and personnel work. The first report on research in group guidance appeared as one of nine parts of a chapter dealing with techniques of guidance and counseling in the 1939 issue (11). In 1942 and 1945 one chapter in each issue on "Guidance through Groups" (12, 13) dealt primarily with group techniques and group processes in relation to group work and the extracurriculum. In 1948 (14) and 1951 (15) the guidance issues of the *Review* contained one chapter each on "Guidance through Groups" with a spread from extracurricular activities and guidance through instruction to the theory of group processes and group psychotherapy. In the 1951 issue there was evidence of increased emphasis in research on problems of students, the school culture, on group techniques in discussion, role-playing, and leadership, on intergroup work, and on group therapy. But the startling evidence of expansion in the field of group approaches to guidance in education comes in the 1954 and 1957 issues with three chapters devoted respectively to the coverage of research in group guidance, group therapy, and the classroom teacher's role in guidance. Chapters dealing with vocational guidance and social information (16–22) have implications throughout for uses of this information in groups as well as in counseling. In the 1960 issue only one chapter (23) is devoted specifically to group procedures while another chapter (24) deals with occupational and educational information. Wrenn's report in 1960 for the Commission on Guidance in American Schools giving planned group services a status comparable to the individual interview in personnel programs would indicate that group aspects of guidance programs are not losing ground (see page 8), but this may mean an intensified need for research in the field.

One would *like* to add that this mounting volume of research and practice in the field of group approaches to guidance is clearly pointing the way to next steps ahead in the program. But when one tries to put all the parts together and see the total picture, the fact becomes evident that we are still on the "growing edge," blazing many new trails, and have not yet reached the stage of laying out a broad highway and putting up the signposts with clear directions to the goals ahead. Many of the paths are merging, not only within the field of education, but with those of other professional fields such as psychology in its many divisions, psychiatry, sociology, and social and religious group work. It is becoming evident through cooperative research and coordinated services among all these fields that each has much to share with the others, and that the advancement of our services to improve human life depends upon this concerted effort.

Research and experience have clarified our concepts of the need for group approaches in guidance, have deepened our perspectives on its purposes, and have provided numerous tested techniques for moving ahead. And, best of all, they are presenting us with the challenge of ever-new problems to solve through continued experimentation and research. The pressure of human need for guidance in learning better how to live has increased. Some of the available research related to group guidance will be drawn upon as we consider various aspects of this service within a guidance or personnel program.

SUMMARY

Guidance is a learning and a therapeutic process. Some aspects can best be carried on in individual face-to-face situations such as the interview; others can best be carried on through some type of group situation such as the classroom, planned discussion group, or social, dramatic, play, or other special-interest groups.

All guidance services in a given institution should be part of a planned and organized program, and all phases should be so interrelated that they will operate harmoniously and helpfully for the individuals to be served. Administrators, guidance or personnel workers, and teachers all make contributions to the guidance program, and each should perform those guidance functions which he can do best and most efficiently.

Many of the activities dealt with in this book as group procedures in guidance are part of every teacher's program. Others require the special training and experience of the personnel worker or the psychologist. All these services should be coordinated and closely interrelated with counseling. Group procedures and counseling implement and supplement each other reciprocally.

The purposes served by group procedures in guidance are those related to the furtherance of learnings leading to self-knowledge and self-direction in making choices, plans, and life adjustments.

Experience and research are clarifying many of the misconceptions of the past regarding the place of group guidance in a total personnel program, and progress is being made in differentiating the various functions of group guidance.

The past two decades have witnessed a rapid expansion of group procedures not only in guidance in the educational field but also in other fields of human service. There is need for continuous research and experimentation to discover best methods of achieving the purposes of these group procedures in guidance.

REFERENCES CITED IN CHAPTER

1. Tyler, Leona E.: "Research Explorations in the Realm of Choice," *Journal of Counseling Psychology,* 8:195–201, fall, 1961.
2. Super, Donald E.: "Book Reviews; Comments on Current Books and the Passing Scene," *Journal of Counseling Psychology,* 8:189–192, summer, 1961.
3. Wrenn, C. Gilbert: *The Counselor in a Changing World: A Preliminary Report of the Project on Guidance in American Schools,* The Commission on Guidance

in American Schools, American Personnel and Guidance Association, Washington, 1961.

4. Cowley, W. H.: "Jabberwocky versus Maturity," in E. G. Williamson (ed.), *Trends in Student Personnel Work,* University of Minnesota Press, Minneapolis, 1949, pp. 342–355.

5. Caplan, Stanley W.: "The Effect of Group Counseling on Junior High School Boys' Concepts of Themselves in School," *Journal of Counseling Psychology,* 4:124–128, summer, 1957.

6. Leino, Walter Bertram: *Evaluation of Outcomes of a Personal Adjustment Course,* doctoral dissertation, University of Minnesota, June, 1956.

7. Stone, C. Harold: "Are Vocational Orientation Courses Worth Their Salt?" *Educational and Psychological Measurement,* 8:161–181, summer, 1948.

8. Bennett, Margaret E.: "The Orientation of Students in Educational Institutions," in *Guidance in Educational Institutions,* Thirty-seventh Yearbook of the National Society for the Study of Education, University of Chicago Press, Chicago, 1938, part 1, pp. 175–195.

9. Richardson, Harold, and Henry Borow: "Evaluation of a Technique of Group Orientation for Vocational Counseling," *Educational and Psychological Measurement,* 12:587–597, winter, 1952.

10. Shostrom, Everett L., and Lawrence M. Brammer: *The Dynamics of the Counseling Process,* McGraw-Hill Book Company, Inc., New York, 1952.

11. Bennett, Margaret E.: "I. Group Guidance," in "Techniques of Guidance and Counseling," in "Pupil Personnel, Guidance, and Counseling," *Review of Educational Research,* 9:217–220, April, 1939.

12. Strang, Ruth: "Guidance through Groups," in "Pupil Personnel, Guidance, and Counseling," *Review of Educational Research,* 12:66–85, February, 1942.

13. Strang, Ruth: "Guidance through Groups," in "Counseling, Guidance, and Personnel Work," *Review of Educational Research,* 15:164–172, April, 1945.

14. Adams, Georgia, et al.: "Guidance through Groups," in "Counseling, Guidance, and Personnel Work," *Review of Educational Research,* 18:184–193, April, 1948.

15. Warters, Jane: "Guidance through Groups," in "Guidance and Counseling," *Review of Educational Research,* 21:140–159, April, 1951.

16. Froehlich, Clifford P.: "Group Guidance Approaches in Educational Institutions," *Review of Educational Research,* 24:147–155, April, 1954.

17. Lifton, Walter M.: "Group Therapy in Educational Institutions," in "Guidance, Counseling, and Pupil Personnel," *Review of Educational Research,* 24:156–165, April, 1954.

18. Arbuckle, Dugald S.: "The Classroom Teacher's Role in Guidance," in "Guidance, Counseling, and Pupil Personnel," *Review of Educational Research,* 24:181–189, April, 1954.

19. Roeber, Edward C.: "Selecting and Using Vocational and Social Information," in "Guidance, Counseling, and Pupil Personnel," *Review of Educational Research,* 24:172–180, April, 1954.

20. Dreese, Mitchell: "Group Guidance and Group Therapy," *Review of Educational Research,* 27:219–228, April, 1957.

21. Cottingham, Harold, and Walter M. Lifton: "The Role of the Teacher and the Instructor in the Guidance Program," *Review of Educational Research,* 27:192–201, April, 1957.

22. Roeber, Edward C.: "Vocational Guidance," *Review of Educational Research,* 27:210–218, April, 1957.

23. Rundquist, Richard M., and Robert Apostal: "Occupational and Educational Information," *Review of Educational Research,* 30:148–157, April, 1960.

24. Hoyt, Kenneth B., and Gilbert D. Moore: "Group Procedures in Guidance and Personnel Work," *Review of Educational Research,* 30:158–167, April, 1960.

ADDITIONAL REFERENCES

Farwell, Gail F., and Herman J. Peters: *Guidance Readings for Counselors,* Rand McNally & Company, Chicago, 1960, pp. 331–368.

Glanz, Edward C.: *Groups in Guidance,* Allyn and Bacon, Inc., Englewood Cliffs, N.J., 1962.

Hardee, Melvene Draheim (ed.): *Personnel Services in Education,* The Fifty-eighth Yearbook of the National Society for the Study of Education, University of Chicago Press, Chicago, 1959, part 2.

Mathewson, R. W.: *Guidance Policy and Practice,* 2d ed., Harper & Row, Publishers, New York, 1955.

Miller, Carrol H.: *Foundations of Guidance,* Harper & Row, Publishers, New York, 1961.

Patterson, C. H.: *Counseling and Guidance in Schools: A First Course,* Harper & Row, Publishers, New York, 1962, pp. 187–206.

Warters, Jane: *Group Guidance: Principles and Practices,* McGraw-Hill Book Company, Inc., New York, 1960.

Willey, Roy DeVerl, and W. Melvin Strong: *Group Procedures in Guidance,* Harper & Row, Publishers, New York, 1957.

2 SOURCES OF THE GROUP APPROACH IN GUIDANCE

Group approaches for guidance, adjustment, or therapy have developed in education, social work, medical and psychiatric practice, and religious education. These programs have emerged from varied professional orientations and have been initiated for varied purposes. Available reports of practices do not provide a concise and comprehensive picture of either historical developments or present status. The present trend toward coordination of research and practice of professional workers in many fields would seem to be especially important in the field of guidance, where the total personality of the individual is the focus of attention. The attempt is made in this chapter to examine various sources from which group approaches to guidance, human-adjustment, and mental-hygiene services have emerged, and to consider how some of these various streams of experience may be merging in the development of group approaches to guidance in education. The purpose here is not to give a comprehensive historical treatment, but to cite illustrations which seem to have significance for present trends.

Sources of the Group Approach in Medical, Psychiatric, and Psychological Practice

Group techniques for planned and organized therapy in this field are chiefly a development of this century. Reports of the use of these techniques indicate that they were first used systematically with patients with physical ailments. J. H. Pratt of Boston is frequently mentioned as the founder of group psychotherapy because of his work with groups of tubercular patients beginning in 1905. These patients were given instruction in personal hygiene and encouraged to maintain systematic health regimens. As a result of his experience with tubercular patients, Pratt (1) extended the method to include patients suffering from other chronic illnesses. The original purpose of these classes was to save time, but as Pratt noticed the emotional uplift the patients received in the groups, he began to emphasize the group psychological factors and his method became known as the "Thought Control Classes."

In 1908 Emerson began to employ the method with a group of under-nourished children at the Boston Dispensary and brought the parents into cooperation in the project. Success was attributed to many factors, including competition in weight gaining and the demonstration of objective results that helped to overcome phobias and prejudices about food. Later, classes were organized for diabetics, persons with cardiac disease, postpartum patients, and those suffering from essential hypertension and peptic ulcers.

One of the earliest recorded instances of the recognition of group influences in the treatment of psychiatric disorders, according to J. W. Klapman in his historical review of theory and practice in this field (2, p. 5), is a comment by two French authors, Camus and Pognies, in a book published in 1904.[1] These authors had noted the quiet and relative good cheer of the psychoneurotic patients on the large ward, the Salle Pinet at the Salpêtrière, as contrasted with the mental state of the wealthier patients in private rooms. However, they had not sufficiently appreciated the influence of the group as a whole on each patient, and the value and practice of group psychotherapy remained to be recognized by other workers.

Klapman lists as pioneer efforts those of L. C. Marsh as early as 1909 and of Edward W. Lazell dating from about 1919. Both these men devised series of lectures for patients. Lazell's lectures were based on psychoanalytic psychology and were expressed in language simple enough for the average patient to understand. Marsh was most interested in stimulating and inspiring patients and in working for a happier state of mind. He was not particularly concerned about the content of lectures. Another pioneer, Paul Schilder, developed group techniques which resembled more closely than his predecessors' the classical analytic technique. Also, he supplemented and complemented his group work with individual psychotherapy. Just as with group methods in guidance in education, experts in group therapy do not claim that it is a substitute for individual treatment, but rather a service that has its own specific values for experiences in reorientation and re-education within a social situation. L. C. Marsh, mentioned earlier, has stated (2, p. 17): "The mental patient should be regarded, not as a patient, but as a student who has received a 'condition' in the great subject of civilization, as most of us understand it, and psychiatry should thus approach him with an intent to re-educate rather than with an intent to 'treat.'"

J. L. Moreno was one of the early experimenters in this field, working in Vienna, first with children (1911) and later (1921) with mental patients through a method which he called "psychodrama," or the "spontaneity theater." The children were encouraged to act out their fantasies,

[1] *Isolement et psychothérapie.*

usually on a primitive fairy-tale level. With other patients, his psychodrama provided opportunity for the cast to act out problem situations and events and for the audience to participate in discussion of the dramatic action presented, thus providing opportunities for catharsis, analysis of acted-out events, and possible insight which may have meant re-education. Moreno came to the United States in the thirties and carried on his psychodrama at Beacon, New York. His method of psychodrama is now used rather widely with mental patients, with adolescents and adults for therapeutic and adjustive purposes, and an outgrowth, sociodrama, with children and adolescents in school.

A tremendous impetus to the development of group psychotherapy came during and after World War II because of greatly increased numbers in the Armed Forces and among veterans requiring psychiatric services. Eventually many workers were led into the use of group-therapy methods, not only because of the impossibility of reaching the increased number of patients by the time-consuming techniques of individual psychotherapy, but also because of the growing evidence that certain results could be achieved better through the group approach than through individual techniques.

Corsini (3), a psychologist, and Spotnitz (4), a psychiatrist, who have included considerable history of the development of group psychotherapy in their writings, illustrate the phenomenal growth of the movement, sometimes called the Third Psychiatric Revolution, by citing statistics on the increase of pertinent professional literature. Spotnitz reports the publication of about 125 papers from 1906 to 1939, four times that number during the next decade, and more than two thousand items listed in the bibliography of group psychotherapy by the end of 1959. He estimates that 200 reports now appear annually, most of them in the professional journals in the field (4, pp. 47–48).

A great variety of methods introduced by various practitioners have stemmed from various schools of thought. Psychoanalysis, the Adlerian school, Rogerian nondirective philosophy, and the group dynamics field, for example, have influenced the development of many new techniques in group psychotherapy. Commenting upon these many approaches described by Corsini (3), Spotnitz (4, p. 49) sees this great diversity as creating a new Tower of Babel, but anticipates that research and experience will eventually stabilize the movement. Out of his long experience with the use of both individual and group techniques, he expresses the conviction that psychotherapy of the future will combine both individual and group therapies, and that the latter will prove to be the more powerful treatment instrument, but not the more effective for *all* types of emotional disturbances (4, p. 265). Methods that have implications for education will be considered in a later chapter.

Some psychiatrists and clinical psychologists, like some social workers, have envisaged educational practices to foster mental health and to help in the prevention of mental illness and personal and social maladjustment. Such an expectancy was expressed by the International Preparatory Commission, which formulated a statement for the International Congress on Mental Hygiene, meeting in London in 1948. This Commission was composed of representatives from several professional fields, including psychiatry. Among their recommendations for practices to conserve mental health were the following (5, pp. 31, 36, 37):

The problem of mental health is one of re-educating people in the whole area of interpersonal relationships in such a way as to give them insight into their own behavior and that of others. While early childhood may offer the best opportunities for education it is essential that education should be carried on among people of all ages and walks of life. . . .

Leadership in mental health education should be undertaken by individuals with special skill in teaching in addition to their understanding of personality and social relationships. . . .

Education in mental health appears to be most successful if it reaches people at critical periods in their lives, e.g., when they are young and impressionable; when they are in trouble; when they are seeking advice, as, for example, mothers of infants; during convalescence; and during periods of transition, such as adolescence, or at the later stage of choosing a career. . . .

The content of this teaching should emphasize mental health rather than mental illness. For the general public the subject is not pathology but why people behave as they do. Every well-informed citizen should be aware of a few simple facts about mental illness and the kind of services that are available, but this is less important than the kind of teaching about human behaviour which helps him to live successfully with other people.

Klapman, in his revised edition (2), which is practically a new book, reveals the same need for group work that every counselor must sense when he comments on how impossible it is to talk to all patients about the many things they would like to have explained.

Spotnitz (4, pp. 268–271) prophesies that responsibility for the emotional training of all children will ultimately be assumed by society just as intellectual training has been assigned to the schools, and that this will prevent many of the damaged personalities that now overwhelm treatment facilities. He expects that treatment for those who need it will be defined as a process of helping them to "grow up," and that, ultimately, we shall know as much about creating the emotionally mature personality as we now know about the culture of flowers. This knowledge can then be utilized to improve the health of society as a whole through helping individuals to learn how to discharge their energy in personally and socially useful ways.

The implications of the generic term *group work* are more varied than those of the term *guidance*. An overview of the decade of group work preceding the organization of the American Association of Group Workers in 1946 includes descriptions of group programs in camping, recreation, health and physical education, child welfare, therapy, intercultural, secular, and religious education, unions, business, industry, government, and various cultural areas (6). The history of group work and descriptions of the varieties of practices are beyond the scope of this book, but a few illustrations are cited that seem especially pertinent to the guidance field.

Group approaches in social work

Social group work has been defined as "a method through which individuals in groups in social agency settings are helped by a worker who guides their interaction in program activities so that they may relate themselves to others and experience growth opportunities in accordance with their needs and capacities to the end of individual, group, and community development" (7, p. 61). In social group work the group itself is utilized by the individual with the help of the worker as a primary means of personality growth, change, and development (7). Konopka (8) credits many disciplines as sources of this group work—sociology, psychology, psychiatry, physical and biological sciences, economics, and history, with roots in religious and humanistic values. Among the conditions necessary for effective group work she includes environment in which the individual feels accepted, worthy as an individual in his own right but capable of accepting dependence as part of the whole group. Wilson (9) has made a distinction between "growth-oriented" and "task-oriented" groups, and this distinction is noted here because the growth oriented type is probably the more closely related of the two types to groups with guidance objectives.

One of the developments in group work during World War II through the various service agencies such as USO and the American Red Cross has significant implications for different aspects of group guidance in large-scale education. Large groups with changing membership became imperative in addition to the small cohesive groups that had been considered essential for personality development, and large groups seemed to provide some of the needed emotional support for participants. Both large and small groups were supplemented by innumerable personal services (6, pp. 115–123).

The professionalization of group work was first undertaken by the American Association for the Study of Group Work, organized in 1936. This became the American Association of Group Workers in 1946 and eventually became a division in the National Conference of Social Work. This group has developed statements of standards for professional practice (7). As in the guidance and personnel field, group activities in social work are considered an integral part of professional services, which include both individual case work and group work.

The group-therapy classes for problem children introduced by S. R. Slavson under the auspices of the Jewish Board of Guardians are well known. These groups as described in his writings provided a permissive environment in which these children could come to feel accepted in a group, work through their frustrations and conflicts, and eliminate egocentricity and psychological insularity. The role of the therapist in these groups is described by Slavson as *neutral* but not *passive*. His task is to provide situations in which children are set free to grow at their own pace through release and the restraint of the others in the group. The total situation is designed to supply substitute satisfactions, give vent to aggression, reinforce the ego, particularly in regard to feelings of failure and inadequacy, counteract deflated self-evaluation, release blockings to expression in some, and build self-restraint in others (10, p. 34).

In commenting on the effects of the group situation, Slavson writes (10, p. 36): "The less conflicted and less frightened group members dissolve fears and resistances in the more neurotic and repressed patients. This is often referred to as the catalytic effect persons have on one another." Methods for adolescents and adults have stressed the development of insight with respect to difficulties through discussion activities.

A great variety of group methods has been developed by various workers in the social-welfare field. Fritz Redl has reported upon methods and results with a puppet club in Detroit, an organization of children who were clients of the Jewish Children's Bureau (11). Here the leaders shared more actively in the group than did those in Slavson's groups. A tremendous variety of play and activity techniques for diagnostic and therapeutic purposes has been developed in social agencies, clinics, and private practice. Experience has shown the need for marked differentiation of approaches and methods with young children, adolescents, and adults. Since this section deals only with sources of the group approach, these variations of method can only be mentioned at this point.

In attempting to envisage the future possibilities of group therapy, Slavson has made some very significant suggestions for group-guidance methods in education. Some of these are included in Chapter 6 in the consideration of possibilities for therapeutic group work in education (see pages 152 and 153).

Group work in religious education

Fellowship in group life has always been a basic characteristic of both Judaism and Christianity. The word *koinonia* appears frequently in modern writings on religious education, connoting a fellowship that is more than a sense of groupness (12). Some of the earliest writings dealing with the dynamics of group work were in the field of religious education, and many of the earliest types of activities now labeled group work were church-sponsored.[2] Both Jewish and Christian centers and associations have a long history of services through group programs, but the development of group work in church education has been spotty. There seems to have been an upsurge of interest in group dynamics since the mid-century. A symposium in 1950 on growing edges in religious education (13), representing many faiths, gave evidence of a leaven very similar to that in social work and secular education with emphasis on life situations and problems and on growth needs of individuals. Another symposium on group dynamics (14) dealt with the interrelationships of religion, psychology, and sociology in the fostering of dynamic fellowship within churches, aimed at the growth of persons in a religious way of life. Training programs in theological seminaries are increasingly preparing, not only for pastoral counseling, but for leadership in group work, in some instances with opportunities for students to experience group therapy as a means of releasing their creative powers to serve others (15). Ernsberger (16) has cautioned against the use of depth psychotherapy by those trained only in counseling, and also against the use of group dynamics as a tool for manipulating individuals and groups rather than for fostering the shared fellowship that may serve individuals in their problem solving and spiritual development.

Many aspects of church and synagogue programs involve group-guidance approaches in religious settings. Among these are discussion groups following sermons to clarify points and guide individual applications, group counseling for the study of personal problems, and family-centered programs for worship, recreation, and study. One interesting development reported enthusiastically from several churches is the rise of small personal groups, sometimes called prayer cells, for spiritual renewal and growth through study, meditation, prayer, and worship. Retreats at various centers are also being used increasingly for this same purpose by both Jewish and Christian churches (17).

[2] L. K. Hall in "Group Work in Religious Education" (6, pp. 52–76) cites *A Social Theory of Religious Education* by George A. Coe, published in 1917, as one of the earliest group-work approaches in religious and character education.

Sources within the Educational Field

In good teaching

In one sense, group procedures of a guidance nature are as old as what might be termed "good functional teaching." By "functional" teaching is meant teaching that guides the learner toward insight into the meaning of life about and within him, and toward application of his growing understanding in his living. All really good teaching has always subsumed these objectives as direct or incidental. Such teaching is inevitably concerned with the individual—his interests, needs, and welfare—and is therefore based on the personnel or guidance point of view.

Doubtless every reader can think of examples of this kind of teaching in his own experiences as learner or teacher: the English teacher who helps one to find significant life meanings in the characters and events of literature as well as to recognize and appreciate beauty of form and style; the social-science teacher who helps one to see not only the succession of historical events but also the interplay of factors within the personalities of leaders and between individuals and groups that produced the events, and opens doors to understanding of similar conditions in oneself or in daily human relationships; the biology teacher who fosters healthful living as the real purpose of learning about bodily mechanisms and functions; the physical-science teacher who strives for both intelligent understanding and skillful use by learners of their physical environment; and the teacher in any field who stimulates the development of interests that might lead to vocations or avocations. Whenever this teaching results in deeper understanding of self and others, better living and life planning, and refined standards of value, it can be said to exemplify the guidance or personnel point of view.

In counseling

Anyone counseling with individuals soon becomes aware of the recurrence of similar problems in different individuals. True, the problem occurs in different settings in each individual, and the same problems occur in an infinite variety of combinations. But the high incidence of certain problems at various age levels has led to awareness of *common* human problems, regardless of individual variations. What has been said about human beings biologically, as to heredity, seems to apply equally well in the field of personality: "The strands are ancient, but each individual is a new knot."

A trained and experienced counselor is also aware not only of the variety of causal factors in human problems but of the common causal factors that reappear so frequently in different individuals with similar difficulties. Here, again, these causal factors invariably appear in unique combinations in the lives of different persons. The active cooperation of the individual is usually essential in seeking causes and in resolving the problems. This means mutual study and learning by both counselor and counselee—a highly time-consuming process in individual interviews.

Over and over again a counselor engages in parallel experiences with individual counselees. Some of this repetition is essential, but some is also quite needless and even undesirable. Experience in group study in which counselees examine some of their common problems, though not necessarily in relation to their own particular difficulties, and recognize their causal similarities has demonstrated two important values of the procedure:

1. It lays a common foundation of understanding upon which counselor and counselee can build effectively in the interview, devoting the period to the unique and special aspects of the counselee's problems.

2. The realization by the counselee through group study that many others are faced with very similar worries or difficulties is a highly valuable therapeutic factor, resulting in much release of tension and the elimination of much embarrassment caused by fear of being different or queer. Thus difficult barriers to rapport and effective individual counseling are removed.

We could illustrate with Mary and John, high school students, who are both concerned about disagreements and tensions in their relationships with their parents. Both think that they are being treated unfairly, and both have felt guilt and shame over their frequent feelings of hatred toward their parents and the temper outbursts in which they have indulged. Mary has brooded over her problems to the point where she has difficulty in concentrating on her studies and is failing in two subjects. John is likewise doing poor schoolwork but does not, at the start, recognize that he is resisting all types of authority as symbolized by teachers and assignments at school as well as parental controls at home.

These adolescents, and all others, need to understand the meaning of the adolescent period as a transition between childhood and adulthood, the many facets of growing up into adulthood, the problems of both parents and children in making adjustments in this period, the nature of emotional ties between parent and child, the naturalness of ambivalent love and hate, the need for mutual understanding and cooperation in the gradual release of parental controls, and the training, self-discipline, and experience required for being truly adult and self-dependent.

With the perspective and understanding gained through group study of what it means to grow up, Mary and John are ready to approach more objectively their particular problems of maturing and gradually establishing changed but happy relationships with their parents. Counseling interviews can help them to assess the unique as well as common problems in their respective home situations, to delve into deeper aspects of emotional involvements, and to work out suitable personal applications of what they have learned about this phase of life.

In many instances conferences with parents and parent study groups will help to bring the parents into active cooperation in this growing-up process of their children. At times joint study of problems by parents and children in the same group will bring insights and a sense of community of interests that may not be achieved in either group alone. Skillful leadership of such groups is important.

Causes of difficulties are rarely single. Mary or John may solve home problems and yet find that poor schoolwork continues. Inefficient methods of study, special problems in a particular subject field, or various personal handicaps such as poor eyesight or nutrition may merely have been accentuated as a result of the emotional tensions created by the home situation. Or all these factors may have had reciprocal influences in intensifying problems in each area suggested above. These possibilities open up need for understanding by adolescents of efficiency methods in learning, individual differences in interests and abilities, and matters of health and hygiene. Here again common learnings can be achieved in groups, and many personal applications of these learnings must be worked out in individual counseling. Our overview of possible causal factors in the problems of Mary and John suggest some of the many possible ramifications of any counseling problems and hence of any program of group study of such problems.

In vocational guidance

The occupational-information aspect of vocational guidance has placed emphasis upon group procedures from the very start. Here was specific content for courses and textbooks that lent itself readily to the traditional type of classroom instruction. The phases of vocational guidance that relate to appraisal of interests and abilities, to techniques of vocational and educational planning, to job orientation and advancement, and to continuous occupational adjustment have been introduced more slowly into group procedures, but are increasingly accepted in special courses or in units in various curriculum areas. The need for specific training in vocational guidance for those who provide either group or individual services is recognized, but practice has not yet caught up fully with theory. Research has yielded evidence of the greater efficacy of the combined group and counseling services in vocational guidance than of either service alone (see pages 16 and 17). Two of the eight areas specified by the Committee on Certification of the American Personnel and Guidance Association as essential in the graduate training program for counselors relate to group guidance. These are the dynamics of group behavior and environmental factors in adjustment, including pertinent occupational, social, and educational aspects.[3]

In orientation programs in colleges

Recognition of the need for orientation of new students in colleges and universities appears to have existed from very early times.[4] There is no record of specific courses for this purpose until 1888, when one was introduced at Boston University for the orientation of its new students. In 1900, a series of lectures was inaugurated for engineering students at Iowa State College, for the purpose of introducing them into a professional atmosphere and acquainting them with staff members and field of work. Reed College, Portland, Oregon, in 1910–1911, seems to have offered the first Freshman Orientation course for which students received college credit; and some type of orientation course was offered during the early decades of the century at a number of other colleges and universities. This period, ending approximately in 1917, was characterized by experimentation with various types of courses, the majority of which dealt more with adjustment to college than with orientation in fields of study.

The period beginning in 1918 witnessed the widespread introduction of War Issues courses and the rapid development of the broad social-studies type of orientation course frequently called a "survey" course and sometimes aimed at introducing the student to various fields of study in the college curriculum. The personnel work done in the Army during World War I and its continuation in the form of student personnel services in colleges, combined with the rapidly increasing enrollments in colleges after the war, gave impetus again to the guidance type of orientation. As a result there were four times as many courses of this type offered in 1926 as in 1917–1918 (18, p. 1302).

Orientation of College Freshmen by Henry J. Doermann, published in 1926,[5] embodies an excellent presentation of the best thinking in this

[3] APGA Committee on Certification, "Professional Training, Licensing, and Certification," *The Personnel and Guidance Journal,* 37:162–166, October, 1958.

[4] Interesting evidence of this early concern is to be found in two fascinating books. The older one, bearing the publication date 1876, is entitled *The Student's Manual, Designed by Specific Directions to Aid in Forming and Strengthening the Intellectual and Moral Character and Habits of the Student.* The author, Rev. John Todd, included chapters entitled "Objects of Study," "Habits," "Reading," "Time," "Conversation," "Politeness and Subordination," "Exercise, Diet, Economy," "Discipline of the Heart," "The Object of Life." Another, by Philip Gilbert Hamerton, published in 1883 and entitled *The Intellectual Life,* has chapters entitled "The Physical Basis," "The Moral Basis," "Of Education," "The Power of Time," "The Influence of Money," "Custom and Tradition," "Women and Marriage," "Aristocracy and Democracy," "Society and Solitude," "Intellectual Hygienics," "Trades and Professions," "Surroundings."

[5] By The Williams & Wilkins Company, Baltimore.

period regarding student personnel practices and now seems prophetic of some of the best practices that have developed in decades subsequent to its publication. Doermann appealed for assistance to freshmen in making an adjustment away from home, in overcoming immaturity, developing a sense of purpose in their college life, and expanding their intellectual interests.

In 1930, Wrenn estimated that from one-fourth to one-third of the standard colleges and universities were giving orientation courses and that one-half to three-fourths of the courses emphasized individual orientation to self and college life. There was evidence during both the twenties and the thirties of a trend toward differentiating the group-guidance type of orientation from other fields of study in the college curriculum. There were also indications of increasing interest in survey courses within major fields of study such as science, humanities, and social science, which did not overlap or duplicate the group-guidance type of orientation. The decade of the thirties also witnessed the development of programs of general education, which are discussed in some detail later in this chapter. This development embraced many of the objectives of orientation and group guidance, and phases of the latter have been incorporated into various general-education courses. In 1943 the Council of Guidance and Personnel Associations, representing 5,000 counselors in high schools and colleges, recommended that orientation courses be provided in high schools and colleges with the objectives of (a) better understanding of occupational and social problems, (b) better personal adjustment, and (c) awareness of the importance of physical fitness, including social hygiene (18, p. 1303).

The War Issues courses of World War I, aimed at motivation of war effort through understanding of the causes and purposes of the world conflict, had their counterpart in lectures and discussions within the orientation program for the Armed Forces in World War II. However, in the latter program greater emphasis was placed on personal orientation with respect to adjustment problems of individuals under conditions of army life and modern warfare. Lecture outlines for officers and for enlisted men had a psychiatric orientation directed to the understanding and control of the emotions engendered by the frustrations and dangers of military life, the prevention of breakdowns, and the maintenance of mental health.

Surveys of orientation programs in colleges and universities in the decade of the forties (19, 20) showed that orientation courses of the guidance type were increasing in numbers. Among the activities included were: how to study, personal-social adjustment in college, traditions, rules, and regulation, extracurricular activities, and vocational guidance. Orientation courses, in addition to Freshman Week, were provided in

70 per cent of the institutions reporting. Two doctoral studies in the fifties (21, 22) indicated that no radical changes in the areas of instruction had occurred since the twenties, with Freshman Week, sometimes with camping experiences, continuing as a very frequent aspect of the orientation program. Small advisory groups were introduced in numerous institutions, with group conferences continuing over a semester or longer period of time.

A national sampling of 340 colleges (including junior colleges) reported in 1958 showed that 44 per cent had orientation courses of at least one semester. The authors, Plutchik and Hoffman (23), state that, while the majority of these colleges were using lecture methods, many expressed a preference for the small-group type of orientation if they could find ways of providing it. The authors of this report emphasize the limited value of brief orientation services in Freshman Week programs unless followed by more intensive services over a longer period. They found that the commonest practice is to center the administration of the orientation in the student personnel service.

In orientation and group-guidance programs in secondary schools

The junior high school, which began to come into the educational picture about 1910, provided a fertile field for the development of group-guidance programs. The initial emphasis at this level upon exploratory and tryout experiences in a more varied curricular program than was available in the usual elementary school meant opportunities for the discovery and development of interests and abilities that could lead to sounder vocational planning. The increased complexity of the junior high school program as compared with that of the elementary school created the need for orientation services to help young pupils to adjust in the new environment.

These same factors influenced the development of orientation and other group-guidance procedures at the senior high school level, where enrollments and the size and complexity of institutions increased rapidly during the twentieth century. Other factors contributing to the group approach in personnel work throughout the secondary school level were: (a) advances in knowledge about individual differences and adolescent needs and problems; (b) recognition of the many common human problems that required pupil study and learning for their solution; (c) the acceptance of self-direction as an ultimate objective of personnel work with the consequent need for the fostering of self-directive techniques in adolescents; (d) the impossibility of serving all students adequately through individual counseling alone; (e) the growing recognition of the values of extended observation of pupils in group situations as well as in the interview for the understanding of their needs and potentialities;

(f) eventually, the recognition of the advantages, therapeutically as well as economically, in providing for certain learnings of a guidance nature in groups as well as in individual interviews (24, p. 928).

Most of the early group-guidance programs at the secondary school level were centered in the homeroom, which continues as one of the most widely used forms of organization. This homeroom program was usually supplemented by freshman-orientation activities, and often by occupational information and vocational planning through social-science, English, or special guidance classes. Historically, some of the earliest efforts at instruction in vocational guidance were begun in English classes. Soon the course in Occupations came on the scene, and this has developed in diverse ways. Many other courses have been introduced into the curriculum dealing with personal, social, and vocational problems and mental hygiene. These courses have been given a wide variety of titles such as Social Problems, Senior Problems, Social Living, Human Relations, Personal Adjustment, Mental Hygiene, Psychology of Living, or Personality Development. Courses in How to Study have also appeared, though this problem has more often been a part of the general group-guidance or homeroom program.

As the name indicates, the homeroom was designed as the home base of the pupil, with a teacher who served as his school parent in helping him to adjust in the new environment and make the most of his new opportunities. This homeroom quickly became the agency through which various administrative routines of the school were carried out. Also, it became an activity center in some of the social and club life and often an organ or unit of the student-body government. Eventually, certain instructional services related to educational, vocational, personal, and social guidance were added, and frequently counseling and personnel record keeping. Considering the facts that few homeroom teachers had special guidance training, that instructional materials were scarce, and that usually no extra time was allowed for the counseling and record-keeping, it is a real tribute to the plan that it has succeeded to the degree that it has in meeting certain guidance needs and has continued as such a widespread type of organization within secondary schools.

During the twenties and thirties some schools added to the homeroom a system of special guidance classes taught by grade advisers who also counseled their students. The plan developed by Richard D. Allen at Providence, Rhode Island, was one of the earliest and best-known examples of this form of organization. Publications describing the organization and administration of the Providence program, and techniques used in the classwork,[6] have widely influenced the development of programs elsewhere.

[6] The Inor Group Guidance Series by Allen and co-workers.

A somewhat different type of program was developing in Pasadena, California, during the late twenties and the thirties, keyed to the 6-4-4 plan of school organization, which was then in effect. The methods used in establishing this program will be described briefly, first because of the way in which these methods led into the next phase of organization and, second, because of the author's conviction that some such methods should be used continuously to keep a program vital and adapted to the needs of each new generation of pupils.[7]

At the junior high school level, trained counselors assigned to each school worked with the director of guidance to plan the over-all program and committee structure, and to bring the entire faculty of each school into active cooperation in both the planning and executing of the project. Committees at each grade level (7 through 10) formulated lists of pupil needs and problems, utilizing data in published research studies, and the suggestions of teachers, parents, and pupils as to interests and guidance problems at each age level. Instructional materials were prepared as guides for homeroom teachers in planning pupil study, discussions, and other activities. These instructional guides were revised frequently on the basis of pooled experience.

Since general curriculum revision was going forward at the same time, the effort was made to include for every subject field suggestions as to guidance implications and ways in which subject teachers, homeroom teachers, and counselors could cooperate in implementing one another's work. The ninth-grade social-science core was utilized to provide occupational information related to each institution, social, economic, and political, as studied; and a unit on vocational planning in this ninth year brought counselors, social-science teachers, and homeroom teachers into close interaction with pupils as they developed their *tentative* vocational and educational plans. Similar cooperation between junior high school and college counselors as pupils moved on into the next level, grades 11 through 14, helped in articulation between the two units.

At the junior college, orientation or group-guidance classes for entering eleventh- and thirteenth-year students were taught for many years by trained counselors. These provided for organized study of adjustment to college, learning techniques, educational and vocational planning, and personal and social problems. Under this setup it was possible to relate the instruction closely to the individual counseling. This program at the junior college level had been begun much earlier than at the junior high

[7] During the period described here, the author was director of guidance and had varying responsibilities also in the development of the curriculum—at first as assistant to the deputy superintendent in charge of curriculum and later as a consultant to the curriculum coordinators with respect to guidance. This relation between guidance and curriculum in the first-mentioned setup opened many possibilities for the development of group approaches to guidance.

school level, and instructional materials had been progressively changed from year to year to meet more fully the expressed needs of students and those emphasized by teachers, counselors, and parents. An informal evaluation of the program by students at one period when they were actively participating in planning the work had given an almost unanimous judgment on unsigned questionnaires that they would elect such a course, or recommend its election by freshmen, if it were not a required course.

Changes in the general pattern of educational offerings resulted in numerous changes from time to time in this group-guidance program. Many of the curriculum changes, particularly at the junior high school, have been outgrowths of this group-guidance program. In the late thirties a system-wide committee, initiated to consider ways of improving the guidance service, made recommendations for changes in the entire curricular structure. Interests and needs of adolescents formerly used as a basis for the group-guidance programs were now reformulated and adopted as the basis of the entire curriculum. Former homeroom units and activities became, in modified form, a basic part of the core or general-education program, now called the block program.

This change resulted in the mid-forties in several modifications in the administrative and educational structure. Guidance became a part of the instructional division; the teachers became, in theory, the counselors; and the office of counselor was abolished in junior high schools. Several experiments with different types of organization were introduced in the various schools. Some evaluations which were attempted will be considered in a later chapter (see page 170). Within a short time there was considerable evidence that much had been lost, at least temporarily, in the change as it was effected. The central guidance office became deluged with requests for special services to individuals, and the junior high school teachers indicated on a committee questionnaire a strong desire for more specialized assistance and for the time and place to do their counseling. One positive aspect of the change was the great interest expressed by many teachers in doing more guidance work with pupils, provided they had more training and assistance and the time and a suitable place for counseling. It is questionable, however, whether increased teacher interest and possible teacher training through actual experience can justify even temporary losses in services to pupils. There are other, though perhaps slower, methods of achieving gains for both teachers and pupils. When California requirements for the certification of pupil personnel workers were reinstated after a lapse in the decade of the forties, credentialed counselors became the leaders of the guidance programs in the junior and senior high schools.

Since this chapter is dealing only with sources of group guidance, the above illustrations have been used merely as examples of how the programs have developed or changed in two systems over many years. The pictures as given are incomplete and would have differed in many ways if other school systems had been chosen for illustration. At present it would appear that homerooms are holding their own for certain guidance functions in many schools and that some phases of group guidance are included in core, general-education, or block programs.

These core, general-education, and so-called life-adjustment programs have received much criticism on the grounds of being superficial, dealing with generalizations, and failing to provide sound foundations for understanding our cultural heritage or for advanced study in the traditional disciplines. Doubtless much of this criticism is justified, though evaluations of some programs have shown core students to compare very favorably with students in traditional courses in gains on tests of achievement, study skills, attitudes, and some types of personal adjustment (25, 26).

Another influence militating against core programs is the strong trend, caused by the race for space mastery and the urgency of national defense, toward increased emphasis upon scientific training, greater intellectualization of education, and the discovery and development of talent. Some schools have reacted to these criticisms by substituting the term *block program* for core. Actually many of the programs called core have never been more than mere groupings of subjects within two or more periods taught by one teacher.

The proponents of a true core or general-education program, however, are remaining firm in their convictions as to its values and are continuing to study how it may become more effective. Hock and Hill (27) describe a general-education program extending from kindergarten through college with focus on the development of basic concepts, breadth of understanding, and the acquisition of tools of intelligent action, including methods of problem solving and critical thinking, needed in all areas of living and working as a mature citizen.

Such a program could subsume the objectives of guidance, and most of the programs include claims of guidance services provided by teachers. However, scrutiny of many descriptions fails to reveal evidence of the kind of guidance recognized as sound by trained personnel workers. One of the most recent and comprehensive treatments of general education (27) fails to list any references in the personnel field, and still another slants the guidance services almost exclusively toward the teacher, considering "how the teacher can relate his guidance functions with those of a guidance specialist *where such specialists are employed*" (25, p. 180).[8] Causes of this seeming lack of coordination between curriculum

[8] Italics are the author's.

and guidance may be found in both fields. The preoccupation of many counselors with programming, scheduling, psychometrics, and record keeping could be one factor. Also, curriculum workers need to take cognizance of the rapid development of a broad spectrum of group services within the personnel field.

In general-education programs in college

Much of the early experimentation with orientation and survey courses at the college level and with group-guidance programs at the high school level grew out of an increasing awareness of the inadequacies of the curriculum in relation to current individual and social needs. This increased awareness of needs stemmed in part from psychological and sociological research, and was an important factor in the introduction of counseling and other personnel services into educational institutions. These services, in both individual and group applications, were in turn instrumental in stimulating and strengthening this awareness and in promoting changes in educational programs. Personnel workers were a leavening influence through their interpretation of needs of students to administrators and teachers; experience with orientation, survey, and other group-guidance courses demonstrated how some of these needs could be met through instruction and also revealed the limitations of having only one type of course for the realization of new objectives of education that were emerging.

An analysis of almost any human problem that was likely to be studied in a group-guidance class points up the interrelationships of many fields of study in the pursuit of these goals. The question of self-appraisal of interest and abilities would require materials from psychology for methods of self-study, from biology for hereditary influences, and from the social sciences for cultural and environmental influences. The problem of improving study or learning methods would make demands not only upon the psychology of learning and of individual differences but also upon health and hygiene and, for applications, upon every field in the curriculum. Problems of sound vocational planning have their ramifications in psychology, health sciences, economics, history, sociology, and all the fields related to preparation for a given area of work. This suggests some of the complexities of the problems to be solved in the application of an educational philosophy which emphasizes education related to individual and social needs, purposeful from the viewpoint of the learner, and functional in his life.

The general-education movement has many roots. It is doubtless an outgrowth, in part, of the earlier orientation and survey courses already described. All these have involved efforts to cope with the chaotic situation that resulted from the elective system with its multiplicity of special courses representing the fruits of research and specialization. Also, the world-wide clash of democratic and totalitarian ideologies has hurled the challenge to educators to discover how the educative process may contribute to the maintenance and improvement of our democratic way of life and discover and develop the talent needed in a technological culture.

For several decades general education has been studied by various committees and commissions, and experiments in new forms of programs have passed beyond pioneer stages. While there is no unanimous consensus on the specifics of content and method, the following statement of aims and objectives of general education would probably elicit but little controversy:

General education is the nonspecialized and nonvocational learning which should be the common experience of everyone. Through general education the individual learns to go beyond the acquisition of facts; he learns to evaluate facts, place them in valid relationship to each other, and integrate them into his total system of attitudes and values.

In the report of the Cooperative Study of Evaluation in General Education sponsored by the American Council on Education, Dressell and Mayhew (28) point out that the movement derived its energy from protest against many practices, such as the compartmentalization of knowledge, the proliferation of courses, and the associated evils of the free elective system. They warn that dynamism of protest is quickly expended, and that general education is in need of a more positive dynamic, a positive integrating principle to replace the principle of protest. While recognizing the validity of the integrating concepts of common knowledge, good citizenship, preparation for adult life, and development of values, they suggest for this post-Sputnik age critical and creative thinking as a positive integrating concept. They emphasize the need for research and experience that will yield insights as to how this concept can be applied in teaching. Also, they suggest that counseling aimed at developing rational methods for problem solving can facilitate work in the classroom.

Mayhew (29) has brought together in one volume descriptions of some of the most promising programs of general education that have emerged in the past several decades. Excerpts from letters of administrators describing their programs and plans for improvements, and expressing considerable satisfaction as to progress, suggest that general education is an ongoing movement with a future if it copes with problems of the space age. Mayhew points out that counseling has emerged as almost a full-time partner of general education.

In adult education

Lifelong education has become a recognized need in our dynamic culture and adult education has become a vital force in our democratic society. Lowy (30) has shown that group work is increasingly used in programs for adults of all ages. The analysis of these programs has indicated that more attention has been given to the group process than to the individual whose self-improvement is a basic goal as well as his contributions to society. Bradford (30) has included this goal in part of his definition of adult education as contributing to the solving of vocational, avocational, personal, family, and civic problems. Programs of vocational guidance through group study and individual guidance for mature persons in a public education setting have been reported by Logie (31, 32). Forums and study groups to assist unemployed adults have been carried on in many centers throughout the nation. Some of these for women have been initiated and sponsored by the Women's Bureau in the Department of Labor; others have been sponsored by service clubs or by civic committees representing a cross section of interested groups. Pasadena's Jobs After Forty Committee illustrates an ongoing program of the latter type with close affiliation with the local office of the State Department of Employment and providing both group and individual counseling services.

A comprehensive summary of research in adult education from 1953 to 1959 (33) gives little indication that guidance services for adults, at least in any organized form, have become an important concern in adult programs, although two chapters of the report deal with the psychology of adults and learning in groups.

Research in human relations

Research in the fields of sociology, psychology, and group dynamics has contributed in large measure to all of the programs in the various service areas mentioned in this chapter. Pertinent findings will be utilized throughout succeeding chapters, especially in Part Two.

RETROSPECT AND PROSPECT

We have seen that group approaches to the study and solution of problems of effective living have been developing in all of the major areas of human service and that most of the programs have many characteristics in common. Also, most of the proponents of group work in fields other than education see it as involving elements of education and of personal development and adjustment, and stress the need for some of these services in very early years. This throws a challenge directly to education.

We have seen that the trends in group guidance and general education for all individuals have been moving toward a new organization of curriculum content in which materials from many subject fields are brought to bear upon the study of significant problems of living of both a personal and a broadly social nature.

What of the future? Perhaps the only statement that can be made with certainty is that it will bring change. The attempts in the educational field to cope with change have often been in the nature of moving from one solution to another instead of evaluating present practice and building soundly on experience, utilizing its lessons fully as we move into the future.

One major issue is that of the relative responsibilities of all teachers and guidance specialists and their interrelationships in a group-guidance program. There are strong indications of a growing realization that special training and qualifications are needed for many aspects of self-understanding, vocational guidance, and personal-social adjustment within the total service aimed at self-direction. This is likely to affect the organization of guidance services profoundly in the future.

REFERENCES CITED IN CHAPTER

1. Pratt, J. H.: "Principles of Class Treatment and Their Application to Various Chronic Diseases," *Hospital Social Service,* 6:401, 1922.
2. Klapman, J. W.: *Group Psychotherapy: Theory and Practice,* Grune & Stratton, Inc., New York, 1946, 2d ed., 1959.
3. Corsini, Raymond J.: *Methods of Group Psychotherapy,* McGraw-Hill Book Company, Inc., Blakiston Division, New York, 1957.
4. Spotnitz, Hyman: *The Couch and the Circle: A Story of Group Psychotherapy,* Alfred A. Knopf, Inc., New York, 1961.
5. *Statement by the International Preparatory Commission,* International Congress on Mental Hygiene, London, lithographed in the United States, August, 1948.
6. Hendry, Charles E. (ed.): *A Decade of Group Work,* Association Press, New York, 1948.
7. Trecker, Harleigh B.: *Social Group Work: Principles and Practices,* Whiteside, Inc., and William Morrow and Company, Inc., New York, 1955.
8. Konopka, Gisele: "The Method of Social Group Work," in Walter A. Friedlander (ed.), *Concepts and Methods of Social Work,* Prentice-Hall, Inc., Englewood Cliffs, N.J., 1958, pp. 116–200.
9. Wilson, Gertrude: "Social Group Work—Trends and Developments," *Social Work,* 11:66, October, 1956.
10. Slavson, S. R.: *An Introduction to Group Therapy,* The Commonwealth Fund, New York, 1943.
11. Redl, Fritz: "Diagnostic Group Work," *The American Journal of Orthopsychiatry,* 14:53–67, 1944.
12. Little, Sara: *Learning Together in Christian Fellowship,* John Knox Press, Richmond, Va.
13. "Growing Edges of Religious Education at Mid-century: Reports," *Religious Education,* 45:195–216, July–August, 1950.
14. "Group Dynamics and Religious Education: A Symposium," *Religious Education,* 47:371–401, November–December, 1952.
15. Jackson, Gordon Edmund: "Conformity and Creativity," *Religious Education,* 55:330–335, September–October, 1960.
16. Ernsberger, David J.: *A Philosophy of Adult Christian Education,* Westminster Press, Philadelphia, 1959.

17. Casteel, John L. (ed.): *Spiritual Renewal through Personal Groups,* Association Press, New York, 1957.
18. Bennett, Margaret E.: "Student Personnel Work: III. Orientation of Students," in Walter S. Monroe (ed.), *Encyclopedia of Educational Research,* rev. ed., The Macmillan Company, New York, 1950, pp. 1302–1305.
19. Kamm, R. B., and C. G. Wrenn: "Current Developments in Student-personnel Programs and the Needs of the Veteran," *School and Society,* 65:89–92, 1947.
20. Bookman, Gladys: "Freshman Orientation Techniques in Colleges and Universities," unpublished doctoral dissertation, University of Wyoming, Laramie, Wyo., 1948.
21. Greene, George H.: "A Study of the Freshman Orientation Course in Small Colleges," summary of doctoral dissertation, Florida A. & M. College, Tallahassee, Fla., 1953. (Mimeographed.)
22. Copeland, Theodore H., Jr.: "Freshman Orientation Programs: A Study of Their Development and Present Status with Special Reference to Middle Atlantic Colleges," unpublished doctoral dissertation, Temple University, Philadelphia, 1953.
23. Plutchik, R., and R. W. Hoffman: "The Small-group College Orientation Program," *Journal of Higher Education,* 29:278–279, fall, 1958.
24. Adams, Georgia Sachs, and Margaret E. Bennett: "Pupil Personnel Work: IV. Orientation and Group Guidance," in Walter S. Monroe (ed.), *Encyclopedia of Educational Research,* rev. ed., The Macmillan Company, New York, 1950, pp. 927–930.
25. Faunce, Roland C., and Nelson L. Bossing: *Developing the Core Curriculum,* 2d ed., Prentice-Hall, Inc., Englewood Cliffs, N.J., 1958.
26. Wright, Grace S.: "Block-time Classes and the Core Program in the Junior High School," U.S. Department of Health, Education, and Welfare Bulletin 1958, no. 6, 1958.
27. Hock, Louise E., and Thomas J. Hill: *The General Education Class in the Secondary School,* Holt, Rinehart and Winston, Inc., New York, 1960.
28. Dressel, Paul L., and Lewis B. Mayhew: *General Education, Explorations in Evaluation,* The Final Report of the Cooperative Study of Evaluation in General Education of the American Council on Education, American Council on Education, Washington, 1954.
29. Mayhew, Lewis B.: *General Education, An Account and Appraisal;* A Guide for College Faculties, Harper & Row, Publishers, New York, 1960.
30. Lowy, Louis: *Adult Education and Group Work,* Whiteside, Inc., and William Morrow and Company, Inc., New York, 1955.
31. Logie, Iona: "Adult Counseling Aids in Retirement Plans," *Vocational Guidance Quarterly,* 3:83–86, spring, 1955.
32. Ballin, Marian R., and Iona R. Logie: "The Counseling of Adults, a Growing Community Need," *Adult Leadership,* 8:200–201, January, 1960.
33. Adult Education, *Review of Educational Research,* 29, June, 1959.

ADDITIONAL REFERENCES

Borow, Henry: "Curricular Approaches to Personal Development: Some Problems of Research," *Journal of Counseling Psychology,* 5:63–69, spring, 1958.
Morse, Horace T., and Paul L. Dressel (eds.): *General Education for Personal Maturity,* William C. Brown Company, Dubuque, Iowa, 1960.

3 COMMON PROBLEMS IN LIVING

The word *problem* as used here does not necessarily imply a difficulty or maladjustment. The Greek root from which the word is derived means literally "something thrown forward." Throughout this chapter the term *common problems* refers to the varieties of imminent or anticipated adjustments which the majority of individuals face at various stages in living. We might, therefore, think of a life problem as some imminent or future adjustment for which some preparation can be made.

These problems of adjustment may be the result of either inner or outer pressures, or usually the interaction of both, and require some kind of activity to meet them. Both human nature and culture present so many alternatives to action that the individual is faced continually with choices among the various possibilities. These choices may lead to satisfying adjustments or to maladjustments with resulting dissatisfactions. One guidance task is that of helping individuals to increase their understanding of implications of various choices and to improve their ability to make wise choices. When problems have not been met satisfactorily, the guidance task becomes that of helping to overcome the maladjustment. Guidance thus serves adjustive, preventive, and remedial functions. Since many of the adjustment problems faced by individuals are related to the processes of maturation and growth within a culture pattern, the adjustive phase of guidance is frequently called "developmental."

Thus, having problems is simply a characteristic of living, which is a continuing process of *becoming* rather than a static state of being. It has been said aptly that living involves not so much a matter of the adjustment to problems as *the adjustment to having problems*. Learning self-direction involves learning to face problems and to deal with them as effectively as possible.

Numerous terms have been used by educators to refer to these common problems of living. The term "growth needs" has often been used to describe the requirements of growing individuals for experiences that would foster wholesome physical, mental, emotional, and social development within their cultural milieu. Some have objected to the word

49

"growth" because it is used to denote physiological development; others have objected to the word "need" because it seemed to them to savor of a laissez-faire educational program adapted to expressed desires or whims of immature individuals. This latter interpretation is, obviously, not a necessary meaning of the word "need," especially when it involves preparation for future adjustments of which a person may or may not be fully aware. Even with respect to immediate adjustment problems, clinical studies have shown that individuals may not recognize what their needs and problems are.

This gap between expressed interests and real needs is pointed up by a study which reports that a lack of relationship was found between the wishes and interests of children on the one hand, and their fears on the other. It apparently occurs to very few children who are burdened with fears to wish that they could be rid of them or could acquire the power within themselves to cope with them. Nor did children with recognizable problems (poor economic and environmental circumstances, broken families, etc.) necessarily relate these conditions to the things they wished for or reported they would like to learn about. It is clear that assessing "growth needs" is a complex procedure (1, p. 69).

Another term which has come into widespread use is "developmental tasks" (2), referring to varieties of learnings essential for satisfactory growth and adjustment at successive age levels. These age levels have been called by Erik H. Erikson the "Eight Stages of Man." Erikson has formulated a list of components of a healthy personality in each of these stages, or, in his words, criteria by which the individual demonstrates that his ego, at a given stage, is strong enough to integrate the timetable of the organism with the structure of social institutions (3, pp. 219–234).

We shall first review briefly these personality needs as described by Erikson, and the "developmental tasks" as presented by Havighurst. Then we shall consider various ways in which the common and unique needs and problems of specific individuals in a particular group may be ascertained as a basis for planning suitable group activities.

Needs and Tasks at Various Age Levels

Some basic needs for wholesome personality development

Some of the characteristic features of the "Eight Stages of Man" in the development and integration of the ego, as depicted by Erikson, are briefly sketched here:

1. *The sense of trust.* This is a development of the very early months and years of life and grows out of the basic satisfactions of experiencing love and affection, of being an inseparable part of a family group, no

matter what one does, and of knowing or feeling that wants will be met by others or can be met by oneself. It is perhaps the foundation of faith in others, in self, and in the goodness of life. Children who fail to develop this sense of trust may go through life unhappily disturbed about their place in life, feeling unloved and unable to love, and lacking any faith in their fellow men or in themselves. Erikson says (4, p. 11):

For most infants . . . a sense of trust is not difficult to come by. It is the most important element in the personality. It emerges at the most vulnerable period of a child's life. Yet it is the least likely to suffer harm, perhaps because both nature and culture work toward making mothers most maternal at that time.

2. *The sense of autonomy* (4, p. 11).

The sense of trust once firmly established, the struggle for the next component of the healthy personality begins. The child is now twelve to fifteen months old. Much of his energy for the next two years will center around asserting that he is a human being with a mind and will of his own. . . . What is at stake throughout these years is the child's sense of autonomy, the sense that he is an independent human being and yet one who is able to use the help and guidance of others in important matters.

Erikson continues (4, p. 13):

Those who would guide the growing child wisely . . . will avoid shaming him and avoid causing him to doubt that he is a person of worth. They will be firm and tolerant with him so that he can rejoice in being a person of independence and can grant independence to others. . . . Just as the child's sense of trust is a reflection of the mother's sturdy and realistic faith, so the child's sense of autonomy is a reflection of the parents' personal dignity.

3. *The sense of initiative* (4, p. 14).

Having become sure, for the time being, that he is a person in his own right, and having enjoyed that feeling for a year or so, the child of four or five wants to find out what kind of person he can be.

Important for this phase of development is the opportunity to try out many types of activities, imitate others, give free rein to his imagination, and express creative powers through various media. Ridicule, criticism, or suppression at this stage may easily curb these creative outlets and stifle wholesome development. Praise and encouragement are essential.

4. *The sense of accomplishment.* This fourth stage, which begins at about six years of age and extends over five or six years, has as its achievement what Erikson calls the sense of industry. The chief danger of this period is the presence of conditions that may lead to the development of a sense of inadequacy and inferiority. This may be the outcome if the child has not yet achieved a sense of initiative, or if his experiences at

home have not prepared him for entering school happily, or if he finds school a place where his previous accomplishments are disregarded or his latent abilities are not challenged. Even with a good start the child may later lapse into discouragement and lack of interest if at home or school his individual needs are overlooked—if too much is expected of him, or if he is made to feel that achievement is beyond his ability.

The primary concern of teachers and of others who are professionally concerned with education is to make sure that both the curriculum and the methods of teaching are realistically planned so that every child will enjoy the feeling of successful accomplishment. Unless the child, at this phase of his development, strengthens the skills he already has and acquires new ones, school will be for him an experience of rejection and failure, rather than an experience which stabilizes his personality.

5. *The sense of identity.* The need for being aware of who one is and what one's relationship is to others becomes pressing during the period of adolescence. The individual is precariously balanced between being a child and being an adult, and he vacillates between one role and the other—seeking to identify himself. In the struggle to formulate a picture of himself that will be consistent with the values he has acquired from others and those he has developed for himself, he takes on a corollary problem—that of formulating a picture of himself as others see him. He is preoccupied with what others think of him, of how he looks to them, of whether or not he conforms to universally accepted standards. He needs to be accepted, to belong. His sense of identity is as much oriented to the conception his peers have of who and what he is as it is to his own evaluation of himself.

6. *Three stages of adulthood.* After the sense of identity, which is the most pressing need of adolescence, has been resolved, the individual is prepared to move into early adulthood. Having established a sound relationship with himself, he is equipped to establish relationships with others. This readiness for *intimacy* in interpersonal relationships is a significant stage of adulthood. Intimacy, as Erikson establishes it, can take many forms: friendship, combat, leadership, love, and inspiration (5).

Where a youth does not accomplish such intimate relations with others—and, I would add, with his own inner sources—in late adolescence or early adulthood, he may either isolate himself and find, at best, highly stereotyped and formal interpersonal relations (formal in the sense of lacking in spontaneity, warmth, and real exchange of fellowship), or he must seek them in repeated attempts and repeated failures.

An important component of the intimacy phase is genitality, the readiness for responsive sexual relationships. As this matures, the adult experiences the desire for *generativity.* This phase of the healthy personality usually manifests itself in parenthood—the eagerness and willingness to assume responsibility for, and contribute to, the development of another generation. In situations in which parenthood is not possible, this phase is sometimes expressed in other types of creativity.

The final phase of adulthood—the summation of the successful realization of all preceding phases of personality development—is *integrity*. It is the sort of maturity that permits acceptance of oneself and of others; that places value on human dignity and love; that sees oneself honestly in relation to other people, to the world of today, and to all the yesterdays which preceded us; and that makes one ready to fulfill his responsibility to himself and to others (5).

Concept of developmental tasks [1]

The classic definition of the developmental task, as advanced by Havighurst is (2, p. 2): "A developmental task is a task which arises at or about a certain period in the life of the individual, successful achievement of which leads to his happiness and to success with later tasks, while failure leads to unhappiness in the individual, disapproval by the society, and difficulty with later tasks."

A developmental task arises for an individual at the time it does because of the interaction of several factors: biological development which precipitates the undertaking; expectations imposed upon the individual from the external world, as determined by the culture in which he lives; his own emerging personality with its individual values and aspirations.

Developmental Tasks of Infancy and Early Childhood. Some of these early tasks are closely related to neurological and physiological development, but cultural patterns of training which give a moral overtone of "social acceptability" to success may infuse them with strong emotional tones that will profoundly affect attitudes in ensuing periods. Among these tasks are: *learning to control the elimination of body wastes; learning to walk; learning to take solid food;* and *learning sex differences and sex modesty. Learning to talk* might be added to this list, though readiness is determined much less by biological development, since the speaking apparatus is fairly well developed. Cultural expectations and individual differences in mental development are among strong contributing factors in the timing of learning to talk.

In the perceptual and interpersonal realms are the tasks of *forming simple concepts of social and physical reality; learning to relate oneself emotionally to parents, siblings, and other people; learning to distinguish right and wrong;* and *developing a conscience.*

Developmental Tasks of Middle Childhood. Basic features of this period are associated with the extension of the sense of trust and of

[1] Summarized from *Human Development and Education* by Robert Havighurst, by permission of Longmans, Green & Co., Inc., New York.

autonomy to relationships with teacher and peers and the need for a sense of accomplishment. It is becoming more difficult to differentiate the tasks in relation to these stages of development, since any one task may contribute to several basic needs. Among the developmental tasks related to the growing sense of accomplishment are: *learning physical skills necessary for ordinary games; developing fundamental skills in reading, writing, and calculating;* and *developing concepts necessary for everyday living.* Additional tasks of this period listed by Havighurst are: *building wholesome attitudes toward oneself as a growing organism* (such as habits of cleanliness, safety, sense of physical adequacy, and wholesome sex attitudes); *learning to get along with age-mates; learning appropriate masculine or feminine social roles; developing conscience, morality, and a scale of values; achieving more personal independence;* and *developing basic attitudes toward social groups and institutions*—an outgrowth of learnings in home and school.

Developmental Tasks of Preadolescence. Many of these relate to more complex stages of the developmental tasks of middle childhood, but appearing on the horizon are those tasks which presage adolescence. Havighurst presents several developmental tasks of this period: (*a*) *achieving an appropriate dependence-independence pattern,* which begins to free the individual from adults and opens up more personal choices; (*b*) *achieving an appropriate giving-receiving pattern,* extended beyond family to teachers, peers, and perhaps pets; (*c*) *relating to social groups,* a beginning of the drive to belong; (*d*) further *development of a conscience* which may become rooted in rules and a sense of fairness, and of right and wrong; (*e*) a new stage in the *learning of one's psychosociobiological sex role* associated with identification with one's own sex group; (*f*) *managing a changing body and learning new motor patterns*—an enormous challenge to the improvement of various skills; (*g*) *learning to understand and control the physical world,* as concepts of space, time, and weight increase; (*h*) *developing an appropriate symbol system and conceptual abilities,* through which cause and effect relationships are perceived; (*i*) *relating oneself to the cosmos,* through the emergence of expanding concepts of reality and God.

Developmental Tasks of Adolescence. Here the sense of identity and the urge to relate with others are in the ascendance as individuals begin to think of themselves in adult terms and strive to perform on an adult level. For this period Havighurst lists as developmental tasks: *achieving new and more mature relations with age-mates of both sexes; achieving a masculine or feminine social role,* often with special problems for some girls, partly because of conflicts between traditional feminine roles and a career-oriented life; *accepting one's physique and using the body effectively,* perhaps presenting problems more frequently to boys with respect to questions of normalcy of the tempo of pubertal development; *achiev-ing emotional independence of parents* and other adults associated with frequent ambivalent feelings; *selecting and preparing for an occupation; preparing for marriage and family life,* a task involving the whole pattern of dating and courtship; *developing intellectual skills and concepts necessary for civic competence,* the urge for which comes with the broadening social consciousness; *desiring and achieving socially responsible behavior,* again a task involving a good deal of ambivalence; and *acquiring a set of values and an ethical system as a guide to behavior*—one of the foundations for self-direction.

Developmental Tasks of Early Adulthood. Here the sense of intimacy, the urge to parenthood, and the drive for integrity, which, in a sense, is a summation of all preceding phases of personality development, are coordinated in the tasks of *selecting a mate, learning to live with a marriage partner, starting a family, rearing children, managing a home, getting started in an occupation, taking on civic responsibility,* and *finding congenial social groups.*

Developmental Tasks of Middle Age. The beginnings of the shift away from parental responsibility, the effort to maintain or improve economic status, and the emergence of opportunities for new creative outlets as responsibilities for children in the home begin to lessen cause a rearranged balance of developmental tasks in this period. Havighurst suggests for this period the tasks of *achieving adult civic and social responsibility; establishing and maintaining an economic standard of living; assisting teen-age children to become responsible and happy adults; developing adult leisure-time activities; relating oneself to one's spouse,* perhaps in new terms as children grow up; *accepting and adjusting to the physiological changes of middle age;* and *adjusting to aging parents,* through the meeting of their needs without impairing the happiness of others.

Developmental Tasks of Later Maturity. In this period there are difficult developmental tasks involving *adjustment to decreased physical strength and health, to reduced income, to possible death of a spouse,* and *to probable narrowing of social relationships.* The maintenance or *establishment of explicit affiliation with one's age group, meeting of social and civic obligations,* and the *adjustment of living arrangements to age demands* as to health and physical activity and to a desirable amount of independence are likely to be associated with rather radical changes in the life pattern.

Interrelations of developmental tasks

In terms of the development of the total personality and the adequacy of the individual to meet the demands which life makes of him, it is perhaps significant to point out that, in general terms, there is both horizontal and vertical integration in performance on developmental tasks. An individual who performs one task well is likely also to perform well in the other tasks for the same period. Also, that same individual is likely to continue to perform well the more advanced developmental tasks in the same category at a later age.

Contrary to what many might anticipate, there is very little evidence that children who perform poorly at one set of tasks compensate by excelling at others (2).

DISCOVERING NEEDS AND PROBLEMS OF INDIVIDUALS

One of the initial concerns in planning a program of guidance services in groups is the discovery of the common and unique needs and problems of the individuals within any particular group. Two major types of understanding are essential for the guidance worker in approaching this task:

1. Understanding of developmental trends and common problems at each progressive age level

2. Knowledge of the various ways in which understanding of individuals within a group may be achieved

There is no dearth of literature regarding developmental trends and common problems, though some periods in the life span have been studied more fully than others. The literature is too voluminous and varied to be summarized here in any helpful detail. A selected list of materials in this field is included in the chapter references.

The significance of a broad overview of the life span (for which Erikson's and Havighurst's approaches were summarized earlier in this chapter), and of more specific trends in planning for a particular group, is to provide perspective on where each individual places roughly on this continuum in various aspects of his present developmental status. Also, it is important for judging to what extent each individual's interests, needs, and problems conform to or vary from those most frequently found within his age group or his developmental level. In other words, understanding of people generally is essential for understanding particular individuals.

Since each person has a unique pattern of potentialities and of development, we do not expect him to conform fully to group norms, but it is through this comparison of the group and the individual that we can arrive at understanding of his uniqueness, and also of the extent of his conformity to general expectancies for his age and developmental status.

Research on common problems has revealed amazingly high incidence of certain problems at various ages and in various environmental situations. Counseling and therapeutic services have likewise revealed this same high incidence of common problems, though always in individual settings. Also, each individual has been seen to have his own unique pattern of development that may involve wide variations in tempo for different aspects of his physical, mental, and total personality development.

After many years of attempting to formulate these common problems for various age groups the writer began to visualize the possibility of a standardized, graded list of basic concerns. Fortunately, before such a graded list was completed evidence began to filter in that shifts were occurring in the emergence of various interests and problems. As the tempo of environmental changes was accelerated it became evident that the patterns of maturing were likewise changing. Some interests and concerns appeared at an earlier age and the nature of others was modified. For example, during World War II concern about marriage appeared earlier for more adolescents than in the previous decades of the century. Differences in intensity and age of appearance of many problems have always been noticeable in comparisons of trends in radically different social or economic groups.

To summarize, while there are general trends with respect to common human problems that must be understood, each group, like each individual, is unique and requires firsthand study of its pattern of needs and concerns in order to provide suitable and helpful guidance services. For guidance purposes this means first the study and understanding of individuals within a group before the group picture can be envisaged. Leadership of a group entails also an understanding of interrelationships within a group, for which techniques will be considered in Chapter 5.

Methods of ascertaining individual needs and problems

Selected research studies will be utilized to illustrate a variety of methods, but specific findings will be summarized only briefly, since the emphasis here is upon *ways* in which understanding of needs and concerns can be achieved.

Free Response in Written Reports. The free-response technique is frequently used to initiate a study of needs, problems, and worries in order to tap conscious concerns and to avoid suggesting problems of which individuals may not be aware. Jersild (6) secured compositions from several thousand young people from the fourth grade through college. They were asked to write on the topics "What I Like about Myself" and "What I Dislike about Myself," and were given no leads as to the nature of their responses. Several persons categorized the data in these compositions independently and Jersild reported a satisfactory agreement among the judges for the purposes of the study, though there were naturally some differences of opinion regarding classification of the great variety of free responses. The effort was made to arrange the categories in an ascending order of psychological maturity, but it was found that, apart from some quite clearly age-linked responses, most of the self-descriptive items prominent at any one age level were also prominent at other levels, though with shifting degrees of emphasis. This was especially true of those involving feelings or attitudes with regard to one's own character traits, emotional tendencies, or feelings toward others (6, p. 30).

Among the characteristics liked in self the following categories were mentioned frequently at all levels: physical characteristics, clothes, ability in sports and play, special talents, personality and character, and social attitudes and relationships. Ability in school work and enjoyment of recreation were noted more often in early years than later, and there was a marked increase over the years in mention of general appearance, inner resources, moral character, and attitudes toward and relationships with others. Matters pertaining to home and family were included among both likes and dislikes much more frequently by the elementary and junior high school pupils than by high school and college students except for eleventh-grade girls. Among items in the disliked traits, physical characteristics decreased and study habits increased in percentage of mention at the college level (6).

Jersild interpreted the findings of this "free-response" survey as indicating a great need in educational programs for assistance to children and youth in self-evaluation and realistic self-acceptance.

PROBLEMS REPORTED IN FREE RESPONSES. The free-response method was used by Little and Chapman (7) on 4,957 high school students embracing an age span of thirteen to nineteen. On the basis of the 19,006 problems which were reported, the following general categories, named in the order of their rank, were formulated: social adjustment, family relations, the use of time, the future, personality, part-time jobs and money, health.

More problems were reported by girls than by boys. Of the general categories listed above, girls registered problems with a higher frequency than boys in the areas of social adjustment, family relations, and personality. There was a higher frequency for boys than for girls in reporting problems related to part-time jobs and money and to health.

Young children who may be unable to formulate and write down problems can reveal many of their wishes, hopes, fears, worries, and interests through free or creative writing or through informal, fairly unstructured discussions in small groups. Pryor (8) has provided delightful suggestions derived from her experiences with what she calls *graphotherapy* in encouraging children to express their thoughts and feelings to release tensions and provide clues to understanding of their problems. Pryor stresses the need for a warm feeling between child and teacher and the avoidance of criticism of form and spelling to bring about free expression of honest reactions. She suggests ways in which the writing period can be used to correct errors without inhibiting spontaneity. Topics might include such themes as the following: "What Makes Me Frightened— or Sad or Glad?" "I Wonder"; "Things I Would Like to Change"; "Things I Like"; "My Hardest Problem." A fight on the playground or some unusual occurrence might lead to a discussion and to writing about its causes.

At any age level it is helpful to have a box available in a convenient spot where anyone can slip in an anonymous statement about a concern or a suggestion for topics or procedures for the group work.

EVIDENCE IN FREE RESPONSE OF ADULT PROBLEMS AMONG GRADUATE STUDENTS. For about twenty years the author has invited various seminar groups of graduate students in personnel work to write statements regarding their unresolved worries and problems, partly to help them gain the feel of approaches with their own students, and also to secure data for use in realistic group discussions of common problems. As these lists have accumulated, the responses have fallen chiefly into the following categories in the approximate order listed as to incidence: Questions related to satisfactory and meaningful achievement in their graduate work; placement or advancement in their chosen work; finding a mate and establishing a home if unmarried; finding time for study, work, home life, and social-civic activities; relationships with co-workers; health problems of self or members of family; financial worries; marital problems with spouse—interpersonal and sexual adjustments; behavior and emotional problems of children; a great variety of worries of a neurotic nature; a search for a more meaningful life.

Obviously, these are common problems of early or middle adulthood in an educational setting. Pursued in group study or individual conferences, they have often provided much evidence of how unresolved difficulties of an earlier period may continue to take their toll in anxieties and frustrations in later years even among individuals who are themselves engaged in personnel work and, in the main, well adjusted.

THE USE OF CHECK LISTS AND INVENTORIES. Items for inventories of problems have often been assembled from written free responses. An advantage of the check list is that it is likely to provide more comprehensive coverage of worries and problems, since some individuals will be inarticulate about expressing difficulties and also may not fully recognize the nature of problems until they see them stated. However, the

free response evoked through a nondirective method offers the opportunity for a complete, uncurbed statement, which may reveal more about
the individual's concern with the problem.

In the use of either method, anonymity may assure freer responses and
prevent hesitation in identifying certain problems with self, though the
approach to a group and their understanding of the purposes of providing the information are likely to be more important than the question of
identification of responses. Both techniques have the limitation of not
tapping some of the problems uncovered in clinical studies that have
shown that individuals are not always aware of the real nature of their
problems. However, there have been enough free-response and inventory
surveys with sufficiently large population samples, so that valuable findings regarding the incidence of problems have been secured.

Problems Reported on Check Lists. Check lists have been developed
for the exploration of the problems of children, youth, and adults. The
SRA Junior Inventory (9) was administered, during its development, to
several thousand elementary school children from schools in all sections
of the country. Although a number of inventories have been applied to
groups of high school students, this represents one of the first systematic
surveys by check list of large numbers of children in this younger age
group. A content analysis of essays on "My Problems" written by hundreds of school children was used as one basis for preparing the items
in the check list. Other sources were the experiences of teachers and
guidance workers in the elementary school field and literature dealing
with children's problems (9, p. 6). Following are brief summaries of
some of the problems checked by 15 per cent or more of the children
under the major headings: [2]

My Health. Colds; dizziness; hungry a lot; get tired of sitting; get
out of breath.

Getting Along with Other People. Want more social and play
skills; need more friends; often say the wrong thing.

About Me and My School. Problems deal with arithmetic, reading,
writing, spelling, grades, tests, ability, lack of good books and membership in a club, heat in schoolroom; dislikes included geography, history,
and school in general; desire expressed for more music and painting.

About Myself. Concern about future work, bad habits such as fingernail biting and temper, wrongdoing, looks, clothes, skill in games,
lack of a pet or a job, fear of being alone at night. Sixteen per cent
checked the item "Sometimes I wish I was dead."

About Me and My Home. Wishes were expressed for one's own room,
more money, movies more often, daddy to be home more, and music

[2] Summaries reproduced by permission of Science Research Associates, Inc., Chicago. The wording of inventory items has not been kept here in the main.

lessons. Twenty-two per cent objected to resting when others were playing.

A variety of health conditions seem to worry the younger children more than the older ones. It has been suggested by the authors of the inventory that many of these children are probably in good health but do not understand the normal working of their bodies. General dislike of school and problems of poor achievement show up more frequently with boys than with girls, though both indicate lack of interest in many subjects and both indicate the desire to improve their skills in arithmetic, reading, or spelling. The large number expressing the wish for more interesting books and for more time spent on a variety of activities, together with awareness of poor achievement, would suggest that conditions related to dropouts and school difficulties at the secondary level are already emerging at the fourth grade (9, p. 2).

Remmers and his co-workers who have conducted the Purdue Opinion Panel over a considerable period of time have attempted to tap teenagers' views on many personal, social, political, economic, educational, religious, and ethical issues by questionnaires as well as check lists. They have reported results for youth classified by various regions in the United States, by sex, high school grade placement, religious affiliation, and family income level (12).

Following is a brief summary of some of the findings from the SRA Youth Inventory [3] and the Purdue Opinion Panel as to worries and concerns revealed by large percentages of teen-agers (10–12):

SCHOOL. Major problems in this area were how to study more effectively, difficulty in keeping mind on studies, expressing themselves orally and in writing, apprehension about examinations, desire for practical work experience, and some doubt about the value of subjects studied.

LOOKING AHEAD. Here was evidence of felt need for more self-appraisal of interests, abilities, and school achievement, for more vocational information (including military service for boys), and assistance in educational and vocational planning for the future.

ABOUT MYSELF. Among concerns about personal adjustment (which might be symptomatic of deeply seated problems or might merely indicate superficial uneasiness) were worry about little things, temper control, stage fright before groups, daydreaming, feeling inferior to others in ability, lack of self-confidence, regret or guilt feelings about conduct or undesirable habits, lonesomeness, impulsiveness, carelessness, compulsion to be "always on the go," fear of failure or humiliation, nervousness, and excitability.

[3] Published by Science Research Associates, Inc., Chicago.

GETTING ALONG WITH OTHERS. The need to be liked and accepted by peers is reflected in the frequently expressed desire to be more popular, concern about being left out of activities, desire to feel important, and need to live up to the ideals of one's group.

MY HOME AND FAMILY. On the Youth Inventory there was a slightly higher frequency of home problems reported at the junior high school level than by senior high school students, and responses did not reflect strongly the generally assumed hostility between teen-agers and parents. Problems checked in this area focused on lack in the home environment, feelings of not being wanted, difficulty with brothers and sisters, fear of telling parents about wrongdoing, and parents' avoidance of discussing sex.

BOY MEETS GIRL. Problems relating to dating and other rituals of courtship are compelling concerns of teen-agers. Among those checked most frequently were lack of friendships and dates with the opposite sex, going steady, retaining interest of the opposite sex, kissing on first date, and desirable conduct for high school students.

HEALTH. Among the most widespread health problems reported were gaining or losing weight, good posture and improvement of figure, and skin problems.

THINGS IN GENERAL. Concern was indicated in the areas of world affairs, religion, and ethical standards of right and wrong.

Problems Reported by College Students. Numerous check-list studies of college students have yielded somewhat different findings as to the incidence of recognized difficulties. Problems of personality have headed the lists in some studies, while budgeting time and standards of work have led in others. Vocational planning usually rates high.

A sampling of college students using the Mooney Problem Check List, which allows for indicating the intensity of problems by encircling the numbers of those which are of most serious concern, was made by Stone (13) with students from the freshman through the senior year. Results are shown in Table 1 as to rank order of eleven categories of problems underlined as present and circled as indicating seriousness. The mean number of items per student was 27.1 underlined, and 5.8 circled as serious. Faculty study of the results of this survey led to the conclusions that certain problems occurred with sufficient frequency to lend themselves to a group approach, that the orientation program should be revised in the light of the findings, that a general-education program geared to meet local needs was indicated, and that the personnel services should be improved.

Koile and Bird (14) administered the Mooney Problem Check List to 442 freshmen at East Texas State Teachers College for the purpose of discovering students' preferences for counselor help on problems.

TABLE 1. RANK ORDER OF ELEVEN CATEGORIES OF PROBLEMS
IDENTIFIED BY COLLEGE STUDENTS

Categories	Rank order of under-lined problems (Stone)	Rank order of serious problems (Stone)	Rank order of problems (Koile and Bird)
Adjustment to college work..............	1	1	1
Social and recreational activities...........	2	6	3
Curriculum and teaching procedures.......	3	5	10
Personal-psychological relations...........	4	3	2
The future—vocational and educational ...	5	2	7
Finances, living conditions, employment....	6	4	6
Health and physical development..........	7	7	5
Social-psychological relations..............	8	9	4
Courtship, sex, and marriage..............	9	8	8
Morals and religion......................	10	11	9
Home and family........................	11	10	11

They believed that contacts with the counselors and group orientation sessions had provided a climate conducive to rather open and free response by students. A total of 8,735 problems were identified by the students with an average of 22.9 problems per student. The rank order of incidence of these problems by category is listed in Table 1 and can thus be compared with the rank order in Stone's survey. These variations are likely to occur between any two groups because of individual and situational differences and different techniques of investigation. Freshmen in the Texas group expressed the desire for assistance in approximately 58 per cent of their identified problems.

Inventoried Problems in Later Maturity. Two investigations, one a survey of the nature and patterns of problems of adjustment of about 3,000 persons over sixty years of age by Cavan, Burgess, Havighurst, and Goldhamer (15), and the other an intensive study of a sampling of 100 people over sixty-five years of age in "Prairie City" carried on by Havighurst and Albrecht (16), have yielded a large store of information about the life patterns and concerns of older people.

An inventory, "Your Attitudes and Activities," used in these investigations included categories of health, family, friends, leisure and recreation, clubs and organizations, employment history, financial security, early life, and attitudes. Biographical data for many individuals filled in the outlines of the summarized results of the inventory to provide a living picture of a large segment of older people in the population. The

items in the inventory were assigned score values by judges on the basis
of comparisons of groups of older individuals who had been classified as
well adjusted or poorly adjusted by interviewers. The median score on
this Attitude Inventory used as indicative of personal adjustment declined from the early sixties until the later periods in the survey group.
Some of the specific trends with increasing age in this sample group
were: *decrease* in the amount of close companionship, in participation
in many activities, in number of hobbies, in plans for the future, in
feelings of satisfaction with health status, in feelings of happiness, usefulness, zest, and interest in life; *increase* in physical handicaps, illness
and nervousness, in religious activities and dependence upon religion,
and in a feeling of economic security, despite a lower income, particularly
on the part of women.

Certain sex differences were noted, which seemed to stem from two
facts—that women live longer than men, and that most women do not
experience complete retirement from work between the ages of sixty-five
and seventy-five as do most men. The most drastic and widespread adjustment for women is that to widowhood and for men to retirement
from employment. Women in the group surveyed participated more than
did men in activities in their sixties and early seventies, but the situation was reversed in later years. Women reported more physical handicaps, had more religious activities, but seemed less happy than men.
Their median score on the Attitude Inventory was lower than the score
for men.

The findings in these two studies are so comprehensive that it is impossible to summarize them adequately in a few paragraphs. They show
that there is the same type of spread in individual adjustments in later
maturity that is to be found in any age group. Also, they indicate that
many of the problems faced by older people are caused not only by the
aging process but also by the influences of the culture as it impinges on
this age group. Havighurst and Albrecht (16) explored the prevailing
assumption of a somewhat hostile, disapproving attitude toward the
aged in our culture by means of a questionnaire entitled "What do you
think about activities for older people?" They interpreted their findings
as negating any widespread blanket disapproval of older people in
America and concluded (16, p. 39): "We think well of elderly people
who make a success of their old age, and we think ill of those who are
unfortunate enough to be failures in their later years."

Investigating Problems through Interviews. Counselors and teachers
have significant opportunities for discovering and clarifying problems
through planned and informal interviews with students and parents, and
through insightful listening to remarks and conversations in groups.
Many problems listed or checked by individuals can be traced back to

sources or to more basic difficulties through skillful counseling and the use of cumulative personnel records. These records will often yield valuable suggestions as to sources of some problems when studied with a view to discovering possible crisis points such as serious illness or accident, new siblings, death or disruption in the family, school failure, and a host of other vicissitudes. When individuals are not aware of their more basic difficulties and are not yet ready to cope with them, the counselor's task in planning group work may be to decide when camouflaged case studies or other approaches can be used helpfully to foster increased insight into real or underlying problems.

Two illustrations of the use of the interview technique for investigating problems are included here.

This method was used by Hunter and Morgan (17) with 200 men and women at Colorado Agricultural and Mechanical College. In order of decreasing frequency of importance, the following problems were reported by one-fifth or more of the students: budgeting time, study time, studying effectively, planning extracurricular activities to avoid interference with academic work, concentrating during study hours, buying and spending wisely, inadequate rest and sleep, deciding on marriage, being self-conscious, lacking in self-confidence, wanting a more pleasing personality, speaking in public.

The Joint Commission on Mental Illness and Health (18) carried out a program of intensive interviews with a group of 2,460 individuals twenty-one years of age and older living at home and constituting "an accurately proportional miniature of the 'normal' adult population of the United States." Interview questions dealt with the way they felt they were adjusting to life; how happy or unhappy, worried or unworried they thought they were; the picture they had of themselves; their attitudes toward three important areas of their lives—marriage, parenthood, and work; how they coped with their problems; where they turned for help; or why they failed to seek help. In addition they were asked to respond to a list of twenty symptom items.

The very detailed report of findings gained from these interviews provides a comprehensive picture of the attitudes and problems of adults of all ages in the areas covered and could not be summarized adequately here.

About 90 per cent said they were very happy or pretty happy, but one-fourth admitted they worried a lot or all the time. Sources of anxiety, and of happiness, were closely related in their judgments to material and economic conditions, but from the viewpoint of security and adequacy of living rather than luxury. The areas of marriage, parenthood, and work were all sources of both happiness and unhappiness, but more than half found their greatest happiness in the home.

Self-perceptions tended to be related more often to external, accepted standards than to individual values and inner conflicts. More than two-thirds believed that in some positive ways they were different from others.

Women expressed more distress than men. Men, on the other hand, blamed themselves more often than did women for marital difficulties and expressed more concern about possible neglect of parental functions. In parental self-criticism by both sexes more emphasis was given to parent-child relationships than to the older cultural emphasis on being providers.

The younger and the better-educated people both tended to worry more than the older and less well educated, but they were happier in the main. The Commission attributed these differences to higher aspirations and expectations on the one hand and to resignation and frustration on the other hand.

Attitudes of men toward jobs were conditioned by several factors, including work status, income, education, and age. Jobs with high status were sources of more worry and distress and also of greater satisfaction than were those of lower status with less ego involvement.

Four symptom patterns seemed to stand out in the group: (a) psychological anxiety, (b) physical health symptoms, (c) immobilization or psychic inertia, and (d) physical anxiety. No clear-cut summary of the incidence of these patterns in various groups can be given briefly, but a few illustrations will be noted. The young presented physical health and psychic inertia patterns frequently. Among the more educated group psychic inertia appeared with high prevalence, due, perhaps, to more complex social and psychological demands. Women and the middle-class group showed more psychological anxiety, and the older group more bodily symptoms. These are only a few of the comparisons of problem patterns teased from the data by the investigators.

One interesting deduction was the indication that happiness does not imply an absence of worries and that the worrier is likely to be more optimistic about the future and more active and positive in his approach to life than the nonworrier. This presumably means that he attempts to cope with his problems rather than being apathetic or resigned about unsatisfying conditions.

One in seven of those interviewed had sought help of some kind in dealing with problems, and about one-fourth said they had worked out their problems themselves.

All of the methods considered previously—written free responses, check lists, and questionnaires—can be utilized together with a wide variety of adjustment and personality inventories to secure clues for helpful procedures in interviews. Item inspection of these instruments will often provide valuable leads to pursue in counseling with individuals, though caution must be exercised not to probe where an individual is not yet ready to face up to or cope with certain aspects of his life or personality.[4]

Frequent interviews with members of a guidance group will keep the leader in touch with group influences upon individuals and be of mutual value in adapting the group guidance to changing individual needs and in helping individuals to apply their learnings in the group more effectively.

Observation Techniques. The observation technique has been defined by Super (19, pp. 26–28) as "the observation of performance, of the personality in action, based on the assumption that people are what they do." He describes the *medium* as either a life situation or an artificial miniature situation, the *method* as recorded observation.

Teachers, counselors, and group leaders have excellent opportunities for assessment of personal needs, developmental trends, and adjustment problems through observation of behavior in life situations in classroom and in discussion and activity groups. Accurate observation and correct interpretation of what an individual does may yield understandings unobtainable from what he writes or says in an interview, or from his responses on tests and inventories. Viteles (19, p. 152) has illustrated the possibility of errors in depending on interviews by pointing out that industrial workers in a motivation study did not reveal to interviewers their hostility to certain management policies or their work slowdown because of fear of being laid off in a depression period. Individuals may often be unaware of what they are withholding in an interview or a written statement.

Observation techniques can, of course, yield highly unreliable data, unless the observer is fully cognizant of the dangers of subjectivity in both his observation and interpretive processes. For years cautions have been sounded concerning the making of anecdotal records, to the effect that they should describe accurately what an individual did in a particular situation, not the recorder's subjective judgment of why the person may have done what he did or of what this behavior indicated as to traits or problems. The value of these cumulated records of behavior over a time span in better understanding of pupils has been amply demonstrated, but the problem of time to make records for all pupils has never been fully solved.

Approaches to measuring leadership in the Armed Services may point to some solutions of this time problem. Situational tests were based on

[4] The Minnesota Counseling Inventory is one of the helpful tools for this purpose. Ralph F. Berdie and Wilbur L. Layton, *Journal of Counseling Psychology*, 7:218–224, fall, 1960.

the analysis of critical incidents in leadership positions, and specific acts of effective leadership were observed and recorded. Prediction based on test performance and agreement among observers were both on the positive side (19, pp. 146–168). Situations in school or activity groups can likewise be analyzed and instruments can be developed that will contain descriptions of types of critical incidents representative of behavior to be observed. These descriptions can then be checked for individuals by the observer with much saving of time. Behavior frequency counts can then be made for specific types of behavior that will help to eliminate subjective judgments. Like the rating scale, this method could narrow observation with respect to all the varied richness of individual behavior and of interpersonal relations in a group. But its use in the study of specific types of behavior may help an alert observer to become more analytic and objective about all aspects of behavior.[5]

Continued observation must ultimately lead to judgments of some kind if it is to be meaningful and useful. Here even more caution and skill are needed than in the observation process. Doubtless most educators are now aware of the need to avoid ascribing motives and judgments of good and bad in interpretation of behavior, and to attempt to understand causal factors and developmental trends in the *becoming* process in every individual; also of the need to enlist the individual himself in the process of interpretation, since the person is in the best situation to know what is going on in his personality.

The complexity of the process of making sound judgments regarding the meaning of behavior may perhaps be illustrated by experimental research in the area of clinical work. Hunt (19, pp. 169–191) has described the use of trained clinicians, trainees, and naïve undergraduates in evaluating clues in clinical data. Results of numerous experiments did not show as great differentiation among the judgments of the three groups as would be desired, but Hunt concluded that, while clinical judgment is sufficiently reliable at present for some practical applications, much further understanding is needed to achieve the desired accuracy in judgments and judges. The use of untrained observers as instruments of precision has been compared to the use of uncalibrated physical instruments in which constant errors may remain unknown. All who attempt

---

[5] Flanagan has prepared a performance record form, with accompanying guide and manual, for the recording of critical incidents in behavior on items under the general headings of personal adjustment, responsibility and effort, creativity and initiative, integrity, social adjustment, sensitivity to others, group orientation, and adaptability to rules and conventions. Blue areas are provided in the form for recording incidents of desirable behavior to be encouraged, and red areas for incidents of undesirable behavior needing improvement. John C. Flanagan, *Performance Record for the Personal and Social Development Program, Teacher's Guide,* and *Manual for School Administrators and Supervisors,* Science Research Associates, Inc., Chicago, 1956.

to understand more about individuals through observation would do well to think of themselves as instruments that will inevitably record errors, some of which can be eliminated by training and experience. Consideration of the fallibility of even highly trained clinicians should cause any observer of human behavior to maintain an attitude of cautious reservation about all judgments.

Studies which have tapped observations of teachers and parents regarding children's problems have shown discrepancies as well as agreements among teachers, parents, and children with respect to incidence and time of emergence of problems. A comparison of two studies (20, 21) showed that many teachers and guidance workers at the elementary school level reported fewer educational problems in grades 7 and 8 than earlier, whereas, in contrast, parents seemed to become increasingly aware of school problems from the elementary through the secondary level. Comparisons of parents' reports of children's problems with children's checking of problems on inventories (20, 9) suggest that parents become aware of some personality difficulties long before children develop concern about them—most often in adolescence. Comparisons of teachers' observations with children's inventories suggest that the extent of children's interests in future work is not adequately recognized by teachers, since percentages of children, grades 4 through 8, checking this interest on the SRA Junior Inventory are much higher than those of teachers checking the incidence of "vocational-adjustment" problems at these grade levels. The wording of items may have influenced this difference. There seems to be more agreement between teachers and children on the lessening incidence of health and social-adjustment problems in grades 7 and 8 in comparison with earlier years. Is life smoothing out in these years, or are children learning to cover up, deal with, or live with their problems; or have many with the most troublesome problems left school?

Life Histories, Case Studies, and Clinical Methods. Some are questioning whether widespread testing and statistical prediction may cause us to lose sight of the total functioning person. Dailey (22), in an appeal to re-emphasize the life-history approach in assessment procedures, has sounded a sharp caution about too great concentration on tests by commenting that "there is no case on record in which a psychological journal published the test scores of a deceased scientist as an adequate description of him as a person."

Longitudinal personnel records should provide much developmental data, but seldom do they afford a lifelike picture of a functioning individual. Analysis and synthesis of long-range records together with current materials such as have been considered earlier in this chapter will yield many clues for envisaging the real person. In group work the group members can participate profitably in formulating their life histories. The autobiography can come alive when assistance is provided through group study in the understanding of hereditary and environmental influences affecting all human lives and of ways to investigate these influences in one's own life. This procedure will be dealt with further in Chapter 10, but is mentioned here to stress the desirability of pooling teacher or counselor observations and personnel record data with information from group members to secure breadth and depth in the understanding of individuals. Prescott (23) in his three-year in-service child-study plan carries out a many-faceted approach aimed to help the teacher see and feel with the child as well as collect, organize, and interpret data in a scientific manner.

Johnson, Stefflre, and Edelfelt (24, pp. 259–260) describe the case method as one of the most important skills for the pupil personnel worker in synthesizing existing and new data about a pupil as an aid in interpreting his difficulties as to nature and causes, and in planning remedial or therapeutic services. This method, which combines techniques from social work and psychological services and generally utilizes medical data also, will usually be limited to a few pupils needing the help of a personnel specialist.

Pressey and Simco (25) used case studies prepared by psychology students to attempt to describe the characteristics of successful as contrasted with "problem" old people. In this comparison of over 500 cases, it appeared that the successful could be differentiated by continuing usefulness, many social relationships, and maintenance of various activities and interests. Studies of the happiness and of the worries of older people suggest that these factors are very important in the maintenance of personally satisfying adjustments in old age. Guidance directed toward long-range planning in youth may help to foster the inner resources that will prevent much of personal bankruptcy in old age.

The Clinical Method. This method will enter into the picture of the school group worker through referral of individuals for special study by those with psychological and psychiatric training. It is likely to reveal problems of adjustment not otherwise discovered or to locate causal factors that may require therapy rather than, or in addition to, group guidance in regular or special groups.

A clinical study of a group of 100 sophomores at Harvard, selected on the basis of their apparent good health and satisfactory adjustment, uncovered some 250 problems. More or less serious problems were recognized by the clinical staff in 91 of the group, and 72, without prompting, presented their own difficulties to the investigators.

In a nontechnical report (26, pp. 70–79) these difficulties were classified as follows:

1. Those pertaining to social adjustment: shyness, feelings of inferiority, overaggressiveness, difficulties in meeting girls or making friends. Only 15 per cent of the boys voluntarily presented these problems, but the staff discerned them in 43 per cent.

2. Adjustments to the family: antagonism against one or both parents, discipline, unhappiness because of parental discord, divorce, illness, or death or religious teaching in the home. About one-fourth of the students mentioned problems in this area.

3. Worries related to sex: love affairs, marriage, and sex relations. Again about one-fourth of the boys expressed concern over these problems.

4. Concern about choice of career. Seventeen per cent of the students raised questions in this area.

5. Personality difficulties. Sixteen per cent of the boys requested discussions about their personalities—their apprehensions and concerns, their life values and purposes. The psychiatrists recognized the need for help with difficulties in 55 per cent of the cases.

6. Academic worries: organization of time, standards of work, choosing a field of concentration, and various dissatisfactions with the college. About 12 per cent of the boys mentioned these academic difficulties, which were identified by the psychiatrists in 10 per cent of the group.

7. Miscellaneous problems: financial and religious problems or difficulties with alcoholism, speech, handwriting, or war or racial attitudes.

It was observed that many of the problems were of a transitory nature and disappeared as the boys matured and adjusted themselves to college life. However, about one-fifth of these "normal" youths were judged to have acute and urgent problems upon which they needed help.

This clinical study has tended to underscore similar findings in many investigations, namely, that students do not always recognize the real nature of their problems and need assistance in gaining such insight before they can cope with them effectively.

Members of the Division of Mental Hygiene of the Department of University Health at Yale University (27) have described the various kinds of psychosocial problems found among the students receiving services through the clinic. Only one problem will be mentioned here because of its possible universality in varying forms and degrees in a period of revolutionary change in a technological world. This problem has been designated as idiosyncratic adaptation in college students. It relates to difficulty of adaptation in a new environment due to habitual adaptive patterns developed within the family that are inappropriate within a new social scene such as the college. This difficulty was presented as one especially characteristic of late adolescence and of college students away from home who are facing the urgent need of achieving a stable organization of adult character. In some degree this is a continuous developmental problem of adaptation as an individual moves through new and increasingly complex situations in school life. A treatment method developed in the Yale clinic included the development of insight into the maladaptive pattern, a gentle, interpretive expression of surprise (an unusual aspect of therapy), and the exploration of appropriate adaptive patterns. This approach may have implications for group guidance at many age levels, though it would usually be essential to avoid undesirable questioning of family patterns before a pupil is ready to achieve independence as an adult. Throughout adolesence the approach may be one of assistance in achieving both awareness of non-adaptive behavior patterns and an insightful acceptance of familial patterns, together with planning for the ultimate achievement of a suitable and satisfying adult life pattern.

Gesell and his co-workers (28, 29) conducted clinical studies of a group through childhood and adolescence that yielded manifestations of peaks and leveling-off periods in health problems, emotional tensions, behavior difficulties, fears, and worries at various stages of development. The authors of this clinical study implied that the cycles of tension and greater poise may be due more to inner patterns of maturation than to the impact of environment. This long-range clinical study is doubtless more valuable in understanding general developmental trends than in the study of a particular individual, whose unique growth pattern is not likely to match perfectly those of his chronological age in the group reported upon.

THE CHALLENGE TO GUIDANCE

The term *common problems* has been used in this chapter to refer to varieties of imminent or anticipated adjustments, usually involving choices of some kind, that the majority of persons may face at various stages in living. It does not necessarily connote maladjustments, though each person doubtless faces some difficulties that might be thus designated at various times in life.

We have surveyed in this chapter some of the needs and developmental tasks that characterize each stage of life. We have examined some of the methods that can be used to investigate the needs, problems, and frustrations of individuals in a particular guidance group, such as free written statements about problems and concerns, use of check lists, inventories, interviews, observation techniques, case method or life histories, and clinical study by specialists. We have examined a few of the findings in research studies utilizing these various techniques. These illustrative studies have been chosen to sample some of the common human problems that confront individuals at the various age levels, as well as to provide examples of the use of the various techniques. The samples of research do not provide a comprehensive coverage of problems and they are not arranged in an order to show a sequence of the emergence of common problems at successive age levels. This sequential approach has been attempted only in the summaries of needs and tasks at various age levels.

While understanding of trends of development is important for judging as to the uniqueness and common traits of individuals, one of the tasks of the leader of any guidance group is that of ascertaining the needs, problems, and concerns of each member of the group. Emphasis has therefore been placed on methods of achieving this understanding. Research findings as to age-level trends with respect to common human problems have been made incidental to the consideration of methods that may be used in exploring these problems with a particular group.

We have seen that failure to cope with inevitable frustrations at one stage may hamper the individual in ensuing stages. When uncompleted tasks and unresolved problems accumulate they may incapacitate a person to the point where the process of maturing is blocked and where it may even be reversed.

Evidence of such results in school dropouts, academic mortality, delinquency, crime, mental illness, divorce, occupational maladjustment, and unhappiness and dissatisfaction with life can be found in every community. The assumption is not intended, of course, that guidance services could prevent all these difficulties. Causes are not thoroughly understood, and doubtless they stem from many biological and cultural sources, differing in combination for each individual.

A challenge to guidance is that of discovering how individuals may best be helped to gain more of the insight, learnings, and skills needed to cope intelligently and effectively with the task and the adventure of exploring and mastering each new stage of life as it emerges. We have some guideposts from past experience and experimentation, but each guidance worker must be an explorer helping to push back the boundaries of our ignorance and uncertainty as to best ways of meeting this challenge. In ensuing chapters we shall examine some of the ways in which group approaches in guidance are being attempted as one means of helping to meet some of our common life needs.

REFERENCES CITED IN CHAPTER

1. Jersild, Arthur T., and Ruth J. Tasch: *Children's Interests and What They Suggest for Education*, Bureau of Publications, Teachers College, Columbia University, New York, 1949.

2. Havighurst, Robert J.: *Human Development and Education*, Longmans, Green & Co., Inc., New York, 1953.
3. Erikson, Erik H.: *Childhood and Society*, W. W. Norton & Company, Inc., New York, 1950.
4. Technical Committee on Fact Finding: *For Every Child a Healthy Personality: A Digest of the Fact-finding Report to the Midcentury White House Conference on Children and Youth*, Midcentury White House Conference on Children and Youth, Inc., Washington, 1950.
5. Erikson, Erik H., and Joan M. Erikson: "Growth and Crises of the Healthy Personality," reprint from Milton J. E. Senn (ed.), *Problems of Infancy and Childhood*, Supplement 2, Transactions of Fourth Conference, Josiah Macy, Jr., Foundation, New York, 1950.
6. Jersild, Arthur T.: *In Search of Self: An Exploration of the Role of the School in Promoting Self-understanding*, Bureau of Publications, Teachers College, Columbia University, New York, 1952.
7. Little, Wilson, and A. L. Chapman: *Developmental Guidance in Secondary School*, McGraw-Hill Book Company, Inc., New York, 1953.
8. Pryor, Frances: "We Can't Afford Not to Write," *Elementary English*, 38:509–512, November, 1961.
9. Remmers, Herman H., and Robert H. Bauernfeind: *Examiners Manual for the SRA Junior Inventory, Form A*, Science Research Associates, Inc., Chicago, 1951.
10. Remmers, Herman H., and Benjamin Shimberg: *Examiners Manual for the SRA Youth Inventory, Form A*, 2d ed., Science Research Associates, Inc., Chicago, 1953.
11. Remmers, Herman H., et al.: *Technical Supplement for the SRA Youth Inventory, Form A*, Science Research Associates, Inc., Chicago, 1953.
12. Remmers, Herman H., and D. H. Radler: *The American Teenager*, The Bobbs-Merrill Company, Inc., Indianapolis, 1957.
13. Stone, L. Gordon: "Student Problems in a Teachers College," *The Journal of Educational Psychology*, 39:404–416, 1948.
14. Koile, Earl A., and Dorothy Bird: "Preference for Counselor Help on Freshman Problems," *Journal of Counseling Psychology*, 3:97–106, summer, 1956.
15. Cavan, Ruth Shonle, et al.: *Personal Adjustment in Old Age*, Science Research Associates, Inc., Chicago, 1949.
16. Havighurst, Robert J., and Ruth Albrecht: *Older People*, Longmans, Green & Co., Inc., New York, 1953.
17. Hunter, Ruth A., and David H. Morgan: "Problems of College Students," *The Journal of Educational Psychology*, 40:79–92, 1949.
18. Gurin, Gerald, Joseph Veroff, and Sheila Feld: *Americans View Their Mental Health: A Nationwide Survey*, Basic Books, Inc., Publishers, New York, 1960.
19. Bass, Bernard M., and Irwin A. Berg (eds.): *Objective Approaches to Personality Assessment*, D. Van Nostrand Company, Inc., Princeton, N.J., 1959.
20. Jersild, Arthur J., and associates: *Joys and Problems of Child Rearing*, Bureau of Publications, Teachers College, Columbia University, New York, 1949.
21. National Association of Guidance Supervisors and Counselor Trainers: *A National Study of Existing and Recommended Practices for Assisting Youth Adjustment in Problems of Elementary Pupils and Their Frequencies as Reported by Schools*, Ann Arbor Publishers, Ann Arbor, Mich., 1953.
22. Dailey, Charles A.: "The Life History Approach to Assessment," *The Personnel and Guidance Journal*, 36:456–460, March, 1958.
23. Prescott, Daniel A.: *The Child in the Educative Process*, McGraw-Hill Book Company, Inc., New York, 1957.
24. Johnson, Walter F., Buford Stefflre, and Roy A. Edelfelt: *Pupil Personnel and Guidance Services*, McGraw-Hill Book Company, Inc., New York, 1961.
25. Shock, Nathan W.: "Gerontology (Later Maturity)," in Calvin P. Stone and Donald Taylor (eds.), *Annual Review of Psychology*, Annual Reviews, Inc., Stanford, Calif., 1951, vol. 2, pp. 353–370.

26. Hooton, Earnest: *Young Man You Are Normal,* G. P. Putnam's Sons, New York, 1945.
27. Wedge, Bryant M. (ed.): *Psychosocial Problems of College Men,* Yale University Press, New Haven, Conn., 1958.
28. Gesell, Arnold, and Frances L. Ilg: *The Child from Five to Ten,* Harper & Row, Publishers, New York, 1946.
29. Gesell, Arnold, Frances L. Ilg, and Louise Ames Bates: *Youth, the Years from Ten to Sixteen,* Harper & Row, Publishers, New York, 1956.

ADDITIONAL REFERENCES

Allen, Richard D., et al.: *Common Problems in Group Guidance,* Inor Publishing Company, New York, 1933.
Ausubel, D. P.: *Theory and Problems of Adolescent Development,* Grune & Stratton, Inc., New York, 1954.
Bath, John A.: "Problems of College Students," *The Journal of College Student Personnel,* 3:33–36, October, 1961.
Better Living Booklets, Science Research Associates, Inc., Chicago.
Blaine, Graham B., Jr., and Charles C. McArthur: *Emotional Problems of the Student,* Appleton-Century-Crofts, Inc., New York, 1961.
De Haan, Robert F., and Jack Kough: *Identifying Students with Special Needs,* Science Research Associates, Inc., Chicago, 1956.
Jersild, Arthur T.: *Child Development,* 5th ed., Prentice-Hall, Inc., Englewood Cliffs, N.J., 1961.
Jersild, Arthur T.: *The Psychology of Adolescence,* The Macmillan Company, New York, 1957.
Loomis, Mary Jane: *The Preadolescent: Three Major Concerns,* Appleton-Century-Crofts, Inc., New York, 1959.
McCreary, William H., and Donald Kitch: "Now Hear Youth: A Report on the California Co-operative Study of School Drop-outs and Graduates," *Bulletin of the California State Department of Education,* vol. 22, no. 9, Sacramento, Calif., October, 1953.
Murphy, Gardner: *Human Potentialities,* Basic Books, Inc., Publishers, New York, 1958.
Pressey, Sidney L., and Raymond G. Kuhlen: *Psychological Development through the Life Span,* rev. ed., Harper & Row, Publishers, New York, 1957.
Sarason, Seymour B., et al.: *Anxiety in Elementary School Children,* John Wiley & Sons, Inc., New York, 1960.
Steckle, Lynde C.: *Problems of Human Adjustment,* rev. ed., Harper & Row, Publishers, New York, 1957.
Strang, Ruth: *The Adolescent Views Himself: A Psychology of Adolescence,* McGraw-Hill Book Company, Inc., New York, 1957.
White, Verna: *Studying the Individual Pupil,* Harper & Row, Publishers, New York, 1958.

TECHNIQUES IN GROUP GUIDANCE AND COUNSELING

PART TWO

TECHNIQUES IN
GROUP GUIDANCE
AND COUNSELING

4 GROUP PROCESSES IN GUIDANCE

Part One of this book has been devoted to the question of *why*, and a preview of the *what*, of group guidance—in other words, to the purposes of group guidance and to the general areas of common human problems and concerns in which it operates. This section, Part Two, deals with questions of *how* and *who*. What are the techniques and who performs them? Both of these questions have, inevitably, crept into the consideration of the *why* and the *what*. The *how* of understanding common problems and concerns of any particular group was used as the means of securing an overview of the *what* for two reasons: First, the difficulty of compressing any adequate picture of research on human needs and problems in one chapter; and second, the importance of always keeping the *how we do it* in the context of the *what* and the *why*. Outside of this frame of reference, techniques are likely to become a meaningless bag of tricks. Part Three deals with various areas in which guidance operates, with emphasis upon group procedures, but always in the light of how these are interrelated with individual counseling.

In Chapter 1, some frequent misconceptions about group guidance were mentioned. Two of these are especially pertinent to the study of group processes as they relate to group guidance: that group guidance, group processes, and group dynamics are all synonymous; and that the major purpose of group guidance is personal development. Another misconception that has an important bearing on techniques is the idea that group guidance is primarily an information service and that only group counseling involves both the affective and cognitive aspects of personality. Of course, whether or not these are misconceptions depends on the techniques that are used. It would be desirable for the reader to review these and other misconceptions noted on pages 20 to 22 before proceeding with the rest of this section. Of course, some may not agree with these statements, but they have been formulated in an attempt to clarify the place of group techniques within the context of the present prevailing concept of guidance.

A few positive statements will be added here to balance the negative ones just made: (*a*) Self-development or self-actualization is, of course, a major goal of guidance shared with all educational and therapeutic services. (*b*) Group processes furnish a medium through which personality development occurs, and their utilization is essential to guidance services. They provide *one* means of achieving certain guidance objectives for individuals—understanding of self and others, life planning and self-actualization, effective interpersonal relationships, and unique contributions to their culture. (*c*) A major task of the guidance worker is to utilize group processes skillfully to serve these guidance objectives for individuals.

Research in the areas of group process and group dynamics has become increasingly active in the last few decades. No longer do we need to depend solely upon theories spun out of the thinking of social philosophers. However, in attempting to utilize the research findings in guidance, we need to bear in mind the caution that tested facts in the area of human relationships are still exceedingly limited in comparison to those in the material realm, and much of the investigation of human groups has been directed to the understanding of group processes and group goals rather than to the question of the influences of these processes upon individuals. In guidance, we need always to consider what is happening to individuals within a group as well as how each is contributing to the group. These are perpetually reciprocal processes in which we are normally interested as members of our culture as well as guidance workers.

This emphasis upon individual goals and welfare within the group process is not intended to exclude the importance of full and free identification of the individual with the group. The Biblical admonition to lose one's life in order to find it doubtless expresses a vital truth regarding self-realization through selfless sharing in the group life. We need merely a caution to keep group goals within the bounds of guidance objectives when we are planning a guidance service. The formulation of a group goal requires that various goals held by individual members be somehow converted into a single goal capable of steering group activities (1, pp. 353–354). One of the over-all goals for a guidance group should be that of mutual aid for all members in working toward self-understanding and self-direction. We shall consider here some of the available research findings that seem especially pertinent for group work in guidance.

THE MEANING OF GROUP DYNAMICS

Cartwright and Zander (2, p. 5) point out that the meaning of this term has become imprecise. They describe three usages of the term: (*a*) a sort of ideology emphasizing democratic leadership, group participation in decisions, and social and individual gains through cooperative activity; (*b*) a set of techniques employed to improve human relations skills; and (*c*) a field of inquiry about the nature of groups, laws of their development, and interrelationships of individuals, groups, and institutions.

This field of research reaches into many traditional disciplines. Sociologists have been most concerned with the study of groups, and psychologists with ways groups influence individuals and the impacts of individuals on group functioning. In group guidance the concern is chiefly with what happens to individuals in groups, but both approaches are pertinent, and objectives for individuals relate to their effective functioning in groups and their contributions to group life as important facets of self-realization through improved self-direction. Much research in group processes is being carried on in small therapeutic groups, and this area will be considered chiefly in Chapter 6.

Contributions of research in group process and group dynamics

The skillful, experienced teacher or counselor will recognize many of the ideas expressed under this heading as understandings which have been gained in working with class groups. Some of the ideas may never have been verbalized consciously. Many of them are embodied in the principles of modern teaching, and in the psychology of group relationships that stems far back in the past.

In recent years there has been an acceleration of research concerning the nature of group life, and the expression *group dynamics* has come into current use together with a whole body of new terms such as are essential in any science for reporting research findings. For example, the term *syntality* is used frequently to describe for the group what we call *personality* for the individual. Syntality refers to all the interrelated attributes or variables by which a group may be described. All these variables are not yet clearly formulated and portrayed by research. The term *synergy* has been coined to refer to the sum total of the energy any group can command, and it has been applied to two aspects of what we sometimes call morale: *maintenance synergy*, or the forces that keep a group intact, and *effective synergy*, or the forces available to move toward the achievement of group goals. *Group structure* refers to all the behavior relationships within a group, such as status gradients depending upon the varying roles of individual members, clique relationships which involve the whole field of sociometry, and the nature of leadership. *Leadership* and *cohesiveness* within groups are being subjected to much study in relation to measures of group performance in their *locomotion* or movement toward goals (2, pp. 14–28).

This new research on the dynamics of group life is being conducted by persons trained in several different disciplines and under the auspices of universities and of other organizations concerned with practical problems of group life. There is a significant body of previous and continuing research in anthropology, sociology, psychology, and all the fields related to human life and behavior to be drawn upon and often reinterpreted by this new group of research workers. As in the field of individual personality, there are wide gaps in our knowledge about group life; but in both areas we need to organize and use what knowledge we have as research expands the boundaries.

What is a group?

Cattell (2, p. 20) has defined a group as a collection of individuals in which their relationships are necessary to the satisfaction of certain of their individual needs. This definition could subsume a variety of individual needs and common goals in working toward the satisfaction of these individual needs. In guidance, the individual goals could include both progress in self-knowledge and self-direction and the achievement of desired status and relationships within the group. For the group itself, the goals may include assistance to all members in working toward their individual goals and many factors related to the group itself as an entity. One of these factors is called *cohesiveness*, or the internal power of the group in holding its members together and the influences it can exert on members to induce changes and achieve cooperation. *Locomotion* is a term referring to the movement of a group toward its goals. The influences of *leadership and followership* in this locomotion are being subjected to much research—the former more than the latter. The term *dynamics* as applied to groups refers to all the interacting forces within groups as they are organizing and operating to achieve their objectives.

What assistance can group dynamics afford the leader of a guidance group? Perhaps the major questions it suggests are: "Do I have a *group* in the sense of the definition quoted previously? If not, how can I help my collection of individuals to become a group? How shall I include myself? What role shall I play in order to be most helpful in the group? What are the common interests of group members? Or how may common interests be developed? How can I help each individual to play his best role in the group? How can I study the syntality and structure of my group and help them to set significant goals and to cooperate effectively in working toward the achievement of these goals? And, most important, how may guidance objectives for individuals be provided for within the group?"

Obviously, the traditional academic teaching methods will not fit into this approach, nor is the alternative to turn this difficult problem over to immature students to handle without adequate guidance. Either of these extremes has been the cause of many failures in homeroom or other group-guidance programs.

Group membership and structure

There are few conclusive findings from research that will aid in the allocation of individuals to guidance groups. Current practices include alphabetical or grade groupings, or whatever system is used to form homeroom, advisory, or special counseling groups, guidance units in various subject fields, small groups with special problems, and, for some purposes, large lecture groups that rarely remain intact as organized groups.

The important considerations would seem to be whether members can communicate and cooperate effectively in setting common goals and share common interests in mutual service for the meeting of individual needs. The optimum number of individuals for full participation in intercommunication is one of the most crucial questions. The larger the group and the shorter the time available, the less each member can interact with others. The wider the range of ability levels, the less likelihood that full sharing of interests and exchange of ideas will be achieved. Studies of the nature of group interaction by Bion (3) and of the personal qualities of members by Stock and Thelan (4) offer some suggestions for the effective formation of groups. Bion's experience with therapy groups led to his recognition of two fundamentally different modes of group life, one dominated by feelings and contagion called *emotionality* and the other by listening and reflection called *work*. These two modes correspond somewhat to two aspects of leadership (see pages 88 and 89) referred to as *emotional and task functions*.

Stock and Thelan (4) studied the personalities of trainees for group leadership with respect to their effectiveness in groups. They identified the following types of characteristic behavior that might occur in different combinations in trainees, each with its counter trend: *dependency* with respect to group moods, ideas, or plans; *fight*, sometimes expressed in argument or negative feelings and attitudes, or in opposite tendencies; *pairing*, expressed in friendly personal relationships, often with one or more intimates in the group or, at the other extreme, in more formal intellectual and impersonal behavior; and *flight*, which might roughly resemble some introvertive-extrovertive tendencies at the two extremes. These brief characterizations do not adequately depict these four tendencies, but anyone working with groups will recognize the general trend in behavior. Stock and Thelan recommend a suitable balance among them for an effective group and, in their training work, concluded that an individual with a strong flight trend coupled with high anxiety was not very trainable. The high fight tendency combined with high anxiety was not considered a serious handicap if the energy associated with anxiety could be directed into work (4, pp. 283–286). This particular finding is probably applicable to the contributions of group members as well as leaders.[1]

School organization does not always lend itself to flexible grouping, but where possible, groups with common problems such as educational or vocational planning, improvement of learning techniques, or personal maladjustments have a good running start toward a workable structure. So many of these problems are common at certain age or grade levels that most groups can formulate a common goal with subgroups working on special phases. For therapeutic work the personality make-up of the group is especially important, and this question will be considered in Chapter 6.

Questions of status gradients, roles of members, and lines of communication within groups are all important aspects of group structure. Status and roles will be considered under leadership later in this chapter and also in connection with various techniques in Chapter 5. A functioning group requires a network of lines of communication among all members instead of the two-way communication between leader and each member common in many classroom situations (1, pp. 641–726).

Factors influencing group cohesiveness or solidarity

A cohesive group may be defined as one in which all members work together for a common goal and all are ready to take responsibility for group chores and endure frustration in their cooperative efforts. This property of cohesiveness is called the internal power of the group and is one criterion of a healthy group. It is evidenced in the various expressions of "we-ness" as compared with "I-ness" and is characterized by a spirit of friendliness and loyalty to fellow members.

Many factors contribute to this cohesiveness. Among them are the obvious factors of a common language and common thought processes, common problems and goals, and definite modes and channels of communication with one another. In the traditional academic class, the members' opportunities for social contacts with others in the group are severely limited, and hence the possibilities for strong group cohesiveness are usually less than in a more informal, permissive type of setup. Other factors encouraging cohesiveness are frequent association, cooperative rather than competitive relationships among members (5), and stabilized organization, with responsibility of each toward the

[1] See Appendix for descriptive statements of these trends.

others, involving a sense of obligation to cooperate in satisfaction of the individual needs of others as if they were one's own. Phillips and D'Amico (6), studying fourth-graders, found positive effects for co-operation but did not find that competition decreased cohesiveness. The number of friendship ties is important, unless these result in cliques which operate to divide or splinter the group. Similar norms as to conduct are helpful and, as will be noted later, a cohesive group will tend to increase the conformity of its members in this respect.

Among the forces which may operate to disrupt or prevent group solidarity are unpleasant experiences, unattractive activities, group frustration, conflicting goals, differences regarding suitable ways to reach an accepted goal, rivalry for status, or interpersonal dislikes.

In guiding a group toward a suitable type of organization, a leader should be aware of both disruptive and cohesive influences and help the group to avoid pitfalls and to strive for solidarity. Research in group dynamics has indicated many of the difficulties which any teacher or leader may encounter if he allows himself to get into a position where he and the group are pitted against each other. Another type of difficulty may ensue, however, if the leader becomes so completely identified with the group that he loses his status as adult counselor. It requires great social sensitivity and real maturity of personality to be in the "we-group" and still not so completely of it that perspective on the adult guidance role is lost.

The cohesiveness of a group is not an end goal in itself, but merely a means to some valued objectives. Experimental research is indicating that there is no necessary relationship between the cohesiveness and productivity of a group. The nature of the leadership within the group, the ability and skills of individual members, and the kind of problem upon which a group is working may all have their influences upon the end product. A few experiments have opened up the question of the effect of group interaction upon creative and critical activity and point to the possibility of the blocking of creative performance under some circumstances (7, pp. 179–184).

In group situations where the guidance of individuals toward greater self-knowledge and optimum self-development are major objectives, it is important that both the leader and the group members keep these individual goals in mind in the process of fostering group interaction. While experimentation is demonstrating that groups may provide significant learning and therapeutic experiences for individuals, we are far from a clear and full understanding of all the factors that are operating in group situations. Warnings are being sounded regarding the possible influences of group pressures on individuals of independent mind and character whose unique contributions to life may need to be protected from the forces leading to conformity within the group (8, p. 362).

Effects of "social climate" on group performance

The extent to which the "social climate" established by a leader affects the performance of a group has been investigated experimentally in situations in which leaders deliberately created relationships which were successively authoritarian, democratic, and laissez-faire (9).

These social climates were created with respect to small groups of ten-year-old boys working together in hobby clubs. The influence of these climates on the performance of the members has implications for all groups that are susceptible to the climate established by a leader.

When the intention was to establish an authoritarian climate, the leader determined the policy of the group; notified the members, step by step, what their activities were to be and what techniques were to be employed; assigned specific shares of the total work load to each member and indicated which members were to work together; issued both praise and criticism in personal terms; and did not directly participate in the activities of the group except when he was demonstrating how a task was to be done.

The leader who was attempting to establish a democratic climate encouraged the group to discuss its policies and reach its own decisions with respect to them; tried to present alternatives with respect to techniques and procedures, and permitted the group to make its choices within the perspective presented by the leader; offered the members the opportunity to divide up the tasks to be done and to select their own working partners; oriented his praise and criticism objectively in terms of group goals; and made himself a member of the group without dislocating himself from the function of leader.

The laissez-faire leader offered virtually no guidance to the group while it was making its basic decisions; established his willingness to supply information when asked but otherwise took no part in allocating work; refrained from participating in the activities of the group and in commenting on the performance of the members.

In these groups it was found that the group members did more work and a better quality of work under democratic leadership than under the laissez-faire climate. The level of work under democratic leadership was also superior to that under authoritarian control, despite the common belief that autocracy ensures efficiency. The quantity of work done in the authoritarian climate exceeded that done under the other climates, but greater originality was manifest under the democratic leadership, and the motivation was more sustained.

Autocratic leadership precipitated many problems in interpersonal relationships, including hostility and aggression, destructiveness, and "ganging up" against scapegoats. There were evidences of rebellion, discontent, and frustration.

While the members of the group were working under authoritarian leadership, they tended to be submissive and dependent, and to lose their individuality. When the same boys were transferred to democratic leadership, there were aggressive outbursts on the part of some that suggested prior frustration. Ultimately, there was an increase in friendliness, an emphasis on the achievements of the group rather than too strong a competitive emphasis on personal achievement, the element of fun became pronounced in the group feeling, and a willingness to share group property was manifested (9).

Flanders (10) compared teacher-centered and learner-centered groups in a school and found in the former more student hostility toward both the teacher and classmates and more withdrawal and apathetic or aggressive behavior. He reported a decrease in interpersonal anxiety, and improved emotional adjustment of participants in the learner-centered group. Other aspects of this question of group climate will be considered in relation to problems of leadership for both the adult leader and members of the group.

Significance of Group Climate for Guidance Objectives. An atmosphere of acceptance and permissiveness is of basic importance for all aspects of group guidance. By acceptance is meant that each individual will be accorded respect and a status of belonging to a cohesive we-group, no matter what his personal characteristics or problems may be at the moment. If behavior is objectionable or disruptive, a distinction will be made between the individual and the unacceptable behavior. Permissiveness connotes freedom to express any ideas or feelings for consideration by the group with awareness that all members will attempt to understand and to continue to accept each other as respected individuals in spite of disagreement with or disapproval of ideas or behavior.

Doubtless even a well-trained and experienced leader will encounter difficulty at times in achieving these two ideals of acceptance and permissiveness, both covertly and overtly. Almost any group would need considerable assistance in developing this type of climate. The leader will contribute by example in attitudes expressed toward members and the entire group. Also, he will need to help the group to establish goals of mutual helpfulness and regulations to assist in working toward these goals. Until a group has achieved a cohesiveness that involves basic consideration for the welfare of all members, and an orderly method of locomotion toward accepted goals, it is usually best not to encourage too much self-revelation that may act as a boomerang causing traumatic reactions. This situation will be present in varying degrees in different groups depending, in part, upon their purposes—whether to study fairly objective problems, or to engage in some social or civic activity, or in an essentially therapeutic experience. Whatever the situation, it calls for thoughtful planning and skillful guidance by the leader to assist a group in developing the climate needed for their purposes.

Leadership in a group

Research in group dynamics has led to new concepts of the nature of leadership. Much of the earlier research and speculation was directed toward understanding of the essential qualities of a leader and many lists of leadership traits have been formulated. More recent studies have investigated the situations in which leadership emerges and have emphasized the working relationships of an individual within a group structure in which he acquires leadership status through demonstrating his capacity for helping the group to carry out cooperative tasks in the achievement of goals. Personal qualities are recognized as important when they contribute to *effective* leadership within a situation, but specific requirements may vary among situations. The interplay between situation and personal characteristics appears to be the matrix within which effective leadership develops (11).

Some of the usually significant personal aspects of capacity for expediting cooperative effort appear to be intelligence (but not too much greater than that of the group), alertness to needs and motives of others, and insight into the nature of situations, further reinforced by such qualities as responsibility, initiative, persistence, and self-confidence (12).

Any of these traits or others that contribute to leadership may be present in varying degrees in group members, and the particular pattern of qualities that a person possesses may qualify him for leadership in one situation but not in another, or for a special type of leadership. Thus a group is likely to have leaders for various purposes rather than *a leader*.

Two major types of leadership have been distinguished in the study of groups: *task or group achievement leadership* that aids a group in reaching some goal, and the morale-building or group-maintenance type that provides a *social-emotional function* in keeping the group together (13, 14). These two types of leadership call for somewhat different qualities and are likely to be performed by different individuals.

The nature of leadership is affected by the power structure of the group, and this power factor is now the object of extensive investigation (1, pp. 727–809). French and Raven (15, pp. 727–744) have suggested five bases of interpersonal power: *attractive* power based on being liked by others, *expert* power based on recognition of superior knowledge, *reward* power dependent on ability to mediate rewards, *coercive* power based on ability to mediate punishment, and *legitimate* power stemming from a recognized right to prescribe behavior. Any of these sources of power may be present in varying degrees in a group. A leader in a school situation needs to examine his own sources of power to understand their influence on the group and the desirability of the influence, as well as to be alert to all the power influences operating among members of the group.

A study of power influences among boys in camping situations (1, pp. 745–765) led to the following conclusions for these groups: A member with high attributed power (based on judgments of the group as to his influence on others) initiates more social influence attempts than others and is more successful. Group members are likely to "contage" from his behavior and show more deference to him than to others. The member with high attributed power is more directive in the manner of influence and is more active in social relations, but not necessarily in program activity, than the low-power members. Physical prowess and personal liking were significantly related to attributive power in these boys' groups, but intelligence level was not significantly related.

These newer viewpoints on leadership and power show them to be determined by systems of interrelationships with varying degrees and kinds of influence and responsibility. With leadership thus conceived as a function of group organization, it would follow that, except in a completely authoritarian group, there would be varying degrees of influence and responsibility among members and, therefore, varying degrees and kinds of leadership within the group.

One of the responsibilities of the leader or guide is to work for the utilization by the group of its leadership potentials and to help all individuals to belong really to the group and to grow through contributing their best services to the group (2, pp. 39–51). The newer concept of leadership provides a helpful approach to these problems by breaking down the older dichotomy between leaders and followers. Each member of a group can be helped to play both roles effectively.

Of course, some individuals will exert more influence on a group than will others. But the trend in interpreting research in group dynamics is toward recognition that any member of a group exerts leadership to the extent that the syntality of the group is modified by his presence. According to this viewpoint, all member actions which help the group achieve its objectives are leadership functions in varying degrees.

Quite as important as the development of leadership skill in suitable areas is that of effective followership in assuming a fair share of the work load, cooperating harmoniously with others, accepting and following through on majority decisions, but working creatively to make known minority views when held.

The Place of the Guidance Leader in the Group. Earlier it was suggested that the guidance leader should become a real member of the "we-group" but at the same time not become so completely of it that the guidance role is lost. This is a difficult balance of roles to achieve, and there are varying points of view among authorities as to its desirability.

Fiedler (16) has found that leaders of task groups who maintain some psychological distance are more effective than those who tend toward warmer and closer interpersonal relations with members. His hypotheses are (*a*) that the first type seem to have better role relations with an emphasis on the task; and (*b*) that the second type may encourage rivalry if he fraternizes only with some members, and may encounter difficulty in disciplining subordinates. Lifton (17) supports the viewpoint that a warm equality relationship in a group is desirable. These differing viewpoints may stem in part from experiences with different types of groups. Fiedler studied task groups in military organizations, as well as a variety of college and business organizations. Lifton reports on groups of counselor trainees undergoing a therapeutic experience. Here the task function may not have been as important as the maintenance of morale, while the fairly mature group was seeking increased personal insight. Also, there may have been some hidden agenda in a university training group no matter how warm, friendly, and equal they were in their group relationships. Lifton provides some very helpful insights for the group counselor in his report of group proceedings.

The answer to this question of the guidance leader's relationship with a group may be unique for each individual. We are recognizing that the personality style of the counselor may be more important than the specific techniques and may help to determine which ones are most effective. One principle that can probably be generalized is that only when an individual is accepted by a group as its guidance leader will he have the power to influence the group in desired ways. What those influences will be depends, of course, upon the purposes of the particular group.

Influence of Leadership on Group and Individual Judgments through Better Utilization of Minority Opinions. Studies which have been made of the results achieved by a group in solving a problem under the guidance of leadership and without such guidance point up the specific contributions which a leader may make. It is significant to stress the fact that the contributions of the leader in such situations do not stem from his intellectual endowments as such. That is, the decisions of the group are better not because the leader has superior wisdom, since he himself does not make the decisions; they are better because through his leadership function he motivates the group to improve its thinking.

Many of these contributions are already generally known: the leader helps the group determine the exact nature of the problem to be discussed; he states the problem in constructive terms in order to evoke constructive reactions to it; he asks provocative questions which will stimulate the thinking of the members of the group. Perhaps not so generally known is the function of the leader in bringing forth minority opinions within the group.

If no leadership is provided in discussions revolving about the solution of a problem, the views of the minority are often submerged. Social pressures are such that those who sense that their point of view is in the minority often fail to advance it for fear of being ridiculed, ignored, disliked, or rejected. The skilled leader assesses this situation and creates the opportunity for the minority point of view to be expressed and to be listened to open-mindedly and without prejudgment. Obviously, the minority opinion does not necessarily carry the day, nor is it *ipso facto* superior to the majority opinion. But, by the same token, the majority opinion of how to solve the problem may not always be the best solution.

The leader's contribution is to make the thinking of the minority available to the group. If the minority opinion is sound, there will be ample opportunity to explore it, and the group may ultimately modify its initial solution to embody the contributions of the minority or may adopt the minority opinion as its own. The group has thus, through services of skilled leadership, improved the level of its problem-solving action and enriched its concept of democratic processes (18).

Effects of Participatory versus Supervisory Leadership on Group Judgment. Some insight into the effect of the quality of leadership on group judgment is provided by an experiment which attempted to determine what leadership traits seemed to influence individuals within a group to change their opinions in conformity with group thinking.

For the purposes of the experiment, leaders of some groups were asked to function in a participatory capacity, others in a supervisory role. The two roles parallel, in general approach, the democratic and the laissez-faire functions described in a previously discussed experiment, with the participatory leaders actively striving to see that all members of the group took part in the discussion, and the supervisory leaders limiting their function to seeing that the discussion was completed within the allotted time and that the group did not wander too far from the subject under discussion.

Everyone who took part in the experiment was given a list of twelve prominent persons; he was asked to list them in his order of preference for the presidency of the United States. The first listing was done individually, before any discussion was held. The second listing was done as a group effort, under the two types of discussion leadership described.

A third listing, after a reasonable lapse of time, was again done as an individual effort.

Analysis of the three listings revealed that the members who had participated in discussions under participatory leadership were more influenced by group judgment than those whose discussion was led by a person who assumed only the supervisory role. In the third listing, done individually after discussion, the "supervisory" members tended to revert to the choices they had initially made, whereas the "participatory" members made choices which more closely reflected the thinking of their group.

Two possible implications are suggested by the results of this experiment: that group opinions formed under supervisory leadership are not very strongly held by the members, and that attitudes change more pronouncedly through a discussion guided by participatory leadership (19).

Importance of Functional Representation for Productivity. Research in the field of group dynamics has extended into many areas, ranging from pure laboratory research to application to existing organizational situations. It is possible, in many instances, for the teacher or counselor to draw implications of value to his specific areas from findings yielded by research in completely different fields.

For instance, a study has been made of the leadership factors which contribute to productivity and morale in industrial organizations. Many of the factors which were studied may not have direct relevance to teaching techniques, but it is of significance to report that the study showed that productivity tended to increase when workers were positively motivated by functional representation. That is, the workers who were most productive were those who felt that they were given some responsibility for deciding how their job was done.

Close supervision, as such, did not seem to contribute as much to productivity as did the factor of the workers' being able to plan their own work and execute their plans; of their feeling that the supervisors would speak in their behalf in their dealings with management; of the existence of easy vertical communication within an industrial organization.

The indications from this study of the need for democratic structuring and for distribution of responsibility within any productive group are as pertinent for groups functioning within the framework of an educational institution as they are elsewhere (20).

Implications for Democratic Planning. These researches on participatory leadership and functional representation have been included to emphasize the importance of active participation of a guidance group in the setting of goals and the planning of procedures. One caution, however, should be noted. A sound guidance service is professional in nature and requires the planning and leadership of trained personnel workers. One of the common weaknesses of homerooms and other group-guidance units results from untrained workers turning the planning and execution of the program over to immature students with the apparent assumption that if they do what they like with enthusiasm and responsibility, good will result. This may be a correct assumption, but it does not follow that guidance will be provided. Guidance requires on the part of the adult leader much knowledge about the group, collectively and individually, some definite guidance objectives, and flexible plans as to how these objectives may be achieved. A guidance group will need skillful orientation with respect to possibilities, and guidance, not imposition, in reaching judgments as to the priority of needs to be met, goals to be set, and possible paths to reach the goals.

Experiments have suggested that unclear group goals and group paths may have negative and inhibiting effects on the group work (1, pp. 395–413). In their study of democratic and autocratic leaders, Lewin, Lippitt, and White (see pages 88 and 89) instructed democratic leaders to provide perspective on the group task and suggest alternative steps toward the goal. Autocratic leaders dictated successive steps toward the goal without an overview of the whole procedure. Sound and effective guidance in a democratic climate requires both professional insight and skill in group leadership.

Effects of group judgment on individual behavior

There has been much research on the nature of group influence on individual judgments, commitments, and behavior, and much remains to be known about this influence. This question is especially significant for group guidance that is aimed toward suitable application of learning in a group to the problems of an individual's life.

Lewin (21), on the basis of experiences in getting people in groups to change food habits, concluded that it is easier to change individual behavior through the influence of group norms than through direct work with the individual. Group decisions have been shown to be effective in stimulating numerous types of behavior change, but no conclusive evidence exists as to how permanent these changes are. Olmstead (22) has pointed out that the question of basic personality changes in response to group influence presents greater complexities than a change in a judgment about some matter or in some particular behavior reaction. But he also cautions that we cannot afford to overlook this more complex problem because of lack of understanding.

Laboratory experiments have shown that some individuals will change judgments of perception about the length of lines, even to the point of unreality, in response to group judgments, while others will not (23, 24). Some studies have indicated that group discussion is a more effective instrument for influencing attitudes than the lecture method. Levine and Butler (25) concluded from their study that the involvement of members in a discussion group opened the way for exposure to new patterns and that decisions arrived at by the group had great carry-over for individuals in their subsequent behavior. The findings in another study by Bennett (26) were interpreted as indicating the importance of unanimity of group consensus on proposed individual action, and the fact that a decision had been made, rather than group discussion and public commitment as influences on individual behavior.

Cartwright and Zander (1, p. 183) point out that group pressures can be directed against uniformity and toward differentiation of roles of members, so that creativeness can be encouraged and freedom of thought respected. The ability to resist group pressures that run counter to individual judgments may be highly important provided channels of informational influence in the group are kept open and negative prejudice or intolerance is not operating. Deutsch and Gerard (27) have expressed this idea clearly in the following statement:

> In other words, normative social influence can be exerted to help make an individual be an individual, and not merely a mirror or puppet of the group. Groups can demand of their members that they have self-respect, that they value their own experience, that they be capable of acting without slavish regard for popularity. Unless groups encourage their members to express their own, independent judgments, group consensus is likely to be an empty achievement. Group process which rests on the distortion of individual experience undermines its own potential for creativity and productiveness.

Guidance groups can provide many opportunities to broaden information and viewpoints and to strengthen open-mindedness, and, with good leadership, can increase respect for variations in opinion and prevent the hampering of individual judgments made in the light of varied possibilities.

REFERENCES CITED IN CHAPTER

1. Cartwright, Dorwin, and Alvin Zander (eds.): *Group Dynamics: Research and Theory*, 2d ed., Harper & Row, Publishers, New York, 1960.
2. Cartwright, Dorwin, and Alvin Zander (eds.): *Group Dynamics: Research and Theory*, Harper & Row, Publishers, New York, 1953.
3. Bion, W. R.: *Experiences in Groups*, Basic Books, Inc., Publishers, New York, 1961.
4. Stock, Dorothy, and Herbert A. Thelan: *Emotional Dynamics and Group Culture*, National Training Laboratories, published by New York University Press, New York, 1958.
5. Deutsch, Morton: "The Effects of Cooperation and Competition upon Group Process," in Dorwin Cartwright and Alvin Zander (eds.), *Group Dynamics: Research and Theory*, 2d ed., Harper & Row, Publishers, New York, 1960, pp. 414–448.

6. Phillips, Beeman N., and Louis A. D'Amico: "Effects of Cooperation and Competition on the Cohesiveness of Small Face-to-face Groups," *Journal of Educational Psychology*, 47:65–70, February, 1956.
7. Crutchfield, Richard S.: "Social Psychology and Group Processes," in Calvin Stone and Quinn McNemar (eds.), *Annual Review of Psychology*, Annual Reviews, Inc., Stanford, Calif., 1954, vol. 5, pp. 171–202.
8. Maxwell, James: "Educational Psychology," in Calvin Stone and Quinn McNemar (eds.), *Annual Review of Psychology*, Annual Reviews, Inc., Stanford, Calif., 1954, vol. 5, pp. 357–376.
9. White, Ralph, and Ronald Lippitt: "Leader Behavior and Member Reaction in Three 'Social Climates,'" in Dorwin Cartwright and Alvin Zander (eds.), *Group Dynamics: Research and Theory*, Harper & Row, Publishers, New York, 1953, pp. 585–611.
10. Flanders, Ned A.: "Personal-Social Anxiety as a Factor in Experimental Learning Situations," *The Journal of Educational Research*, 45:100–110, November, 1951.
11. Petrullo, Luigi, and Bernard M. Bass (eds.): *Leadership and Interpersonal Behavior*, Holt, Rinehart and Winston, Inc., New York, 1961.
12. Stogdill, Ralph M.: "Leadership, Membership, and Organization," *Psychological Bulletin*, 47:1–14, 1950.
13. Gibb, Cecil A.: "Leadership," in Gardner Lindzey (ed.), *Handbook of Social Psychology*, Addison-Wesley Publishing Company, Inc., Reading, Mass., 1944, vol. 2, pp. 877–920.
14. Warters, Jane: *Group Guidance: Principles and Practices*, McGraw-Hill Book Company, Inc., New York, 1960, pp. 27–56.
15. French, John R. P., Jr.: "A Formal Theory of Social Power" in Dorwin Cartwright and Alvin Zander (eds.), *Group Dynamics: Research and Theory*, 2d ed., Harper & Row, Publishers, New York, 1960, pp. 727–744.
16. Fiedler, Fred E.: "The Leader's Psychological Distance and Group Effectiveness," in Dorwin Cartwright and Alvin Zander (eds.), *Group Dynamics: Research and Theory*, 2d ed., Harper & Row, Publishers, New York, 1960, pp. 586–606.
17. Lifton, Walter: *Working with Groups*, John Wiley & Sons, Inc., New York, 1961.
18. Maier, Norman R. F., and Allen R. Solem: "The Contribution of a Discussion Leader to the Quality of Group Thinking: The Effective Use of Minority Opinions," *Human Relations*, 5:277–288, August, 1952.
19. Preston, Malcolm G., and Roy K. Heintz: "Effects of Participatory vs. Supervisory Leadership on Group Judgment," *Journal of Abnormal and Social Psychology*, 44:345–355, 1949.
20. Kahn, Robert L., and Daniel Katz: "Leadership Practices in Relation to Productivity and Morale," in Dorwin Cartwright and Alvin Zander (eds.), *Group Dynamics: Research and Theory*, Harper & Row, Publishers, New York, 1953, pp. 612–628.
21. Lewin, K.: "Frontiers in Group Dynamics," *Human Relations*, 1:5–42, 1947.
22. Olmstead, Michael S.: *The Small Group*, Random House, Inc., New York, 1959.
23. Asch, S. E.: *Social Psychology*, Prentice-Hall, Inc., Englewood Cliffs, N.J., 1952.
24. Berenda, Ruth W.: *The Influence of the Group on the Judgments of Children*, King's Crown Press, New York, 1950.
25. Levine, Jacob, and John Butler: "Lecture vs. Group Decision," *Journal of Applied Psychology*, 36:29–33, February, 1952.
26. Bennett, Edith: "Discussion, Decision, Commitment, and Consensus in Group Decision," *Human Relations*, 21:251–273, 1955.
27. Deutsch, Morton, and Harold B. Gerard: "A Study of Normative and Informational Social Influences upon Individual Judgment," *Journal of Abnormal and Social Psychology*, 51:629–636, 1955.

Additional References

Bonner, Hubert: *Group Dynamics: Principles and Applications*, The Ronald Press Company, New York, 1959.

Gordon, Thomas: *Group-centered Leadership*, Houghton Mifflin Company, Boston, 1955.

Hall, D. M.: *Dynamics of Group Action*, rev. ed., Interstate Press and Publishers, Danville, Ill., 1957.

Hare, A. P., et al. (eds.): *Small Groups: Studies in Social Interaction*, Alfred A. Knopf, Inc., New York, 1955.

Heider, Fritz: *The Psychology of Interpersonal Relations*, John Wiley & Sons, Inc., New York, 1958.

Knowles, M., and H. Knowles: *Introduction to Group Dynamics*, Association Press, New York, 1959.

Ross, Murray G., and Charles E. Hendry: *New Understandings of Leadership*, Association Press, New York, 1957.

Smith, Lois: *Group Processes in Elementary and Secondary Schools*, Department of Classroom Teachers, American Educational Research Association of the National Education Association, Washington, 1959.

Stogdill, Ralph M.: *Leadership and Structures of Personal Interaction*, Ohio Studies in Personnel; Bureau of Business Research Monograph No. 84, Bureau of Business Research, College of Commerce and Administration, Ohio State University, Columbus, Ohio, 1957.

Thelan, Herbert A.: *Dynamics of Group Work*, University of Chicago Press, Chicago, 1954.

Thibaut, John W., and Harold H. Kelly: *The Social Psychology of Groups*, John Wiley & Sons, Inc., New York, 1959.

White, Ralph, and Ronald Lippitt: *Autocracy and Democracy—An Experimental Inquiry*, Harper & Row, Publishers, New York, 1960.

Whyte, William H., Jr.: *The Organization Man*, Simon and Schuster, Inc., New York, 1956.

5 GROUP TECHNIQUES

This chapter deals primarily with what will be termed *learning techniques* applicable in most types of guidance groups in which the purposes relate to choices, plans, and activities involved in the various areas dealt with in Part Three. The term *therapeutic techniques* will be used in Chapter 6 to refer to some of the methods used with small groups for therapeutic purposes. This distinction between learning and therapeutic techniques is somewhat artificial, since some type of learning certainly occurs in an effective therapeutic situation, and learning that involves movement in problem solving and clarification of life purposes and plans may well be therapeutic in many respects. Also, many similar techniques are applicable in both learning and therapeutic groups as these terms are used here.

THE LEARNING PROCESS IN GUIDANCE

The term *learning techniques* is used here to direct attention to the learnings, involving new insights and changes in attitudes and behavior, that may occur for individuals through various group approaches in guidance. It seems plausible to assume that the *learning processes* fostered through guidance are basically the same as those in all other phases of learning. The differences are likely to reside in objectives, the nature of learning situations, and the techniques employed. The learning that occurs in the traditional academic classroom is likely to be quite different from that which takes place in the informal, permissive group coming to grips with problems of self-appraisal, self-direction, and interpersonal relationships.

Guidance through groups may involve the same *learning* processes as guidance through interviews. Here again the differences may lie in the different learning situation, the more direct approach to individual concerns in the interview, and the possibilities here for learning on deeper levels of the personality than in the group situation. This last-mentioned difference may not be true of group psychotherapy as compared with clinical counseling. There are, of course, many variations in learning situations among different types of interviews, and some interviews will not touch as vital aspects of learning as will some types of group work.

Effective guidance through groups generally requires the same permissive and friendly atmosphere of understanding and acceptance of individuals as does counseling. The requirement presents to the leader of a group not only the necessity of expressing these attitudes himself toward the entire group, but of fostering the same attitudes among members of the group in their relationships with each other. This probably describes the ideal learning situation for any purpose, but it is especially important where emotionally tinged personal concerns may be scrutinized in a group. Investigations of the processes of group interaction are providing helpful insights about best ways of creating good learning situations.

SPECIFIC GUIDANCE TECHNIQUES

In group guidance, as in all teaching, one of the basic principles in the use of methods is that of flexibility in the selection and adaptation of varied techniques to meet new and changing conditions. Many of the techniques considered here are useful in a variety of teaching situations. Here our concern is with their bearings on guidance services.

Preplanning by the leader

In many school programs, the curriculum may provide for particular areas of study in the guidance field at designated grade levels or in specific subjects. Examples of these areas of study include orientation, educational and vocational planning, self-appraisal, understanding human behavior, improving learning skills, getting along with others, and school citizenship. These specific areas require the same careful planning as any other subject area with respect to objectives, content, materials, and activities. This statement may seem to some too obvious to warrant inclusion here, but there are plenty of situations where such planning is not done, particularly when homerooms carry the whole burden of group guidance, or when counselors meet only occasionally with their counselees.

One phase of preplanning especially needed in the guidance field is that of exploring all the subject areas in the curriculum to ascertain what contributions they are making to areas dealt with in guidance. The purposes of this exploration are twofold: to avoid undesirable repetition, and to help students to utilize learnings from their various studies in their solving of guidance problems. The second purpose can help to make all of their learning experiences more meaningful through concrete applications in planning and living.

If this preliminary exploration is carried on cooperatively with the entire faculty it is likely to result in much more vital teaching in every area. This method can be used very profitably between levels in a school system as well as within one school. The writer recalls the surprise and satisfaction expressed by a group of elementary school teachers when they learned in a meeting with secondary school counselors that their anecdotal records were proving invaluable in helping counselors to understand and serve pupils better. They commented that their hours of labor would no longer seem drudgery.

Another type of preparation, when the membership of a group is known, is to study their personnel records to learn as much as possible about them before the first meeting. In some situations personal interviews may also provide significant information, and members may already be known to a leader through former teaching or counseling.

Among questions for this preview are: Will it be a fairly homogeneous group or one of wide variation in general ability, academic achievement, social and economic background? Are there likely to be cliques and rejected individuals? What are some possible needs, interests, and concerns of group members that may serve as starting points for group study and discussion?

In making these suggestions for preplanning, it is assumed that no group-guidance leader will be prejudiced in any way by information about individuals that may indicate possible behavior or adjustment problems. This question of the desirability of preknowledge about students has been argued pro and con interminably. For any suitable leader of a guidance group it could seem to have no negative implications.

Significance of the leader's personality

The influence of personality has been studied more in relation to individual counseling than to group work. Some of the findings for counseling may well be applicable to group services. At least they seem to harmonize with some of the writer's experience with groups and hence will be noted here as suggestive.

Fiedler (1), in a study of therapeutic relationships, found the chief differences were between experienced and inexperinced clinicians rather than in the specific techniques used. Combs (2) has stated with reference to the nature and competencies of "helpers," "The expert is not a neophyte with better methods—he is a different breed of fish."

There is increased recognition that many types of personalities can be effective in the "helping relationship" and their methods may be widely diverse. Rogers (3) emphasizes the importance of the helper being a real person in his own right and using his personality as a means of achieving the same goal for those he serves. Combs (2) suggests that good and poor helpers can be described in terms of their perceptions rather than their behavior. Among these perceptual aspects he includes a hopeful, causation-oriented frame of reference; seeing people as unthreatening and worthy; altruistic and accepting attitudes; openness to experience and tolerance of ambiguity. Among appropriate methods, Combs mentions permissive as superior to authoritarian, acceptance as superior to appeasing, vital as superior to lifeless.

As applied to groups we might summarize these points of view in the statement that the personality style of the leader should determine the techniques used and the way he uses them. This does not imply any deemphasis upon training or experience, but rather that both will be used creatively with respect, acceptance, and, insofar as possible, understanding of both self and group members.

Another interesting and somewhat new idea in counseling and psychotherapy may have significant implications for group guidance—that of self-disclosure by the therapist. This has been, and probably still is, considered very undesirable by many. Jouard (4), admitting that the surface has only been scratched here, claims that it is important that the therapist respond freely and spontaneously as a real person in response to what a patient has expressed. But he cautions that these responses must differ importantly from the spontaneous responses of a friend or relative, since the therapist has no vested interest in preventing growth or change in the patient. Presumably vested interests, if any, for the therapist with integrity would lie in the opposite direction.

It is quite obvious that this self-disclosure technique could be fraught with dangers if used by an untrained person lacking insight into the dynamics of his own and others' personalities, and a mature self-mastery. It might be especially dangerous, or at least unsuitable at times, with immature children or adolescents. Yet it has many possibilities in the using of self to help other selves in an honest, open relationship.

The writer has used this technique cautiously, even gingerly, with groups for many years. Sharing some personal experience, thought, or feeling has often seemed to serve as an *open sesame* to barriers of repression in members of a group, influencing much as does the recognition that supposed idiosyncrasies are really common human problems. The leader must needs have the same concern for himself that he has for members of the group—that disclosures will not act as boomerangs because of some unresolved problems; also, that the social amenities suitable for the group are observed. This last statement refers not only to the content of the disclosures but also to the danger of engaging in reverie that is merely satisfying to the sharer and boring and meaningless to the group. Of course, preaching, not an uncommon practice in group guidance, must be added to the proscribed methods.

The whole field of leader personality in group guidance is pretty much unexplored and uncharted through research. To what extent we can carry over research and experience from the counseling field is uncertain. Probably few would disagree that a major requirement is for a person who has come to terms with himself and with life in a way that enables him to release energy freely, happily, and unselfishly in a shared, helping relationship with others. We could add to this adequate awareness and acceptance of self and others, a growing system of life values, an openness to new experience, and enough basic life satisfactions to prevent one from using groups to meet one's own needs in undesirable ways. Certainly the leader will grow along with the groups he serves, gaining ever new and fresh insights into previously unforeseen possibilities.

Some might wish to describe the suitable guidance leader as emotionally and socially mature. If these terms connote a person who is basically concerned with the welfare of all other individuals as much as with self, and has the other qualities just mentioned, they may be an adequate designation. But, as with the term mental hygiene, there seems to be increasing diversity of opinion as to just what is meant (5).

Democratic leader-group planning and participation

Guidance cannot be "taught" like a traditional subject in the curriculum, even with the most modern methods. Guidance needs and interests of any particular group of individuals cannot be fully mapped out and suitable content thoroughly preplanned by a leader, though he can and should prepare himself by securing an excellent background of understanding about the needs, interests, and typical adjustment problems of individuals generally in the age group with which he is working. One of the first tasks with a specific group is to learn as much as possible about persons in the group as individuals. Then one is ready to study the group with a view to understanding its syntality and structure. This will require time and considerable interaction within the group and is an ongoing process for which the leader has much responsibility. How to make this process democratic rather than leader-manipulated is a crucial issue.

The procedure of letting a group choose a problem and organize immediately with elected officers is not necessarily democratic [1] and frequently fails to weld a really cohesive group out of a collection of individuals. Some are likely to be left out in the cold, and a topic of ap-

[1] A travesty on this method was once observed in a fourth-grade class. On the first day the teacher asked the group, "What would you like to study this year?" Hands waved and some cried, "Boats." Presumably the previous fourth grade had had this center of interest. Others made additional suggestions, but none came from the teacher. A vote was taken and "boats" won!

parent interest may soon pall on the group. The teacher or guide has the responsibility of providing opportunity for enough orientation and exploration within a field of study or activity and for enough intercommunication among individuals to tap common, fundamental interests and to help each individual to begin to find a satisfying place within the group structure. It requires keen insight and skill to know when the emerging group is ready for each successive step in assuming more responsibility for group action. It is always wise for the guide to be cognizant of his own best role to serve the group as it emerges, or he may find himself undesirably isolated on the one hand, or perhaps too much the center of attraction or power on the other hand, to serve the best interests of the group.

Previous knowledge about individuals in the group and understanding of common problems of the particular age group will provide a leader with many clues as to desirable orienting activities. The activities may create opportunities for interaction of members in becoming acquainted with each other, and they may stimulate the beginnings of a group structure of interrelationships that can pave the way for real group organization and leadership. A leader may find it desirable to present an overview of possibilities for the particular group, stimulate group discussion about them, secure written suggestions to tally and report, initiate some buzz sessions with reports to the group, and perhaps use some problem inventories or free-response writing about interests and problems. These are only a few of myriad possibilities.

The pooling of suggestions by group members as to personal problems, worries, and interests, either orally or in writing, will usually provide adequate data for a good group starting point on common problems. From here group and committee planning with the leader will generally open more vistas than can be explored. This democratic planning involves much more than merely pooling ideas and voting. It is a leader's role to stimulate thinking, broaden the horizon of possibilities, and provide (or lead the group to gain) enough background understanding about areas or problems suggested for study, so that group judgments will not be made blindly. Of course some immediate interest, such as etiquette at a party, can lead into many related questions of dating, boy-and-girl relationships, parent-child relationships, and school citizenship.

Any really democratic group must, of course, have a feeling of "we-ness." The previous discussion of group processes in Chapter 4 has included suggestions from research as to ways in which this group cohesiveness may develop. The teacher or leader has a responsibility to help establish a friendly, permissive atmosphere in which all may feel at ease and have the desire and the self-confidence to participate as democratic members of the group. Naturally, there will be different tempos at which this sense of belonging develops.

The question of when or whether a group will organize with elected officers depends entirely on the nature of the group, the problems to be studied, or the activities to be planned. When a group is learning methods of self-appraisal, or techniques of vocational planning, one should not expect an inexperienced class member to assume a major role as leader. There may be many activities carried on in connection with such study where class leaders will be highly valuable. But class organization and parliamentary procedure for suitable class activities should not be confused with democratic participation in class study in the meaning of free and full interpersonal communication in thinking, judging, and problem solving. The guiding of this process is a challenge to a highly skilled leader.

Thelan (6) has emphasized the importance of keeping functioning subgroups in a class to a minimum number, in order that each individual will have the largest possible amount of participation. He describes the function of the whole class as that of developing need for specific activities and learnings on the part of each member, of analyzing requirements of learning for the subgroups, and of serving as a clearinghouse and an interpreter of over-all progress.

Beyond these initial stages the leader or guide should strive to be an integral part of a cohesive group with common interests in which each member senses that he has a respected place and a unique role to play in helping the group to reach its own group-determined goals.

Appraising Group Needs and Structure

The interpersonal structure of the group will have a pervasive influence upon the group climate, and this needs to be studied frequently to shed light on problems of acceptance, rejections, closed subgroups or cliques, and any other factors that may prevent the free intercommunication and cooperation important for a cohesiveness that will include everyone in a respected status and suitable and satisfying roles. Sometimes assistance may be given through key leaders; again it may involve direct study by the entire group as to how their democratic processes can be improved. It has been aptly said that democracy must be taught as well as caught.

There is a rapidly growing body of research and experiential data on how democracy can be taught through discussion groups. Much of the research data has not yet been adapted to use at all ages levels, but a group leader can carry on firsthand "action research" in helping a group to study and improve their own democratic processes. Such study may be initiated to investigate a particular problem of which the group has become aware—perhaps how to equalize duties or responsibilities fairly in a project, how to choose leaders wisely, how to control a discipline problem that is interfering with group progress—or it may result from general interest in trying to make the group more democratic. Before the interest appears it is likely that a leader may find it helpful to initiate more subtle methods of studying the interpersonal structure of the group as one means of getting effective group processes under way.

Sociometric techniques

These are techniques, first introduced by Moreno (7), to study the various interpersonal relationships within a group through providing opportunity for individuals to express preferences for companions in various activities. Numerous methods of graphing these preferences have been developed to depict the structure of relations existing at a given time among members of a group.

The sociometric test is quite simple and adaptable to many group situations. It may consist of a single question, such as "With whom would you like to sit?" or "With whom would you like to work on a committee?" The question may refer to any situation or activity within a particular group and should be realistic, in that the pupils know that the activities will occur and that there is a definite point in their expressing preferences for work or play companions. A pupil is usually asked to write down his first three choices, and the fact is made clear that not everyone can be given his first preference.

The following points have been stressed as important in administering a sociometric test and using the results (8–12): (a) Members of a group should know each other well enough to make valid choices (a reason for some initial activities such as have been suggested). (b) Questions should be worded so that children understand how and when results are to be used. (c) It should be emphasized that any boy or girl may be chosen, so as to approve in advance any direction a choice may take. (d) The test should be presented with interest and enthusiasm, but at the same time the procedure should be kept casual. A comment that we work or play better when we are with others we like might help to make the question seem casual. (e) The individual preferences written on slips of paper should be kept completely confidential. (f) Pupils' choices may be tabulated for individual members and for groups such as boys and girls, mutual pairs, mutual rejections, and other subdivisions that will show great varieties of interrelationships.

The first tabulation may be made by listing the names of group members along the top of a form and in the same order down the left-hand side. The rank order of each member's choices (1, 2, or 3 if three choices were requested) is entered in the row after his name, in the columns under the names of those chosen. In this way the number of choices for each individual can be totaled by rank and a partial picture of the choice status of each member can be seen. The sociogram depicts these relations graphically.

A number of sociogram forms have been developed (8–11), and Warters (12) has brought these together and interpreted them helpfully, and has summarized much pertinent research in sociometry. The handling of the test results for a fairly large group is very time-consuming. Some methods of processing the data for use with electronic computers have been developed for extensive research projects.

A sociogram can highlight the salient points in the structure of a group: who are the stars of attraction, who are rejected, who are the isolates, where the chains occur (one person choosing another, who in turn chooses another), where we find closed triangular situations, where small groups are separated into islands, to what extent choices are reciprocated, and to what degree the entire group is integrated.

The findings of a sociogram can be put to many uses in guiding a group in evolving effective relationships. The most immediate use is to apply the sociogram in carrying out the original rearrangement which was promised to the group. In doing this it should be pointed out to the entire group that it is not possible for every person to be grouped with his first choice, but that the regrouping has been carried out on the democratic principle of meeting most of the needs of as many as possible.

To effect an equitable regrouping, it has proved desirable to observe the following rules: If there are pupils who have not been chosen by anyone, try to give those pupils their own first choice. It is better to give a pupil a reciprocated choice than a first choice. If a pupil has been chosen by those he did not choose, give him his first choice. Avoid throwing a specifically rejected student into a group made up of students who asked not to be with him. And, finally, if the technique is to be effective, every student in the group should be placed with at least one of his indicated choices.

Sociometric data for a given individual needs to be studied carefully in the light of all available personnel data and teacher observation in order to interpret what it may reveal about him. Any guidance to individuals with respect to the sociometric findings should be given without reference to the findings themselves. This is especially important, of course, with respect to conditions of rejection, knowledge of which may lower morale and self-respect. Individual guidance should usually follow any group discussion of qualities which make us liked and accepted and should not be related to specific facts of rejection by peers on the socio-metric test.

Some Variations of Sociometric Techniques. Sometimes a teacher may invite members of a group to name individuals with whom they would not wish to carry on some activity. This procedure might be indicated if certain tensions existed within the group. No definite number of names will be suggested for these negative responses. It is possible to assign scores to individuals on the basis of number of times chosen or rejected and arrange a rank order of ratings ranging from the person who has the largest number of choices to the one who has the largest number of rejections. This practice of inviting negative responses has been questioned by some workers, who fear that the rejection responses may be discussed outside the classroom and lead to wider rejection of certain children. Also, the rank-order method of rating children will not always reveal the actual situation. A pupil may be rejected by some and chosen by others and receive a middle-range rating that is difficult to interpret.

Thompson and Powell (13) investigated the merits of a rating-scale approach to the measurement of social status with a sixth-grade class. In addition to the usual types of sociometric questions involving three choices in order of preferences of boys or girls for school and out-of-school activities, but with no request to specify those with whom they would least like to do various things, they asked each pupil to rate every other classmate on a seven-point scale for each of four activities: to help in making up work, to sit near, to choose to play on a team, and to invite to a party. Each classmate was rated at one of the following points: (*a*) would be the very first one chosen; (*b*) one of the first three; (*c*) one of the first six; (*d*) I might or might not choose; (*e*) one of the last six; (*f*) one of the last three; (*g*) would be the very last one I would choose. After several test-retest trials, and comparison of results of the two methods, the investigators concluded that the rating scale provided more stable results over the period of the study, made it possible to differentiate between social rejects and social isolates (or neglectees), and did not appear to cause any stigmatizing of children as rejects. The rating scale was found to be more cumbersome than the rank-order method, which provided a slightly more stable classification of "stars" and rejects. They expressed the opinion that the rating method merited further study of its possibilities.

Justman and Wrightstone (14) investigated the relative merits of a variant of (*a*) the Guess Who test, in which pupils were asked to designate classmates suitable for described roles in a play, of which six were negative and six positive characterizations; (*b*) a modified form of the Ohio Social Acceptance Scale, advanced series, in which each pupil was asked to rate each of his classmates on a five-point scale: (1) very, very best friends; (2) good friends; (3) not friends, but O.K.; (4) don't know them; (5) not O.K.; and (c) a modification of Moreno's original approach, in which each pupil was asked to select the three classmates he liked best and the three he liked least. The authors concluded from comparisons of results on the three approaches that the Moreno approach and the Ohio Social Acceptance Scale may be used interchangeably, but that the Casting Characters technique (the Guess Who test) appears to measure somewhat different aspects of pupil status than the other two.

The use of any of these methods of securing negative responses or of asking for choices that are unrelated to actual activities in a group should probably be questioned for a guidance group where a climate of acceptance is important, unless there are evidences of tensions or conflicts that need to be understood. These techniques are primarily valuable for research. Adaptations of the Guess Who type of test might be used effectively in connection with some phase of role-playing to increase both leader and member insights.

Sociometric techniques have revealed some of the limitations of teacher observation of pupil status, and have aroused interest in searching for ways of improving both pupil status and interpersonal relationships within a group. They are distinctly informal instruments for the teacher, to help in her understanding of individuals and groups, and the data should not be shared with pupils.

Any sociometric technique can be used as a springboard for very valuable group discussion which will develop insight in the field of interpersonal relationships. Without betraying the confidences implicit in sociometric tests and without revealing to any student what his rating is with his peers, a group can be directed in a discussion of what makes one liked by one's classmates. Emphasis can also be placed, through group procedures, on the gains to be derived from knowing and liking all kinds of people. It is often valuable, too, to point out to pupils that their choices may change—that, as they develop or as they get to know members of their own group better, they may enjoy reaching out and choosing other associates. Or, that the classmates they choose to work with on a committee may not be the same as the classmates with whom they would like to share a recreational activity.

It is probably an open question whether sociometric techniques are more valuable to place individuals in compatible situations for activities or to provide insight to the leader about group structure. Both uses are doubtless valuable, but certain cautions are needed in the interpretation of results. Olmstead (15) has suggested that the insight of perhaps broadest significance is the discovery of a "psyche-group" and a "socio-group" within even a small average group. The former is a more personal group held together by bonds of liking and friendship, while the latter is a more impersonal, working group. Some limitations of socio-metric results need to be kept in mind, and Olmstead has summarized these (15, pp. 98–99): (a) They do not necessarily record actual asso-ciations, but only what people say or write. (b) They are conscious opinions and may not represent unconscious feelings. (c) They do not necessarily portray the essence of group life with its task-oriented activi-ties as well as affective relationships. In spite of limitations, however, they have real value and repeated at suitable intervals may show im-portant developments in group structure.

Discussion techniques

The discussion class has been defined ideally as (16):

. . . a cooperative attack on a common set of problems, based on a common set of data, materials, and experiences, in which the problem is pursued to as complex and deep a level as possible. The instructor, ideally, in a discussion class helps the group focus on the common problem, helps them extend and deepen the problem, brings whatever resources he may have to the attack and finally helps the group recognize when the problem has been solved as well as the further implications of the solution.

This definition is somewhat academic for some types of guidance prob-lems, and it would need to be adapted to maturity levels other than col-lege. However, the definition and the research reported here have some important implications at all levels.

Bloom, whose definition is quoted above, studied ingeniously the thought processes of college students in lectures and discussion classes by the method of Stimulated Recall. Sound recordings were made dur-ing entire class periods and played back to students within about forty-eight hours. The playback was stopped at critical points, and students were asked to report the thoughts they had in the original situation at these points. Classes varied widely in the percentage of reported thoughts which were relevant to the lecture or discussion. Each of the *lectures* studied was superior to the average discussion class in the *amount* of relevant thinking reported. However, four-fifths of the *discussions* evoked more thoughts which involve synthesis of ideas and attempts to solve problems or questions raised than did the average lecture. Bloom char-acterizes the discussion class as still an extremely blunt educational in-strument and one that requires time and training on the part of students in order to develop competence in its use for problem solving.

Learning to Listen. One of the major problems for each participant in a discussion group is that of forgetting self and learning really to listen to all others in the group attentively, with the purpose of understanding and evaluating each contribution and working cooperatively with the entire group toward some consensus of judgment. This may or may not mean unanimity of judgment but will involve judicious consideration of all pertinent points of view or solutions.

Listening has been described (17) as an ability which develops through various stages during childhood. These stages have been described as: (a) little conscious listening and easy distraction; (b) half listening, but holding fast to one's own ideas; (c) listening passively, but with no reaction; (d) listening, forming associations, and responding with items from one's own experience; (e) listening and reacting to what is said through questions and answers; and (f) listening and reacting with genuine mental and emotional participation—a real meeting of minds.

Obviously, the early stages of listening ability are not confined to childhood. One of the responsibilities of the leader is to help all members of the group to grow in their listening ability to the point where it becomes part of a creative act as described in the last stage.

Duker (18) has summarized research on listening and provided helpful bibliographies for testing and teaching techniques for listening at both elementary and secondary school levels.[2]

Contributing to Discussion. In using discussion productively as a learning technique, the leader may find it helpful to be able to recognize and identify the roles which may be assumed by members of a discussion group under democratic structuring (19).

Although students are rarely aware that they are enacting these roles, each function in the following enumeration makes an affirmative contribution to the group experience, and the teacher who is aware of them can guide students toward making such contributions.

Among characteristic member roles in a democratic group in which functional leadership is diffused are: *Initiator,* the person who suggests new activities, new ideas, new problems; *Orientor,* the person who stimulates a group to define its goals and determine its direction; *Facilitator,* the communications expert within the group, who sees that all members are informed of the particular skills of other members and who calls for restatements, definitions, summaries, in order that the group can assess its progress; *Encourager,* the member who stimulates others to perform at their best level; *Harmonizer,* the member who makes it possible for all sides to be heard, reconciles differences, reduces tensions; *Summarizer,* the person who reports back to the group from time to time on the ground which has been covered; *Fact-seeker,* the member who recognizes and indicates the points on which additional information is needed; *Fact-giver,* the member who is able to contribute information from his own experience or from his familiarity with authoritative sources

---

[2] A film, *Effective Listening,* by Conboy and Buehler (1959), would be valuable in this training.

in the field; *Compromiser,* the member who, himself a proponent of a challenged position, is able to yield in order that the group may move ahead; *Expediter,* the member who handles the mechanical and physical arrangements for the group; *Spokesman,* the person on whom the group relies to represent its point of view to outside groups; *Status role,* the person generally accorded respect from other members of the group because of his accomplishments or abilities and who, by his participation, gives status to the group; *Recorder,* the member who records the official action of the group; *Evaluator,* the person who reports to the group in terms of the progress it has made toward its goals (as distinguished from the summarizer who reports substantive progress); *Analyzer,* the member who maintains a group awareness of how it is functioning *as a group.*

Perhaps it should be pointed out that in addition to the constructive roles which are listed above, there are a number of negative roles which are often enacted in group discussions. They include the aggressor, who attacks the status of others; the blocker, who habitually opposes everything; the recognition-seeker, who places his own ego needs above the needs of the group; the dodger, who refuses to become involved with the group; the dominator, who has a need to show authority or display superiority; the help-seeker, who exploits the sympathies of the group; the special-interest pleader, who "lobbies" for a particular solution or decision; the blamer, who is always critical of others and who himself is faultless (19).

All students should have some understandings of what the elements of good discussion are, how to participate in discussion, and some of the techniques of leading a discussion.

So much emphasis is currently placed on leadership techniques that many participants in group activity tend to forget that the responsibility of a good discussion is shared by everyone in the group. In developing this sense of responsibility among the members of a student group, some of the elements which might be stressed are:

1. In group discussion, very often the whole is greater than the sum of its parts. Something emerges from the *group* approach which has a life of its own, which is more than the mere adding up of the thinking of a number of individuals. The productiveness of a group in generating this creative quality is directly related to the level of participation of its members. In other words, a group which is dominated by three or four vocal members, with the other members remaining passive, never attains this group quality. It does not come to life as a functioning entity.

2. Participation thus becomes a primary responsibility of everybody in group discussion.

3. Participation means not only the ability to talk but also the ability to listen and, most important, the ability to synthesize what is said.

4. It is the responsibility of all group members to come to a discussion prepared. They should know what is to be discussed, have some familiarity with the subject, and understand what the scope of the discussion is to be. If the group has agreed that a specified amount of reading or research should be done in preparation for the discussion, every member of the group should fulfill his responsibility in this respect.

5. Members should make every effort not to digress from the subject under discussion, and should share the discussion time with everybody else who wants to talk.

6. Good manners are indispensable to good group discussion. Participants should remain good-tempered and good-natured; they should not indulge in personal remarks; they should respect what others have to say and how they say it.

7. Student members should be made aware of the temptations to use a group-discussion situation to serve their own needs, rather than to advance the discussion. They should be trained to guard against converting a group discussion into a vehicle through which they can fortify their egos or work off their hostilities.

Functions of the Discussion Leader. One of his first functions is to establish a pervasive climate of warm friendliness within the group that fosters a sense of acceptance and permissiveness on the part of everyone. The importance of acceptance and permissiveness has been noted earlier, acceptance implying respected membership in the group and permissiveness connoting freedom to express ideas, feelings, or opinions, or to remain silent.[3] Hoffmann and Plutchik (20) suggest four ways in which a discussion leader can encourage a genuine sense of acceptance: to be nonjudgmental with respect to all contributions from the group, often using the reflection technique to help clarify statements; to give equal attention and weight to every statement; to call attention to existing limits when necessary (and we might add, help the group to set their own limits when possible); to avoid preaching, advising, or moralizing.

Other functions of the leader are:

1. To provide conditions that will facilitate free and full intercom-

---

[3] This emphasis upon a warm, accepting climate does not carry the connotation that sweetness and light will always prevail in a permissive group. Feelings of hostility may often be expressed through aggressive or other types of negative behavior. Important learnings for group members are the gaining of fuller understanding of the sources of hostility, and of its normalcy as a form of emotional expression; also, the development of skill in directing the energy associated with this feeling into constructive and socially acceptable behavior. Limitations set by the leader and the group in the interest of general welfare are almost always desirable if they stem from an understanding and accepting spirit and are not merely repressive in nature. This matter of hostility will be considered in Chapter 6 in connection with the question of therapeutic relationships in small groups.

munication. An informal circular seating arrangement is one helpful device. Another is to serve as a tactful traffic officer to facilitate the participation of all. This involves skill in curbing members who may tend to monopolize discussion without antagonizing them, and in encouraging the less talkative members without embarrassing them. Another important service is to help a group to utilize minority opinions effectively when group decisions are pending.

2. To help the group to set goals, to explore the ramifications of problems to be studied, to serve as a resource of information and materials, and to bring other resource people to the service of the group when the need is indicated. Hoffmann and Plutchik (20) comment on the uses and abuses of the *deflection* technique—that is, being used as an information giver or a question answerer. The chief disadvantage of overuse is the encouragement of a dependency attitude which may discourage the fullest initiative and creativity within the group.

3. To introduce helpful techniques to keep desirable movement in the discussion.

There are a number of specific techniques which are used in group discussion to break through the initial reluctance which many people have to talk, and to help build up rapport among members of the group. For example, there are many people who can talk easily and well if they are faced with only two or three other persons but who "freeze" when they try to talk in a group of twenty-five or thirty. To aid people to transfer their sense of ease from small groups to large groups, the "buzz" session technique is often used as a warm-up in group discussions. A group is broken down into subgroups of five or six members. Each subgroup holds a brief, informal discussion for five or ten minutes. Sometimes all the subgroups will discuss the same subject, and sometimes each group will be asked to take on a specific phase of a broader subject. At the end of the brief buzz session, each subgroup through its spokesman reports to the full group the feeling of his subgroup on the subject under discussion. Several useful functions are served by this technique. The most important one is that the device has quickly and painlessly precipitated a great many people into the discussion. A second useful function is that as the buzz sessions are reported out, it is possible to assess quickly what the major areas of agreement and disagreement within the group are, since sometimes these areas crystallize in a few minutes of discussion. Buzz sessions are also useful, in many instances, because they automatically generate leadership material from within the group.

Brainstorming has become a rather popular technique in some situations as a means of getting a wide variety of suggestions before a group considering a particular problem. Individuals are urged to pool their ideas spontaneously without critical reserve and with no critical responses from the group. While this technique may produce a wealth of suggestions, it has not always stood up well in research when results have been compared with the quality of more critical individual thinking. Favorable results of brainstorming exercises have been reported.

4. To keep discussion within boundaries relevant to the problem, and at times to summarize so that the group members are aware of how much or how little headway they have made, in what areas they seem to have reached agreement, and what questions are still unsolved; eventually to help the group evaluate both their techniques and their conclusions.

5. To care for special difficulties that may arise within the group. Often there will be some members of a group who present problems, either of nonparticipation or of interference with the participation of others, perhaps through undue talking, wandering from the topic, or unpleasant arguing. Study of the causes of their conduct will usually reveal approaches to help them. Information about special interests of a shy individual may be used to draw him tactfully into discussions. Suggestions to the more active disturbers in individual interviews may help. Always, the effort should be made to build up a feeling of belonging and respected status in the group rather than of isolation and censure. Direct study by the entire group of how to improve its procedures may often care for many problem situations without the intervention of the leader.

Bales has subjected the interaction of small groups to very rigorous and detailed investigation in the Laboratory of Social Relations at Harvard University. A chart used in this study for recording observations of the behavior of participants in groups (21, p. 9) includes three types of categories: (a) positive social-emotional behavior, which contributes to solidarity, release of tensions, and group consensus; (b) active cooperation in the group task through giving and asking for suggestions, opinions, and orientation with respect to problems; and (c) negative social-emotional behavior, which tends toward disagreement, tensions, and antagonisms within the group. A check list of illustrative types of behavior under such categories could prove helpful to a group in studying its interaction problems and in working for improvement of its interaction-learning process.

Problem-solving techniques

In a world in which conditions about us change rapidly and in which we ourselves are always in a state of change in various ways, it is essential that we develop techniques for maintaining a balance between these inner and outer forces. If education is to help prepare individuals for the lifelong adjustments they will be called upon to make, guidance in the problem-solving process must be a component of education.

Problem solving is used here to connote the creative process by which individuals evaluate changes in themselves and their environment, and make new choices, decisions, or adjustments in harmony with life goals and values, which may also be in a state of flux. Thus conceived, problem solving is a fundamental technique of living in a democratic social order.

Students can profitably be made aware that an organized approach to the solution of a problem is productive. Many of the mental disciplines which are applied to problems in the area of the sciences are also pertinent for problems in the field of interpersonal relationships, although obviously the range of variable factors enormously complicates the situation.

Through group demonstrations it will be helpful to guide students toward identifying the steps through which problems can be approached and solutions arrived at. The steps can be formulated as follows:

1. The individual must be aware that a problem exists and must recognize that it is necessary or desirable to solve it.

2. He must understand the nature of the problem; that is, he must be sure that he is aiming directly at his target, and not obscuring the problem by failing to define it accurately.

3. Once a problem has been brought into correct focus, action can be initiated. The first action step is a broad one: gathering all facts which may be relevant.

4. With a body of information on hand, the problem should be examined and analyzed in terms of these facts.

5. Thus equipped with an identified problem which has been examined in terms of pertinent facts, the individual should be prepared to advance tentative solutions to the problem.

6. The next step is one of evaluation. The proposed solutions should be weighed and thought through, in order to determine what effect they will actually have on the problem.

7. Finally, the tentative solution should be exposed to some testing and observation, so that the individual can determine finally whether it is to be accepted or rejected.

It is clear that the foregoing steps call for an objectivity and a discipline which are not readily mastered, particularly when the problem being considered has emotional implications. Observations of students who have been exposed experimentally to the problem-solving process point up some of the obstacles to applying these techniques effectively and ways of removing them.

These obstacles can be summarized briefly as follows (22):

1. No amount of application to a problem is effective if the problem itself is not correctly understood.

2. The individual who does not grasp *relationships* between one situation and another, between one set of data and another, is at a disadvantage in solving problems. One must be able to apply what one has already experienced and learned to what is yet unsolved.

3. The systematic step-by-step approach to a problem is more constructive than the stop-and-start, intuitive, emotionally charged approach.

4. Lack of self-confidence, reliance on snap judgments, and interjection of personal biases are deterrents in solving problems.

Perhaps the most useful contribution which can be made in equipping students with facility in problem solving is through acquainting them with the *thinking process*, making them conscious of the steps in this process, and affording them opportunities in a group situation for practice in applying these methods. Both classroom experience and extracurricular group activity can provide many situations through which students can recognize what is involved in sound thinking, and how its principles can be applied to varied situations. Principles which should be stressed in group experiences of this type might include: the need for accurate and complete observation, giving meaning to our observations through both analysis and synthesis, the techniques of interpreting data validly so that they yield sound generalizations, and the need to verify our conclusions.

A group of students at the University of Chicago whose poor work on comprehensive examinations was thought to be due in large part to poor techniques in problem solving was given special training in these methods. There is substantial evidence, although much of it is admittedly subjective, that this remedial training was effective. The students themselves reported good results from the training, indicating that it had increased their self-confidence and trained them to be analytical and systematic in approaching problems. Faculty members also reported evidences of improvement in the students, stressing the increased confidence of the students and their willingness to participate in classroom discussions, as well as an improved level of problem solving. This observed improvement was also supported, to some extent, by improvement in grades received in examinations (22).

Many areas in group guidance afford the opportunity for both group and individual applications of problem-solving techniques to specific problems. The leader can help a group formulate and analyze a problem, search for available information bearing on various aspects, examine their findings, and reach both group and individual conclusions with respect to the problem. In fields where research of a reliable nature is not available, students can be guided in discovering and planning things they can do to tap helpful experience of others who have faced similar problems, or ways in which they may conduct their own experiments to reach or verify tentative solutions that may serve as bases of action.

One task of the leader is that of deciding in what areas this approach is suitable for various levels of maturity and types of problems. Another is to provide guidance to individuals in adapting group solutions to their own unique situations. The habit of approaching life situations through these problem-solving techniques is one of the basic techniques of self-direction, and each individual should improve his skill from year to year in this objective and rational approach to living. "Facts" which the individual learns may change, but a problem-solving technique, if broadly oriented to include all pertinent aspects of a problem, may be serviceable for a lifetime.

Role-playing as a learning device

Role-playing is a device for developing skills and insights in the realm of human relations by "acting out" situations which parallel real-life problems. As used in a class group, it is likely to include the following steps: (a) sensitizing the group to the need for training in some type of situation—for example, if the role-playing grows naturally out of a discussion of a problem of child-parent relationships, this step is cared for naturally; (b) the warm-up, role-taking, and definition of the situation; (c) helping the audience group to observe intelligently; (d) evaluating the initial role-playing; and (e) replaying the situation after evaluative discussion. There are, of course, many variations of procedure for different purposes (23).

Role-playing usually takes the form of psychodrama or sociodrama. The inherent difference between the two forms is that the educational [4] psychodrama concerns itself with the *individual* involvement of a person with other people (such as the rebelliousness of an adolescent toward parental authority), whereas the sociodrama deals with problems lodged in a societal situation (such as undemocratic attitudes toward members of a minority racial group.) Apart from these content differences, the two forms are similar in techniques, goals, and underlying philosophy.

The techniques of the educational psychodrama and the sociodrama can be applied, as a group method, with equal effectiveness at any age level—from nursery school to adult groups. The important considerations are that situations which are chosen for acting out bear a relationship to recognizable problems for the age group which is involved, and that individuals are not subjected to traumatic experiences through situations that are embarrassing or beyond their depth, and that cannot be utilized by the leader for wholesome learning within the group.

---

[4] "Educational psychodrama" is used here to distinguish the form used in schools from the therapeutic psychodrama used by psychiatrists or other clinicians with individuals who have serious emotional problems.

Although general recognition of the usefulness of the techniques of the psychodrama and the sociodrama is a fairly recent development in American education, and research in the area is currently being very energetically carried on, the underlying philosophy has been familiar to students of American education for more than thirty years. The roots for today's acceptance of the psychodrama and sociodrama lie in the writing of J. L. Moreno, who articulated the theory of *spontaneous* learning.

Moreno's premise is that a significant aspect of the learning process is learning through active response—as differentiated from "content" learning, in which the learner is a relatively passive recipient, taking in what he is taught and feeding it back on request. He contends that the most valuable aspects of learning, in terms of total-life application, occur in the field of human relations; and that in this area, the individual will function at his best if he learns to act and react with spontaneity, free of blocks, capable of working through his frustrations, evaluating each situation in terms of its actual components rather than in terms of preconceived stereotypes.

This is the type of learning which can be achieved through judicious and skilled use of the psychodrama and the sociodrama.

Although both these dramatic devices are unrehearsed performances, they are by no means unplanned. The teacher or counselor who is responsible for directing the group activity structures the situation, that is, selects a problem or a relationship for dramatization which needs clarification for the group, or which is creating tensions which ought to be resolved. The preplanning includes, in addition to selection of situation, defining the roles which will be acted out, assigning them to individuals whose interpretation of the roles will illuminate the problem, and involving the entire group—actors and spectators alike—in the activity.

In other words, the dramatic activity, as such, is not the total scope of the psychodrama and the sociodrama. For the device to be effective, both as a therapeutic and an educational technique, it is important for the entire group, whether they take part in the acting situation or witness it, to recognize the problem which is being treated and to develop insight about the people who are role-playing. Each member of the group—including the leader—reacts to the manner in which the problem is being handled, evaluates it as a demonstration of either a constructive or destructive solution of a conflict in human relations. It can be seen that for maximum results from the psychodrama and sociodrama, the presentation itself must be linked to a full discussion by the entire group.

Although the importance of discussion and analysis in relation to psychodrama and sociodrama may sometimes be somewhat de-emphasized in current studies, in favor of the fascinating dramatic techniques themselves, they are indispensable components of the entire learning process. Sometimes the discussion can precede the presentation, as part of setting the stage. It can be made clear what problem is to be explored, and what roles are to be enacted. After the presentation, all members of the group contribute their own reactions to the situation; how the presentation affected them; what new insights were provided; how they would have handled the problem differently; how goals might better have been achieved through other courses of action.

In other situations, there is no prepresentation discussion. Only the members of the group who take roles—the actors—are briefed on the situation, and it is unfolded before unprepared spectators. In such situations, the postpresentation discussion carries the full burden of recognition, identification, and evaluation. Regardless of where the discussion is placed in relationship to the presentation, it is imperative that a psychodrama or a sociodrama be accompanied by a complete talking-out, in order that everyone gets a full learning experience, a total sense of being involved, of belonging to the problem, and of having shared in the solving of it.

In general terms, the psychodrama and the sociodrama can be classified functionally as diagnostic, therapeutic, or educational, although it is obvious that any sound presentation probably has some of the elements of all three.

The diagnostic presentation is, in effect, a dress rehearsal. It is a device for determining in advance whether an individual or a group is prepared to handle a situation which will occur in the future, by putting them through the paces of the anticipated situation. For example, suppose a student leader is to serve as chairman of a student-council meeting at which a crucial question is to be discussed, and the leader himself has some misgivings about his ability to handle the meeting without bias, since he has strong personal feelings about the issue, and recognizable hostility toward some of its proponents. A psychodramatic situation could be structured, in which the leader enacts his own real-life role. Other students are assigned to represent typical points of view and attitudes which will occur at the forthcoming meeting. The agenda for the meeting is carried out, and the leader and the group together evaluate his preparedness to handle the situation.

The problem which has just been delineated can, of course, be treated at a broader level than the diagnostic one. It could involve one of the most effective techniques of the psychodrama—that of role reversal. If this were done, the role of the student leader would be assumed by another member of the group, and the real-life leader would take the role of the member of the student council whom he most ardently opposes. By playing out the situation from this new perspective, the leader and the entire group see a whole new set of dynamics in effect, develop deeper understandings about human interaction, and are better prepared to meet the actual situation. Such a session is, in effect, a training device as well as a diagnostic one.

The therapeutic psychodrama can be effectively used by trained clinicians and by psychiatrists who are employing the group approach for therapy. Its use within school systems should of necessity be guarded, and should not be extended beyond the counselor's ability to assess and control the situation. However, since the group techniques within any professional field have some application to all other fields, the following summary of therapeutic psychodrama suggests its usefulness (24): [5]

In-so-far as it is concerned with present therapy, psychodrama attempts to produce individual or group self-integration so that effective action is free to take place and adjustment to problems of living is successfully brought about. In order to do this, problem scenes are dramatized which have caused blocks, frustrations or inhibitions with the intention that dramatic catharsis will clear these blocks away and healthy integrated action will take place spontaneously.

In-so-far as it is concerned with preventative therapy or prophylaxis, psychodrama attempts to anticipate those situations which may produce maladjustments, and to help the subject to be better prepared to meet them. For this purpose anticipated scenes which the subject fears, and perhaps has avoided in the past, are dramatized. In so doing the individual or group gets continued practice by attacking the problem situation with the direction and support of the audience and the psychodramatic director. On the stage he feels free to fail without punishment, and therefore gains security and confidence, eventually learning how to successfully face any problem.

The psychodrama or the sociodrama which is educational in intent might conceivably take several courses, and, as has already been pointed out, any dramatic presentation of a problem situation has educational implications. The presentation might serve the purpose of testing and developing skills; it might be used to point up didactically a broad educational concept. For the purposes of our concern with this device, we might consider the educational function of a psychodrama in the realm of vocational guidance. Suppose that several members in a group of high school students have indicated that they want to prepare for professional work in the social-welfare field. A series of situations could be structured and enacted, in which the students would be performing the actual functions of a social-welfare worker. Through the dramatic presentation and the discussion which followed, several gains might be scored: the students would learn concretely and directly what a social worker does; they would derive from their own experience and from the evaluation of the spectators some cognizance of whether they had any aptitude for handling these functions; they would experience some crystallization of their own feelings with respect to the vocation they had tentatively chosen.

[5] Reprinted by permission of the publisher, Beacon House, Inc., New York.

There are many variations of the techniques of the psychodrama and the sociodrama, in addition to the direct enactment of a problem situation, and the technique of role reversal which has already been described. These variations are limited only by the imagination and resourcefulness of the director of the group. Among the techniques in which research has been carried out are: having one of the actors depict an absent person, toward whom feelings can then be displayed without inhibition; an individual acting out his real-life role, not as he sees it, but as he thinks others see it; the enactment of a complete situation through fictitious characters, completely unanchored to real-life roles; dramatization of dream material; having a single actor depict several roles simultaneously; purging a situation of verbal limitations by presenting it entirely in pantomime.

Among the contributions which the psychodrama or sociodrama makes to the learning process are the following:

1. It permits people to act out their true feelings with reference to a situation in a permissive atmosphere, and thus effects a catharsis.

2. It develops flexibility in handling situations and tests the resources of the individual in facing unanticipated circumstances.

3. It enables the individual to make mistakes and to experience failure in a sheltered situation, without fear of consequences, and thus enables him to try himself out in situations without being damaged in the process.

4. It removes the teacher or the counselor from the authoritarian role, in which communication is a one-way process, and instead places her in a sharing position, in which experience and learning are joint achievements. Toward this end, it is often helpful for the teacher or counselor actively to assume roles, other than their own, in psychodramas and sociodramas.

5. It develops understanding of our own motives, aims, and drives and those of other people; points up, through direct, spontaneous, creative experience, what happens when these elements interact and how both the situation and the persons are reshaped by the interaction; and demonstrates how deeper insights, *commonly experienced,* aid in effective and constructive human relations.

Some Cautions about the Use of Role-Playing. Like any other educational technique, role-playing can be overused to the point where it becomes hackneyed and tiresome. Also, beyond a certain point it may result in an uneconomical and disproportionate use of the total time available for a particular type of learning. Still more important is the consideration of possible attitudes which may be engendered toward real-life situations, where one does not often have the opportunity to try out various roles or techniques before engaging in the real business of living through a situation. Here the preliminary tryouts must usually be experienced mentally, through imaginative anticipation and creative thought processes.

When and how to use role-playing or discussion methods depends upon many factors, including the age and other characteristics of the group, the personality and skill of the leader, the group climate and structure, and the problems being studied. An interesting observation of one group therapist [6] is that well-adjusted individuals tire of role-playing more quickly than do neurotic individuals. Undoubtedly the latter group often find greater satisfaction through dramatization because of their difficulties in becoming wholeheartedly engaged in the activities of real life.

There has been only meager evidence through research that role-playing can produce personality change. Jones and Peters (25) reported evidence of improved overt behavior in a group of schizophrenic patients who engaged in psychodrama dealing often with interpersonal problems of members. In a review of experimental research Mann (26) pointed to the need for valid answers to such questions as these: What personality characteristics may be most affected? Are all role-playing techniques equally effective? Is preplanning better than spontaneous role-playing?

An experimental research project by Mann and Mann (27) in the use of leaderless role-playing with several small groups selected from a graduate education course yielded significant gains for the experimental role-playing groups over the control groups engaged in leaderless group discussion, in interpersonal relationships as expressed in the criteria of "desirability as a friend," "aiding in the attainment of group goals," and "cooperativeness."

The case method

This method has an ancient lineage. We might cite the parables in the Bible and many old legends and folk and fairy tales as early illustrations of attempts to depict human motives and to influence human behavior. Materials in elementary school readers reflect varying approaches in different generations to the questions of character and citizenship education and of teaching aimed at the improvement of human relationships.

During recent decades there has been increased interest in the method and much experimentation with its possibilities in many fields. Among guidance workers, Richard D. Allen, of Providence, Rhode Island, did much pioneer work in the development of case-conference problems for use in group-guidance classes (28). Usually, these problems dealt with some adjustment difficulty of a teen-ager or some ethical or guid-

[6] George R. Bach, *Intensive Group Psychotherapy,* The Ronald Press Company, New York, 1954.

ance problem. The description carried the situation to a point where some judgment or solution was needed, and then questions were added to open up class discussion about the problem. In his writing and in practice, Allen emphasized the importance of the leader's avoiding any moralizing, of encouraging free expression by students of their feelings and thoughts regarding the situation, and of guiding the class discussion toward some kind of group consensus or judgment. Allen's materials were published before present-day terminology about permissive atmosphere and the dynamics of group relationships appeared, but we find in them the seeds of contemporary approaches.

The case method has been used in a great variety of adaptations in units in core, general-education, and life-adjustment programs, utilizing selections from literature and motion pictures illustrative of human relationships and adjustment problems. Publishers and organizations have developed many new films as teaching materials for these areas. Sociodrama techniques are being increasingly used through spontaneous role-playing of characters in a problem story or a real-life situation. One report of this method (29) describes how the question of intergroup relations is approached with a seventh-grade class through a story about three boys, one of them Jewish, who become involved in a problem of trespassing on an exclusive camp site, but in the process save another boy's life. The story is carried to a crucial point where the promised reward of two weeks at camp, offered by the rescued boy's father to the three boys, is changed for the Jewish boy to a bicycle because he would not be admitted to the camp. At this point the story is turned over to the class for discussion or role-playing of the denouement. The ensuing class activities may include experimentation with many possible solutions of the dilemma.

The authors of the report on this method emphasize the following (29, pp. 39–41): "*Each problem story intended as warm-up to role-playing must deal with a developmental task of the age for which the story is intended. Only then will it have real meaning and importance for the group working to solve its dilemma.*"

A teacher or group leader can develop his own materials to suit the needs of his group, either for the problem story or for the case conference. Knowledge of individual and group problems will be the starting point. The materials presented should be sufficiently camouflaged so that no individual or small group will be singled out for identification with the characters described. Also, it is important that these characters retain a respected status as individuals in the opinions of the leader and the group, even though their conduct may be criticized. Only thus can an individual who comes to identify himself with a character retain or develop self-acceptance and self-respect as he strives to solve his problem.

One valuable means of achieving this objective is to help groups to probe for causes of behavior and to think of possible solutions directed at these causes rather than the symptoms evidenced in the observable behavior. The case method used in a great variety of situations should help to develop desirable habits of studying the behavior of self and others in such a way as to gain real insight into its dynamics and to improve self-direction and social facility.

The case method is widely used in legal education and in training in many other professions. Wallace Donham, who has used the method extensively with graduate students in business education, has emphasized the significance of this approach in all phases of responsible living (30). This emphasis is based upon the thesis that in an ever-changing world, situations are never repeated exactly. This means that an intelligent, effective technique of coping with each new situation depends upon skill in analyzing its components, in utilizing past experience, and in learning creatively to make new adjustments to the new situations. Learning and adjustment in this sense can never be static or achieved, but must always be in a state of healthy flux. The process of learning and adjusting thus becomes more important than any specifically acquired knowledge, which is only a means to an end—its intelligent use. Whitehead's oft-quoted statement "Knowledge keeps no better than fish" is particularly meaningful in this context.

Castore (31) found that the attitudes of a group of students toward the case method of instruction were more critical during the second half of a semester than during the first half and that their participation in the class was reduced. He questions whether this change may have been due to the fact that the burden of responsibility placed on the student by this method became more difficult as the work progressed. Perhaps one should also question whether teacher leadership remained at the same level of skill throughout the semester, since no method will carry itself without suitable stimulation.

A recent report on the case method by a college instructor contains the following comments (32):

The case is only a description of reality, however accurately written. It is only a skeleton which the student's imagination must clothe with flesh and blood and infuse with feeling. He may, if he will, refuse to do this or he may be unable to do so. But there is another reality from which he cannot escape. It is the reality of the classroom itself, the community, albeit a temporary one, of his fellow students. For insofar as the "case method" means anything at all, it means a process of learning by discussion. Its essence is to present a problem for joint solution, and the student is thus plunged into group endeavor with his fellows. This is his real laboratory of social relations and the task of the teacher becomes then one of helping him to learn what he can from it. . . .

The "case method" is directed primarily toward the development of insight and skill rather than erudition, toward behavior rather than knowledge. . . .

There are few among those practicing "case method" teaching who would argue that it should be the only method of instruction countenanced in institutions of collegiate level. What we do insist is that there is a desperate need for this kind of educational experience along with others.

A few case descriptions with questions to guide in the probing for causes of difficulties and the planning of helpful ways to improve adjustment are in the Pasadena Pupil Judgment Test in the Appendix. Such tests have been used to stimulate interest in understanding motives and causal factors underlying behavior, both to foster better human relationships and to pave the way for a wholesome, objective approach to the study of self. More information about each individual, as described in this test, is needed, and a case conference leader should be prepared to supply it at appropriate points in the group discussion. Additional information for a particular case can often be drawn from knowledge about actual individuals in the group, provided it is sufficiently camouflaged to avoid identification. Gradually, through such study, the idea of common problems is certain to emerge, and individuals can thus grow in their awareness of their ties with other human beings in mutuality of problems. Such identification can be thoroughly wholesome in releasing tensions and in overcoming barriers to self-understanding, self-acceptance, and progress toward self-improvement.

The use of the case method in vocational guidance with college students is described in Chapter 11 (see pages 291 and 292). Raines (33) has also reported on its effective use with college freshmen in ways that reached into a variety of educational, vocational, and social problems. The Problems in Vocational Planning in the Appendix have been used widely with high school students, and the form could be adapted to a variety of case situations.

Any of the techniques already considered—discussion, problem solving, and role-playing—can be utilized effectively in the case method. A variety of films, stories, biographies, and plays can be drawn upon as source materials.[7]

---

[7] Lists of films and sources of films are included in the Appendix. For literature a good reference is Hilda Taba, *Reading Ladders in Human Relations,* American Council on Education, Washington, 1949. Librarians are increasingly joining the ranks of personnel workers by assuming responsibility for the location and utilization of source materials. A bulletin of the University of Illinois Library School describes a plan in which counseling functions related to various areas in the student program are distributed among the library staff of the Chicago Undergraduate Division of the University of Illinois. This plan is described by David K. Maxfield, in *Counselor Librarianship: A New Departure,* Occasional Papers, no. 38, March, 1954.

INDIVIDUAL APPRAISAL TECHNIQUES

This area will be dealt with in considerable detail in Chapter 10, but certain aspects of technique will be emphasized here.

Approaches and techniques in a self-appraisal unit or course

In planning for direct study of self-appraisal methods with high school or college students, consideration should be given to the total program of student appraisal within the institution in order that this directed study may draw upon information already available through personnel records. This statement does not imply that all such information will be transmitted to students, but rather that it will be used as background for the interpretation of data secured by students in group study. Interviews of students with counselors are usually necessary for such interpretations, but group study of sound appraisal methods and experience in using them in collecting some data about self will serve to enhance the value of these individual conferences immeasurably.

A unit or course on self-appraisal should clarify what objective tests and other methods may *not* reveal, as well as what they may indicate, regarding the potentialities of individuals. Also, it should clarify the functions of a counselor or psychologist, who can help the pupil interpret scientific data and his own subjective information about himself, and perhaps inform him about *probabilities* of success in various fields of study or work, but who is not a fortuneteller or one who can make decisions or choices for him.

Too often appraisal units provide for administration of tests and the supplying of profiles of results to students without adequate explanations of both the limitations and contributions of test data and without interpretations by trained workers in the perspective of long-range data for each individual. Psychologists with years of training and experience are frequently puzzled by inconsistencies in such data. We can scarcely expect that teachers without much specialized psychological training and immature students with little or no psychological background can make wise interpretations of some of the test data that are frequently made available to students and their parents.

Recognizing these difficulties should not deter us from advancing in our efforts to provide guidance in self-appraisal, but should alert us to the complexity of the problem, so that we avoid the pitfalls of pseudo science. One help in meeting this difficulty is to include within a unit on self-appraisal the study of various pseudoscientific methods of personality appraisal and of the possibilities and limitations of modern, scientific methods.

Judging the Soundness of Appraisal Services. The problem of evaluating the various consultant services in this field that are offered to the lay consumer in a community is complicated by a number of factors: the range of such services is almost limitless; the terminology used to describe the practitioners is often misleading; and the field is not subject to the same rigid licensing controls in most states as are applied to other, related professions.

Some of the more palpable forms of quackery can easily be identified, and it can readily be established with students that no valid professional help can be expected from such sources. It is fairly generally accepted, by now, that no reliance can be placed in the shady arts of physiognomy, phrenology, and other ready-made routes to "character analysis." Less difficult to discern are the merits of a large number of persons who label themselves "psychologists." Some unqualified individuals have been sufficiently clever in the use of psychological terminology to confuse some educators and even psychological and psychiatric workers.

The following guides will be helpful in training students to make sound judgments with respect to appraisal services:

1. The more sweeping and grandiose a consultant's promises are, the less likely he is to be professionally adequate. Students should be alerted to the dangers of the practitioner who has the easy and quick answer; who will solve all problems in three sessions on a money-back guarantee; who glibly offers cut-rate fees or other bargains.

2. Useful criteria in evaluating a consultant include his professional training in psychology and personnel work, membership in accepted professional organizations, certification in those states which license psychologists, and affiliation with responsible public or private institutions or agencies.

3. All students will be benefited by some broad consumer education with respect to what they can reasonably expect from psychological appraisal, and what must be rejected as an unreliable promise. When students can differentiate between the plausible and the impossible in this area, on the basis of a realistic acceptance of the limitations of psychological appraisal techniques, they will be better equipped to approach their own problems of self-appraisal.

Appraising Aspects of Personality through Psychological Methods. Psychology, as a science, is relatively new, but the vistas which it has opened up often tempt us to move beyond the boundaries of research and proved experience. In the early days of psychological testing there was a tendency to assume that if enough test records for a given individual were accumulated, somehow a picture was gained of his personality. Often the parts, as in a kaleidoscope, would become rearranged in time, and the worker would be confronted with a seemingly new personality.

As our knowledge about the human personality—how it develops and what makes it tick—has grown, we have come to recognize that standardized, objective tests, important as they are, sample only certain aspects and certain levels of personality and may frequently fail to tap the potentialities which we seek to understand. Never can a group of objective tests depict the whole personality in all its ramifications and dynamic interrelationships. But they give us much information which, interpreted in relation to other data, is essential for wise educational and vocational choices and plans.

Many so-called "projective techniques" have been developed which provide opportunity for an individual to react to more unstructured material than in the objective tests, and these often yield many insights with respect to the dynamics of personality and levels of integration. We might think of a continuum from projective clinical techniques on the one hand to all the unstructured methods on the other hand by which teachers and personnel workers observe and study children, adolescents, or adults in the varied situations in school or college. Some of these informal approaches to the study of self are described in Chapter 10 (see pages 242 to 246).

Doubtless the most significant outcomes of a unit or course in self-appraisal lie in the attitudes toward, and techniques for, self-study which any student acquires and which he can continue to apply beyond school as he evaluates his ongoing experience. We can never afford to overlook William James's caution that, like the iceberg, the greater part of the personality is submerged from our view.

Sampling and the Normal Probability Curve. Perhaps one of the most useful contributions to be made by a group approach to the problems of self-appraisal is to acquaint students with the framework within which psychological measuring is done. No matter how eager students may be for yes-or-no answers, for evaluations of themselves in terms of absolutes, it should be firmly established, *before any self-appraisal tests are administered,* that the only reliable results which can be expected from objective psychological measuring techniques are results stated in terms of *relative placement* in comparison with others in some group.

To establish this concept, the nature of the normal probability curve should be made clear as a graphic representation of the way individuals tend to vary with respect to the strength of various traits. A class group can usually demonstrate this tendency roughly by graphing their heights or perhaps their scores on a reading or arithmetic test, and then trying to interpret the placement of each individual in terms of the number of students he exceeds or who exceed him with respect to the particular characteristic being graphed. For many tests the students' scores will be translated into percentiles, and the concept of relative placement within a hypothetical group of 100 will need to be developed. The maturity of the class and the tests to be used will determine whether other statistical concepts with respect to placement on the normal probability curve will be required.

The need for all of us to find quick and all-encompassing answers is a common one, and the temptation for students to read more into self-appraisal techniques than the method can support is understandable. It should be counteracted by developing as lucid an understanding of the methods as possible, in such terms as these:

All we are measuring in this test is trait X.

This test cannot give you an absolute answer to the question: Am I X?

It may indicate that you are probably, at present, more X than 60 per cent of the boys of your age who, like you, are also in the tenth grade.

And you should be warned that if you took this same test on another day, you might place, say, at the 65th percentile instead of the 60th; or you might perhaps place at the 54th. So do not peg your whole appraisal of yourself on the fact that your X rating is 60. It is only one of many ways by which you will want to find out things about yourself.

It is to be hoped that in any appraisal program enough test and other data would be accumulated for each individual to enable each person to discover his own spread of characteristics, weak, average, and strong, on his own distribution curve. If the concept of personality development through the interaction of hereditary and environmental factors has been developed with a group, it will be possible to stimulate thinking with respect to the possible effects of these factors on test results and the possibilities of utilizing environmental opportunities for further development of desired characteristics. The importance of the *pattern* of characteristics, rather than the mere strength or weakness of any one trait, should always be stressed.

Norms. For practical purposes with a given group of high school or college students, an all-important question is that of deciding with what particular group each student should compare himself. Should his relative placement be established in terms of others of his age? sex? previous experience? training? background? An individual considering an art, or perhaps an engineering, major should know whether his percentile or other placement represents a comparison with art, or engineering, majors of his present grade placement, high school or college; students in general; or a random sampling of all people. Norms are frequently available for different types of institutions, such as public or private, and many institutions develop their own norms, which will enable counselors to help students estimate their probabilities of success in various fields of study in that institution. This type of approach to the interpretation of tests helps to prevent students from classifying themselves abstractly with respect to one or more characteristics.

Rating scales and inventories sometimes present a slightly different problem of interpretation. A number of interest and personality inventories have percentile norms for particular age or interest groups, but most rating scales will include only a few categories such as superior, average, and inferior. Each of these categories may be subdivided and the number thus expanded to perhaps five or seven. Interpretations will depend upon methods used by the raters.

Steps in the development of a self-appraisal project

Approach with Students. Understanding of both possibilities and limitations of one cross-section appraisal of self is the first essential step. Some of these considerations have been noted. Next in importance is the realization that everyone has both strengths and weaknesses and that the pattern of abilities, interests, and other personality characteristics is more significant usually than any one strength or weakness. Any group leader would do well to examine his own evaluation of various human potentialities such as intelligence or scholastic aptitude as compared with, say, mechanical or artistic abilities or social facility, since with prejudices in favor of high scholastic aptitude, he can unconsciously prevent, instead of facilitate, the progress of some individuals in accepting and respecting their unique patterns of potentialities.

When a group of students knows that the results of tests and other appraisal methods are for their own use in self-understanding and planning, cooperation in the testing and rating is likely to be on a high level and results are likely to be more reliable than when the group feels no special personal interest in the results.

Selecting a Battery of Appraisal Instruments. This selection will depend, of course, upon the maturity of members of the group, personnel data already available, and the immediate uses to be made of results. Members of the student group, with the guidance of the leader, can helpfully prepare a tentative list of the things they wish to know about themselves. The leader and consultants can then consider what data are available on personnel records; what information needs rechecking during the present study; which types of information can be secured (*a*) through objective tests, (*b*) through interest or personality inventories and rating scales, (*c*) through various projective techniques, (*d*) through autobiographies and self-estimates, (*e*) through parent conferences or some other means of communication with parents, (*f*) through counselors, teachers, or other leaders who know members of the group, (*g*) other sources. This type of preanalysis will prevent a narrow approach to the self-appraisal task with its limited and perhaps erroneous information.

CRITERIA FOR THE SELECTION OF TESTS. This problem of selection of suitable tests requires considerable training in testing and diagnostic techniques and calls for the cooperation of a trained psychologist. The difficulties to be encountered have been treated helpfully by the Joint Committee of the American Psychological Association, the American Educational Research Association, and the National Council on Measurements Used in Education in their report entitled *Technical Recommendations for Psychological Tests and Diagnostic Techniques* (34).

Anyone planning a testing program can avoid many pitfalls by studying in this report the specifications enumerated for reporting information about tests. These specifications are aimed at encouraging producers of tests to provide adequate data as to standardization and bases for interpretation of tests, and helping users to select and interpret tests wisely. These recommendations apply to any types of tests such as are discussed in this section. Because of the frequent lack of adequate norms and validation data, it has been suggested by one authority that test users might well develop their own norms for some tests and that test publishers might help in this process (35).

Administration and Scoring of Objective Tests. Results of objective tests will be meaningless unless favorable conditions prevail in the group during the testing periods, exact instructions are followed, and timing is checked accurately, usually with a stop watch. No tests should be administered without careful preparation on the part of the tester, who must (*a*) be thoroughly acquainted with the manual of instructions; (*b*) have all necessary supplies conveniently at hand; and (*c*) be able to establish and maintain an atmosphere in the group conducive to alertness and active effort of individuals without undue tension or strain that may inhibit or hinder their best work.

If students score the tests, care should be exercised to prevent the results for any one student from being known by other students without his permission. If scoring by machine or trained clerical workers is not possible, there should be sampling checks of accuracy of student scoring or, perhaps, rechecks of the total scoring process.

The making of both class and individual graphs of results of tests is helpful, but individual graphs should never be interpreted by themselves out of the context of other personnel data.

Securing the Composite View of Personality. No appraisal project is complete without some plan for bringing together all types of information secured and graphing or charting them in such a manner as to reveal the *pattern* of characteristics, weak, average, and strong. This composite picture should be available for reference as students learn about the demands of various occupations and as they formulate their vocational plans.

Interpreting Test Data. Both group discussion and individual conferences are important at this stage. Group discussion will generally deal with what each test measures, how reliable and valid results are likely to be according to statistical studies, and what the statistical probabilities are for results varying on a retest. Such considerations will help to prevent individuals from classifying themselves too rigidly on the basis of one test.

Students can also be helped to evaluate the dependability of various test results by suggestions as to how they can compare them with other data yielding indications of possible abilities, such as marks in subjects and various kinds of achievement in school, on jobs, in hobbies, recreational activities, at home, etc. Such comparisons may suggest the need for further steps in evaluation where test results and actual achievement do not agree. Individual study by a psychologist or counselor may be indicated in some instances to discover causes of discrepancies in data.

Individual conferences provide the opportunity to interpret test and other data in relation to long-range personnel records. Also, misunderstandings or unwholesome attitudes that may have been acquired through the group study can be detected and overcome by the skillful counselor.

Any interpretation of self-appraisal data is likely to lead into a consideration of the heredity-environment issue. Students should, of course, be helped to think realistically about their personal limitations as well as their best potentialities. However, since any characteristics appraised in adolescence or adulthood are usually the result of lifelong interaction of nature and nurture, it is probably wise to avoid too categorical interpretations of innate abilities. Comprehensive data indicating the relative strength of various qualities, compared with standards for entering various training and vocational fields, will usually provide answers to questions of immediate choices and planning without any judgments of finality with respect to *real* abilities. There is always an element of the unknowable in a developing personality that warrants caution in our guidance.

Outcomes of a Self-appraisal Unit. (*a*) Each student should have increased understanding of the complexity of the self-appraisal problem and improved techniques for continuing the process of learning more about self. (*b*) Each student should have increased knowledge about his strengths and weaknesses and increased respect for, and acceptance of, his own unique pattern of characteristics as well as those of others. (*c*) Each student should have made plans and taken steps for developing and using his talents and for improving or overcoming his liabilities or for adjusting to them effectively. The development of strengths or talents has been mentioned first, since too often in the schools we have probably conscientiously stressed weaknesses and the need to overcome them ahead of the discovery and use of talents.

A Review of Some Principles Underlying Self-appraisal Techniques

These principles are summarized partly to emphasize necessary precautions as well as to point up possibilities.

1. Self-appraisal is a lifelong task, and approaches in any unit of study should emphasize sound methods, as well as increased self-knowledge, as foundations for continued appraisal.

2. Personality has many facets, of which only a few can be partially appraised through objective tests or other measures.

3. Group tests are more reliable for the appraisal of groups than for individuals.

4. Reliable tests are valuable as indicators of possible characteristics and problems; as means of exploration and measurement of interests, aptitudes, and achievement; and of validation of other data. Cross checks on test data are also essential.

5. No test data can be interpreted soundly for an individual except in the context of his comprehensive, long-range personnel records or developmental history.

6. When the findings from tests of ability do not harmonize with related achievement, causes for the discrepancies must be located before any conclusions as to potentialities can be drawn.

7. Aptitudes have their unique patterns of development and can rarely be measured accurately by one test sampling at one particular time.

8. Interests can be developed as well as discovered. They may help to suggest abilities but cannot be used to predict them.

9. All types of human abilities must have a respected status in the value judgments of a group and a leader before individuals can accept wholesomely their relative strengths and weaknesses with respect to these varied abilities.

10. Individual variations with respect to the strength of most potentialities usually follow a normal probability curve in an unselected population.

11. Every individual has some strong, mediocre, and weak abilities. No one can expect to be strong in every characteristic, and everyone should be helped to accept and respect his pattern of abilities without conceit or embarrassment.

12. The *pattern* of abilities, strong, average, and weak, is likely to be more important for life planning than the strength or weakness of any one characteristic.

13. No individual should be furnished with information about himself

that he is not ready to use constructively. This is a difficult point to interpret wisely. One should be aware of enough strengths to build self-confidence before facing weaknesses. And perhaps the latter should be faced only when something specific can be done about them or they need to be fitted suitably into a plan for the future.

14. Because of prevailing attitudes toward IQs, it is doubtful whether these should ever be supplied to individuals as part of their self-appraisal data. Percentile placements or other interpretations of scholastic aptitude are likely to be more useful and less harmful.

15. Personality traits and trends would seem to be more amenable to change than so-called "aptitudes." A variety of approaches, objective and subjective, structured and unstructured, is essential for significant information in this area of personality.

16. The self-attitudes and the techniques of self-appraisal developed in group study and counseling are more important than the specific information about self acquired in any one unit or course.

REFERENCES CITED IN CHAPTER

1. Fiedler, F. E.: "The Concept of an Ideal Therapeutic Relationship," *Journal of Consulting Psychology*, 14:239–245, 1950.
2. Combs, Arthur W.: "A Perceptual View of the Nature of Helpers," in *Personality Theory and Counseling Practice*, papers presented at First Annual Conference, University of Florida, Gainesville, Fla., Jan. 5–7, 1961, pp. 53–58.
3. Rogers, Carl R.: *On Becoming a Person*, Houghton Mifflin Company, Boston, 1961.
4. Jouard, Sidney M.: "Self-disclosure and Other Cathexis," *Journal of Abnormal and Social Psychology*, 59:428–431, 1959.
5. Eilbert, Leo R.: "A Tentative Definition of Emotional Immaturity Utilizing the Critical Incidence Technique," *The Personnel and Guidance Journal*, 35:554–564, May, 1957.
6. Thelan, Herbert A.: "Group Dynamics in Instruction: The Principle of Least Group Size," *School Review*, 57:139–148, March, 1949.
7. Moreno, J. L.: *Who Shall Survive?* 2d ed., Beacon House, Inc., New York, 1953.
8. Jennings, Helen Hall: *Sociometry in Group Relations*, 2d ed., American Council on Education, Washington, 1959.
9. Taba, Hilda: *Diagnosing Human Relations Needs*, American Council on Education, Washington, 1955.
10. Taba, Hilda: *With Perspective on Human Relations*, American Council on Education, Washington, 1955.
11. Northway, Mary L.: *A Primer of Sociometry*, University of Toronto Press, Toronto, 1952.
12. Warters, Jane: *Group Guidance: Principles and Practices*, McGraw-Hill Book Company, Inc., New York, 1960, pp. 93–169.
13. Thompson, George G., and Marvin Powell: "An Investigation of the Rating-scale Approach to the Measurement of Social Status," *Educational and Psychological Measurement*, 11:440–455, fall, 1951.
14. Justman, Joseph, and J. Wayne Wrightstone: "A Comparison of Three Methods of Measuring Pupil Status in the Classroom," *Educational and Psychological Measurement*, 11:362–367, fall, 1951.
15. Olmstead, Michael S.: *The Small Group*, Random House, Inc., New York, 1959.

16. Bloom, B. S.: "Research on Teaching by Discussion," *College and University Bulletin*, Association for Higher Education, Department of the NEA, vol. 6, no. 8, Feb. 1 and 15, 1954.

17. Barbe, Walter B., and Robert M. Meyers: "Developing Listening Ability in Children," *Elementary English*, 31:2:82–84, February, 1954.

18. Duker, Sam: "Listening," *Review of Educational Research*, 31:145–151, April, 1961.

19. Benne, Kenneth D., and Paul Sheats: "Functional Roles of Group Members," in Kenneth D. Benne and Bozidar Muntyan (eds.), *Human Relations in Curriculum Change*, The Dryden Press, Inc., New York, 1951, pp. 98–104.

20. Hoffmann, Randall W., and Robert Plutchik: *Small-group Discussion in Orientation and Teaching*, G. P. Putnam's Sons, New York, 1959.

21. Bales, Robert F.: *Interaction Process Analysis: A Method for the Study of Small Groups*, Addison-Wesley Publishing Company, Inc., Reading, Mass., 1950.

22. Bloom, Benjamin S., and Lois J. Broder: *Problem-solving Processes of College Students: An Exploratory Investigation*, University of Chicago Press, Chicago, 1950.

23. Hendry, Charles E., et al.: "What Is Role Playing?" in Kenneth D. Benne and Bozidar Muntyan (eds.), *Human Relations in Curriculum Change*, The Dryden Press, Inc., New York, 1951, pp. 223–240.

24. Levy, Ronald B.: "Psychodrama and the Philosophy of Cultural Education," in Robert B. Haas (ed.), *Psychodrama and Sociodrama in American Education*, Beacon House, Inc., New York, 1949, p. 227.

25. Jones, F. D., and A. N. Peters: "An Experimental Evaluation of Group Psychotherapy," *Journal of Abnormal and Social Psychology*, 47:345–353, 1952.

26. Mann, John H.: "Experimental Evaluations of Role Playing," *Psychological Bulletin*, 53:227–234, 1956.

27. Mann, John H., and Carol Honrath Mann: "Role Playing Experience and Interpersonal Adjustment," *Journal of Counseling Psychology*, 6:148–152, summer, 1959.

28. Allen, Richard D., et al.: *Case-conference Problems in Group Guidance*, Inor Publishing Company, New York, 1933.

29. Shaftel, George, and Fannie R. Shaftel: *Role Playing the Problem Story*, National Conference of Christians and Jews, New York, 1952.

30. Donham, Wallace Brett: *Education for Responsible Living*, Harvard University Press, Cambridge, Mass., 1945.

31. Castore, George F.: "Attitudes of Students toward the Case Method of Instruction in a Human Relations Course," *Journal of Educational Research*, 45:201–202, November, 1951.

32. Gibson, Hilden: "Case Method," *College and University Bulletin*, Association for Higher Education, Department of the NEA, vol. 6, no. 9, Mar. 1, 1954.

33. Raines, Max R.: "Helping College Freshmen Identify Problems through a Case Conference," *The Personnel and Guidance Journal*, 34:417–419, March, 1956.

34. Joint Committee of the American Psychological Association, American Educational Research Association, and National Council on Measurements Used in Education: *Technical Recommendations for Psychological Tests and Diagnostic Techniques*, American Psychological Association, Inc., Washington, supplement to *Psychological Bulletin*, vol. 51, no. 2, part 2, March, 1954.

35. Super, Donald E.: "Dilemma for Test Users," *Occupations, The National Vocational Guidance Journal*, 29:174–176, December, 1954.

ADDITIONAL REFERENCES

Bingham, Alma: *Improving Children's Facility in Problem Solving*, Bureau of Publications, Teachers College, Columbia University, New York, 1958.

Boltz, Joseph K.: *Problem Solving*, Wayne University Press, Detroit, 1955.

Caldwell, Edson: *Group Techniques for the Classroom Teacher,* Science Research Associates, Inc., Chicago, 1959.

Cleary, Florence D., et al.: *Individual and Group Guidance,* Wayne University Press, Detroit, 1953.

Detjen, Ervin W., and Mary F. Detjen: *Elementary School Guidance,* 2d ed., McGraw-Hill Book Company, Inc., New York, 1963.

Goldman, Leo: *Using Tests in Counseling,* Appleton-Century-Crofts, Inc., New York, 1961.

Grolund, Norman E.: *Sociometry in the Classroom,* Harper & Row, Publishers, New York, 1959.

Gulley, Halbert E.: *Discussion, Conference, and Group Process,* Holt, Rinehart and Winston, Inc., New York, 1960.

Klein, Alan F.: *Role Playing in Leadership Training and Group Problem Solving,* Association Press, New York, 1956.

Lindzey, Gardner, and Edgar F. Borgatta: "Sociometric Measurement," in Gardner Lindzey (ed.), *Handbook of Social Psychology,* vol. 1, Addison-Wesley Publishing Company, Inc., Reading, Mass., 1954, pp. 449–487.

Munson, Harold L.: *How to Set Up a Guidance Unit,* Science Research Associates, Inc., Chicago, 1957.

Parish, M. M.: "Psychodrama: Description of Applications and a Review of Techniques," *Group Psychotherapy,* 6:63–89, 1953.

Phillips, Beeman N., et al.: *Psychology at Work in the Elementary School Classroom,* Harper & Row, Publishers, New York, 1960.

Remmers, H. H., et al.: *A Practical Introduction to Measurement and Evaluation,* Harper & Row, Publishers, New York, 1960.

Ross, Vivian: *Handbook for Homeroom Guidance,* The Macmillan Company, New York, 1954.

Rothney, John W. M., et al.: *Measurement for Guidance,* Harper & Row, Publishers, New York, 1959.

Russell, David H., and Elizabeth F. Russell: *Listening Aids through the Grades,* Bureau of Publications, Teachers College, Columbia University, New York, 1959.

Spoerl, Dorothy (ed.): *Tensions Our Children Live With,* The Beacon Press, Boston, 1959.

Super, Donald E., and John O. Crites: *Appraising Vocational Fitness by Means of Psychological Tests,* rev. ed., Harper & Row, Publishers, New York, 1962.

Thorndike, Robert L., and Elizabeth Hagen: *Measurement and Evaluation in Psychology and Education,* John Wiley & Sons, Inc., New York, 1961.

Thrall, R. M., et al. (eds.): *Decision Processes,* John Wiley & Sons, Inc., New York, 1954.

Traxler, Arthur E.: *Techniques of Guidance,* rev. ed., Harper & Row, Publishers, New York, 1957.

Weiss, Jerry M.: *Guidance through Drama,* Whiteside, Inc., and William Morrow and Company, Inc., New York, 1954.

Willey, Roy deVerl, and W. Melvin Strong: *Group Procedures in Guidance,* Harper & Row, Publishers, New York, 1957.

Zeleny, Leslie D.: *How to Use Sociodrama,* no. 20, How to Do It Series, National Education Association, Washington, 1955.

The term *group counseling* has become very popular, and practices under this name have been introduced rather widely in school systems. One might almost call it an epidemic. Usually the term refers to small groups, perhaps not larger than eight to ten individuals, meeting to discuss problems with a counselor in an informal setting. The term *multiple counseling* has been introduced by at least two authorities—Froehlich (1) to refer to small groups with a common problem, and Driver (2) to refer to situations in which group and individual counseling are always combined in the service. The term *group therapy* has frequently been borrowed from the field of psychotherapy, which is the province of psychiatrists and psychologists. In their field the term *multiple therapy* usually refers to the use of two therapists with a single group of individuals.

These differences have been noted merely as an introduction to consideration of what group counseling may connote. The reports of practices are so varied that it would be quite impossible to provide an accurate picture of its present meaning. Most of the reports do not present any clear-cut formulation of the theory upon which practices are developed.

These statements are not intended to be derogatory. They are made for the purpose of raising questions on whether we are building our group counseling practices upon sound foundations of theory establishing what we are trying to accomplish and why. If we seem to be groping toward the light in the personnel field we can at least take comfort from the fact that we have many psychotherapists as traveling companions. Two fairly current articles by psychotherapists begin with the following statements: "Somebody has described psychotherapy as the art of applying a science that does not yet exist" (3); and the other, "Once upon a time there was a method for treating mental problems called psychotherapy" (4). Both of these writers present evidence of widespread professional anxiety regarding the lack of satisfactory proof in research of the nature of outcomes of psychotherapeutic services— certainly a wholesome attitude for anyone trying to serve human beings with either common or uncommon problems.

Frank (5) has pointed to the role of adherence to a particular school of thought, such as Freudian, Adlerian, or Rogerian, as providing a certain confidence for therapists,[1] but summarizes findings of a questionnaire survey by Wolff (5) showing that while 70 per cent of the respondents believed their treatment to be the best, only 25 per cent were satisfied with their theory.

Well, let's face it—there's an appalling void in our understanding of human life. But there are also an alarming number of people in distress who want help on their problems, and there are many more who need help and don't know it, or are unwilling to seek help or uncertain how to get it. Also, those who work with children and adolescents face the responsibility for services that may prevent the development of many maladjustments or help individuals to overcome those that have not become deeply embedded in the personality or have not yet seriously warped it. So, if we are to help serve these needs in the guidance or personnel field, we have to learn to live with our uncertainties and move ahead with all the courage, caution, and wisdom we can muster. It takes a good bit of courage, and perhaps even audacity, to attempt to write about a field where there are still so many unknowns.

Implications for guidance of group psychotherapy

We have learned much from individual psychotherapy about preventive services in individual counseling and in education. Group psychotherapy is likewise revealing many possibilities for remedial, preventive, and developmental services in group work in the personnel field. In fact, many psychotherapists claim that many of the serious difficulties with which they deal could be prevented with proper education; also, that they are borrowing many educational methods in their work with patients. For these reasons a brief overview of some of the developments in group psychotherapy will be introduced before we consider what is happening with respect to group counseling.

One encouraging fact is the almost unanimous enthusiasm of psychotherapists about their experiences with group therapy, even among those who confess to have tried it somewhat skeptically because of the pressure of numbers to be treated. How much this enthusiasm is due to the interest and inspiration resulting from new experience, and how much to the basic values in the group situation and group methods probably remains to be proved through experimental research. Spotnitz was quoted in Chapter 2 (see pages 29 and 30) as prophesying that group therapy would prove to be a more powerful instrument than individual therapy,

---

[1] Frank (5, p. 22) illustrates this point facetiously by quoting the remark of a young doctor in classical analyst training, "The good thing about this training is, even if the patient doesn't get better, you know you are doing the right thing."

but not the more effective for *all* types of emotional disturbances. Like most other psychotherapists he stresses the importance of combining group and individual treatment; also, the fact that group treatment is more demanding and requires more skill than treating one person alone.

What advantages are claimed for group psychotherapy?

1. The group provides a more realistic life situation than the interview in which an individual can engage in reality testing with other members. Since most human problems develop in interpersonal relationships, the group provides a lifelike situation in which these relationships can be examined and new techniques of relating to others can be tried out in a protected environment in which learning can result from both failures and successes without undue traumatic aftereffects.

2. The group experience is almost certain to reveal many common problems, though always in unique patterns. Some therapists have commented on the fact that communication in the group tends to accentuate the universal and the commonplace in human experience. Recognition of the common nature of problems tends to reduce tension and anxiety about one's own situation.

3. This bond of common concerns fosters an altruistic desire to help one another, so that the therapeutic service is extended beyond the therapist to include the group.[2] Also, this interest in others may break through the vicious circle of preoccupation with self and help members to lose themselves in the group experience.

4. An intimate, cohesive group tends to resemble a primary family group in which many common themes will be explored: first, relationships with parents and sibs; next, with peers and with authority figures. It may also tend to relieve a feeling of loneliness and isolation. Members may come to symbolize some of these figures for each other and spread the transference effects (to use a psychoanalytic term)[3] beyond the therapist, who may become identified by many with an authority figure. This transference tends to spread manifestations of hostility and of affection beyond the therapist into the group. The group can then absorb much of the energy of these drives, though some individuals may not be able to endure the resulting group pressures with equanimity and benefit and may require removal for individual therapy.

5. Mutual acceptance, affection, respect, and helpfulness within the group tend to develop improved self-concepts and act as a force toward normalcy. One therapist has expressed this force as the tendency of the group to heal itself and its members.

---

[2] Not all therapists would agree with this statement. They would recognize the therapeutic value of the group situation but not the members as therapists.

[3] See pages 139 and 140 for a brief description of this school of thought.

These are only a few of the advantages of group therapy. Spotnitz (6, p. 265) has cautioned that we know more about the constructive use of group procedures than about their destructive potentialities. We need always to be alert for undesirable influences that may indicate the need for individual assistance.

How do the various schools of psychotherapy differ?

Here again we are considering differences in a fairly nontechnical manner for background in examining our therapeutic approaches in guidance. Whatever brief statements are made about these schools are certain to be inadequate. It appears that so many techniques are being borrowed and applied in group counseling, perhaps without full awareness of their original purposes, that an overview of their sources is essential for deciding what techniques might be of value in a therapeutic —not a therapy—situation.

The Psychoanalytic Field. The word *field* has been used to point to the variety of adaptions of original Freudian ideas. These variations make it difficult to summarize the major themes. Miller (7, pp. 341–342) quotes the following definition by Rangell as a succinct statement of basic ideas:

It is a method of therapy whereby conditions are brought about favorable for the development of a transference neurosis in which the past is restored in the present, in order that, through a systematic interpretive attack on the resistances which oppose it, there appears a resolution of that neurosis (transference and infantile) to the end of bringing about structural changes in the mental apparatus of the patient, to make the latter capable of optimum adaptation to life.

This doesn't sound like anything we want to try to do in the schools, does it? Yet some counselors have asked how they could learn to use these techniques and some claim they are using them without any training!

Now, in case this definition does not entirely clarify the meaning for everyone, we shall add this one from Corsini (8, p. 33).

Psychoanalysis is the uncovering of unconscious emotions and conflicts. This uncovering leads eventually to insights, that is, to understanding on the part of the patient of the role that formerly repressed ideas and feelings are playing in his pathological state of mind or behavior. The transformation of unconscious processes into conscious ones takes place through the recall of forgotten memories by the process of free association and other techniques which overcome resistance.

Probably the most valuable contributions of psychoanalysis for the guidance worker relate to the concept of repression of earlier experiences, and the various defense mechanisms that develop to maintain a workable relationship with the environment. The id as the source of instinctual drives, the ego as the mediator between the id and the external environment, and the superego, or conscience, developed through identification with standards of parent surrogates, have come into common usage to refer to forces that cause conflict and repression. There are varying theories as to the nature of the interaction of these forces. One claim is that a strong, compelling superego causes painful conflict with id and ego drives that results in repression. Another is that too weak a superego may result in behavior that causes guilt and anxiety. And still another that a weak ego may result in repression due to fear of the consequences of unsocial behavior.

As to group counseling, the prevailing view is that only conscious or slightly preconscious factors should be dealt with, and deeply repressed aspects of the unconscious should be left to treatment by the psychotherapist. Many psychotherapists are claiming that wholesome preventive and development influences in home and school at an early age could prevent much of the repression that leads to later maladjustment. Most of the techniques advocated for early school years that are dealt with in this volume could be classified among these influences, such as opportunities to express, accept, and direct varieties of emotional drives.

Foulkes (9) is frequently mentioned in psychiatric literature as an outstanding exponent of group psychoanalytic procedures. He encourages members of his group to talk about anything which comes to mind without selection. This free-floating discussion or conversation may be compared with the free association of the psychoanalytic interview, though Foulkes warns that his group analysis is not psychoanalysis in groups nor a substitute for it. He cites three basic assets created by the group situation as he worked out his methods in the Northfield Military Hospital in England:

1. Active participation of members, which awakens interest and opens the door to new experiences

2. Communication in a permissive atmosphere, which necessitates formulating meanings and exchanging ideas

3. Observation in a social setting, which provides the therapist with a living history and a living diagnosis and prognosis, and the patients with self-observation as they compare themselves with others

From this type of group therapy, the patient gains activation, adjustment or adaptation, and insight. This insight is considered to be especially important as a concomitant of adjustment. Foulkes questions the adequacy of some techniques, such as the psychodrama with emphasis on catharsis, because they do not always eventuate in insight which may guide future adjustments or adaptations.

The Adlerian School of Individual Psychology. Adler proposed that man is essentially a social and a goal-seeking being and that he develops his basic life style in his goal seeking within his social interrelationships. Dreikurs (10, pp. 30–32), who has interpreted Adler's theory, has labeled children's goals as *attention,* based on a primary drive for social belonging; *power,* involving the desire to control self and others; *revenge,* stemming from frustration of the two primary goals just mentioned; and *defeat,* meaning that the struggle for the other three goals has been given up. While one of these goals may be dominant in a particular life style, each person has a hierarchy of complex goals. Compensation for some sense of inferiority is one of the behavior mechanisms recognized in this school of thought.

A continuum of awareness is stressed rather than the Freudian idea of the conscious and unconscious, and the life style of the person is assumed to determine the experiences of which he is aware. Dreikurs (10, p. 91) comments that when the person changes his concept of himself and of life, his early recollections change. Disturbances are attributed, not to emotions, which are considered expressions of thought, but to erroneous concepts about self.

Treatment is directed toward changes in concepts of self and of life —a reorientation type of learning involving changes in social values and the direction of life movement. Evidences of resistance during therapy are interpreted as due to conflict between the goals of the therapist and the patient, who is free to choose his own goals. Basic techniques include encouragement and efforts to develop faith in self, self-confidence, and a sense of personal responsibility for one's own self-direction toward a social orientation that integrates self-interest with that of others. Dreikurs (10, p. 93) points out that in all successful therapy there is a change in the value system and movement toward a mature type of self-esteem and of social cooperation.

Adler initiated a type of group treatment in Vienna where he counseled children before groups of trainees to demonstrate his procedures. He observed that the group situation seemed to improve his relationships with the children and had an effect on the observers. When Dreikurs, Adler's pupil, came to America he introduced several kinds of group therapy, among them the multiple therapy with two therapists, family counseling, and what he terms a learning procedure with groups. This last-mentioned type provides for free discussion among members in which the therapist strives to understand their goals and life style. Then he interprets to each individual how he is operating and why, and helps each to learn how he can change his goals or develop more effective ways of reaching them. Dreikurs describes the steps as establishment and maintenance of the proper relationships, understanding each person, providing insight to help each one understand himself, and lastly, reorientation or change (10, p. 81).

Corsini (8, pp. 180–197) has described family counseling as developed by Dreikurs. The personnel of one of the so-called Adlerian centers includes a counselor-therapist, a receptionist, a social worker, and a playroom worker. Members of the parent group are interviewed by the social worker to secure a personal history. The counselor interviews the parents and children of a particular family before the group, but not before each other. Children are in the playroom while the parents are being interviewed, and the parents leave the group while the children are interviewed briefly. With the results of these interviews and reports from the other personnel, the counselor engages the group members in discussion of the situation, interprets to the parents what he understands as the factors involved in the family problem, and is quite directive in suggestions for improvement. Family councils meeting in the homes with rotating chairmen to consider problems are the final step in this group work.

Dreikurs (8, pp. 31–32, 11) has applied the Adlerian theory to what he terms guidance in the classroom—a directive process in which the individual is taught improved ways of behaving and persuaded to try them out. The assumption is that success with better ways of operating will result in satisfaction and internal change.

The Rogerian or Client-centered Theory. Rogers (12) has defined therapy as a *helping relationship* in which the therapist gives of himself in helping the client to utilize his inner potential of growth to find his own solutions and direct his own life. He claims that his system is one that is developing through experience and research and it is, therefore, difficult for anyone to summarize it in any conclusive way. In some of his writing, Rogers (13) has described what he sees as characteristics of the therapist who can provide this helping relationship, and some of the evidences of personality change that occur in the process of successful therapy.

The characteristics of the therapist have been expressed by Rogers in a series of questions. Here we shall merely summarize a few of the characteristics implied by these questions. They include *being a person* perceived as trustworthy with attitudes of warmth, caring, liking, and respect for the client, with acceptance of one's own feelings as well as unconditional acceptance of the other person, secure enough to enter fully into the world of the client and still retain separateness for both, sufficiently sensitive in the relationship to free the client of any sense of threat of external evaluation, able to reflect the client's feeling and personal meanings in a way to clarify his perceptions, and able to accept both client and himself as in a *process of becoming.*

Rogers has developed a tentative scale for measurement of process in therapy. Here again, it is difficult to summarize briefly, and Rogers's own descriptions need to be studied by those who would attempt to utilize his approach. First, one should understand how Rogers uses the word *feeling*. He has defined it as "an emotionally tinged experience with its personal meaning" (12, p. 117). The writer has observed that those who are not well oriented in the client-centered approach often tend to think of feelings and emotions as some sort of separate entities rather than an integral part of the total personality.

Rogers depicts personality change in therapy on a continuum extending from rigid personal constructs based on ways in which the individual has construed past experience with little recognition of his immediate, inner feeling life, through what is described as a gradual loosening of rigidities and the merging of streams of experience into a full awareness of the flow of the inner life in all its richness of detail. The self becomes the subjective awareness of experiencing, personal constructs are reformulated but held loosely in this continuous flow of experience, in which effective choices of new ways of being can be made (13, p. 140). One aspect of this shift on the continuum is from incongruence to congruence between the experiencing of the individual and his conceptualizing of this in his awareness. We might say that he is moving into a fuller awareness of reality. Still other streams on this continuum involve movement toward a free expression of present self-related feelings, an increasing recognition of self-responsibility for problems (found also in the Adlerian theory) and a movement from fear of relationships to a free experiencing within relationships.

The therapist, theoretically, serves as a sort of mirror to reflect back the feelings of the client in a way to clarify his personal meanings. This is, of course, a very different concept than that of interpretation by the psychoanalyst. It may assume a neutral attitude on the part of the therapist as he allows himself to be used in the helping relationship. Frank (5, p. 31) has questioned the extent to which full neutrality operates even in nondirective therapy. He reports a study of a nondirective protocol in which ratings of the therapist's approving or disapproving comments were closely coordinated with the rise and fall of client's statements that were classified as responses to the approving or disapproving reactions. Of course, one protocol can prove nothing, but Rogers himself may be moving away from strong emphasis on neutrality in his more recent description of the therapist as a real human being in his own right as he participates in the therapeutic relationship. Rogers recognizes clearly that the therapist is growing along with the client in their shared experiencing.

Client-centered or nondirective techniques are probably used more extensively in group counseling in educational institutions than any other techniques, except perhaps where a psychiatrist or psychologist is conducting the group work. It is often difficult to distinguish between various methods, since the activities of the leader may appear to be the same even though theory and purposes may differ.

Hobbs (14), whose methods exemplify the group-centered, nondirective approach, strives for a permissive, accepting attitude between leader and group and among members. The group is helped to become a therapeutic agent along with the therapist. The latter attempts to communicate what members are saying and feeling (the reflective technique) but delays his action enough to allow group members to play active roles. He is in the group pitching, but not in a directive fashion. Hobbs sees the following outcomes: greater acceptance of self, new perceptions of self and others, and an internalization and continuance of the therapy process.

The Spontaneity-Sociometric Theory of Moreno. This is considered by Corsini (8, p. 34) to be one of the major fields of psychotherapy. Moreno's sociometric and role-playing techniques were described in Chapter 5. His spontaneity theory is based on the idea of man's creativity as a part of God, and he views psychotherapy as a means of helping man to regain his spontaneity.

The Semantics Approach. The central idea in General Semantics has been used in group therapy in the treatment of traumatic neuroses (15). It has some significant implications for all of education as well as for group counseling, since it is concerned with faulty meanings that may become attached to words as symbols of experience and the distortions of reality that may result from these meanings.

General Semantics is a movement to establish a system of thought designed to release individuals from the authoritarian grip of language symbols. Korzybski (16), a leader in the movement, expressed the belief that our verbal methods of education do serious damage to growing children. He stressed the importance of providing the child with personal experience in his physical and social environment before words describing or attaching values to events and objects are brought into his experience. When word symbols such as good, love, hate, honesty, sin, and fear are learned before their attributes can be inferred from actual experience, they may become associated with specific and inappropriate infantile reactions and prevent growth in our understanding of their possible meanings. Thought is thus brought under the control of automatic, infantile reactions. Rational behavior involves the control of these automatic responses and the choice of action on the basis of growing, realistic value systems.

Through an early conditioning process, a word symbol may come to stand for only a part of an object or experience, or it may be extended to include much more. The child may also identify the symbol with the thing itself and fail to distinguish between the two. For example, experiences associated with the symbols "mother," "father," or "teacher" at any particular time may carry over and affect reactions to these same people under very different circumstances or may influence reactions to other people with similar attributes. A child may develop fear or hatred of his father due to certain experiences, then identify "father" with all men or with those exercising authority over him, and come to fear or hate all these people without cause.

Korzybski emphasized the need for our "dating" each event or experience as we abstract meaning from it, thus preventing ourselves from confusing or identifying similar but different experiences. When we realize that all people, including ourselves, are in a continuous process of growth and change, we may free ourselves from the tyranny of emotionally tinged words that we have carried over from past experience and are applying inappropriately to later experiences. Much hate, fear, suspicion, disillusionment, prejudice, and misinformation might be wiped out through this change in thinking.

WHAT IS MENTAL HEALTH?

All of the schools of psychotherapy have as their objective assistance to distressed and maladjusted individuals in achieving a status of mental health that will enable them to function as happily and effectively as possible. At a less serious level of adjustment we have the same objective in group counseling services where these are provided for individuals with special problems rather than as a part of the guidance service for everyone.

Our concepts of the nature of mental health have undergone much change as our knowledge about personality has expanded, and some hesitate today to define its nature in any precise way.[4] One of the earlier

[4] There has been a controversy among some psychologists as to whether the term *mental illness* is a misnomer except where brain pathology is involved. Szasz (17) has explained mental symptoms as expressions of inability to cope with problems of living and of ethical choice and responsibility. Mowrer (18) has explained them as due to guilt stemming from unacknowledged sin. Ausubel (19) has refuted both explanations as untenable, though he admits they may be factors in a personality disorder that should be diagnosed as disease. This question is too technical to consider here in detail, but references are given for those who wish to explore the matter further. One value of such a controversy is to highlight the need for caution in labeling as "abnormal" behavior that might appear to be a natural resultant of causes if all the causal factors were known.

concepts of mental health placed it on one pole of a continuum from severe mental illness to optimum mental health with the assumption that an individual could be characterized as manifesting a degree of either extreme. One trend today is toward recognition of qualitative differences, but there are varied concepts of the nature of these qualitative differences. Maslow (20) argues for an open concept of mental health that can embrace new understandings of human potentialities as our knowledge about human life expands. Jahoda (21), who has reviewed and interpreted the many current concepts of mental health, comments that one value seems compatible with almost all of them: that an individual should be able to stand on his own feet without making undue demands or impositions on others. Norms with respect to this self-dependence would, of course, be adjusted to age and maturity expectancies. Jahoda (21) stresses the need for a multiple criterion approach to mental health and organizes current concepts under six criteria. They are summarized very briefly here [5] without reference, usually, to the sources of the concepts.

1. *Attitudes toward the Self.* Healthy self-attitudes embody correctness of perception of the real self, the congruence of concepts of the real self and the ideal self, acceptance of self with recognition of strengths and weaknesses, self-confidence, self-respect, and a sense of identity, described by Erikson as the inner capital accrued from all past experience.

2. *Growth, Development, or Self-actualization.* Jung has described self-actualization as the fullest, most complete differentiation and harmonious blending of all aspects of one's personality. The mental-hygiene meaning of growth and development has been interpreted in terms of *motivational force* toward goals beyond basic need, and *investment in living* comprising the range and quality of concern with other people, things, and activities considered significant. The healthy personality does not center concern in self, and the basic direction of growth is forward.

3. *Integration.* This may mean balance and relatedness of all processes and attributes in an individual with a unifying philosophy that gives a sense of purpose and meaning in life. It would be associated in the healthy personality with resistance to stress, or an anxiety-frustration tolerance that gives a resilience to ego strength in withstanding adversity without inner damage; also, the ability to lose oneself in things of the world adjudged of prime value.

4. *Autonomy.* This has been defined as an inner regulation of behavior based on conscious discrimination by the individual of environmental factors he wishes to accept or reject. The autonomous individual can

[5] By permission of the publisher, Basic Books, Inc., Publishers, New York.

make independent decisions and determine the appropriateness of conformity or nonconformity in response to the social pressures he experiences.

5. *Perception of Reality.* Here one important factor is that of keeping
perceptions free from distortion caused by individual needs. Another
aspect is that of broadening and deepening the field of reality perception.
Rogers (22) has called this "openness to experience." Maslow (20, p. 7),
commenting on efficient perception of reality, says, ". . . the healthier
persons become, the more of the inner world becomes available . . .
more of the unconscious becomes conscious and, therefore, available."
To Rogers (22) this means, in a climate of freedom, growth toward a
harmony of value directions for all who are experiencing this expansion
of reality awareness.

6. *Environmental Mastery.* This criterion embodies themes of success
and adaptation: adequacy in love, work, play, interpersonal relations,
and efficiency in meeting situational requirements; and a workable
arrangement between environment and the individual whereby either
or both may be modified through individual initiative. The healthy person can change his inner balance of psychic forces as well as the external world, and thus is more resourceful in reaching solutions to problems and in implementing his decisions.

There is a growing awareness that guilt is a wholesome aspect of the
good life when it is a response to really bad behavior and is associated
with change. Maslow (20) finds humor in the creative, healthy personality, and a certain childlikeness in the mature, responsible person. Also,
he stresses the importance of humility in the light of our ignorance about
psychological health, and this means, of course, a searching for—and
openness to—new understandings as our horizons widen.

All of these six criteria have implications for group counseling at successive maturity levels. One of the guidance objectives for the fostering
of wholesome personality development is the growth in understanding
and application of these criteria by each individual. Doubtless, one of
the most significant ways in which a group leader can prepare to assist
others toward this goal is to attempt to understand and apply them with
respect to his own personality and interpersonal relationships. Of course,
for both self and others, the wholesome emphasis is upon what one is
becoming with due respect to age and maturity, rather than upon any
present status. A rigid standard, lacking humility, tolerance, and humor,
could seriously militate against the acceptance of self and others that is
so central in our understanding of what constitutes positive mental
health.

SOME ASPECTS OF GROUP COUNSELING

Theoretical orientation

The orientation of a group leader with respect to both psychology and psychotherapy will help to determine what his approach to group counseling will be. Reports of group practices in both psychotherapy and guidance indicate that within these relatively new fields there has been much borrowing and interplay. Many of the approaches appear to be quite eclectic, so that it is often difficult to judge just what theoretical orientation underlies the techniques. All except the purely didactic methods, which seem not to be entirely extinct as claimed by one writer, have a common theme of free intercommunication among group members.

A major concern in group counseling is that of determining its boundaries. It has already been noted that one suggested boundary is that which differentiates between difficulties that lie within the conscious realm, or mild repressions, and those which stem from deeper unconscious repressions. This is not easy to determine. The Adlerians question the existence of the "unconscious" and claim that many of our best motivations and highest aspirations come from the realm of which the individual is "unaware" at a given time. Progoff (23, p. 103), Director of the Institute for Research in Depth Psychology at Drew University and a former student of Jung, claims "Man is not a bundle of repressions, but a bundle of possibilities, and the key to therapy lies in reactivating the process of growth" that has been blocked.

Probably the best criteria for the group counselor in judging as to the boundaries of his suitable activities are (a) the degree to which the behavior of an individual appears to be within the broad spectrum of "normalcy" and (b) his own degree of confidence in ability to understand and help an individual. It is better to err on the side of caution than courage if the services of a specialist are available.

Composition of groups

Most of our information on the nature and size of groups comes from therapy rather than counseling sources. The size of most permissive groups is kept small, but there is no full agreement among therapists as to the optimum number. The minimum number might be from three to five in order to form an effective social unit, and the maximum from ten to twelve. Selective criteria for a group seem to depend upon many factors varying with the organization and the methods used. Compatibility or congeniality of members would be important under most conditions, though the leader and the entire group can play an important part in welding members into a cooperating unit. It has been suggested that a variety of personalities in the group with shy, extroverted, introverted, overconscientious, or irresponsible trends can often help to foster group cohesiveness through efforts of the group to suppress undesirable traits. Bach (24, pp. 19–22) uses four personality criteria for exclusion from groups—insufficient reality contact, extremes of culturally tabooed or illegal behavior, the dominant character who would be a chronic monopolist of discussion, and those with psychopathic defenses and impulsiveness. Bach follows the same policy reported by Powdermaker and Frank (25) who, in their Veterans Administration Mental Hygiene Clinic procedure, found it helpful to place patients in the same group who showed great differences with respect to diagnoses, education, race, religion, cultural background, economic level, age, and experience. At the University of Minnesota Students' Mental Hygiene Clinic (26), it was found that groups composed of patients with various complaints and symptoms were much more active than those of segregated types.

In some group counseling situations there has been a tendency to form groups with similar problems such as underachievement or acting-out, aggressive behavior. Driver (27), in her descriptions of multiple counseling, mentions ten as the limit of numbers for a small group organized for a common personal interest or need, with equal numbers of male and female members, and heterogeneity in personality type and racial and cultural background. She suggests possibilities for breaking up larger groups into smaller ones for achieving some of the values of small-group counseling. A few examples of groups with heterogeneous problems will be cited later.

Types of leadership

Several major types can be distinguished: (a) those in which the leader is the didactic teacher and authority, providing re-education with respect to factors in life adjustment; (b) those in which the leader is the activator or catalyst in a permissive, nondirective atmosphere and helps the group to interpret their experiences, gain insight into their difficulties, and use the group experience for therapeutic growth; (c) those in which both methods are utilized by the leader to serve varied purposes within a group in which various forces of group life may be brought to bear upon the situation as therapeutic agents; (d) the leaderless group. This last type, stemming frequently from the influence of Bion (28), seems to be used most often by those who stress the importance of eliminating a tendency toward dependency upon the leader and of fostering more independence and responsibility for dealing with personal decisions and difficulties. In some instances it has appeared to the writer that this leaderless approach was a substitute for a basic orientation and plan. It is likely to be uneconomical as to time and effort, and oftentimes the same results can be achieved by democratic, catalytic leadership that can also provide some valuable resources for the group. Positive values have been reported for leaderless-group experiments where the authoritarian influence would have been difficult to eliminate with the presence of a leader.

Foulkes (9), whose approach is psychoanalytically oriented (see page 140), uses a technique which he calls "leadership by default," in which he simply invites his patients to answer their own questions as they are directed to the leader.

Interrelationships of Leader and Group. These relationships are especially significant in permissive groups. The leader must be a member of the group and must also allow himself to be used by the group to serve their needs as they uncover motives and drives and learn through group action to redirect them into desirable channels. One great advantage of the permissive type of group situation is that the leader has the opportunity to wean the group from being led and to help them assume responsibility for independent action.

When emotional problems are involved in group study there may be frequent silences, and both leader and group should recognize these as important phases of the group process when something important may be happening in the experiences of individuals. Of course, too prolonged silences may sometimes be stupid, according to one therapist, and call for some tactful action on the part of the leader.

If hostility and resistance mount, the leader can often, by inactivity, prevent too great concentration of these negative feelings upon himself. Members may become the symbols of rival siblings or other roles and dissipate some of the antagonisms that otherwise might be directed to the leader, especially as an authority figure. The leader must be able to accept resistance and hostility if it develops in order to serve as a therapeutic agent. Limits should be set, however, in most school groups, cooperatively if possible.

The group leader is responsible for the correct timing of interpretations of causes of difficulties and disturbances of individuals or the group, but his aim is to let the materials for these interpretations come from the group itself. Learning how to use inner and outer forces to achieve individually and socially desirable goals is one of the essentials for effective living.

Techniques in group counseling

All of the techniques considered in Chapter 5 are applicable at some points in group counseling. A few additional techniques utilized in group therapy have been noted in the illustrations of group methods in the various schools of psychotherapy, such as the free-floating discussion used in psychoanalytic groups, the reflection technique in Rogerian, client-centered groups, and didactic methods in Adlerian groups. Still others will be noted that have possibilities for adaptation in group counseling.

Interpretation plays varying roles in these groups. In psychoanalytic techniques it may involve the sharing by the therapist of insight about unconscious motives and drives; in reflection techniques interpretation is not likely to go much beyond the awareness of the client, though the responses of the therapist may be aimed at movement toward deeper insight. In Adlerian techniques the interpretation moves directly toward increase of insight regarding life style, goals, and behavior mechanisms that appear to the therapist to need attention.

Perhaps a general rule with respect to interpretation in group counseling would be that it should not go beyond what the individual is ready and able to cope with in some constructive manner. It is easier to state this rule than to gain all the insights necessary to carry through on it. And skill in gaining these insights calls for much training, experience, and power of empathy.

Numerous specific techniques can be noted in the descriptions of group therapy and group counseling cited next.

Illustrations of group therapy and group counseling

In a permissive, group-centered type of therapy, the group is usually so arranged, for example around a table or in easy chairs, that all can participate easily and informally. The leader is responsible for establishing the informal, permissive atmosphere and for maintaining a therapeutic situation. He may be active, neutral, or passive at various times, depending on the demands of an ever-changing, evolving situation. At the start he may initiate the process by explaining the purposes of the group meetings and introducing members to each other. There is little or no authority exhibited by the leader, though he may unobtrusively manipulate situations to create desirable therapeutic conditions.

Bach (24), with an eclectic approach and a group-dynamics orientation, takes considerable initiative in getting various programs under way at different stages in the progression of the program. He describes three different functions of group leadership in his groups: procedural, catalytic, and interpretative. He introduces various techniques at points where he judges that the group will benefit from them, such as dream reporting, role-playing, projective drawings, psychometric assessment, analysis of the social interaction, or "going around" in the reporting of experiences or symptoms. He gives much attention to peer-group structure and to the interpretation of the various roles played by various members in the main groups and subgroups. An interesting comment on growth within the group is to this effect (24, p. 388): "Advanced patients sense they no longer play roles, that they no longer participate segmentally in the group life. This transition from role-living to full ego-participation is an aspect of emotional learning during the psychotherapeutic process mediated through group participation."

Some Types of Therapeutic Group Work with Children and Adolescents. The work of Slavson (29) with children and adolescents in a social-work setting has yielded some valuable suggestions for educators. Slavson experimented with "activity group therapy" of a permissive nature with children, and with "group interview therapy" with adolescents —both age groups having behavior and adjustment problems. He considers the activity therapy, through permissive play and club situations, suitable only for children below middle adolescence. Age is his first criterion for grouping, and he suggests a limit of age range of a year and a half to two years. He considers unsuitable for these permissive groups children with extreme problems of a neurotic nature or with extreme aggressive behavior disorders, psychopathic personalities, and usually psychotics. Experience has indicated that these noncompetitive and nonthreatening groups have been beneficial to children with latent or arrested schizophrenia.

The therapist is described as neutral, but not passive. It is essential that he be a person who has no unresolved emotional problems that would tie down the children and impede their growth. His task is to set the children free to grow at their own pace through emotional release and the restraint of others in the group. The aim is a new orientation toward environment and people. The total situation is designed to supply substitute gratifications, give vent to aggression, reinforce the ego, particularly in regard to feelings of failure and inadequacy, counteract deflated self-evaluation, release blockings to expression in some, and build self-restraint in others. Four basic needs of the children to be met through the group therapy are stated as: (*a*) need for security and unconditional love; (*b*) building up of ego and sense of self-worth; (*c*) creative self-expression; (*d*) acceptance by the group (29, pp. 30–36).

Unlike activity-group therapy, the interview-group therapy aims at developing insight into problems and feelings and some understanding of the causes of behavior and attitudes. The methods used are similar to those already described under permissive-group therapy. Slavson, who has a psychoanalytic orientation, emphasizes as the dynamics of interview groups: (*a*) transference relationships, (*b*) catharsis, (*c*) insight and ego strengthening, and (*d*) reality testing.

The diffusion of latent hostility and aggression throughout the group of sibling figures, as well as the parent figure represented by the leader, is made clear as an advantage in group therapy. Also, Slavson stresses the importance of the discharge of hostility and warns that the therapist must not fall into the trap of reacting to provocative behavior (29, pp. 36–38).

Slavson summarizes some of the therapeutic means employed in the group methods as follows (29, pp. 135–136):

1. To provide emotional support through group relationships.

2. To activate emotional release in the area of specific anxiety-ridden conflicts; in particular to encourage the release of pent-up aggression.

3. To reduce guilt and anxiety, especially through the universalization of common forms of conflict.

4. To provide opportunity for the testing of various forms of social reality as personified in individual members of the group or in the group as a whole.

5. To provide opportunity for the modification of the concept of the self in the direction of increased self-esteem and recognition of constructive capacities. This in turn tends to increase the acceptance of other persons and tolerance for frustrating experience.

6. To foster the development of insight arising from an actual living out of emotional drives in the context of the multiple relationships within the group. Interpretation is employed only when the expression of specific emotional trends has been sufficiently solidified.

Play Techniques for Diagnostic and Therapeutic Work with Very Young Children. From the viewpoint of the therapist, child-centered play therapy has been described by Moustakas as (30, p. 2) "a set of attitudes in and through which children may feel free enough to express themselves fully, in their own way, so that eventually they may achieve feelings of security, adequacy, and worthiness through emotional insight." This writer emphasizes three basic attitudes in play therapy: faith, expressed as a pervasive belief in the child's ability to work out his difficulties and discover what is best for him; acceptance, shown through encouraging the child to express his feelings and himself fully and to explore his attitudes freely; respect, manifested in the relationship with the child in ways to convince him that his self is regarded as worthwhile and important (30, pp. 2–6). Most of the writings in this field contain descriptions of play procedures, their use in diagnosis of difficulties, and reports of changes occurring in the behavior of the children during the period of therapy.

A review of research on nondirective play therapy (31) suggests that it may have a considerable history, extending back to Rousseau who studied the play of the child to understand his psychology. But the reviewer of the research on this technique finds little objective evidence of what happens in the process of therapy. A comparison of three available studies of this process yielded the following conclusion (31, p. 179):

They would seem to indicate that nondirective play therapy is an objectively measurable process; that children's emotional expressions are altered in a discernible manner; and that maturation appears to be related to the type of expression of therapeutic change. Beyond such statements the studies substantiate few of the philosophical aspects of play therapy.

This reviewer, Lebo, also examined evidences of success of nondirective therapy used in the treatment of allergies, in the study of mental deficiency, in the treatment of children's personality disorders and of physical handicaps, in the handling of race conflicts and of reading disabilities. While he criticizes most of the studies as to methodology because of the lack of control groups, which prevents clear-cut conclusions as to what specific procedures effected changes, he finds evidence of some type or degree of improved adjustment with respect to most of the problems studied and concludes that (31, p. 182) "the effects of play therapy . . . would seem to be lasting, particularly in the area of personality adjustment." He recommends carefully planned experimentation to investigate its effectiveness in relation to other procedures. This same recommendation is perhaps equally applicable to all techniques which are directed at changes in the complex structure and functioning of personalities.

One experiment with group-play therapy in a first-second grade in a school situation reports observable gains, substantiated by sociograms, in the degree of social acceptance for those who had had the therapy. It was suggested that permissive attitudes in the entire classroom may have been partly responsible for the increased social acceptance of these children (32).

Play therapy doubtless has a promising future, but as in all other types of group therapy, much research is needed to steer the course of its development.

Group Counseling Experiments at the High School Level. Out of numerous illustrations of group counseling that might be cited from school experience, the following has been selected primarily because it represents the combined use of several approaches. The group was composed of seven eleventh-grade obese girls who were selected by the school physician as probably having no endocrine involvement in the overweight condition. Membership in the group was voluntary, and meetings were held once a week for a semester during assembly period.

The directive aspect of the program included informal talks by the physician and the psychologist about possible causes of obesity, and the development of individual weight charts, which included approximations of ideal weight, and of desirable weekly goals for weight reduction. The girls were warned that these weekly estimates were highly unreliable and that reduction would not take a steady course. Meetings were held for the girls and their mothers to study with a nutrition specialist the safest and most nutritious reducing diets.

Initial medical and psychological data were secured for each girl, the latter including Wechsler-Bellevue and Rorschach tests and cumulated personnel data. The Rorschach patterns showed some interesting similarities with respect to emotional and ego development.

The group discussions were, in the main, nondirective and during the course of the semester brought into the open many emotional problems of members. Two that appeared to be common to all of them were some feelings of rejection or of discrimination in the home and of fear as to how effectively they might play their roles in boy-girl relationships if they achieved physiques which would attract boys and enable them to date. Many ramifications of these two problems and of their struggles in controlling food intake were examined in their informal discussions.

A TOPS club (Take Off Pounds Safely) was formed—without any tie-up with the national movement by this name. The queen chosen at the end of the semester had lost twenty pounds, and each girl reported some loss.

Three of the girls began to date boys before the end of the semester, their first experiences with boy friends. One of them eventually announced that her problems were solved because she was now going steady! A fourth married during the summer and reported a happy marital adjustment in the fall. A fifth, with one of the most extreme obese problems, had surgery recommended by her physician, but did not remain in school long enough for a check on the efficacy of the results with respect to weight reduction. No observable marked changes occurred with the other two girls while they remained in school.

A Group Counseling Experiment at the College Level. A group of eight freshmen and sophomore students, men and women, were assigned to this group by the college counselors. They met with the psychologist in an informal office setting for a two-hour period once a week for a semester.[6] The age range was from eighteen to fifty, all but one being in their late teens or early twenties. The desirability of admitting the man fifty years of age was questioned, but this resulted in the introduction of a very interesting feature into the group situation. All members of the group were interviewed by the psychologist before the first meeting, and WAIS and Rorschach tests were administered.

After a brief discussion by the leader of possible purposes and opportunities in group counseling, responsibility was shifted to the group with the leader serving as a resource member who offered suggestions

---

[6] This two-hour period never seemed too long, but the prevailing opinion in published reports seems to be that it *is* undesirably long.

at times as to possible procedures in studying problems and supplied reflective, clarifying, or interpretive comments when it seemed that they would be helpful.

One development that interested the writer was an occasional request from the group for either reading references or discussion by the leader to increase their understanding about some aspect of a problem. Both types of requests were met, thus introducing a didactic element at times, but the effort was made to prevent undesirable dependence upon the leader or evasions by members of their emotional problems.

An interesting relationship developed between the younger group members and the fifty-year-old man, who revealed a rigid, authoritarian type of personality. Intense hostility was expressed for a time regarding his autocratic control of his adolescent children and his apparent lack of real companionship and any recreation with his wife. He retaliated with severe criticism of the irresponsibility of two young men in the group who were serious underachievers. Before the end of the semester the older man withdrew from college to take a full-time job for which he had been preparing. On leaving the group he thanked them for their criticisms and explained that he was now holding some democratic family councils, had joined a church group with his wife, and was planning time for recreation with her. The two underachievers reciprocated with expressions of appreciation for his criticisms of them and admitted that he had stimulated their thinking about life values. The parent-child relationships that were involved in this situation can readily be seen.

One amusing incident occurred when the group went to the art laboratory for freehand painting after having attempted to analyze each other's spontaneous drawings in their regular meeting place. They ganged up on the leader and asked her to leave for a specified time. When she returned, the paintings were lined up and she was asked to identify them. This was done accurately except for two, and then the two members whose paintings were questioned explained that they had played a practical joke by one trying to copy the other's technique.

Excellent cohesiveness and camaraderie developed within the group, and consternation was expressed when it was officially disbanded to make way for a new group. Several members continued to meet by themselves, and one or more returned to the psychologist's office frequently to discuss some problem that was puzzling the group. Not all of the members have been followed up, unfortunately, but the scholarship of the underachievers did improve over the year that contact was maintained. One young woman whose problems were doubtless the most serious and deep-seated sent an announcement four years later of graduation from a professional training course and of her engagement to be married.

These two examples at the high school and college levels have been introduced to illustrate the use of a variety of techniques and some possibilities in a school situation where work pressures may not always allow for carefully controlled experimentation. Experimental research is, of course, greatly needed in a field as relatively new as group counseling.

One experimental study with a control group for multiple counseling of boys with behavior problems reported by Caplan was mentioned in Chapter 1 (see page 15). Evidence of improved citizenship and scholarship was reported. An elaborate experimental study in group counseling of underachieving adolescents at the University of Illinois (33, 34) led to the conclusion that three of four groups achieved significant growth. Possible changes were noted in improved scores on an achievement test, increased acceptance of self and of others, and improved ability to relate to peers, siblings, and parents. The researchers commented that the neurotic pairing of two members seemed to account for the lack of productivity in the fourth group.

Experimental research and experience will undoubtedly open up many new possibilities in this field of group counseling as well as indicating limitations in our present practices.[7]

Implications of a therapeutic environment

Many suggestions for a school environment can be drawn from a description by Maxwell Jones (35) of a "therapeutic community" organized in England to provide treatment for a heterogeneous group of patients "who were generally regarded as being both untreatable and unemployable." This project grew out of earlier experiments during World War II with service personnel suffering from "effort syndrome." Lectures and discussions about their symptoms and a reorganized hospital society to create a lifelike community had yielded results that encouraged more intensive experimentation in other situations. The description of how a "hard core" of unsocialized and mentally ill persons were welded into a "therapeutic community," in which a sense of belonging, mutual helpfulness, and active participation in work, play, and study in a fairly natural life situation brought healing or improved

[7] A group counseling project, financed by a Federal grant, is being conducted under the direction of C. C. Dunsmoor, Board of Cooperative Educational Services, Bedford Hills, New York. The objective of this project is to demonstrate the effects of group counseling for underachieving junior high school boys with acting-out behavior; also to investigate teachers' attitudes toward this type of student and to evaluate the change that takes place through group discussion. (Group Counseling Project D 040, First Quarter Progress Report, Nov. 30, 1961.) This project may shed new light on this puzzling problem of helping the underachiever, as well as on group counseling practices.

adjustment to many, is inspiring evidence of some of the possibilities inherent in group therapy.

The educational methods described by Jones included the use of daily meetings with the entire patient population, in which social problems and real-life situations were discussed, acted out in psychodrama, or presented in documentary films. Doctors and the entire group were involved in attempts to arrive at constructive attitudes in relation to problems raised. Intensive group therapy was provided in small groups, and the entire hospital personnel and the patients cooperated in planning and carrying out work routines, projects, and recreation.

Jones comments that in their educational procedures individual responsibility could not be separated from the group climate. "What appears to matter most," he wrote, "is the degree of 'group learning'—the extent to which the community accepts an idea which then becomes an integral part of the group culture. Patients seem to accept new ideas much more readily when these have behind them the weight of group acceptance" (35, p. 160).[8]

A follow-up, through intensive interviews, of the adjustment of 104 patients from this Industrial Neurosis Unit of desocialized patients with severe character disorders (including drug addicts, prostitutes, prison offenders, schizoid personalities, sexual perverts, aggressive psychopaths, etc., over 85 per cent of whom had had a previous history of psychiatric treatment), six months after a duration of treatment of three to four months, yielded adjustment estimates as follows: poor, 34 per cent; fair, 22 per cent; and satisfactory, 44 per cent. These estimates of adjustment were based upon many factors such as employment, expressed attitudes, and evidence concerning interpersonal relationships in the home and elsewhere (35, pp. 96–146).

If this could happen in a few months with patients considered untreatable and unemployable, what *might* we do throughout the period of formal education in preventive and remedial as well as developmental programs for all youths?

Increasingly psychiatrists and other workers in the mental health field are urging the expansion of services in the schools that may lessen the number of individuals needing psychotherapy. Spotnitz, a well-known group psychotherapist, has expressed the belief that the time is not far off when society will assume responsibility through the schools for what he calls emotional training. He claims that teaching children how to handle their feelings is as important as teaching them how to work with letters and figures and other intellectual concepts: [9]

---

[8] Reprinted by permission of the publisher, Basic Books, Inc., Publishers, New York.

[9] Reprinted by permission of the publisher, Alfred A. Knopf, Inc., New York, 1961.

They need to understand why they feel angry, melancholy, or tearful at times and what is healthful and socially appropriate for them to say and do in these states. The desirability of thinking and talking about troublesome feelings and the undesirability of discharging them in asocial behavior are lessons which every person should learn early in life. The distinction between the "sayable" and the "doable," so vital for emotional health, is one which many adults have to be taught today in the course of psychotherapy. Emotional education at an early age would obviate the need for such reeducation. Children can learn how to discharge their energy in personally and socially useful ways. Proper instruction makes it second nature for them to behave accordingly and pleasurable enough so that they don't want to behave in other ways (6, p. 269).

The ultimate task of the psychotherapist will be to eliminate the need for his services. Just as various dread diseases have been conquered by vaccine, improved sanitation, and other preventive measures, diseases which respond to psychological treatment will eventually cease to be medical problems. In the course of time these conditions will yield to social and educational programs, to be conducted through the home, the school, industrial enterprises, and other community settings (6, p. 274).

In planning all aspects of group guidance, including group counseling, we must, of course, recognize the limits of our training and experience and move ahead only as rapidly as we can develop the needed competencies, and only so far as communities are ready for the services. But, without doubt, the readiness in both areas extends well beyond present practice.

SUMMARY

The term *group counseling* is being applied to a variety of guidance services in small groups. Usually these small groups are formed to provide therapeutic services for individuals with special problems, but they are also used for intensive help on almost any phase of guidance.

Many of the techniques used in group counseling have been borrowed from the various schools of psychotherapy. The theories and techniques of some of the major schools have been reviewed briefly to stimulate thinking about the basic orientations that may underlie various group counseling practices.

Since much of the group counseling is of a therapeutic nature, directed toward improved personal adjustment, current concepts of mental health have been surveyed as a basis for examining purposes and objectives of this therapeutic service. These concepts are grouped under six headings: attitudes toward self; growth, development or self-actualization; integration; autonomy; perception of reality; and environmental mastery.

Some programs in group psychotherapy and group counseling have been described to illustrate applications of theory and techniques in varied situations at different age levels. Advantages of group methods, their interrelationship with individual services, and some of the outcomes indicated through research have been reviewed.

Psychotherapists are envisaging possibilities through developmental and preventive guidance and educational services of reducing the need for intensive remedial and curative help.

REFERENCES CITED IN CHAPTER

1. Wright, E. Wayne: "Multiple Counseling: Why? When? How?," *The Personnel and Guidance Journal*, 37:551–556, April, 1959.
2. Driver, Helen I., et al.: *Counseling and Learning through Small-group Discussion*, Monona Publications, Madison, Wis., 1958.
3. Meehl, Paul E.: "The Cognitive Activity of the Clinician," *The American Psychologist*, 15:19–27, January, 1960.
4. Austin, Alexander W.: "The Functional Autonomy of Psychotherapy," *The American Psychologist*, 16:75–78, February, 1961.
5. Frank, Jerome D.: "The Role of Influence in Psychotherapy," in Morris I. Stein, *Contemporary Psychotherapies*, The Free Press of Glencoe, A Division of the Crowell-Collier Publishing Co., New York, 1961, pp. 16–41.
6. Spotnitz, Hyman: *The Couch and the Circle: A Story of Group Psychotherapy*, Alfred A. Knopf, Inc., New York, 1961.
7. Miller, Arthur A.: "A Survey of the Development and Evolution of Psychoanalytic Treatment," in Morris I. Stein, *Contemporary Psychotherapies*, The Free Press of Glencoe, A Division of the Crowell-Collier Publishing Co., New York, 1961, pp. 338–354.
8. Corsini, Raymond J.: *Methods of Group Psychotherapy*, McGraw-Hill Book Company, Inc., Blakiston Division, New York, 1957.
9. Foulkes, S. H.: *Group Analytic Psychotherapy: Studies in the Social Integration of Individuals and Groups*, William Heinemann, Ltd., London, 1948.
10. Dreikurs, Rudolf: "The Adlerian Approach to Psychodynamics," in Morris I. Stein, *Contemporary Psychotherapies*, The Free Press of Glencoe, A Division of the Crowell-Collier Publishing Co., New York, 1961, pp. 60–94.
11. Dreikurs, Rudolf: *Psychology in the Classroom*, Harper & Row, Publishers, New York, 1957.
12. Rogers, Carl: "The Characteristics of a Helping Relationship," and "A Tentative Scale for the Measurement of Process in Psychotherapy," in Morris I. Stein, *Contemporary Psychotherapies*, The Free Press of Glencoe, A Division of the Crowell-Collier Publishing Co., New York, 1961, pp. 95–127.
13. Rogers, Carl R.: "A Process Conception of Psychotherapy," *The American Psychologist*, 13:142–149, April, 1958.
14. Hobbs, Nicholas: "Group-centered Psychotherapy," in Carl Rogers, *Client-centered Therapy: Its Current Practice, Implications, and Theory*, Houghton Mifflin Company, Boston, 1951, pp. 278–319.
15. Kelley, Douglas M.: "The Use of General Semantics and Korzybskian Principles as an Extensional Method of Group Psychotherapy in Traumatic Neurosis," *The Journal of Nervous and Mental Disease*, 114:189–220, September, 1951.
16. Korzybski, Alfred: *Science and Sanity: An Introduction to Non-Aristotelian Systems and General Semantics*, Science Press, New York, 1933.
17. Szasz, Thomas S.: "The Myth of Mental Illness," *The American Psychologist*, 15:113–118, February, 1960.
18. Mowrer, O. H.: "'Sin,' the Lesser of Two Evils," *The American Psychologist*, 15:301–304, May, 1960.

19. Ausubel, David P.: "Personality Disorder *Is* Disease," *The American Psychologist*, 16:69–74, February, 1961.
20. Maslow, Abraham H.: "Some Frontier Problems in Psychological Health," in *Personality Theory and Counseling Practice*, papers presented at the First Annual Conference on Personality Theory and Counseling Practice, University of Florida, Gainesville, Fla., January, 1961.
21. Jahoda, Marie: *Current Concepts of Positive Mental Health*, Basic Books, Inc., Publishers, New York, 1958.
22. Rogers, Carl R.: "The Developing Values of the Growing Person," in *Personality Theory and Counseling Practice*, papers presented at the First Annual Conference on Personality Theory and Counseling Practice, University of Florida, Gainesville, Fla., January, 1961.
23. Progoff, Ira: "The Psychology of Personal Growth," *The Atlantic Monthly*, 208: 102–107, July, 1961.
24. Bach, George R.: *Intensive Group Psychotherapy*, The Ronald Press Company, New York, 1954.
25. Powdermaker, Florence B., et al.: *Group Psychotherapy: Studies in Methodology of Research and Therapy*, Harvard University Press, Cambridge, Mass., 1953.
26. Hinckley, Robert G., and Lydia Hermann: *Group Treatment in Psychotherapy: A Report of Experience*, University of Minnesota Press, Minneapolis, 1951.
27. Driver, Helen Irene: *Multiple Counseling: A Small Group Discussion Method for Personal Growth*, Monona Publications, Madison, Wis., 1954.
28. Bion, W. R.: *Experiences in Groups*, Basic Books, Inc., Publishers, New York, 1961.
29. Slavson, S. R.: *The Practice of Group Therapy*, International Universities Press, New York, 1947.
30. Moustakas, Clark E.: *Children in Play Therapy: A Key to Understanding Normal and Disturbed Emotions*, McGraw-Hill Book Company, Inc., New York, 1953.
31. Lebo, Dell: "The Present Status of Research on Nondirective Play Therapy," *Journal of Consulting Psychology*, 17:177–183, June, 1953.
32. Davis, Ruth G.: "Group Therapy and Social Acceptance in a First-Second Grade," *Elementary School Journal*, 49:219–223, December, 1948.
33. Broedel, John, et al.: "The Effects of Group Counseling on Gifted Underachieving Adolescents," *Journal of Counseling Psychology*, 7:163–170, fall, 1960.
34. Cohn, Benjamin, Merle Ohlsen, and Fred Proff: "Roles Played by Adolescents in an Unproductive Counseling Group," *The Personnel and Guidance Journal*, 38:724–731, May, 1960.
35. Jones, Maxwell: *The Therapeutic Community*, Basic Books, Inc., New York, 1953.

Additional References

Balser, Benjamin Harris (ed.): *Psychotherapy for the Forgotten Age*, International Universities Press, New York, 1957.
Bonney, Merle E.: *Mental Health in Education*, Allyn and Bacon, Inc., Englewood Cliffs, N.J., 1960.
Dreikurs, Rudolf, and R. J. Corsini: "Twenty Years of Group Psychotherapy," *American Journal of Psychotherapy*, 110:567–574, 1954.
Frank, Jerome D.: *Persuasion and Healing: A Comparative Study of Psychotherapy*, Johns Hopkins Press, Baltimore, 1961.
Ginott, Haim G.: *Group Psychotherapy with Children*, McGraw-Hill Book Company, Inc., New York, 1961.
Gorlow, Leon, et al.: *The Nature of Nondirective Group Psychotherapy*, Bureau of Publications, Teachers College, Columbia University, New York, 1952.
Kaplan, Louis: *Mental Health and Human Relations in Education*, Harper & Row, Publishers, New York, 1959.
Kornberg, Leonard: *A Class for Disturbed Children: A Case Study and Its Meaning*

for Education, Bureau of Publications, Teachers College, Columbia University, New York, 1955.

Mahler, Clarence A., and Edson Caldwell: *Group Counseling in Secondary Schools,* Science Research Associates, Inc., Chicago, 1961.

Moustakas, Clark E.: *Psychotherapy with Children: The Living Relationship,* Harper & Row, Publishers, New York, 1959.

Papenek, Helene: "Combined Group and Individual Therapy in the Light of Adlerian Psychology," *International Journal of Group Psychotherapy,* 6:136–146, 1956.

Scheidlinger, Saul: "Group Factors in Promoting School Children's Mental Health," *The American Journal of Orthopsychiatry,* 22:394–404, 1952.

Slavson, S. R.: *The Fields of Group Psychotherapy,* International Universities Press, New York, 1958.

Warters, Jane: *Group Guidance: Principles and Practices,* McGraw-Hill Book Company, Inc., New York, 1960.

Witty, Paul A. (Chairman): *Mental Health in Education,* Fifty-fourth Yearbook of the National Society for the Study of Education, University of Chicago Press, Chicago, 1955, part 2.

7 PROBLEMS OF PERSONNEL

Who are the group-guidance workers?

The discussion of this question will relate primarily to schools, colleges, and universities. In social work, leaders of group activities are, in the main, those who have been trained in the social-work field. It was noted in Chapter 2 that schools of religion are increasingly providing training for religious workers in group leadership. In the educational field there is great diversity of practice. Subject and homeroom teachers, teacher-counselors, advisors, counselors, deans, and other administrators, and psychologists are among the leaders of various group activities in different institutions. And the practices seem to vary as much as the leadership.

In 1957 the writer attempted to secure an overview of the situation in the public schools through a questionnaire to the state directors or supervisors of guidance. Returns from 43 states, or 86 per cent, yielded the following rank order of patterns of organization for group-guidance services within the schools: homeroom, the most frequent center; special guidance classes, next in frequency; and core classes, a close third. In estimates of patterns that are emerging and may prevail in the next ten or twenty years, special classes headed the list with 19 responses, the homeroom was checked by 13, special units within certain subjects by 3, core programs by 3, every subject by 2, the cocurriculum by 2, and no response on this point by 2. Thirteen commented on the need for specialized training to carry on this work, and one supervisor wrote that combined group and individual guidance will be handled by specially trained personnel—training to include interdisciplinary study in education, psychology, anthropology, sociology, personnel and social work. From one state where the core program has been widely developed came the suggestion that counselors will be working closely with teachers in classrooms and will hold special group meetings. Doubtless a current survey would show a fairly large number of very small groups led by counselors or psychologists, often termed group counseling or group therapy (see Chapter 6). Some colleges and universities are providing group therapy or psychotherapy with psychiatrists or clinical psychologists.

Qualifications for workers in guidance

Obviously the diversity of organizational patterns in the schools presents a complex problem with respect to qualifications of workers. Most homeroom, core, and subject teachers are not likely to have had much training in the guidance field.[1]

The replies from state supervisors of guidance to the questionnaire in 1957 brought the following responses regarding adequacy of teacher preparation for their guidance functions: poor, 1; inadequate, 18; only partially adequate, 4; "O.K.," 5. Others commented that there was little or no released time for guidance functions; elementary teachers were usually superior to others in training related to guidance; less than one-fourth of all teachers had had any guidance training; recent graduates were better trained than others; there was a great need for in-service training. Among the specific inadequacies mentioned were basic training, testing and interviewing competence, sensitivity to pupil needs, and understanding of teacher functions in the guidance program.

The desirable qualifications of counselors have been the subject of intensive study by several professional organizations for a goodly number of years. The need for such study was evidenced in a survey in 1953 of the training of individuals then serving as guidance specialists in public schools in a six-state area in the Middle West. This survey (2, p. 150) indicated that only two-thirds of the guidance personnel had had an introductory course in guidance, and scarcely more than a third had had a course in occupational information. Half or more had had courses in advanced educational psychology or individual differences. Only 40 per cent listed a mental-hygiene course. Not quite 3 in 4 had had a general course in educational measurement, and about 1 in 10 had had a clinical course in measurement.

Since 1953 there has been an increase in the number of states legislating mandatory or optional certification of counselors, though where these requirements apply only to those engaged half-time or more in guidance services there are many loopholes. An Office of Education report on certification in 1957 (3) showed that 34 states required certification for school counselors, and this was optional in seven states. The

---

[1] A check through a national summary of 1960–1961 state requirements for certification of teachers (1) yielded the following information: health education listed for several states; child study or growth and development, 3 states; adolescent psychology at the secondary level, 2 states; guidance or mental hygiene, 3 states, optional in 2 of these; tests and measurements, 2 states; educational and occupational information, 2 states; guidance in the core program, 1 state. Requirements in guidance for administrators, and for counselors where there was no state credential, were slightly more numerous but not sufficient to provide assurance of adequate background.

figure had increased to 38 states by 1960. The nature of these state certification requirements has varied widely (4).

One of the greatest spurs to the improvement of counselor training at the secondary level has been the provision of counselor and guidance training institutes created under the National Defense Education Act of 1958. This act also provided for appropriations to state educational agencies to assist in establishing and maintaining programs of testing and counseling. It has been reported that about 80 per cent of these state funds have been used for purposes related to counseling (5). This legislation indicates recognition that guidance occupies a place of crucial importance in our nation for the discovery and development of our human resources needed to preserve our way of life. Estimates of the number of counselors needed to meet recommended ratios of counselors to students are much more than double the present number of full-time counselors.

The U.S. Office of Education bulletins describing preparation programs in colleges and universities for guidance and student personnel workers (6, 7) reveal a wide diversity of training programs. Since preparation for group guidance is the concern here, the nature of over-all training programs will not be considered at this point. The most significant aspects of these reports for group guidance are the following: of 223 institutions offering preparation programs at the graduate level for guidance and student personnel workers, only 32 per cent offered courses specified as dealing with group procedures at the Master's level, and 46 per cent at the Doctor's level. At these training levels 91 per cent and 86 per cent, respectively, provided offerings in educational and occupational information—an area related to both group and individual service. Of course, every area might be considered as contributing to group procedures, but the counseling area of preparation is included by title in 93 and 97 per cent of the Master's and Doctor's programs. Some ambiguity could enter into interpretations at this point, since the term counseling is now being used frequently to refer to both individual and group methods.

In these government reports, group procedures received a rank order of 8 among 12 areas of preparation on the basis of the percentage of institutions offering courses in group work. One group of high school counselors who evaluated their formal preparation gave group guidance the lowest rating (ranks ranged from 1 to 15) as to adequacy of the preparation. This suggests a possible lack of background by those providing these training courses, at least from the viewpoint of needs in the schools, or perhaps the lack of a well-developed discipline in this area (8).

In evaluating the present status of preparation for group-guidance services in the schools it may be desirable to consider the fact that within the field of psychiatry standards for the training of group psychotherapists are based on the assumption that this preparation will be built upon the regular training for psychiatric practice. In the schools a prevailing assumption in the past has been that the group guidance could be performed by any teacher. However, awareness of the falseness of this assumption is growing, and it is likely that many trained personnel workers who have done group guidance or counseling may agree with psychiatrists who claim that the group work is much more difficult and exacting than individual therapy (9).

Emerging standards for guidance and personnel workers

Three tentative reports of recommended standards for counselor education were issued by professional groups in 1961.[2] Some of the common elements of these recommended standards are summarized here on the basis of the assumption that much of the group-guidance service requires as rigorous training and as high personal qualifications as does individual counseling.

Level and Length of Training. All groups recommended a minimum of two years of study in a graduate school or division in which a sequence of courses are taught by qualified specialists who understand the relationships of their fields to counseling.[3]

Content of Counselor Education. Major recommendations are for a broad interdisciplinary training. The Committee of the Division of Counseling Psychology (10) gives basic emphasis to psychology, including differential, developmental, learning, personality, and social psychology fields, and adds as professional areas vocational psychology, appraisal procedures, psychology of counseling, professional relationships and ethics, together with group dynamics and/or human relations, statistics, measurement, and occupational, educational, and personal-social information. The Special Committee of APGA (11) recommends concentration in four major areas: the behavioral and social sciences, bio-

[2] These reports were from the following: a committee in the Division of Counseling Psychology, American Psychological Association, Walter F. Johnson, Chairman; the Commission on Guidance in the American Schools, supported by a grant from the Fund for the Advancement of Education and administered by the American Personnel and Guidance Association, C. Gilbert Wrenn, Director; and a Special Committee for the Preparation of the APGA Policy Statement on Counselor Education, Willis E. Dugan, Chairman.

[3] The statements issued by the three groups naturally vary considerably in wording. The effort is made in this brief summary to avoid distortions of any of the three reports, but the statements may conform more closely to one report than another at certain points. Some specific recommendations from each group are added to the items of general agreement, with the usual numbered references to the chapter bibliography.

logical sciences and humanities, processes of education, and professional studies in counseling. The Commission on Guidance in American Schools (12) emphasizes two major cores, one in psychology, including developmental and child psychology, personality growth and dynamics, and group psychology, and a second major in the study of societal forces and culture changes, including graduate areas of sociology, anthropology, economics, and international relations.

All three reports give major emphasis to the necessity of a supervised practicum in counseling, and the Commission report (12) adds supervised experience in planned group situations.

Also included in this report are applied and techniques courses, research methods, basic educational philosophies, curriculum patterns, and ethical and legal responsibilities in counseling.

Selection of Candidates for Counselor Training. The Special Committee of APGA (11) gives considerable emphasis to the importance of the personal qualities of the school counselor such as belief in the inherent worth and potentialities of each individual, commitment to human values, and ability to communicate. Recommended multiple criteria for selection to ensure high-quality candidates include high academic ability. Recommendations of all groups stress the importance of well-adjusted, emotionally mature individuals with interests typical of persons successful in interpersonal relationships.

It has been suggested that selection should be a reciprocal process on the part of the training institution and the trainee, with the latter taking an active part in the decision and in planning his career, whether in guidance or in another field. Hill (13) has provided a review of current selection procedures together with recommendations for improvement.

Another recommendation that is included in many reports is the need for counselor trainees to improve their understanding of themselves through some form of personal guidance. Opportunities for group therapy or counseling for trainees are being introduced in several graduate programs of counselor education and in some in-service training programs in schools. Lifton (14) has described his group work with university seminars for counselor trainees, and Mariner and others (15) have described a two-year group psychotherapy consultation program with public school pesonnel.

Gazda and Ohlsen (16), in evaluating the effects of short-term counseling on prospective counselors, found evidence of apparent changes in a healthful direction in manifest needs as measured by their research instruments, and also in the self-judgments of the experimental subjects in a fourteen-month follow-up. They concluded that, while strict statistical interpretations did not indicate any major improvements in the

mental health of these essentially normal individuals, there was perhaps
sufficient evidence of the value of group counseling in the follow-up
reports of the clients to show that they were happier and better able
to relate to others as a result of the experience.

For both the in-service training and further degree work, the author
would suggest as one of the most effective types of training that of undergoing group-guidance experience, in relation to one's own problems
of self-appraisal, planning, and life adjustment, ranging from informal
and objective self-appraisal to simple group therapy in small discussion
groups. There is no better way of "getting the feel" of how to provide
the group-guidance services for others than of experiencing it oneself.
This statement assumes, of course, that teachers and counselors have
basic foundation in educational psychology and growth and development
in personality, and are acquiring or improving the other competencies
for guidance work.

Such firsthand experience in group guidance should not only increase
professional competence but should bear fruit in improved personal adjustment and happiness, factors that seldom reach the optimum state in
any life. Leadership of trained counselors or psychologists in the school
system, of psychiatrists, or psychiatric social workers in the community,
or of university faculty members who are providing training for guidance
work in nearby universities can usually be secured for a school group.
In the area of vocational guidance, the community will offer many opportunities for firsthand experience or on-the-job training.

The emphases on quality of personnel and depth and breadth of
education in all of the current reports on counselor selection and training, together with government recognition of the basic importance of
the guidance service in our national life, augur well for its quality in
the future.

Identifying and training teachers for guidance functions

The need for identifying suitable teachers for some of the guidance
functions is now widely recognized. Research on this problem has been
directed primarily to the study of teacher attitudes toward and interest
in guidance. Koile and Treat (17) attempted to discriminate between
student-oriented and subject-oriented teachers at the secondary school
level, using a Professional Activity Inventory for Teachers. Koile (18)
also studied the characteristics of college teachers interested in faculty
counseling of students. Characteristics associated with student-oriented
interests did not appear to be as sharply differentiated among public
school teachers as among college teachers. At the high school level
teachers of vocational subjects attained higher student-oriented interest

scores than did teachers in three other subject groupings. Younger and older groups had lower scores than those who had taught eleven to twenty years. At both the high school and college levels women tended to be more interested than men in counseling. In colleges greater interest in counseling was shown by those of lower faculty rank and without the doctorate, by the middle age group rather than the youngest and the oldest, by those teaching in the applied arts and sciences as compared with those in the humanities and natural sciences, by those with a larger number of years of noncollege teaching experience, and by those in state teachers colleges and state regional colleges as compared with those in liberal arts colleges.

Koile remarked that administrative policies, such as reduction in instructional load, might have a bearing on attitudes toward counseling, and stressed the need for controlled research to identify characteristics of effective faculty counselors. These two studies suggested that there may be a potentially larger pool of student-oriented teachers for guidance in the public schools than in colleges. Another study by Stewart (19) of factors influencing teacher attitudes toward and participation in guidance yielded findings similar to those in the two studies just summarized.

Teacher Training for Guidance Functions. Three articles in a series, "Basic Approaches to Mental Health," in *The Personnel and Guidance Journal* deal with guidance for prospective teachers in self-understanding and human relationships. Moustakas (20) reported upon a human-relations seminar at the Merrill-Palmer school where the trainees were concomitantly engaged in guided group counseling for themselves and in free discussions of problems with their elementary school children, thus being able to analyze their own responses and difficulties encountered in the group guidance with children.

At the Nebraska Human Resources Research Foundation, a team approach with students in special classes at Teachers College is described by Hall (21). Instruction in theory of effective human relations, combined with activity projects involving personal investment in a wide range of services with children, teen-agers, families, alumni, parents, and student groups, in which effort was made to give recognition for desirable behavior and for social values and contributions, was aimed at personality cultivation and improved human-relations skills of the students in training.

At the Bank Street College of Education a program described by Biber and others (22) combined intensive personal counseling of teacher trainees with their supervised teaching experience, providing the opportunity for self-examination by the student teachers of their own emotional and intellectual reactions in their varied experiences with children and of their understandings of the children and the suitability of their methods in the teaching and guidance process.

The organization of the group guidance program

Throughout this book emphasis has been placed upon the need for cooperative planning by an entire school staff. The values to be derived from such planning reside not only in the enrichment of the guidance program through ideas from many sources, but also in the feedback into the total educational program, and the more insightful cooperation of all members of the school staff as they envisage the interrelationships of the group guidance and their specific administrative, teaching, or extracurricular functions. One feature of this collaboration might well be that of self-appraisal by each staff member of his best potential contributions to the service and his training needs to perform this service effectively. This would be comparable to the reciprocal appraisal suggested for guidance trainees in a graduate training program.

Little has been said in this book regarding administrative organization for group guidance, other than to stress the need for a close coordination of group work and counseling. It is assumed that the group work would be an integral part of the guidance or personnel program if there is an official responsible for that program. The possibilities have been noted for the use of the homeroom, special guidance or orientation classes, core or general-education classes, various informal-discussion groups, remedial or laboratory services, and the relationships of the total curriculum and extracurriculum have been explored. There are as yet few directives from research as to the best types of administrative organization for group guidance.

The results of one very rigorous research investigation of the relative merits of the homeroom and the special guidance class seemed to favor the homeroom setup in many respects. However, one feature of the situations studied should not be overlooked in the interpretation of the findings. The principal of the school in which the homerooms were evaluated had told the author many years before the investigation was made that if he were ever forced to abandon all but one feature of his school program, he would choose to retain the homeroom. One can never afford to underestimate the influence of the administrator in any program.

The trend toward combined group and individual counseling carried on by trained counselors appears to be gathering momentum as the need for special qualifications and training for guidance is increasingly recognized. This trend does not eliminate the services of teachers for many aspects of guidance. It calls for job analyses of the work to be done and the distribution of functions according to *who can do best what needs to be done.* This requires a well-planned organization of the program in which each person understands the nature of his functions and their relationship to the total service; also, lines of intercommunication that facilitate full interplay and cooperation of everyone involved in the program.

A school plant providing facilities for large-, average-, and small-group activities, such as is recommended by Trump (23), will be most helpful to care for all the varieties of group guidance in a well-organized program.

Problems of evaluation

Our modern concept of guidance, as concerned with the total person in his social culture and with his self-direction in the whole gamut of his life activities, presents us with a complex problem of evaluating outcomes of services. Still other complicating factors are the need for new techniques in evaluating effectiveness and outcomes for individuals of experiences in groups, and the fact that well-planned group-guidance services by trained personnel are relatively new features of guidance programs. We cannot conclude from many attempted evaluations of former or existing programs what the possible outcomes of suitably organized and adequately staffed services might be. This situation is true to a degree of all evaluations of educational programs. We have often been prone in the past to draw conclusions and make recommendations on the basis of prevailing practices rather than on the results of experimental investigations of more ideal situations.

Borow (24), in an overview of research methods in group-mediated personnel work, has noted that high values have not been placed on these group procedures until fairly recent times; that former arguments of economy for group techniques are now being supplanted by claims of certain substantial advantages for them which are presumably not offered by counseling; that they are seen increasingly as performing a complementary role with counseling in personnel work; and that it is in this perspective that many research studies are now conceived.

Borow has succinctly summarized the current situation as to research in the following paragraph (24, pp. 219–220):

Published research in this area falls into three categories: (*a*) the study of group methods as preparation for counseling; (*b*) the study of group and individual counseling methods as integral aspects of the total helping relationship; (*c*) the comparative study of outcomes of group and individual methods. Several workers have called attention to the need for supplementing research on interview process and counselor strategy with studies of client motives and perceptions in counseling. While findings have by no means been decisive, there seems now to be sufficient preliminary evidence at hand to support the belief that the inappropriate motives, perceptual sets, and expectations with which many students enter upon counseling can be modified by a group experience, either preparatory or parallel to individual work. There have, furthermore, been a number of research reports which suggest the increased effectiveness of combining individual and group techniques in student counseling at both the secondary-school and college levels. Such studies as have compared the independent effects of individual counseling and group work upon short-range educational and vocational outcomes have generally failed to confirm the presumed superiority of the former. On the strength of this sort of research activity, one may be encouraged to hope that the experimental attitude has finally taken root in the group-methods field. Yet, the research has not generally been of a high order, and much of the significance of currently available studies is negated by the stringent evaluation placed upon them by our changing research methodology, with its increasingly exacting requirements for acceptable experimental design.

Research pertinent to various aspects of group guidance has been summarized at various points throughout this book. Caution is needed in generalizing from any of the available findings, and there is a continuous need for fresh and creative evaluation in any evolving program. Elaborate controlled experimentation is not possible at every stage in the development of a school program. However, we could doubtless do much more of it than in the past if members of a school staff working for advanced degrees could fully utilize the living laboratories of a school for their research, and if full advantage were taken of possibilities for cooperative research with graduate schools that have counselor education programs. Advantages that accrue to the graduate school can be multiplied manyfold through the influence of guidance trainees upon other group-guidance programs.

In addition, there are many informal, less exacting, and less time-consuming methods that can be used profitably by everyone. The term *action research* is coming into the educational vernacular to refer to informal experimentation with varieties of approaches and techniques, the efficacy of which can be judged partly by observation of activities and partly by the normal outcomes of procedures that are evaluated in some manner under any circumstances, through pupil behavior, attitudes, and achievement.

The estimates by members of a group of the relative values of different aspects of their work can yield invaluable information to a group leader, especially if these judgments are made in unsigned notes or questionnaires. Oral appraisals can be secured continuously as a part of leader-group planning of activities. All members of a school staff can collaborate in observing and recording changes in pupil behavior, attitude, social facility, learning techniques, thinking, and problem-solving abilities, and specific types of achievement in subjects and in scholarship.

There are various check lists for judging the adequacy of guidance services that can be used by the school staff or by outside judges. Members of a school group can develop their own check lists keyed to the objectives and organization of their own program. For group guidance this procedure is likely to be fully as helpful as the use of standardized check lists, since most of the available ones do not bear as fully on group approaches as on counseling, individual study, and appropriate record keeping.

Excerpts from "A Check List for Appraising a Secondary School Guidance Program" (25), which gives excellent emphasis to group-guidance procedures, are included in the Appendix.

SUMMARY

The lack of professional standards for guidance workers in the past has caused great diversity of practice in the assignment of guidance functions in the schools and wide variety in the educational preparation of counselors and teachers for the performance of guidance services. There has been widespread lack of recognition of the need for special qualifications for group aspects of personnel work.

The rapid spread of state certification requirements for counselors and the impetus of counselor-training institutes established under the provisions of the National Defense Education Act of 1958 have led to improved counselor-education programs in graduate schools. Training for group guidance has not yet received as full recognition in these programs as has that for individual counseling. There is increasing evidence in the recommendations of professional groups for counselor qualifications that group aspects of guidance are being recognized as coordinate with counseling and requiring as rigorous training.

Procedures for identifying teachers best suited for guidance work have been investigated through studies of their interests in and attitudes toward guidance. Group counseling experience is being provided for teacher and counselor trainees in numerous educational programs for purposes of improved self-understanding and adjustment, and is also being used in some in-service training programs in schools.

Coordination of the group and individual guidance functions of all members of a school staff is essential for a well-organized and effective program.

Methods of evaluation of group guidance and counseling are being expanded and refined in response to emerging concepts of the place of group procedures in personnel programs. Continuous creative and experimental research is needed to guide new and improved developments in these services.

REFERENCES CITED IN CHAPTER

1. Woellner, Mrs. Robert C., and M. Aurilla Wood: *Requirements for Certification of Teachers, Counselors, Librarians, Administrators, for Elementary Schools, Secondary Schools, Junior Colleges,* 26th ed., 1961–1962, University of Chicago Press, Chicago, 1961.
2. Jones, Arthur J., and Leonard M. Miller: "The National Picture of Pupil Personnel and Guidance Services in 1953," *Bulletin of the National Association of Secondary-school Principals,* 38:103–195, February, 1954.
3. Brewster, Royce E.: *Guidance Workers Certification Requirements,* U.S. Department of Health, Education, and Welfare, Bulletin 1957, no. 22, 1957.
4. Hill, George E., and Donald A. Green: "The Selection, Preparation, and Professionalization of Guidance and Personnel Workers," *Review of Educational Research,* 30:115–130, April, 1960.
5. Tyler, Leona E.: *The National Defense Counseling and Guidance Training Institutes Program: A Report of the First 50 Institutes,* U.S. Office of Education, 1960.
6. MacMinn, Paul, and Roland G. Ross: *Status of Preparation Programs for Guidance and Student Personnel Workers,* U.S. Office of Education Bulletin 1959, no. 7, 1959.
7. MacMinn, Paul: *Preparation Programs and Course Offerings in School and College Personnel Work,* 1959–1960, U.S. Office of Education Circular 591, 1959.
8. Harmon, Donald, and Dwight L. Arnold: "High School Counselors Evaluate Their Formal Preparation," *The Personnel and Guidance Journal,* 39:303–306, December, 1960.
9. Spotnitz, Hyman: *The Couch and the Circle,* Alfred A. Knopf, Inc., New York, 1961.
10. Division of Counseling Psychology, American Psychological Association: *The Scope and Standards of Preparation in Psychology for School Counselors,* memorandum to members of the division, July 25, 1961.
11. Special Committee for the Preparation of the APGA Policy Statement on Counselor Education: "The Policy Statement on Counselor Education," *The Personnel and Guidance Journal,* 40:401–407, December, 1961.
12. Wrenn, C. Gilbert: *The Counselor in a Changing World; A Preliminary Report of the Project on Guidance in American Schools,* The Commission on Guidance in American Schools, American Personnel and Guidance Association, Washington, 1961.
13. Hill, George E.: "The Selection of School Counselors," *The Personnel and Guidance Journal,* 39:355–360, January, 1961.
14. Lifton, Walter M.: *Working with Groups: Group Process and Individual Growth,* John Wiley & Sons, Inc., New York, 1961.
15. Mariner, Allen S., et al.: "Group Psychiatric Consultation with Public School Personnel, a Two-year Study," *The Personnel and Guidance Journal,* 40:254–258, November, 1961.
16. Gazda, George, and Merle Ohlsen: "The Effects of Short-term Group Counseling on Prospective Counselors," *The Personnel and Guidance Journal,* 39:634–638, April, 1961.
17. Koile, Earl A., and Carol L. Treat: "Identifying Student-oriented Teachers," *The Personnel and Guidance Journal,* 40:344–348, December, 1961.
18. Koile, Earl A.: "Characteristics of College Teachers Interested in Faculty Counseling Activities," *Journal of Counseling Psychology,* 2:32–34, spring, 1955.
19. Stewart, James A.: "Factors Influencing Teacher Attitudes toward and Partici-

pation in Guidance Services," *The Personnel and Guidance Journal*, 39:729–734, May, 1961.
20. Moustakas, Clark: "A Human Relations Seminar at the Merrill-Palmer School," *The Personnel and Guidance Journal*, 37:342–349, January, 1959.
21. Hall, William E.: "The Program at the Nebraska Human Resources Research Foundation," *The Personnel and Guidance Journal*, 37:276–281, December, 1958.
22. Biber, Barbara, et al.: "Teacher Education at Bank Street College," *The Personnel and Guidance Journal*, 37:558–568, April, 1959.
23. Trump, J. Lloyd: *Images of the Future: A New Approach to the Secondary School*, National Association of Secondary-school Principals, Department of the National Education Association, Washington, 1959.
24. Borow, Henry: "Frontiers of Personnel Research in Education," in *Personnel Services in Education*, Melvene Draheim Hardee (Chairman), National Society for the Study of Education, 1958 Yearbook, University of Chicago Press, Chicago, 1959, part 2, pp. 210–258.
25. Kitch, Donald E., and William H. McCreary: "Improving Guidance Programs in Secondary Schools," *Bulletin of the California State Department of Education*, vol. 19, no. 8, Sacramento, Calif., December, 1950.

ADDITIONAL REFERENCES

Arbuckle, Dugald S.: *Guidance and Counseling in the Classroom*, Allyn and Bacon, Inc., Englewood Cliffs, N.J., 1957.
Barr, John: *The Elementary Teacher and Guidance*, Holt, Rinehart and Winston, Inc., New York, 1958.
Coleman, William: "The Role of Evaluation in Improving Guidance and Counseling Services," *The Personnel and Guidance Journal*, 35:441–444, March, 1957.
Cottingham, Harold F., and William E. Hopke: *Guidance in the Junior High School*, McKnight & McKnight Publishing Company, Bloomington, Ill., 1961.
Fusco, Gene C.: *Organization and Administration of Pupil Personnel Service Programs in Selected School Systems*, U.S. Office of Education Bulletin 1961, no. 22, 1961.
Gordon, Ira J.: *The Teacher as a Guidance Worker*, Harper & Row, Publishers, New York, 1956.
Hatch, Raymond N., and James W. Costar: *Guidance Services in the Elementary School*, William C. Brown Company, Publishers, Dubuque, Iowa, 1961.
Johnson, Mauritz, Jr., et al.: *Junior High School Guidance*, Harper & Row, Publishers, New York, 1961.
Johnson, Walter F., et al.: *Pupil Personnel and Guidance Services*, McGraw-Hill Book Company, Inc., New York, 1961.
Johnston, Edgar G., et al.: *The Role of the Teacher in Guidance*, Prentice-Hall, Inc., Englewood Cliffs, N.J., 1959.
Lloyd-Jones, Esther, and Margaret Ruth Smith (eds.): *Student Personnel Work as Deeper Teaching*, Harper & Row, Publishers, New York, 1954.
Martinson, Ruth A., and Harry Smallenburg: *Guidance in Elementary Schools*, Prentice-Hall, Inc., Englewood Cliffs, N.J., 1958.
Moustakas, Clark E.: *The Teacher and the Child: Personal Interaction in the Classroom*, McGraw-Hill Book Company, Inc., New York, 1956.
National Association for Evaluation of Secondary Schools: *Evaluative Criteria*, The Association, Washington, 1960.
"Guidance and Counseling in the Secondary School," *Bulletin of the National Association of Secondary-school Principals*, 43:1–122, 1959.
Noble, Jeanne L., and Robert H. Mathewson, "Evaluating a Program of Counselor Training through Group Conferences," *The Personnel and Guidance Journal*, 34: 285–288, January, 1956.

Ryans, David G.: *Characteristics of Teachers,* American Council on Education, Washington, 1960.

Wattenberger, J. L.: "Competencies Needed by Core Teachers," *Educational Research Bulletin,* 32:181–185, 1953.

Willey, Roy DeVerl: *Guidance in Elementary Education,* rev. ed., Harper & Row, Publishers, New York, 1960.

Wrenn, C. Gilbert: *The Counselor in a Changing World,* The Commission on Guidance in American Schools, American Personnel and Guidance Association, Washington, 1962.

PART THREE

THE AREAS FOR
GROUP GUIDANCE

8 ORIENTATION

Orientation, in the sense of adaptation to new situations, is taking on new meaning as the increased tempo of change in our technological world is continually transforming our environment. Assistance in adjusting to new school situations, which are increasingly complex at successive levels, has long been recognized as essential. Now we are all faced with orientation and reorientation problems throughout life, and we need the attitudes, understandings, and skills that will enable us to meet and utilize new situations effectively at every stage in living. Orientation is, therefore, not only a process within each new school situation, but also a lifelong process. The objectives of orientation services to students in schools are thus twofold: immediate for the new school situation, and long-range for the continuous orientation within changing situations throughout life. If both objectives are kept in mind for orientation services, each progressive step in schooling should become easier, and students should be preparing in an important way for life beyond school as well as experiencing more satisfying and fruitful living within each new school or college.

Another aspect of orientation is the mutuality of the process between new students and their new institution. We might say that orientation is a mutual process of *learning* on the part of new students, the faculty, and student body of an institution, whereby each group becomes better acquainted with the others, and each participates in an ongoing process which will help the new students to become an effectively functioning part of the institution and help the institution to become responsive to the needs of a changing student body. Such a learning process cannot be confined to a small group of administrators and student leaders nor to a few events of a freshman induction program, though both may be significant aspects of the process.

Reports of orientation programs in schools and colleges show that the services are now being initiated much earlier than formerly. For secondary schools the programs frequently begin with cooperatively planned activities of the two school levels, elementary and junior high school or junior and senior high school, initiated months before the transfer of students occurs. For colleges and universities there are many types of preadmission and pre-enrollment programs; and with the increased populations in institutions of higher education, guidance programs for college preparatory students in secondary schools are being initiated much earlier than in the past. Still another trend is to extend the orientation service for a longer period within any one level. This trend is based on the recognition that not all problems of adjustment within the new situation are faced or can be met in the early days or weeks in the new school situation.

The increased mobility of our population has led to another orientation problem, that of assisting students who enter new schools at various times throughout the school year. Reports of new services for these late entrants at all levels, including elementary schools, are appearing in educational literature.

Other developments in the use of orientation procedures have occurred in military programs to assist in the induction into military service and in the preparation for meeting conditions of war, and in hospital programs of lectures and discussion to assist patients with mental and emotional difficulties in adjusting to hospital life and as preparation for more intensive group psychotherapy. There is little essential difference in the purposes of these various programs in spite of the wide variations in setting and practices. The term *precounseling orientation* is now frequently used to apply to group services aimed at informing students about the nature of the counseling process and preparing them to cooperate in the interview helpfully (1, 2).

The broad purposes of orientation can be subdivided into several specific goals such as the following:

1. To help the newcomer become acquainted with the new institution—its history, traditions, purposes, physical plant and facilities, faculty and student body, rules and regulations, curricular and extracurricular opportunities and special services—in order that he may adjust himself happily in the new environment through participating effectively in its life, and that he may utilize its opportunities for furthering his personal development.

2. To guide the newcomer in a reconsideration of his goals and purposes in relation to increased self-knowledge and in the perspective of his new opportunities for personal development as a basis for *wise choices of experiences.*

3. To assist the newcomer to improve his skill in *making desirable adjustments* within the new environment and in utilizing his various new opportunities and thus contribute to his *increased skill in self-direction.*

4. To help and inspire the newcomer *to make his own best unique contributions* to his new school home.

5. To guide the newcomer in *the interpretation and integration of his*

varied experiences in a wider social environment, in order to help him to broaden and deepen his perspective on life and plan more intelligently for the future.

6. To provide opportunities for the faculty and student body to become acquainted with the newcomers, to become aware of their needs and their potential contributions within the institution, and, in cooperation with them, to re-examine and adapt curricular and extracurricular opportunities in the light of this new understanding.

7. To help all individuals to develop the perspectives and skills that will enable them to meet and utilize new situations throughout life more effectively.

Orientation, thus conceived, can foster the personal growth of all who are involved. It serves as a catalyzer or a ferment within an institution to keep it flexible and responsive to a changing population, and at the same time as a conserver of intrinsic and enduring values.

Several aspects of the orientation process will be examined in relation to various age levels.

ORIENTATION PROGRAMS

In nursery school, kindergarten, and elementary school

Preadmission Services. The success with which the child has met his developmental tasks in traversing the period of infancy and earliest childhood will determine in large degree how he meets the new opportunities in a school group. Parent- and other adult-education programs and the study of parenthood in high school and college years should contribute through the parents to the child's readiness for entrance into school life.

Meetings and conferences with parents preliminary to, or concurrent with, the opening of a new school year afford opportunities for mutual parent-teacher study of children, the interpretation to parents of school experience, and the joint planning of ways in which home and school can cooperate in helping to make this first big adjustment from the sheltered home environment to the wider school group a happy adventure for children. Where physical examinations are provided by the school or the community, sometimes in summer clinics, conferences of parents, physician or nurse, and, ideally, guidance workers and teachers when available can help to bring mutual awareness to home and school of health and developmental problems, for the solution of which both parents and teachers should cooperate. Sometimes the health data must be supplied directly to teachers and guidance workers by the health officials. Bulletins from the school to the parents of children entering nursery school or kindergarten are frequently used to explain school programs and to suggest ways in which parents can help their children to adjust in the new school environment.

Most teachers of very young children are now well trained in methods of helping them to make the transition from home to school by serving temporarily as parent surrogates, and by creating an environment in which children will feel accepted and learn to share happily in experiences with other children. Opportunities for parents and children to explore the new environment together before the children are on their own can help to relieve anxieties and tensions.

Postadmission Orientation. These services are so much an integral part of an elementary school program where children stay with one teacher that it is difficult to separate them for consideration. At the beginning of each new term there is the "get-acquainted" task, which not only provides the teacher with valuable information about each child but also helps to weld the group into a cohesive unit. Get-acquainted games and reports by children of how they have spent vacation time, of their pets, hobbies, interests, and what they would like to learn about during the year are a few of the many ways in which all can get to know one another better. A simple list of goals for the term, and a few simple rules for working and playing together, prepared cooperatively by teacher and pupils, can serve as a starter for democratic planning.

Opportunities for the children to talk about their new school experiences in little informal groups may be as important for kindergarten and elementary school children as for college students. Increasingly, child psychologists are emphasizing the importance of this talking-out process with respect to attitudes and emotions as early as nursery school years.

With accelerated mobility of population the problem of orientation for late entrants is present at all levels in the school system. As a newcomer enters a group, pupils can strengthen their own sense of belonging by planning how to help the new pupil to feel at home, to find his place in the group, and to make his best contributions to group projects. Martin (3) sees mobility as a challenge for enriching the experience of all members of a group by utilizing the varied experiences of newcomers, often from different cultures, to help them feel accepted and to increase the skill of all in a group in interpreting and adjusting to change.

As children progress through the grades, they encounter new orientation problems that appear with the demand for the development and use of new subject, social, and play skills. Variations in the readiness and ability of children to acquire reading and other skills and the cumulation of difficulties and maladjustment on the part of children in the middle grades who have not acquired necessary skills have led to recognition of the need for help in special remedial groups.

It may seem farfetched to introduce a comment about preorientation for college or other advanced training at the elementary school level. Nevertheless, some of the tragedies of individuals in relation to planning for college date back to this early period. No teacher or test can predict with complete accuracy the potential scholastic ability of an elementary school child. But the elementary school period is a golden time to discover and foster a child's strongest assets and to build up child and parent pride in these talents, be they manipulative, social, artistic, or academic. Many parents, and therefore children, set up unrealistic college ambitions at an early age, only to have them shattered when the requirements for college entrance are not met. At the elementary school age, it is possible to work *positively* on the development of suitable interests without reference to the negative aspects which must be faced later if ambitions and abilities are not harmonized.

Another side of this question relates to the academically favored child who, for some reason, does not master his reading or arithmetic skills and is, therefore, unable to achieve in secondary school the scholastic excellence needed to pursue college work. This individual is being denied his birthright if we do not provide the kind of remedial assistance in special groups necessary to overcome his handicap. Clinical studies at the high school level reveal too many young people whose earlier group mental-test records and grades are low and whose real ability is of college caliber, as shown by individual-ability tests where reading skill does not count so heavily. Elementary school is the place to discover these discrepancies between records and abilities.

In junior and senior high school

Preadmission Services. Successful adjustment and achievement at one school level is one good type of insurance against difficulties at the next stage. However, the anticipation of entrance into junior or senior high school is frequently associated with anxiety on the part of both children and their parents, and much can be done before entrance to allay fears and provide helpful preparation.

Among the variety of approaches that are used are bulletins or brochures describing opportunities at the new school and dealing with questions about such matters as appropriate dress, time schedules, transportation, supplies, rules and regulations, marking system, study methods, choosing subjects and activities, student government, parent study groups and meetings, and special services. Administrators, counselors, and student leaders may meet with groups of prospective pupils and their parents; pupils and parents may visit the new school to see the program in action, attend classes, and meet faculty and pupils. Movies or filmstrips may bring glimpses of the new school to the pupils and their parents. Radio, and more recently television, have been used to reach more parents in the home both to inform them about the purposes and nature of the new school and to present challenging questions for parent and child discussion.

A comprehensive preadmission program for seventh-graders in a new school district reported by FitzPatrick and Plattor (4) started in November at the sixth-grade level when the seventh-grade counselor began spending one day a week in the district's elementary schools meeting with sixth-grade students and teachers. Administrators, guidance and teaching staffs, students, and parents in elementary and junior high school planned the over-all program together. In March planning began for panels of junior high school students with sixth-graders in assemblies at their elementary schools. Visits were then arranged for two sixth-grade classes per day at the junior high school where pupils met with administrator, counselor, and seventh-grade "buddies" whose classes were attended for four periods, followed by a building tour and luncheon conference with opportunity for questions and discussion. A parent meeting was held immediately after the tours were completed, with a panel program and discussion. Continuing activities in the sixth-grade classes included discussions of the mechanics of the junior high school, and lessons on study habits, testing, and the relationships of broad occupational categories to subjects studied in school. In June counselors gave out handbooks during their meetings with sixth-graders in their schools. All of this preadmission program was preliminary to an orientation program described later, that was carried on through seventh and eighth grades anticipating subject choices in the ninth grade.

An extended preadmission orientation program for high school has been described by Nielsen (5). Beginning in February of the year before transfer, units on opportunities in the new high schools are introduced in the social-studies classes of the contributing elementary schools, followed by two interviews with the new counselor and visits to the new school. In April ninth-grade programs are made out with the assistance of the eighth-grade teacher. During the first week prior to the opening of school, meetings are held with parents and teachers.

A program of summer conferences of the guidance director with prospective ninth-grade freshmen and their parents has been described by Blecha (6). During these conferences various information blanks are completed, class programs and tentative four-year schedules are mapped out using available personnel data, various aspects of the school organization are explained, and questions are answered. Like many other orientation programs now being reported, this is only one phase of a long-range process.

Ellis (7) reports a cooperative program of a junior high school with senior high schools, in which units on educational and vocational guidance were offered in junior high school followed by a Career Day for these students in December at one of the high schools with opportunity to tour the new building and meet high school students and teachers. During the year curricular and cocurricular assemblies are held in junior high school, with parents invited, providing information from high school faculty and students regarding opportunities in two different schools with visitation later for interested students to the technical high school.

There is increasing emphasis upon the need for improved articulation between all levels from elementary to college through mutual study of pertinent problems and the exchange of information between workers at the various levels to achieve understanding of what they expect of each other and to improve the transfer of information about students to the higher level and feed back information to the lower level (8).

Among specific suggestions for improving this articulation are representatives from different levels on committees, exchange of positions and materials, the carry-over of some familiar activities such as a block-time program, and more follow-up activities (9).

Postadmission Orientation. A homeroom or block-time group is often the center for orientation though school-wide assemblies and social events will be used to welcome new pupils into the wider life of the school. If preplanning by administrators, counselors, teachers, and pupils, perhaps including representatives of entering groups, has been done, there is likely to be a wealth of suggestions and of materials to be drawn upon for both class and school activities. English or social-studies classes of the previous year's freshman groups may have written compositions about their orienting experiences; art and mechanical-drawing classes may have prepared clever posters and building and ground plans; commercial and printing classes may have helped to prepare duplicated or printed materials for the freshmen; dramatics and music classes may have prepared skits to portray some phases of school life; school leaders will have planned interesting get-acquainted methods and ways of initiating the new pupils into citizenship in the student body. A pal for each newcomer is frequently assigned. Always there will be opportunities to practice school songs and yells.

In the small class groups, orientation may be just one phase of a larger group-guidance program. Here, the freshmen have the opportunity not only to be informed about a multitude of new conditions, rules, and regulations, but also to pool their individual questions and difficulties for helpful consideration by teacher, counselor, or older student and tackle thoughtfully their problems of how best to use their new opportunities and what they as new citizens will be able to contribute over the years to their school democracy.

Among the topics that are usually studied by a freshman group are:

The new school plant

The purposes of education at their level

History and traditions of the new school

Rules and regulations—their purposes and how they might be improved through democratic procedures

School citizenship and democratic leadership and followership

Special services and how to use them

Getting acquainted and making friends

Conserving time, energy, and health

Using new opportunities to the best advantage

Curricular offerings—their purposes and values

Extracurricular opportunities—their purposes and values

Formulation of personal goals for the school years ahead

Formulation of plans for well-balanced living at the new school level —through work, play, and citizenship

Study and learning in the new situations (see Chapter 9)

Development of personal life values

A plan for evaluating progress toward goals

Group plans for contributing to the life of the school

Evaluation of orientation services as guides for improved services to the next freshman group

In schools where a group-guidance program is fairly continuous throughout the high school years, some of these topics will not be included in the initial orientation. Assistance in self-appraisal is essential, of course, as a foundation for goal setting and for vocational and educational planning. These phases of guidance are dealt with in later chapters and are not included specifically among the topics for orientation except in the sense of a general look ahead. The re-examination of previous interests and achievements with the guidance of a group leader and conferences with a counselor about indications of interests and abilities in personnel records will provide some of the background needed for tentative and realistic goal setting.

A list of specific learnings related to the topics listed for orientation at the secondary level is given on pages 195 and 196. These learnings are similar in the high school and college, but are faced at different maturity levels. They will amplify the topics in this section, though they are stated in a form more appropriate in general to the college than the high school level.

Two current trends are the extension of the orientation program over a longer period of time and the participation of the counselor in the group activities. These trends will be noted in the following illustrations drawn from several orientation programs. Blecha (6) has described the first day of school set aside for freshmen.[1] The guidance director welcomed them in a general meeting, and members of the student council guided them to their homerooms where they received class schedules and then began a program of shortened classes. Near the end of each class the guidance director explained over the public-address system the general activities for the next period, and then a period was provided for the freshmen to explore the entire building. Another phase of the program in this school is a daily thirty-five-minute activity period for all students, used twice weekly for freshmen orientation for several months to provide assistance in fitting into the total school program and in the understanding of values inherent in the various subject fields. The next phase deals with school clubs and encourages freshmen to become active in at least one but not more than two. Before semester exams the freshmen are given time for extra study in activity periods. One of these periods per week is set aside for group guidance or individual counseling by the homeroom teacher for all students.

At another school [2] the counselor meets with eighth-grade students—sophomores in a six-year high school—once a week for three weeks in regular classes to help them plan their programs for grades 9 to 12. These meetings are supplemented with a handbook and a parents' meeting. This use of regular classes, sometimes combined with larger auditorium groups and also with smaller counseling groups, is becoming a fairly frequent practice and will be considered later in relation to other aspects of group guidance.

Orientation through Each Class and Activity. Each teacher and each club or group leader has an orientation responsibility for getting a group acquainted and organized, for formulating specific goals for the term, both group and individual, and for understanding and use of the best study and learning techniques for the particular field.

Coordination of Orientation Activities. Councils or committees to plan and coordinate various phases of the orientation program are essential for a well-knit program. Possibilities for representation on such a coordinating group have already been suggested. Many schools have homeroom or guidance councils with representatives from each guidance group that provide reciprocal communication between these smaller groups and the over-all school organization. Often these councils are an integral part of the student-body organization. Administrators and faculty need to participate fully in this reciprocal communication to keep their practices responsive to these ongoing group processes.

Orientation for Late Entrants and Foreign Students. Population mobility has created in the high school the same problem mentioned for

[1] At Preble High School, Green Bay, Wis.
[2] Plainview High School, New York (4).

the elementary school, that of new students entering at many times during the school year. These late entrants and students from foreign countries sometimes present a similar problem, a cultural background different from that which prevails in the community, and may, therefore, need a special type of orientation to fit easily into the school life. Language and widely different experiences may call for special assistance. As in the elementary school, it is important to utilize their unique experiences when feasible in order to help them bridge gaps, to enrich the lives of other students, and to foster increased skill in adjusting to change. Special orientation problems of foreign students are considered further on page 193.

For the college and technical school level

Preadmission Services. The educational guidance throughout secondary school years that acquaints students with varied college-entrance requirements and helps them to acquire information about various colleges and other training schools as a basis for choosing appropriate institutions for further training may be considered a part of preadmission services to students. College visiting days for students or personnel workers, or both, provide firsthand precontacts with neighboring institutions. Varied College Day programs are frequently held in high schools to bring college officials or high school alumni from colleges into meetings with prospective college students where questions relating to choice of institution and entrance can be discussed. If carefully planned, these College Days can provide a wealth of opportunities for students to learn about differences among the colleges and to acquire background for intelligent choices of institutions (10). Series of College Days for different institutions are becoming recognized as more valuable than one affair into which are crowded all of the confusing opportunities to learn about many schools, colleges, and universities. Study of college bulletins and brochures under the guidance of a counselor will widen the foundations for these students' choices.

With intensified competition for admission to college and the emphasis upon the identification and development of talent among youth, many schools are initiating college-motivation programs early in the high school years, and also providing students at an early date with information about scholarship opportunities. These early steps are important in motivating those with good academic potentialities to achieve scholastic records that will keep college and scholarship opportunities open for them. This phase of guidance will be considered in greater detail in Chapter 12.

Entrance into college means for many students leaving home and adjusting in a totally new environment. The distance between college and most homes precludes many of the types of group procedures used within a school system, but colleges have worked out ingenious plans for helping students to make this transition. Letters to students who have been accepted, visits of college officials with parents and students in their home communities, and invitational conferences with parents and students at the college during the summer are among these pre-admission procedures.

The Allegheny College Educational Guidance Clinic (11) illustrates an intensive precollege guidance service. Begun in the decade of the thirties this clinic has drawn its staff not only from the local college but from other colleges and universities and from high school guidance staffs. The summer Clinic Week provides opportunity for juniors and seniors in high school and their parents to secure a realistic picture of college life and of requirements for success in college, as well as guidance in the choice of a college and formulation of educational goals. Personnel data for each counselee include a wealth of information secured from past history and achievement and current medical and psychological examinations. Attendance in classes, laboratories, group discussions, and social events are combined with lengthy interviews with counselors, leading to increased understanding by prospective students and their parents of the predictive expectancies of college success. McCracken and co-workers report also improved articulation between high school and college through exchange of information, follow-up studies, and participation or visitation of high school guidance workers and teachers.

These summer clinics for incoming students are now being used widely. Reports from Michigan State University show that almost 80 per cent of new freshmen and most transfer students attended such clinics, thus cutting down Freshman Week time by two or three days.[3]

Postadmission Orientation. Preplanning for orientation of freshmen or new students through cooperative work of administrators, personnel workers, faculty, heads of residence, and student advisers is quite general for Freshman or Orientation Days or Week.[4] Student groups with faculty guidance frequently prepare freshman manuals (12) and plan many of the social activities to welcome new students, start acquaintanceships, and provide opportunities for campus tours and for conferences with student advisers. The training of student advisers and the preparation of faculty advisers, heads of residence, and others for their

[3] Thomas A. Goodrich and Rowland R. Pierson: "Pre-college Counseling at Michigan State University," *The Personnel and Guidance Journal,* 37:595–597, April, 1959; also notation from Walter F. Johnson.

[4] *Orientation* is tending to replace *Freshman* to include services to new upperclassmen as well as the first-year students, and to tie these services into the total orientation program.

services are increasingly the responsibility of administrators and personnel workers.

Former freshmen may contribute to this planning by their English compositions about their orienting experiences and how they might have been improved. It has been suggested by some that sophomores often make excellent student advisers for freshmen because they are nearer to their problems than the older students. In any event, student advisers need to be carefully chosen, trained as thoroughly as possible, and cautioned as to the desirable limits of their advisory services. One phase of their training is to learn to recognize what problems need to be referred where.

FRESHMAN OR ORIENTATION DAYS OR WEEK. This custom of bringing freshmen together before classes begin is one of the most common orientation practices. It serves the double purpose of caring for some administrative problems, such as registration and testing of freshmen, and for initial services of acquainting the new students with the campus, getting them settled in dormitories or other living groups, introducing them to student and faculty advisers and administrators, and helping, through social functions, to make them feel at home. A practice has grown of spending a few days in camp life in some pleasant place near the campus where a spirit of informal camaraderie may prevail.

At one time Orientation Week was relied upon in many institutions as one of the chief means of orienting new students. Gradually it was recognized that too much was crowded into a few days, that lectures on adjustment problems to large groups did not function too effectively, because of both the method and the timing. Also, extensive testing schedules and registration preempted too much of the total available time and left too little for interesting personal contacts.

Among the changes that are being introduced in some institutions to overcome these difficulties are the following:

1. Initial testing is being held down to a minimum of a scholastic-aptitude test and an English or reading test. Other aptitude tests and interest and personality inventories may be administered in an orientation or other guidance course where students can be made aware of the purposes and values of the tests and perhaps use some of them in self-appraisal, and where more suitable testing conditions are likely to prevail than in the exciting, confusing Freshman Days. A study which may have significant bearing on all of the testing done during Orientation Week showed that scores on aptitude tests taken upon college entrance have a definitely lower average in high-anxiety students than in low-anxiety students but that the relation between the two groups in college-grade average is slightly reversed.

2. Registration procedures have been streamlined to reduce long hours in waiting lines; and advanced registration during the summer is provided for students who can come to the college.

3. Physical examinations are extended beyond Orientation Week into the first semester to eliminate crowded schedules.

4. Small-group discussions are scheduled with faculty and student advisers and housing personnel to consider many of the problems formerly dealt with in large lecture groups.

5. More orientation procedures are being extended over a longer period through the traditional orientation course in small discussion groups with an orientation counselor or often a faculty leader.

THE ORIENTATION COURSE. Beyond the initial introduction to the campus in Orientation Week comes the long pull during which the new student is confronted by many novel situations and adjustment problems. The orientation course, if it is sufficiently flexible, can provide many helpful opportunities for learning self-direction through guided study of ways of meeting these new challenges. This assistance is most frequently met through a regularly scheduled orientation course, designated by varied titles. The great majority of these courses are now of the personal-adjustment or guidance type. The older survey, or subject-orientation, approach appears to have found its way frequently into general-education programs, though in radically changed form. This shift is also true of some of the guidance-type courses, but we shall not distinguish between these organizational differences in examining the orientation process. Some approaches are chiefly through lectures; others combine lectures with discussion groups; a few use chiefly the small informal-discussion group. One promising development is the use of faculty advisers for these small groups (13), an approach that is likely to coordinate group study and individual counseling in a way that has not been feasible with many of the larger class groups, except where the latter have been taught by counselors or personnel workers.

Hoffmann and Plutchik (14) have described an orientation program at Hofstra College carried on through small groups under the leadership of faculty members with the over-all objective of helping students to modify their attitudes in ways to become more understanding of and more receptive to all that the college has to offer. A few of their suggestions for conducting these discussion groups were considered in Chapter 5. Lloyd-Jones has characterized this type of program as higher education in some of its more creative aspects (14, p. x).

Raines (15) has reported helping college freshmen identify many of their own personal-social problems through case conferences in which they analyzed possible causes of difficulties in case descriptions that involved problems believed to be common to the group and mapped out suggested solutions. This year-long program includes units on study and social skills, vocational planning, and life philosophy in addition to initial acquaintance with college.[5]

THE CONTENT OF ORIENTATION COURSES. In tracing the history of the orientation movement (see pages 37 to 39), it was noted that orientation courses had not changed much as to content during the past thirty years. Copeland (16, p. 113) found among 52 colleges in the Middle Atlantic region that at least 75 per cent of all the orientation programs included the following four topics: Study Habits, College Rules and Regulations, Extracurricular Activities, and College Citizenship. Fifty-six per cent of the colleges made provision for elective topics in their programs. Greene's report (17) of orientation programs in 36 colleges in all parts of the country added to those already mentioned such topics as Sex, Marriage, and Courtship (11 per cent), Philosophy of Life or Christian Living (8 per cent). Personal Appearance and Social Etiquette were included in 19 per cent, but these questions might also have been embraced in the topic of Social Development reported in other studies.

The question of whether these traditional areas of study in orientation courses are meeting present-day needs of students depends in large degree, of course, upon how the topics are treated. All of them relate to some of the problems of college students reported in Chapter 3 (see pages 62 to 72), but apparently many colleges are not providing opportunities for guidance through their group orientation programs with respect to a good many of the problems on which students have expressed desire for assistance. It would seem highly desirable for colleges to re-examine their orientation programs frequently in the light of the many surveys of student needs and problems to ascertain how these programs might be made more responsive to student concerns. Other valuable techniques are those of securing suggestions regularly from each succeeding group of students as to their pressing concerns and of having student representatives on committees for continuous re-examination of desirable changes in the content and methods of the orientation program. Copeland (16) found that faculty members were not represented in the planning of the program in many institutions where this function was primarily a responsibility of the administration. With faculty advisers performing some of the guidance functions in so many colleges, it would seem highly desirable for them to participate in the planning of this important aspect of student guidance together with administrators, counselors or personnel workers, and students. Representatives of nonadvisory faculty members might also prove a leavening influence in teaching in various subject fields. The value of this college-

[5] Appalachian State Teachers College, Boone, N.C.

wide participation is felt not only in the orientation course but throughout the faculty and the student body.

The content of a specific orientation course will depend in part on what other opportunities are available in the institution for student guidance with respect to their personal problems of adjustment and of educational and vocational planning. If provision is made elsewhere— say, in a broad general-education program—for vocational guidance and the study of personality and physical and mental hygiene, the orientation course may be more limited in scope than if it carries the whole burden of group approaches to learning in all these areas. Also, concerns regarding placement and orientation in occupational life, and marriage and the establishment of a home, are more pressing for most upperclassmen than for freshmen, though personal qualities, educational preparation, and social experience gained throughout college years are vitally important for these later adjustments and should certainly be anticipated early enough in the college career to do something about them. Problems of vocational choice, educational planning, dating and social activities, health, and success in college work will, of course, be the more immediate concerns of freshmen.

Orientation for Foreign Students. The orientation of a student from one culture to an educational institution in a different culture presents special problems that call for a special type of guidance service. In addition to probable language handicaps are problems arising out of cultural differences in the purposes of education, differences in educational practices, and in mutual difficulties of faculty member and foreign student in understanding each other's motives, value standards, and differences in perception that stem from differences in cultural background. Moore (18) has illustrated cultural differences in educational values by comparing the Japanese idea of education as training to fit one for his established niche in society (19) or the Indian idea of education as the means by which man understands his own nature and his relationship to other beings and to the universe (20) with the emphasis in the United States upon the development of talents of all levels and of educated men who can put their "skill to work to provide for the welfare of all." He has summarized the problem of the orientation of foreign students as requiring (*a*) an understanding of American education, (*b*) the understanding of the goals and functions of education in other societies, and (*c*) the ability to make meaningful comparisons that explain likenesses and differences in such a way as to make the information useful. He adds:

It seems clear that those who plan and execute orientation programs are engaged in the process of acculturation and that the real test of the skillfulness of their work is the extent to which faculty member and student come to appreciate differences and likenesses in human culture and adapt teaching, learning, and personal relationships to a mutual appreciation of them.

Kiel (21) has outlined the many types of orientation and adjustment problems faced by students from other countries with their widely differing cultural patterns, has described the services of orientation centers established under the auspices of the U.S. Department of State and various universities, and pointed out the many mutual advantages in the international exchange of students. International clubs, with membership including United States students, and special faculty advisers for groups of foreign students are valuable aids in the acculturation process.

Orientation Services for Admission to Professional Schools and for Imminent Life Adjustments. Increasingly services are provided for upperclassmen in colleges to study requirements for admission to professional schools and the nature of offerings in these schools, and to appraise their suitability for the type of training contemplated. Some colleges also offer courses at the junior or senior level related to imminent problems of life adjustment such as vocation and marriage.

Orientation at the adult level

Very little has been done until quite recently in the nature of group preinduction in adult education programs. Bulletins, radio and television programs, and local newspaper announcements offer information about training opportunities. Some institutions have prepared movies depicting offerings and provide counseling services for the choice of subjects. Many adults who enter community colleges or university extension courses face wide gaps between present and previous work and need reorientation services to help them reformulate their educational goals and review and resharpen their learning techniques. Also, orientation is a needed service in every course with respect to its purposes, values, and specific learning techniques.

Recognition of this need is evidenced in a 1961 bulletin of the California State Department of Education describing orientation, counseling, testing, and group-guidance services for adults (22). Logie, who contributed to this publication, and her co-workers initiated a group-guidance service at the Marina Evening High School in San Francisco in 1949 to provide educational and vocational guidance (22, pp. 70–74). Since 1959 the adult counseling service in the San Francisco program has included orientation classes dealing with school adjustment, study methods and use of the library, conferences, assemblies, student-body organization, school activities, and also group guidance and counseling for older adults.

Important learnings through orientation

To avoid repetition this discussion will include possibilities for high school, college, and adult years. Many of the desired learnings are similar but on different maturity levels and in different situations. A few comments will be made about some of the more obvious immediate orientation tasks, but considerations about *learning to learn* will be dealt with in the next chapter, and those about personality and interpersonal relationships and vocational and educational planning in Chapters 10 through 15.

1. Learning about school or college facilities and the community. On the surface this would seem like a fairly simple task. However, understanding and appreciation of all the possibilities for cultural development and occupational training within either a high school or college and the surrounding community are not easily achieved.

2. Learning how to use available services and resources within the professional personnel of the institution. Ways of using health, financial, guidance, placement, and library services should be thoroughly understood by every student. Opportunities to meet representatives of these services and learn about best procedures for utilizing them is one very specific aspect of orientation. Tours of offices and movies showing services in action can be used as helpful supplementary devices. Possibilities for phases of vocational guidance through the entire faculty are sometimes overlooked. A survey of the occupational experiences of faculty members is often very revealing, even to the administration, especially since so many opportunities for service outside of education have opened up.

3. Getting acquainted widely in the student body, making new friends, and learning to work and play with both sexes. Some individuals need much more learning than others to achieve these goals. Skill in conversation, dancing, and all the various social amenities may affect success in this area, together with personal appearance, poise, self-confidence, and tact. The etiquette of dating is a sure-fire topic of deep interest and one in which adolescents need to exchange views and build up standards.

4. Learning more about self as one basis for making choices and plans and for continued sound self-appraisal.

5. Learning about the purposes and values of curricular offerings and how to choose subjects wisely.

6. Learning about the values and opportunities in extracurricular offerings and how to choose them wisely and enter them.

7. Learning more about the world of work as one basis for the formulation of long-range plans in harmony with interests and abilities.

8. Learning how to study and learn effectively and to evaluate progress.

9. Learning how to participate effectively as a citizen in the institution, through good leadership, followership, and democratic social interaction.

10. Learning how to grow up and achieve desirable self-dependence, dependability, and social sensitivity.

11. Learning self-direction in all aspects of living.

12. Developing a set of values as criteria for choices and life adjustments.

Doubtless this list could be expanded still more, but enough points have been listed to emphasize the fact that orientation should not be a superficial service to be dispensed through a few lectures.

Suitable methods for orientation

In general terms the answer to this question lies in an analysis of learnings to be fostered and the consideration of the conditions under which the learnings can best be achieved. In an actual school or college setting, one of the questions that usually predominates is, "What funds and what personnel are available to do the job?" These factors, coupled with large enrollments, especially at the college level, are partial keys to the widespread use of lectures for much of the orientation work. Opinions of both faculty and students are tending strongly toward the greater value of small discussion groups, and many of the lecture plans are combined with opportunities for discussion. Enthusiastic reports of the values of the very small counseling groups of ten or fifteen members and the growing number of plans for the improved training of faculty advisers to do more than help students make study programs are indications of a new and valuable development in college personnel services. This same trend is seen in secondary schools in the growth of block-time programs with teacher-counselors. Professional study and cooperative planning with trained personnel workers would seem essential if this trend leads to a sound guidance service.

Special clinic, laboratory, or enabling groups

Recognition of the great variety of needs of individual students for making successful adjustments in college has led to the establishment of many specific services that could provide the particular assistance that was indicated. Examples of clinic services can be cited from the program at Stephens College, Missouri, where students can secure personal assistance in such areas as reading, personal appearance, clothing, posture, health, English usage, speech, vocational guidance, personal finance, or religion. Early in the development of the General College at the University of Minnesota, laboratories were inaugurated where a student could receive special help on any phase of his work, on vocational guidance or other personal problems. Such types of special groups have become a part of student services in many institutions. Opportunities for group study of personal problems range from informal-discussion groups in dormitories or housing units under the guidance of a leader to group therapy for serious maladjustments carried on by psychiatrists and clinical psychologists in the health service or the personnel department in some colleges and universities. Enabling courses have been established in some universities to assist students in developmental reading, in a variety of educational, vocational, and personal problems, and in social and leadership techniques (13, p. 58). Some schools within universities provide subject-orientation courses to aid students in selecting a subject field for specialization.

Evaluation of orientation programs

No comprehensive research investigation of the outcomes of orientation is at present available for current programs. In 1942 Nelson (23) reported the results of his evaluation of the effectiveness of orientation at fourteen colleges. With few exceptions he found that students in colleges with well-organized orientation programs made on the average better scores than did students in colleges without orientation courses on tests which he had designed to measure knowledge and attitudes in the areas of library usage, college study, the student's college, student citizenship, personality and health, vocational choice, worthy home membership, and religion in college.

An earlier evaluation by the author (24) of an orientation course for eleventh-year and thirteenth-year students at a four-year junior college, using control groups with no orientation to compare with the experimental orientation groups was reported in Chapter 1 (see pages 16 and 17).

A comprehensive evaluation of the general-education program of the General College, University of Minnesota, reported by Eckert (25) has bearings on orientation because of the guidance objectives inherent in the program. Tests keyed to the program, student judgments, evidences of students' adjustments, and a follow-up of students beyond the college years pointed to gains in understandings fundamental to good personal, sociocivic, and vocational orientation and adjustment, and to marked changes in the direction of more appropriate and realistic vocational ambitions for those students who had taken advantage of both instruction and counseling for vocational guidance.[6] Some gains were noted in social adjustments and in health attitudes, and about half of the former students acknowledged help from the General College in dealing with

[6] A study by Harold Stone of the vocational-guidance program is reported in Chap. 1 (see p. 16).

personal problems. Because of evidence of the relative stability of many attitudes and traits, despite teaching and counseling efforts, the author of this report propounded the question significant for all educators: "What dynamics of action are not yet touched by even a highly progressive educational program which has made notable strides in selling itself to its consumers?"

Arbuckle (26) reported an investigation to compare directive and nondirective techniques in a course in personal adjustment at the School of Education, Boston University, using hypothetical case studies as a basis for discussion in small groups of ten each. Checks on adjustment before and after the course by two adjustment inventories yielded superior gains for the students in the nondirective group.

Copeland (16) gathered some data on the evaluation of orientation courses in 1953 through his doctoral study. He reported that almost all the colleges included in his survey conducted an evaluation of some kind and 86 per cent of these evaluations involved more than one person or group. Few of these were available in written reports. Only 40 per cent of the colleges included the freshmen themselves in the evaluation process. During a five-year period the attitudes of the freshmen toward the program were reported to have remained the same (in 34 per cent of the colleges) or to have improved (in 47 per cent). Copeland suggests as a result of his study that the students should be brought into active cooperation in the planning of the program together with the administration and the total faculty through a committee of representatives from all three groups with the dean of students as chairman; that small group meetings be used insofar as possible; and that upperclassmen be assigned to each group to assist the leader.

During a period when the author was working with such a committee as is suggested by Copeland, in the development of a college-orientation course, the percentage of students who checked on unsigned questionnaires that they would recommend it as a required course for all freshmen rose from approximately 50 per cent to 95 per cent. This percentage dropped rapidly when a gap occurred in student participation in the planning of the work.

A recent overview of improvements needed in Orientation Week included the suggestions to get the whole campus—all the campus offices, student leaders, and faculty—into the work and spirit of Orientation Week, to provide a more adequate instruction and training program for student and faculty leaders in the program, and to restate aims and review all projects to meet the revised aims (27). A similar procedure would doubtless be helpful for the entire orientation program.

Mennes (28) secured the following order of value ratings by high school students on various aspects of a continuing program of orientation carried on before and after school entry: (1) student handbook, (2) orientation unit in social studies, (3) help from students through the student council, (4) special assemblies, (5) group guidance, (6) help from teachers, (7) individual conferences with counselor.

Lindeman (29) concluded on the basis of questionnaire responses from 37 colleges in the Middle West having orientation programs that the trend was toward distributing the orientation services over a longer period than a few days at the beginning of a school year and toward becoming a more vital adjunct of the guidance program, with increasing cooperation of the entire faculty. Also he concluded that there was evidence that a properly organized and administered plan has tremendous values for new students, though much remains to be done to achieve an ideal service.

Froe and Lee (30) found significant gains for college students on reading and study skill tests following a two-week orientation program in which 65 groups of seven students each met with faculty members to consider their test profile sheets, study techniques, use of the library, and selection of courses.[7] Ford (31) and Wall (32) have made tentative reports of evaluations being conducted at The Pennsylvania State University of the preregistration counseling program for entering freshmen students and their parents from May to September each year. This program includes lectures, interviews, and informal discussions of test data, educational and vocational planning, and the varied phases of university life, utilizing a larger number of the university staff members, including counselors and deans. In the beginning the program was limited chiefly to interviews, but after group methods were introduced it was estimated that 1,200 man-hours of work were saved in one summer and the quality of the service was improved, partly as a result of better use of the shortened interview time because of the preparation given in the group sessions. One evidence of the influence of the program was the fact that approximately 20 per cent of the students counseled in one summer made curriculum changes following the service and others canceled their admissions on the advice of counselors. Questionnaires administered to parents before and after participation in the program indicated the development of more realistic attitudes toward university standards of achievement and toward their expectations for their children, more accurate appraisal of their children's vocational interests, and favorable reactions to all aspects of the preregistration program.

Tautfest (33) has reported as an evaluation technique for orientation programs a survey of the interests in orientation topics of a sample of high school seniors who were prospective Purdue University freshmen. Five topics received high ranks by 60 to 89 per cent of the respondents:

[7] Morgan State College, Baltimore.

academic responsibilities and study habits; academic program planning; familiarization with the campus; extracurricular activities, student organization, and intramural sports; and handling finances in college. As a result of the findings more emphasis was given to academic and intellectual areas of college life in the orientation program. Also, consideration was given to the question of how other topics of proved value could be made more vital in ways to elicit student interest.

REFERENCES CITED IN CHAPTER

1. Froehlich, Clifford P.: "An Investigation of Precounseling Orientation," *The Vocational Guidance Quarterly*, 4:103–104, spring, 1956.
2. Brammer, Lawrence, and Everett L. Shostrom: *Therapeutic Psychology; Fundamentals of Counseling and Psychotherapy*, Prentice-Hall, Inc., Englewood Cliffs, N.J., 1960, pp. 126–127.
3. Martin, Francis: "Mobility," *Childhood Education*, 3:25–28, September, 1957.
4. FitzPatrick, R. E., and E. E. Plattor: "The Role of a Comprehensive Program of Orientation in a New School District," *Bulletin of the National Association of Secondary-school Principals*, 42:154–161, November, 1958.
5. Nielsen, Lloyd: "Ninth Grade Orientation and Programming," *Bulletin of the National Association of Secondary-school Principals*, 42:149–151, November, 1958.
6. Blecha, Edward J.: "Preble's Freshmen Orientation Program," *Bulletin of the National Association of Secondary-school Principals*, 45:129–132, May, 1961.
7. Ellis, U. Berkeley: "Ninth Grade Orientation for Senior High School," *Bulletin of the National Association of Secondary-school Principals*, 45:133–136, May, 1961.
8. Riccio, Anthony C., and Joseph H. Maguire: "Interdependence of Guidance Services at the Various Levels," *Bulletin of the National Association of Secondary-school Principals*, 45:136–142, May, 1961.
9. Johnson, Mauritz J., William E. Busaker, and Fred Q. Bowman: *Junior High School Guidance*, Harper & Row, Publishers, New York, 1961, pp. 44–64.
10. Forrester, Gertrude: "How to Run a College Day," *Occupations, The Vocational Guidance Journal*, 27:373–380, March, 1949.
11. McCracken, Charles W., William P. Wharton, and Gretchen Graff: "The Precollege Clinic Week," *The Personnel and Guidance Journal*, 34:437–440, March, 1956.
12. Trumpe, Richard M., and Lee E. Isaacson: "The Student Handbook, a Bridge to Better Understanding," *The Vocational Guidance Quarterly*, 7:231–235, summer, 1959.
13. Grier, Daniel J.: "The New Student Arrives at College," in Esther Lloyd-Jones and Margaret Ruth Smith (eds.), *Student Personnel Work as Deeper Teaching*, Harper & Row, Publishers, New York, 1954, pp. 46–61.
14. Hoffmann, Randall W., and Robert Plutchik: *Small-group Discussion in Orientation and Teaching*, G. P. Putnam's Sons, New York, 1959.
15. Raines, Max R.: "Informal Observations in Guidance: Helping College Freshmen Identify Problems through a Case Conference," *The Personnel and Guidance Journal*, 34:417–419, March, 1956.
16. Copeland, Theodore H., Jr.: "Freshman Orientation Programs: A Study of Their Development and Present Status with Special Reference to Middle Atlantic Colleges," unpublished doctoral dissertation, Temple University, Philadelphia, 1953.
17. Greene, George H.: *A Study of the Freshman Orientation Course in Small Colleges*, Florida A. & M. College, Tallahassee, Fla., 1953. (Mimeographed.)
18. Moore, Forrest C.: *Some Ideas on Orientation and Cultural Relativism: Implications for Orientation Programs*, paper presented at the 1961 American Personnel and Guidance Association Convention, Denver, Colo. (Mimeographed.)

19. Buchanan, Daniel C.: "Japanese Character and Personality as Revealed in Their Culture," in William A. Parker (ed.), *Understanding Other Cultures*, American Council of Learned Societies, Washington, 1954, pp. 67–70.

20. Atreya, B. L.: "Indian Culture," in C. C. Berg et al. (eds.), *Interrelations of Cultures*, UNESCO, Paris, 1953.

21. Kiel, Norman: "Learning with Students from Other Lands," in Esther Lloyd-Jones and Margaret Ruth Smith (eds.), *Student Personnel Work as Deeper Teaching*, Harper & Row, Publishers, New York, 1954, pp. 199–214.

22. De Gabriel, Eugene M.: "Guidance Services for Adults," *Bulletin of the California State Department of Education*, vol. 30, no. 7, Sacramento, Calif., August, 1961.

23. Nelson, Erland: "The Effectiveness of Freshman Orientation at Fourteen Colleges," *School and Society*, 55:138–139, Jan. 31, 1942.

24. Bennett, Margaret E.: "An Evaluation of an Orientation or Group Guidance Program in a Four-year Junior College," *Abstracts of Dissertations*, Stanford University, Stanford, Calif., 1937–1938, pp. 121–128.

25. Eckert, Ruth E.: *Outcomes of General Education: An Appraisal of the General Education Program*, University of Minnesota Press, Minneapolis, 1943.

26. Arbuckle, Dugald S.: "College Experiment in Orientation," *Occupations, The Vocational Guidance Journal*, 28:112–117, November, 1949.

27. Guthrie, William S.: "Orientation Week: Results Obtained and/or Improvements Needed," *Educational and Psychological Measurement*, 11:715–717, winter, 1951.

28. Mennes, Arthur: "Orientation of New Students to High School," *The School Review*, 44:64–66, February, 1956.

29. Lindeman, W. W.: "Trends in College Freshman Orientation," *Educational Forum*, 21:63–65, 1956–1957.

30. Froe, Otis D., and Maurice A. Lee: "A New Emphasis in Freshman Orientation," *The Personnel and Guidance Journal*, 34:360–365, February, 1956.

31. Ford, Donald H.: *Changing Individual Behavior through Group Counseling*, presented at the National Meeting of the American Personnel and Guidance Association in Philadelphia, Apr. 11, 1960. (Mimeographed.)

32. Wall, Harvey W.: *Counseling Students by Counseling Parents*, presented at the National Meeting of the American Personnel and Guidance Association in Philadelphia, Apr. 11, 1960. (Mimeographed.)

33. Tautfest, Patricia B.: "An Evaluation Technique for Orientation Programs," *The Journal of College Student Personnel*, 3:25–28, 32, October, 1961.

ADDITIONAL REFERENCES

References for students

Bennett, Margaret E.: *College and Life: Problems of Self-discovery and Self-direction*, 4th ed., McGraw-Hill Book Company, Inc., New York, 1952.

Bennett, Margaret E., and Molly Lewin: *Getting the Most Out of College*, McGraw-Hill Book Company, Inc., New York, 1957.

Chandler, John Roscoe, et al.: *Successful Adjustment in College*, 2d ed., Prentice-Hall, Inc., Englewood Cliffs, N.J., 1958.

Cieslak, Edward C.: *The Foreign Student in American Colleges*, Wayne University Press, Detroit, 1955.

Daane, Calvin J., et al.: *Introduction to College*, Allyn and Bacon, Inc., Englewood Cliffs, N.J., 1958.

Detjen, Mary Ford, and Ervin Winfred Detjen: *Your High School Days*, 2d ed., McGraw-Hill Book Company, Inc., New York, 1958.

Fisher, Margaret Barrow, and Jeanne L. Noble: *College Education as Personal Development*, Prentice-Hall, Inc., Englewood Cliffs, N.J., 1960.

Landis, Paul H.: *So This Is College*, McGraw-Hill Book Company, Inc., New York, 1954.

Riley, Clara M.: *Getting the Most Out of College: A Guidebook,* based on the text, *Getting the Most Out of College,* by Margaret E. Bennett, William C. Brown Company, Publishers, Dubuque, Iowa, 1960.

Robinson, Clark: *Making the Most of School and Life,* The Macmillan Company, New York, 1955.

Sifferd, Calvin S.: *College and You,* McKnight & McKnight Publishing Company, Bloomington, Ill., 1952.

Townsend, Agatha: *College Freshmen Speak Out,* Harper & Row, Publishers, New York, 1956.

Traxler, Arthur E., and Agatha Townsend (eds.): *Improving Transition from School to College: How Can Schools and Colleges Best Cooperate?* Harper & Row, Publishers, New York, 1953.

Voeks, Virginia: *On Becoming an Educated Person,* W. B. Saunders Company, Philadelphia, 1957.

Weigand, George, and Walter S. Blake, Jr.: *College Orientation: A Study Skills Manual,* Prentice-Hall, Inc., Englewood Cliffs, N.J., 1955.

Additional references are included in a list of group-guidance materials for students in the bibliographies for Chapter 12.

9 LEARNING TO LEARN

When we think of learning as a technique to be used throughout life, it becomes broader in scope than learning to study in school. As the curriculum becomes more functional in the sense of learning about life and providing more opportunities for full and fine living at each successive maturity level, methods of learning in school and out of school may become more similar, though for the majority of individuals there is likely always to be more concentrated study in school than in later years. Study and learning are one's major occupation in school, comparable to one's vocational work in adult life.

The challenge of helping individuals see the pertinence of learning methods in school for learning and adjustment throughout life is likely to broaden and deepen the perspective of any teacher or counselor with respect to educational and guidance services. Learning must thus be seen not only as the acquisition of skills, knowledge, attitudes, and values, but as a whole way of life, which involves ever-increasing power in the control and direction of inner and outer forces.

So many textbooks and guides on how to study are available that it seems unnecessary to consider here the tremendous variety of approaches to problems that may be included in units, classes, or laboratories for the purpose of improving study and learning.

Suggestions will be limited primarily to areas of controversial practices, to some of the newer approaches, and to reiteration of a few fundamental principles.

How Well Are We Meeting This Need?

Studies of the problems of individuals at various age levels have shown that the educational program does not always give adequate emphasis to the development of power in learning to learn. In surveys at both the high school and college levels, students invariably list aspects of how to study among their major problems or worries. At all levels, counselors or psychologists have discovered learning difficulties among the causes of maladjustment for many individuals who require special assistance. The psychiatrist at Yale University reported that one-half of the freshmen with whom he had consulted were emotionally concerned over scholastic difficulties and that the majority of these students had never learned to study systematically (1). Similar findings are reported widely in the literature that is concerned with the needs and problems of students.

The desire so widely expressed by high school and college students for assistance in how to study provokes many questions. If this were chiefly a recent phenomenon, one would be tempted to ask whether the present chaotic state of our theory regarding the nature of learning might not be reflected in teaching and hence in confusion on the part of students concerning learning methods. Increased enrollments at the secondary and college levels are suggestive of other reasons for this demand, especially to the extent that teaching methods and curriculum content have not been adapted to the learning needs of the heterogeneous student population. It is always easy to ask whether an earlier school level has performed its task sufficiently well in preparing students to succeed at the next higher level. And perhaps the most challenging question of all is whether this insistent interest in learning how to learn better is not the natural result of the desire to succeed in one's work— meaning for students scholastic success and preparation for occupation and the kind of living made possible by vocational success. Can we add here real, intrinsic interest in learning for learning's sake as well as for living, at least for some individuals?

The role of guidance is twofold in this learning-to-learn process: first, to help individuals to enter into learning situations free of emotional and attitudinal obstacles to optimum progress; and second, to provide needed services to pupils, teachers, and parents that may facilitate the process. Guidance services directed toward the elimination of emotional blocks to learning are required for some pupils before effective work can be done in helping them to develop intrinsic motivation for study and to understand and apply sound principles of learning.

Wellington (2) has illustrated the first role of guidance vividly in the story of a little second-grade boy who persisted in spending his time lying on the floor staring at the ceiling. Before it was decided to place him in a slow-learning group, a counselor discovered that he was a highly gifted but bored youngster who was visualizing math problems and stellar constellations on the ceiling! Students may be helped through group guidance as well as individual study to discover and overcome emotional handicaps as well as to find real purposes for study and acquire increased mastery of learning techniques.

How Does One Learn to Learn?

A generalized answer to this question is very easy to give. Presumably it involves the application of principles of learning in situations in which one is supposed to be learning. However, principles should be deduced from knowledge about the nature of the learning process, and our theories of learning are undergoing much controversy among psychologists who are engaged in experimental research on learning. There are various schools of thought. Some interpret all learning as the result of a stimulus-response mechanism which becomes enormously complicated as it is manifested in most types of human behavior. Others posit more than one type of process, and view learning as the result of a complicated interaction of the personality and the environment in which insight into certain relationships may produce learning which is not necessarily accounted for by any recognizable stimulus-response pattern. The fact that insight into certain relationships in a learning situation appears often to result in rapid progress, rather than the slower increments of improvement that appear with practice of a skill, is one type of evidence that various processes may be occurring during learning. The questions of effect in learning and of latent learning are two crucial aspects of the present controversy.

Despite gaps in our knowledge, educators and guidance workers are faced with very practical and urgent demands to help individuals to improve their learning techniques, and hence must carry on their services on the basis of the most plausible hypotheses in view of available research and experience. We shall review a few of these hypotheses briefly.

All characteristically human behavior is learned

Dollard and Miller (3, p. 25), who have constructed a theory of learning to be applied in psychotherapy, state: "The field of human learning covers phenomena which range all the way from the simple, almost reflex learning of a child to avoid a hot radiator to the complex processes of insight by which a scientist constructs a theory." They posit four fundamental interrelated factors in learning: drive, response, cue, and reinforcement. They summarize the relationships of these factors as follows (3, p. 29–30): [1]

The drive implies responses, which are usually also determined by cues from other stimuli not strong enough to act as drives but more specifically distinctive than the drive. If the first response is not rewarded by an event reducing

[1] Reprinted from John Dollard and Neal E. Miller, *Personality and Psychotherapy: An Analysis in Terms of Learning, Thinking, and Culture,* 1950, by permission of the McGraw-Hill Book Company, Inc., New York.

the drive, this response tends to drop out and others to appear. The extinction of successive non-rewarding responses produces so-called random behavior. If some one response is followed by reward, the connection between the cue and this response is strengthened, so that the next time that the same drive and other cues are present, this response is more likely to occur. This strengthening of the cue-response connection is the essence of learning.

The concept of all *human* behavior as being learned carries the learning process far beyond what we can observe as occurring in any educational situation. We know that the individual, when we receive him in school, is the resultant of much unintentional or "unconscious" learning as well as intentional. Often we tend to overlook some of this unintentional learning, which continues to occur throughout the period of schooling and which, together with early preschool learning, may profoundly affect the total learning process.

The psychiatrist Lawrence S. Kubie has called to the attention of educators that the Latin word curriculum had as one meaning a two-wheeled open carriage drawn by two horses abreast. He compares the two horses to the head and the heart and stresses the need for keeping "emotional maturation" abreast of intellectual development in education (4). His clever figurative approach emphasizes the harnessing of emotional drives and interests of learners to any learning task or situation.

Incentives in the nature of interests and motivating purposes are vitally important in learning

No educator needs to be reminded of the importance of this principle. The problem here in group approaches is to plan ways of starting with the immediate interests and concerns of pupils about how to study, which appear to be very widespread and very real, of helping them to gain rewards for their purposeful efforts in improved achievement, and of guiding them toward a mastery of learning techniques adapted to their unique patterns of abilities that may become an integral part of self-direction of learning throughout life. Such a plan must reach beyond a How to Study course or unit to bring all their learning experience in the curriculum and extracurriculum into the picture. This means that all other phases of group guidance are involved and that an entire faculty must participate in planning and carrying out a learning-to-learn program.

Another requirement is the involvement of the total personality of the pupil, emotionally as well as intellectually, in the process. Kubie (4) has warned educators that expressed interests of individuals may be "an erratic and undependable compass," because conscious interests may be symbols of unconscious yearnings, hopes, fears, anger, and regrets—all interacting in a complex pattern. He cites as an illustration the apparently deep interest of a girl in all aspects of early Greek culture—until she learned that there were different cultural expectancies for men and women in that culture as in our own. Similarity of Greek dress for both sexes had presumably made the initial appeal because of her comparison of herself with her brother—meaning to the psychiatrist a manifestation of the unconscious sex-envy pattern. The interest in Greek culture disappeared abruptly.

One of the implications for learning to learn is that negative emotional factors in ineffectual methods of learning must be understood and brought under conscious control, and positive emotions enlisted in the development of improved techniques. This may carry the process of improvement far beyond any immediate study of learning habits into self-appraisal, as considered later. It may require counseling or special clinical help for individuals who have serious and persistent learning difficulties that do not appear to be related to ability, physical or health handicaps, or training deficiencies in specific skills such as reading or arithmetic.

A common study problem of students, particularly at the high school and college levels, is that of dealing with a wide variety of interests and drives to action. Conflicts in choosing how to spend time and the control of the timing of attention to various interests often present a greater problem than a specific study skill. Dollard and Miller (3, pp. 431–434) have proposed a theory for the control of neurotic conflicts that has valuable implications for academic learning. They suggest that the process of unconscious *repression,* which leads to so many emotional difficulties, must be replaced by a learned and conscious *suppression* of drives to action which are inappropriate or impossible of realization at a particular time and the substitution of the immediately possible or appropriate activities. They comment that this process can be learned like any other type of human behavior.

Efficiency methods can improve quality as well as quantity of learning

Efficiency methods cannot be summarized in a few simple rules. They vary somewhat with the type of learning and the characteristics of the learner. Students need assistance in discovering how best to adapt efficiency methods to themselves, and how to adapt them to each field of study and each type of learning.

Only a few examples of problems related to efficiency methods will be mentioned here, since these are the tools of every educator's profession:

1. How to arrange environmental conditions for study that will elim-

inate undesirable distractions, provide optimum illumination and atmospheric conditions, conserve time through suitable study materials, and foster physical and mental fitness

2. How to utilize motivation and attitudes to serve the learning process through clear-cut purposes and directed interests

3. How to plan and budget study time to the best advantage to avoid fatigue and the effects of retroactive inhibition due to interference of similar types of learning

4. How to use spaced repetition and whole or part methods in skill learning and memorizing

5. How to use meaningful relationships of facts or concepts and the values of insight to the fullest advantage

6. How to improve efficiency in reading

7. How to improve the quality of one's thinking

8. How to make good notes as a basis for review and continuity in learning

9. How to prepare for and take examinations

10. How to evaluate progress

11. How to use library and other learning facilities

12. How to make learning more meaningful and permanent through its continuous use in applications in living

APPROACHES TO THE TEACHING OF LEARNING TECHNIQUES

There has been much controversy regarding the relative merits of providing assistance through special classes on how to study and learn and of handling the problem through each class or subject. Involved here, also, is the question of the relative merits of direct and indirect approaches to improvement in learning to learn. Evaluation of outcomes of How to Study programs have almost invariably revealed significant gains in reading and other learning techniques as a result of direct approaches. Wide differences in individual gains, and variations in the results for different subject fields, present questions for careful study in attempting to determine the best approach to the problem.

The question of special How to Study classes versus the learning of study techniques in each subject has many facets. It would seem incontrovertible that some skills and thought processes could best be learned through manipulation of subject content under the guidance of a teacher specially trained in the particular field. However, the teacher trained in the specific subject is not always trained in the learning techniques in his field. Nor is he always proficient in the over-all psychology of learning and in the understanding of individual difficulties in learning. The ideal situation might well be for the subject teacher and the special How to Study teacher to supplement each other, with the special teacher proficient in over-all techniques of efficient learning and in clinical methods of studying individual learning problems.

The clinical study of individuals with learning difficulties has convinced the author that few subject teachers can be expected to discover all the serious mental and emotional handicaps of learners and develop remedial programs within the regular classroom situation. The judgment will be hazarded, however, that if more direct attention were given, both in regular and special classes, throughout the period of schooling to training in all the various techniques of learning, there would be a tremendous reduction in the number of learners who develop learning handicaps and therefore require clinical study and remedial assistance.

If better methods of learning are among our major objectives in education, it would seem that one step toward our goal would be to enlist the active cooperation of the learner. On the other hand, any good teacher knows that many subtle aspects of learning do, and perhaps must, occur spontaneously and without conscious effort. The differentiation between these unconscious by-products and the consciously planned and self-directed learnings combines high degrees of science and art on the part of the educator.

The answer, then, to the question of whether our approaches to learning techniques should be direct or indirect—whether they should be carried on in every class or subject or in special classes—is probably "Both." Research and experience do not yet define clearly and explicitly the boundaries of each approach, and each teacher must, to some extent, shape her own approach in terms of specific circumstances.

Grade placement of direct approaches to learning techniques

As with self-appraisal methods, the *direct approach* is more frequently made at the high school or college level than in elementary school. However, even at the elementary school level there are teachable moments when the direct approach is both suitable and effective. Most of these occur when new techniques in reading, arithmetic, spelling, or any of the skill subjects are required, when snags or plateaus in progress are encountered by any group within a class, when "research" or other new study technique is needed, when new social, play, or athletic skills are being acquired, or when some problem of group relationships develops which requires new understandings, attitudes, and behavior.

Most elementary teachers will feel that they do all this, perhaps incidentally and informally, as a part of the day's work. The crucial question is how much careful planning and direct, though perhaps informal and permissive, discussion with pupils are necessary to develop the insights and attitudes which will carry over into new adjustments when similar but new problems arise.

During many visits to modern elementary classrooms to observe individual pupils who have been referred for special study, the author has often wondered why more temporary groups have not been formed to assist pupils encountering similar problems of learning in reading, arithmetic, or other skills. It was recalled that many years ago groups of elementary school pupils sometimes asked to stay in at recess time to secure drill on arithmetic processes. This may have an unnatural sound to present-day elementary teachers, but do we sometimes forget, in our desirably rich and varied modern programs, the satisfaction that comes to young learners from a sense of mastery of a simple but important skill? This is no appeal to return to meaningless drill, but merely a comment on the basic need for a sense of achievement in purposeful tasks.

Still another aspect of the learning problem at the elementary school level is the extent to which all pupils reach their best levels of achievement in relation to ability. For example, pupils from all reading groups in a primary class with similar problems could be grouped together temporarily to study how to improve a specific aspect of reading. Such temporary groups would be comparable to some How to Study classes at higher levels. Frequently a brilliant student is encountered at the college level who could have profited immensely from such special assistance in learning techniques at a very early age, and who has been continually handicapped by a specific disability that need never have dogged his footsteps over many years. Time, energy, a balanced sense of values, and almost superhuman resourcefulness on the part of elementary school teachers are a few of the requirements to grapple with all these problems of individual learners.[2]

At the junior and senior high school levels, the direct approaches to improvement in study or learning methods are frequently concentrated in core, general-education, social-studies, or English classes, homerooms, or special group-guidance or orientation classes. No recent surveys are available showing the exact placement and extent of offerings in How to Study or learning techniques. The trend over many years has been to offer assistance of this type at points where pupils enter a new school level, or where new or improved study techniques are especially important, such as in the beginning of a foreign language or other college-preparatory subject that may require certain scholarship standards. A

[2] It is not assumed, of course, that this attention to problems of learning techniques will solve all the problems of achievement in relation to ability. It is mentioned by itself here because this section deals with learning techniques, and because difficulties with specific learning techniques may prevent a bright pupil from taking advantage of opportunities for enriched experiences suited to his interests and abilities.

recent survey of school graduates in several California high schools revealed widespread recognition by the students who went on to college of difficulties in the transition to higher education. One of the most frequent suggestions of one group of graduates was for the teaching of good study habits. Another was for the use of more "college-type" instruction to prepare them for the transition (5).

At the college and university level, special assistance in how to study is most frequently offered at the freshman year as a part of orientation, as a special course, through lectures, or through a more individualized laboratory situation in which students may receive special help on special problems.

Principles of learning versus rules of study

Textbooks, manuals, and curriculum guides dealing with learning techniques can usually be grouped roughly according to one or the other of these approaches, though some combine both. The chief consideration here is which will be most useful in a wide variety of situations and in the development of individualized techniques. After experimenting with both approaches, the author's preference is for the approach through general principles of learning, which individuals can be helped to apply to various types of learning and to their own idiosyncrasies.

For some processes it is necessary, with the present incomplete state of our knowledge about learning, merely to present available research findings and guide the individual in experimenting to discover probable best methods of learning for him. For example, in the learning of vocabulary and rules of grammar in a language, there will be wide differences among individuals in the need for spaced repetition and the types of association, visual, auditory, or kinesthetic, that will prove most serviceable. Even in the fairly concrete aspect of environmental conditions for effective study, we find wide differences in individual reactions to noise, degree of relaxation or tension, and atmospheric conditions. Here, as in all phases of group guidance, adaptation of techniques to individual difference is of paramount importance.

Specific techniques

It would of course be impossible and even undesirable to attempt to list all the varieties of techniques that could be developed and used in a unit or course on How to Study. Numerous volumes on this subject are available. Here are a few suggested criteria for the selection of techniques.

1. They should be planned with a view to helping individuals to envisage the nature of the learning process as realistically as possible—to see what happens when we learn and under what conditions.

Several good films depicting animal or human learning are available for these purposes (see Appendix). Reports on or actual demonstrations of the teaching of tricks to pets are sure to arouse interest and emphasize important aspects of learning, such as conditioning and motivation.

2. Learning through actual use of study and learning processes is more effective than merely studying about how to learn.

The entire educational program, including home study, provides an immense laboratory for firsthand experiences in this area. There should be no need for artificial projects and exercises. One of the chief problems in planning the work is that of keeping a balance between the isolation for study of specific techniques such as reading, note taking, remembering, etc., and the approach to the total learning process in action. Analysis of specific processes is essential to understanding and to self-appraisal of learning strengths and weaknesses, but practice and evaluation of the synthesized process in actual work is also important for improved habits of study and learning.

Daily assignments, class and laboratory activities, individual and group reports, term papers, preparation for and taking of examinations; practice of manual and motor activities of various sorts in music, art, crafts, athletics, typing, shop, or home-economics work; club, social, or assembly activities can all be brought under scrutiny analytically and tried out in actual performance. Role-playing within the How to Study group is frequently valuable where experimentation in the real performance may be unsuitable. But with the understanding and cooperation of all teachers, valuable tryout experience may be secured in real rather than artificial practice situations.

3. Individual students should have guidance at each step in applying all learnings to their own problems of study so that they can understand how to adapt these principles and techniques to their own unique learning potentialities.

Varieties of check lists, charts, and work guides are valuable in this assistance to individuals. Experimentation with various learning and study methods is both interesting and helpful in enabling individuals to discover and plan their own best techniques. Among such experiments could be testing of time budgets with specific allocations of study periods for various subjects, best methods of association for effective remembering, optimum spacing of drill, environmental conditions for study, prevention and control of fatigue. All such projects have many ramifications in the psychology of learning. For some we do not have conclusive evidence in experimental research as to best practices for individuals, and each individual must be helped to discover which of several methods are best for particular purposes.

Learning to think soundly, critically, and creatively

Through the Purdue Opinion Panel, Remmers (6) found that his wide sampling of American teen-agers did not seem to be particularly independent or individualistic in their patterns of decision making. While evidencing the normal adolescent drive for independence, large percentages of the group revealed dependence upon adults and their peers for the formulation of their opinions on a variety of personal, social, economic, and political issues and for decisions as to conduct. Remmers and others such as Reisman and Whyte (7, 8) point up the urgent need in a democratic free society for the development in its citizens of the desire and the ability to weigh issues, recognize propaganda, and think critically and independently rather than being "other-directed." Added to this necessity for citizens in a democracy is the requirement in a technological world for a creative, problem-solving technique that will enable each person to face up to ever-changing situations, analyze them clearly and critically, and work out ever-new adjustments between inner and outer forces that may promote both individual and social welfare.

The word *creative* is used here in its newer sense of describing a potentiality in all individuals. What is new in the idea of creativity is the recognition, resulting from research in the life sciences, that personality development is a creative process that can and must be nurtured through education in a free society if that society is to maintain itself (9). Creativity as used here in connection with thinking, problem solving, and decision making connotes, not some new or unusual product, but a process that involves seeing new relationships among recognized aspects of shifting, changing situations and thereby gaining new insights, new meanings, about self, others, and life. This can occur on a very simple level with a child in the elementary school or on progressively more complex levels through adolescence and adulthood. This ability has been characterized as the most important outcome of education in a democratic society (10).

The thinking process has been subjected to experimental study for many years, but psychologists admit that we still know all too little about it, though great advances have been made. The subjective and complex nature of the process makes it difficult to study. However, experimentation has provided many suggestions as to how various types of thinking can be fostered through planned group processes.

Critical Thinking. Glaser (11) carried on a ten-week experiment in teaching high school students some of the essentials in logic and the psychology of thinking with practice in the recognition of errors and critical evaluation of newspaper articles (12, p. 497). Results on the Watson-Glaser Tests of Critical Thinking yielded significant gains for the experimental over the control group. One conclusion was that while no subject can be depended upon by itself, as ordinarily taught, to improve thinking, any subject or project can be so taught as to help pupils to guard against bias and hasty or uncritical generalizations.

Creative Thinking. Roe, in her studies of leading artists and scientists in several fields, noted that they were characterized by unusual energy output and perseverance. She posited that this might mean a very high level of motivation. Many scientists emphasize the need to "load up with the facts" (12, pp. 436–437). No one seems to have improved on the four steps in creative thinking outlined by Graham Wallas (13): preparation—hard, systematic analysis of the problem and accumulation of knowledge; incubation—the stage of rest or suspended effort; illumination —when the "happy idea" strikes; and verification—a critical process of testing out the result.

Freedom to experiment and flexibility in attack on problems are essential requirements for creativity that can be provided in a permissive, accepting atmosphere. However, Murray has warned that not every spontaneous impulse is constructive (9, pp. 96–118). Understanding and artistry are needed by the teacher or guide to determine when to encourage and when to limit or redirect spontaneity in the interests of creativity. Rogers (9, pp. 69–82) is convinced through his experience with therapeutic techniques that when an individual has been released from inner conflicts and repressions and is open to all of his experiences his behavior will be creative. He stresses the importance of a climate in which external evaluation is absent and the individual is accepted as of unconditional worth—not softness or indulgence, but permission to be free, meaning that one is responsible.

Problem Solving. There is much disagreement among researchers concerning the nature of human problem solving. In a review of research in this field published in 1958, Corman (14) reported how a group of forty distinguished researchers failed to delimit the area or agree on much of anything. While recognizing that direct classroom applications are sparse, he expressed optimism for the future if the present level of interest is maintained.

The scientific method provides some practical leads as to techniques in problem solving, but suitable steps may vary with the nature of the problem. The following steps are usually included in the problem-solving type of thinking: formulate and define the problem clearly in order to understand its nature; assemble all available pertinent facts; analyze the problem in the light of these facts; arrive at tentative solutions; evaluate each solution in terms of its bearing on the problem; observe and experiment with each chosen solution to check its effectiveness.

For most life problems all of the needed facts are not likely to be available, and one must then consider to what extent human experience and best judgments should be utilized in thinking through problems in this area.

Group processes in problem solving are similar to those carried on by an individual, and these were considered in Chapter 5 in connection with various group-guidance techniques.

Decision Making. Improvement of this process, a part of almost any problem solving, is the central focus of guidance for self-direction. We need more understanding of its nature than research has yet yielded. Doubtless, no one is fully aware of all of the factors that influence a particular decision. Attitudes, values, aspirations, goals, self-concepts, and a multitude of conscious and unconscious motives may enter into some choice. Only to the extent that we are aware of these influences can we learn to exercise some rational control over the direction of our lives. Traditional logic does not always enter into thinking about our choices (15). Whatever we can learn about ourselves and others may contribute to this rational self-direction. Kostick (16) reported evidence in an experiment in group decision making of the efficacy of class discussion for raising students' levels of scholastic aspiration. This level of aspiration is, of course, a basic motivating factor in effective learning.

How Can One Learn to Improve Thought Processes? Research has been carried on for many years to attempt to discover the various factors that may be involved in thought processes. The findings in this research do not yet seem too helpful for practical application in group learning situations. Most of the research on tests of thinking indicates a general reasoning factor (interpreted by some as "ability to define problems"), verbal comprehension, spatial and visualizing ability, perceptual speed, and ability to perceive relationships. This list is not complete, and technical names have not been fully used (12, pp. 390–444). Tests that are useful for various age levels may be available eventually, so that individuals may learn about their assets and liabilities in thinking.

Doubtless every teacher and counselor can contribute to the improvement of thinking by guiding individuals in the thoughtful and systematic study of real-life problems suited to their maturity levels, helping them to acquire a rich store of pertinent knowledge that is used in a discriminating manner; to become increasingly alert to the influences of bias, prejudice, inflexibility, and other deterrents to clear thinking; and to see how the various subject fields may provide interrelated understandings of our many-faceted lives. Materials prepared by the author to guide college students in the improvement of their thinking can be adapted readily for use at other levels (17, pp. 170–193).

Remedial work

In any sizable group of individuals there will be a few with learning handicaps of some sort sufficiently serious so that they cannot benefit fully from group work alone. Their need is for careful diagnosis, usually by a trained psychologist, of the causes or sources of their difficulties, and special remedial treatment. The recognition of this need has led to the addition to many school staffs of adjustment teachers, clinical psychologists, or other special workers. Such services will not be considered here in detail.

While warning workers without special training against snap judgments regarding possible causes of apparently serious learning handicaps, the author would emphasize the importance of careful observation of such individuals to detect at least obvious causes. Not a few pupils with visual, auditory, or temporary language handicaps, for example, go undetected for some reason until real remedial problems develop. Knowing what pupils are thinking and feeling and what has happened to them at crucial points in their lives is a fruitful way of detecting what may often be fairly simple emotional problems in their early stages. Noting discrepancies between test data and behavior or achievement is another important type of observation that may sometimes lead to changed expectancies for a pupil and new opportunities for development.

Some high schools and colleges have laboratories or clinics where students can go or be referred for special study and help with respect to reading techniques, or sometimes for any type of study or learning difficulty. Some of these laboratories work primarily with class groups, but others have been planned to provide assistance to any student with respect to a particular study problem—preparing a report, writing a letter, improving vocabulary, solving mathematics or science problems, best methods of learning a foreign language, improving spelling. This is essentially a tutorial service. Many so-called "supervised study periods" could be improved through this type of service if adequate and sufficient teacher personnel were available.

Evaluating progress

If students are to be encouraged to think of themselves as active participants rather than passive recipients in the process of learning to learn, it is important that they share with teachers in the evaluation of their own progress. To this end, it is helpful for students to understand techniques for measuring the rate of learning, and for them to be oriented to the significance of the grading system used in their institutions.

The technique of plotting learning curves as a gauge for depicting the effectiveness of practice in accelerating the learning process can productively be shared with students. The curves can measure either the decreased amounts of time required to perform a specified unit of work or the increased amount of work which the student can perform, with practice, in a specified unit of time. Although visually these two curves are diametrically opposite, in effect they both reflect the same type of learning progress.

If your how-to-learn group projects involve actual experiments in which students plot learning curves, two considerations should be emphasized. First, it should be pointed out that there are generally believed to be physiological limits beyond which one should not expect much improvement. That is, students should not be disappointed if the "amount-of-achievement" line stops soaring at some point; nor if the "amount-of-time" line fails to diminish at some point. The direction of the curve is more significant than its finite stopping point.

Second, students should be familiar with the phenomenon of plateaus in the learning process—periods in which no measurable improvement is made. It is possible that during these fallow periods latent but not demonstrable improvement does take place—improvement which sets in motion the next upward spurt. Somewhere between the unrealistic expectation that one's learning facility will improve ad infinitum and the premature discouragement which stems from interpreting the first plateau as the end of the line lies a wholesome attitude toward learning.

Most institutions rely primarily on a system of grading as the device for enabling students to evaluate their progress. It is important that students (and their parents, as well) understand the basis on which grading is done so that they can properly interpret their records. Some schools issue grades as an index only to mastery of subject matter. Others grade in terms of the student's development. In still other schools, grades are computed on a competitive basis, in terms of how an individual student ranks with respect to the performance of his classmates. And in some schools grades are an index of the extent to which the student has made use of aptitudes he has revealed on the basis of previous testing.

Although not all systems of grading place the same emphasis on the skills of scholarship as such, there is among students a certain amount of status attached to good grades and, conversely, an onus attached to poor grades. It is healthy for students to realize that aiming for high grades is not the sole goal of the educational experience, and that scholastic excellence should not be pursued at the expense of well-rounded development of the individual.

On the other hand, it is well to instill in students respect for scholastic prowess as such, on the premise that their school years are probably the one span of their life which will be devoted to systematic mastery of certain learnings and their success in learning is a direct measure of how well they are doing their job.

A wide range of reasons may lie behind the failure of any individual student with respect to attaining acceptable scholarship standards. These can best be ascertained by examining the circumstances and background of the individual student and by guiding group study of causes of poor scholarship applied to self. The possible reasons include limited aptitude in the field being studied, inadequate preparation in previous courses, lack of motivation, poor study habits, physical deterrents, or personality attributes not conducive to scholastic aims.

Obviously not all the foregoing problems are equally susceptible to treatment, but the skilled teacher or counselor will assess the problem to the best of his judgment and help the student to develop a plan of attack based upon perspective of scholastic achievement in relation to his total goals, and upon optimum use of his existing strengths to effect improvement in instances in which improvement is possible.

SOME ASPECTS OF GUIDANCE IN LEARNING TO LEARN

Responsibilities and cooperative planning of all teachers

Since group guidance always should lead to individual applications of learnings, it is essential that subject and guidance teachers are continuously informed regarding what each is doing with respect to this problem of learning to learn. Among the outcomes of this close cooperation will be:

1. Challenges to subject teachers to re-examine the learning techniques in their respective fields in relation to general principles of learning

2. Deeper understanding of individual differences and greater efforts to adapt work to individual needs

3. Increased understanding by guidance teachers of the demands of various subject areas and improved ability to guide students in their educational and vocational planning

4. Mutual respect and confidence between subject teachers and guidance workers, through which each is likely to serve students more helpfully

Each teacher might profitably ask the following questions while planning the work for and with a group:

Do I know the state of readiness of all my pupils for their learning tasks?

To what extent is this readiness dependent upon maturation, neurological and physiological, and to what extent on experience?

What can I do to foster and improve this readiness through providing needed experiences?

Am I starting with my class where they are or where I am?

Am I and the class mutually aware of general purposes and goals to serve as guideposts or directive points?

Is each specific task related meaningfully to these over-all purposes and goals?

Have I helped each individual to formulate suitable goals and plans within the group pattern, and do I help each to evaluate successive steps and to analyze the snags or problems encountered? (This may call for some outline or check list, adapted to the class or subject, which each individual can fill out and check over frequently with the teacher, unless the class is small enough for regular conferences.)

Are all incentives for learning being utilized, including immediate significance in students' lives, intrinsic interest in the subject, and implications for personal development and preparation for future work and living?

Have my students planned how to be systematic and efficient in their study methods, arranging as ideal conditions as possible with respect to a quiet place, essential materials conveniently at hand, suitable and adequate time for study with brief rest periods? (Radio and television *may* be forcing new powers of attention and concentration, but it is doubtful that they are doing so.)

Do I know the reading proficiency of each member of the class, and am I providing assistance in the vocabulary-building and specific reading techniques required for the subject?

Is there a similar plan for any other necessary basic skills such as arithmetic, spelling, written and oral expression, and listening?

Is the class having assistance with the types of thinking required to manipulate and use concepts peculiar to the subject field?

Do they know the best methods of learning to retain essential data, such as vocabulary and rules of grammar in foreign languages, principles and formulas in mathematics and science, and the interrelationships and continuity of events in history?

Is the class organized to carry on helpful group learning activities, and are they aware of the learning possibilities in the give-and-take of group interaction?

Do members of the class know how to keep serviceable notes or records of class and study experiences as means of review and of orderly progress?

Are there group and individual plans for frequent evaluation of progress that are more meaningful than a mere grade on a test?

Does the group plan with me how to use evaluation findings in moving ahead in the learning process?

And as an over-all question at every stage: Am I striving always for meaningful experiences for students, even when drill or repetition may be indicated, and for the rewarding and satisfying results of successful achievement for each individual at his optimum level that will spur him on to further learning?

Naturally, these goals will never be achieved perfectly. But if all teachers in a school or college planned cooperatively to emphasize best methods of learning to learn in their respective classes in accordance with some general outline of approaches such as is suggested above, it is very likely that a new spirit and a new level of learning would be achieved in the institution, and not at the cost of interest, spontaneity, or creativity in any class. If, in addition, students had the opportunity to examine their learning assets and liabilities in a guidance group, to formulate suitable time budgets to care for work, play, health, leisure, and rest, to learn how to use the library and other learning facilities, to study best ways of capitalizing on assets, and then have the opportunity to overcome handicaps through remedial measures, they would be likely to make rapid progress toward mastering the tools of their job of learning to learn.

Caution is needed in any concerted effort of a school staff to help students improve their learning techniques, so that it does not become a competitive race among teachers or departments for higher scholastic standards. This could bring undue tension and strain into the situation for many and defeat the purposes of the effort which should center around making the learning process interesting, satisfying, and more meaningful. Advantages of a special guidance class in learning techniques are that attention can be directed more fully to the over-all problems and needs of individuals; that the planning of suitable time and effort for each field of study can be balanced in relation to individual abilities, interests, and goals; and that possible confusion over divergent methods of different instructors can be studied and resolved from the viewpoint of individual differences in learning abilities and the varied methods in different disciplines. This approach requires good psychological background on the part of the teacher-counselor.

Research and recommendations

Very few directives are available from experimental research as to best methods of teaching how to study and learn. Krumboltz and Farquhar (18) report an experiment with college students utilizing three methods: an instructor-centered approach with lectures and assignments, a student-centered approach with discussion and cooperative planning, and an eclectic approach combining aspects of both of the other methods. The criterion instruments appraised facts, study habits, student attitudes and opinions, interests, and achievement motivation. Highest motivation was shown in the eclectic method, but only for women; the instructor-centered method rated second on motivation, and the student-centered method rated third. There were no significant differences in other outcomes. The method most pleasing under one instructor was not most successful under another instructor at a different time of day. Those who originally expressed preference for the instructor-centered method increased their self-ratings on the study-habits inventory, while the reverse occurred for those who had expressed preference for the student-centered approach. The authors of this study emphasize the desirability of an intermediate method that combines the lecture and group types of approach, also the need for further experimentation with various methods.

Blake (19) has summarized some operating principles for a college-level study skills program as part of a broader orientation program. These include diagnostic testing to disclose study skill needs; emphasis on a developmental program for all students, with the remedial aspect secondary but an integral part of the program; instruction preferably in small groups of twenty or less, student-centered rather than content-centered, and providing integration of reading, writing, speaking, and listening as aspects of the single process of communication.

Preston (20) has provided some excellent suggestions for parents, teachers, and counselors as to how they may foster valuable learning skills from early childhood through college. He deals with four crucial requirements of study: interest in learning, self-discipline in study, skill in gathering and assimilating information, and a good memory for mastering material studied. While emphasis is placed on the first two requirements for the preschool and kindergarten period, and the last two for high school and college years, Preston points out that all four of the learnings are interrelated and that an individual should improve in each of them at every stage of development. His suggestions for instilling curiosity, wonder, an atmosphere of excitement about new learning, and the desire for deeper inquiry are especially challenging.

Methods may ultimately be influenced significantly by the recommendations of a commission of the National Association of Secondary-school Principals stressing the need for pupils to spend much time in individual learning. To provide such opportunity the suggestion is made that school plants should have individual study spaces equipped with varieties of modern devices for learning, in addition to large-group and small-group spaces. This type of setup would allow for multiple approaches to guidance in learning to learn (21).

References Cited in Chapter

1. Fry, Clement C.: *Mental Health in College*, The Commonwealth Fund, New York, 1942.
2. Wellington, Jean: "The Role of Guidance in the Enhancement of Learning," *The School Guidance Worker*, 13:9–12, October, 1957.
3. Dollard, John, and Neal E. Miller: *Personality and Psychotherapy: An Analysis in Terms of Learning, Thinking, and Culture*, McGraw-Hill Book Company, Inc., New York, 1950.
4. Kubie, Lawrence S.: "The Psychiatrist Considers Curriculum Development," *Teachers College Record*, 50:241–246, January, 1949.
5. McCreary, William H., and Donald E. Kitch: "Now Hear Youth: A Report on the California Co-operative Study of School Drop-outs and Graduates," *Bulletin of the California State Department of Education*, vol. 22, no. 9, Sacramento, Calif., October, 1953.
6. Remmers, H. H., and D. H. Radler: *The American Teenager*, The Bobbs-Merrill Company, Inc., Indianapolis, 1957.
7. Reisman, David, et al.: *The Lonely Crowd: A Study of the Changing American Character*, Yale University Press, New Haven, Conn., 1950.
8. Whyte, W. H., Jr.: *The Organization Man*, Simon and Schuster, Inc., New York, 1956.
9. Anderson, Harold H. (ed.): *Creativity and Its Cultivation*, Harper & Row, Publishers, New York, 1959.
10. Bentley, Edward, and J. Cecil Barker: "Education for Making Decisions," *California Journal of Secondary Education*, 31:402–408, November, 1956.
11. Glaser, E. M.: *An Experiment in the Development of Critical Thinking*, Teachers College Contributions to Education, No. 843, Columbia University Press, New York, 1931.
12. Johnson, Donald M.: *The Psychology of Thought and Judgment*, Harper & Row, Publishers, New York, 1955.
13. Wallas, Graham: *The Art of Thought*, Jonathan Cape and Robert Ballam, Inc., New York, 1931.
14. Corman, Bernard R.: "Learning: II. Problem Solving and Related Topics," *Review of Educational Research*, 28:459–467, December, 1958.
15. Wasserman, Paul, and Fred S. Silander: *Decision-making: An Annotated Bibliography*, Graduate School of Business and Public Administration, Cornell University, Ithaca, N.Y., 1958.
16. Kostick, Max: "An Experiment in Group Decision," *Journal of Teacher Education*, 8:67–72, March, 1957.
17. Bennett, M. E.: *College and Life: Problems of Self-discovery and Self-direction*, 4th ed., McGraw-Hill Book Company, Inc., New York, 1952.
18. Krumboltz, John D., and William W. Farquhar: "The Effect of Three Teaching Methods on Achievement and Motivational Outcomes in a How-to-study Course," *Psychological Monographs, General and Applied*, 71:1–26, American Psychological Association, Washington, 1957.
19. Blake, Walter S., Jr.: "A Basic Study Skills Program for Colleges and Universities," *The Personnel and Guidance Journal*, 34:289–291, January, 1956.
20. Preston, Ralph Clausius: *Teaching Study Habits and Skills*, Holt, Rinehart and Winston, Inc., New York, 1959.
21. Wesley, Emory J.: "Briefing the Journals," *The Vocational Guidance Quarterly*, 9:253, summer, 1961. (Summary of "Individual Learning," *Overview*, 2:45–52, March, 1961.)

Additional References

Bartlett, Sir Frederic: *Thinking, an Experimental and Social Study*, George Allen & Unwin, Ltd., London, 1958.

Berg, Irwin A., and Bernard M. Bass: *Conformity and Deviation*, Harper & Row, Publishers, New York, 1961.

Blackwood, Paul E.: *How Children Learn to Think*, U.S. Office of Education Bulletin 1951, no. 10, 1957 (reprinted 1955 and 1957).

Burton, William Henry, et al.: *Education for Effective Thinking: An Introductory Text*, Appleton-Century-Crofts, Inc., New York, 1960.

Guilford, J. P.: "Factors that Aid and Hinder Creativity," in "Perspectives 1961–1962," *Teachers College Record*, 1961–1962.

Russell, David H.: *Children's Thinking*, Ginn & Company, Boston, 1956.

Stein, M. I., and Shirley J. Henize (eds.): *Creativity and the Individual*, The Free Press of Glencoe, A Division of the Crowell-Collier Publishing Co., New York, 1960.

Trow, William Clark: *The Learning Process*, Department of Classroom Teachers, American Educational Research Association of the National Education Association, Washington, 1954.

References for students

Armstrong, William Howard: *Study Is Hard Work*, Harper & Row, Publishers, New York, 1956.

Bennett, Margaret E.: *College and Life*, 4th ed., McGraw-Hill Book Company, Inc., New York, 1952, pp. 85–211.

Bennett, Margaret E., and Molly Lewin: *Getting the Most Out of College*, McGraw-Hill Book Company, Inc., New York, 1957, pp. 47–84.

Chandler, John Roscoe, et al.: *Successful Adjustment in College*, 2d ed., Prentice-Hall, Inc., Englewood Cliffs, N.J., 1958, pp. 29–70.

Cole, Luella: *Student's Guide to Effective Study*, rev. ed., Holt, Rinehart and Winston, Inc., New York, 1960.

Dudycha, George John: *Learn More with Less Effort*, Harper & Row, Publishers, New York, 1957.

Farquhar, William W., John D. Krumboltz, and C. Gilbert Wrenn: *Learning to Study*, The Ronald Press Company, New York, 1960.

Garrison, Roger H.: *The Adventure of Learning in College: An Undergraduate Guide to Productive Study*, Harper & Row, Publishers, New York, 1959.

Morgan, Clifford T., and James Deese: *How to Study*, McGraw-Hill Book Company, Inc., New York, 1957.

New York State Counselors Association: *Tips on How to Study*, Delmar Publishers, Inc., Albany, N.Y., 1956.

Preston, Ralph C., and Morton Botel: *How to Study*, Science Research Associates, Inc., Chicago, 1956.

Robinson, Francis P.: *Effective Study*, rev. ed., Harper & Row, Publishers, New York, 1961.

Stanton, Thomas F.: *How to Study; High School Edition*, American Guidance Service, Minneapolis, Minn., 1959.

Voeks, Virginia: *On Becoming an Educated Person: An Orientation to College*, W. B. Saunders Company, Philadelphia, 1957, pp. 20–91.

Weigand, George, and Walter S. Blake, Jr.: *College Orientation: A Study Skills Manual*, Prentice-Hall, Inc., Englewood Cliffs, N.J., 1955.

Wrenn, C. Gilbert, and Robert P. Larsen: *Studying Effectively: A Manual*, rev. ed., Stanford University Press, Stanford, Calif., 1955.

10 UNDERSTANDING SELF AND OTHERS

We shall deal here primarily with self-understanding, but *self* and *others* have been included in the chapter title because these understandings are mutually interdependent, each contributing to the other. This is one great advantage of group approaches to self-appraisal. The similarities of human beings are probably greater than the differences; also, awareness of self and concepts of self develop to a large degree through relationships with others. One indication of how members of a group can help each other in self-understanding is the finding that ratings by peers may often give more useful information in some areas than ratings by adults or superiors (1, pp. 518–523, 582).

SELF-UNDERSTANDING IS A LIFELONG PROCESS

It is essential for the guidance worker planning a self-appraisal program with a group to recognize that self-understanding is a lifelong process and that any one cross-section approach can yield only partial insights—sometimes grossly distorted ones. Important outcomes beyond limited findings are the increased understanding of human personality and of ways of assessing it, and increased skill in applying this understanding in future planning and living.

These objectives of a group approach should serve also as a perpetual caution to a teacher or counselor in attempting to interpret and apply any available personnel data in guidance with an individual. The simile of the largely submerged iceberg is always applicable to human beings, together with the realization that each individual is always, to a degree, an unpredictable emergence. The would-be self-appraiser needs also to understand these limitations, and the fact that what one is becoming may be more important than one's present status.

SOME DIFFICULTIES AND FRUSTRATIONS IN SELF-APPRAISAL

One of the deepest frustrations for a group leader, that must be faced also by group members, stems from the state of uncertainty and confusion in psychology with respect to theories of personality and reliable and valid ways of assessing it. Tremendous progress has been and is being made through research, but there are no simple, easy ways of reaching understanding about this most complex manifestation of life.

In the 1930s, Alexis Carrel (2) estimated that it would require about twenty-five years of uninterrupted study for one gifted individual to master all the various sciences concerned with human life, so that he could apply them effectively to its improvement. By uninterrupted study he meant a dedication to this work that would result in the renouncing of common modes of existence and the living of a fully contemplative life. He warned that our present civilization contains the seeds of its own destruction if this knowledge of mankind cannot be put to effective use in the development of human personality, and suggested the need for an institution capable of providing for uninterrupted pursuit for at least a century of the investigations concerning human life to provide the information needed to develop a civilization really serviceable to man.

The years since Carrel made this suggestion have witnessed a tremendous expansion in research in the various sciences related to human life. Supplementing the vast amount of individual research, universities and foundations have established cooperative research centers in which scientists from medical, biological, psychological, and sociological fields have pooled their efforts to push forward in the understanding of mankind and his human relationships. The task of mastering this vast and continuous accumulation of knowledge has probably become far greater than Carrel's estimate. Practitioners in fields serving human beings, such as medicine, psychiatry, psychology, education, and social work, cannot keep their practice fully abreast of this mounting tide of research findings. And another tide appears to be swelling instead of receding in crime, delinquency, mental illness, and various forms of maladjustment. In addition, mankind must face the possibilities of extinction if it does not learn quickly enough how to utilize for human betterment the forces inherent in matter which the physical scientists have unleashed.

The possibilities for good or ill in the present situation are staggering to contemplate. To attempt such contemplation must inspire both deep humility and dedication to high endeavor on the part of any worker unselfishly interested in human beings and human destiny.

One aspect of this task related to the subject of this chapter is that of helping individuals to increase their understanding of themselves and of their fellow human beings and to improve their interpersonal relationships with a view to creating a way of life in which human potentialities can be more fully developed and used for human betterment.

Every statement of educational or guidance objectives includes some direct approaches to self-knowledge, but obviously the essential learnings cannot be achieved in the interview time allotted to each individual in even the best personnel program.

Psychotherapists may spend hundreds of hours helping a relatively few maladjusted or mentally ill individuals to learn how to master themselves and their life situations. Many of them are suggesting that education can help to prevent much maladjustment through the wise nurture of mature personalities.

We can, doubtless, start safely with the assumption that a person, at any stage of his development, is the product of interplay between inherited potentialities and environmental influences, but we have limited understanding of the relative strength of these factors. They probably vary somewhat in strength of influence with each individual and certainly for different aspects of development. The question of the relative influence of nature and nurture in general mental ability has been debated for years, without any complete resolution of the issue, though present evidence seems to give more weight to nature, but by no means rules out nurture. Some researchers, as we shall see later, are willing to claim varying weights for these two factors in some characteristics of personality. We do have enough understanding about the *nature of the influence* of both heredity and environment to help individuals to gain considerable insight about them in their own lives and to learn how to utilize inner potentials and outer influences creatively.

A second difficulty to be met is that of selecting suitable methods and instruments for self-appraisal from the vast array of tests, inventories, questionnaires and other less structured techniques. A good psychological background is needed for this selection and also for their administration and interpretation. If a leader does not have this background to an adequate degree, it is his responsibility to enlist the cooperation of a co-worker competent in this respect, and to limit the appraisal to those methods and those instruments with which he can cope professionally.

One basic principle that always applies in appraisal is this: never use one type of data out of the context of comprehensive information about the total functioning person. Gardner Murphy has given us a comforting thought regarding this complex problem of personality appraisal in the statement: "The great teachers whom I have known are forever alert to the fact that the individual, whether two or twenty years old, can tell us more about his unrealized potentials than can any norm prepared in any office" (3, p. 317).

The Impact of Self-knowledge on the Individual

Any sound and fairly comprehensive self-study will reveal strengths, weaknesses, and mediocre characteristics—many things we shall like and many that we shall dislike about ourselves. Gaining this information about self can be a painful and traumatic experience, particularly to one who already lacks self-confidence and ego strength. One way in which the group leader can prevent negative effects is to build up understanding in a group of the nature of human variation, both among individuals and within any person. Parents and teachers are prone to stress excellence of achievement for every child, particularly in areas involving academic ability. Therefore, a realistic understanding of the normal curve as it applies to most human characteristics, and of the greater importance of the total pattern of one's potentialities than of any one trait or ability is basic to a wholesome approach to self-appraisal. Equally important is an attitude of profound respect for every type of human ability and for every individual with his unique pattern of abilities and its many hidden and undeveloped resources.

Each member of a group must be helped to gain wholesome self-acceptance with respect to both assets and liabilities, and to develop suitable plans for making the most of strengths and the best of weaknesses. Also, any one cross-section study must eventuate in realization of the tentative nature of its findings and open doors to further exploration. A leader needs always to be alert to note when a group member needs individual counseling to resolve emotional conflicts or misunderstandings.

Reasons for Self-appraisal

These reasons can be stated very simply and concisely. First, understanding of self is essential for any realistic planning of educational, vocational, and personal-social goals, and for self-direction in progressing toward them. This self-knowledge cannot be secured in a few interviews. It requires closely coordinated group study and individual counseling. Second, techniques of self-study are essential throughout life for the continuous adjustments and adaptations necessary for everyone in an ever-changing world. These techniques must be taught, learned, and developed through use. Third, individuals at all ages show eagerness to understand themselves and others at their levels of maturity in situations where they can accept and respect themselves and others in a mutually helpful and skillfully guided process.

CONDITIONS ESSENTIAL FOR WHOLESOME SELF-APPRAISAL

A warm friendliness between leader and group and between members of the group is one of the first essentials for the study of personality. Every individual should feel secure in his acceptance by the group as a respected and contributing member. This sense of acceptance and belonging is especially important in personality study, since identification of self with characters or particular problems may engender feelings of shame, embarrassment, or a sense of being different if one does not feel himself to be an integral part of the group. If one feels accepted because of *who* he is, he can more easily face with equanimity *what* he is with respect to weaknesses as well as strengths. Recognition of the inevitability of weaknesses in every personality and of the possibility of doing something about them is, of course, a prerequisite for wholesome study of self.

The leader's personality is probably the factor of first importance in determining the climate of the class or group. If he has achieved the state of maturity where he has come to fairly reasonable terms with his conflicting drives, has accepted his basic human nature as normal and wholesome when harnessed to long-range goals, has learned to endure frustration but at the same time has found creative outlets in a well-balanced, satisfying life, and has grown into an emotional maturity which identifies his interests and welfare with those of his fellow beings, he can enter into guidance relationships with immature personalities helpfully. If he is still essentially immature and self-centered, he *may* easily establish rapport and camaraderie with a youthful group, but he will not have adequate insight and perspective to help them move forward in their personal and social growth.

If he has not gained some major insight into the varied forces and influences in his life that have made him what he is, and has not achieved emotional acceptance of himself, a leader is not ready to help immature personalities in this task. Inevitably he will project some of his conflicts into his work and perhaps unconsciously reject some of the individuals who most need sympathetic acceptance and understanding by others. A misunderstood sense of guilt may be expressed in attitudes as well as words or deeds of disapproval or condemnation of others. When this happens between a guide and any members of a group, one can scarcely expect to influence all members of the group to accept, respect, and help one another.

Jersild (4), who has studied the problem of self-understanding with many teachers through discussion, interviews and inventories, reported some of his findings as to their concerns about self under the headings of anxiety (as a response to conflict or danger from within as con-trasted with fear as a response to danger from without), loneliness, the search for meaning in life, and hostility. He concludes that when teach-ers really face themselves through struggle they gain a compassion that links acceptance of self and of others, and releases the power to feel with others, to love both self and others, to find self-fulfillment, and to help others in the search.

The person who has experienced and *resolved* severe conflicts may be unusually insightful and helpful with others, but he must have climbed out of the mire of resentment and self-pity into happy accept-ance of his past and present and eager anticipation of the future, before he is ready for this service.

Casual objectivity, sympathetic understanding, and absence of shock or disapproval are basic attitudes for the guide when discussions of behavior are under way. This does not mean that unsocial behavior will be condoned, but merely that it will be temporarily accepted as the resultant of certain causes which must be understood as a step toward changing it. If a camouflaged case study should be used in discussion of a problem, the description should always include some admirable qualities that will enable an individual who may identify himself with the person described to retain his self-respect. If the climate of the group allows for direct study of its members, the member himself must always be distinguished from undesirable behavior so that respect and accept-ance as a person can be differentiated from any form of behavior that may be condemned.

Approaches with Young Children

Assistance to young children in self-understanding will be in large degree indirect, but many very important foundations will be laid for the increasingly direct approach with older children, adolescents, and adults. Much of the emphasis in early years will be upon emotions, fears, living and working with others, their interests, and their achievements and difficulties in learning.

The challenge to educators to help children understand themselves has come from Lawrence S. Kubie, a psychiatrist, who has stated this challenge in the following terms (5, p. 246): [1]

The next problem which education must solve is how to lessen the dichotomy between conscious and unconscious levels in human personality. The goal of psychotherapy is always to expand the area of conscious control in human personality. The goal of education should be to prevent, correct and limit this fatal and universal dichotomy in human development. . . .

[1] Reprinted by permission of the publishers.

Instead of bringing up infants and children under a system of taboos which make it impossible for them to talk about themselves or to adults about their hates and fears, their jealousies, their bitterness against the adult world, their bodily shames and envies and lusts, all of this could be lived out, acted out, and talked out in groups from the nursery years on. This would be a process of socialization for the savage human infant and child which would tend to block and to counteract those forces which exist in everyone and which make us repress into unconsciousness the most vital emotional problems of our development.

I have sometimes called this the Fifth Freedom, the child's right to know his own feelings and thoughts and impulses—not to act them out blindly, but to be consciously aware of them. This is where education and preventive psychiatry merge. And this is where new techniques which have nothing to do with curricular developments are sorely needed.

Dollard and Miller (6) have indicated desirable boundaries between this service through education and that which the psychotherapist provides, and have suggested important techniques for the educational service as a means of helping to prevent neurotic disabilities that require psychotherapy as a special type of "remedial" teaching. They contrast the mechanism of *repression* and *suppression*—the one an unconscious process beyond the control of the individual, the other a conscious, self-directed process which brings control of responses within one's power. One aspect of psychotherapy is described as the process by which the person is helped to unlearn, or remove, his repressions and to learn new modes of adjustment that will keep responses under conscious control. This psychotherapeutic process subsumes a highly complicated and often very lengthy process of learning that is not in the sphere of the educator's activity. The authors distinguish between the task of educators in helping children to deal with emotional conflicts which are primarily in the conscious realm or involve only mild repressions, and the task of the psychotherapist in helping individuals to cope with their conflicts connected with deeper unconscious repressions.

They illustrate the values of suppression as compared with repression by the experiences of a fourteen-year-old boy, George, who was suddenly deprived of a carefully planned Saturday holiday by the illness of his companion. When George received the telephone message that the other boy could not go, he was intensely disappointed but pretended to accept the circumstances. Soon he was fighting with his younger sister and eventually was sent to his room for the remainder of the morning. George's mother had failed to see the situation as a case of displaced aggression which had been caused by anger at the original frustration. It is suggested that the mother might have helped George to verbalize his natural disappointment and anger over the interrupted trip at the time of the telephone call and to make other plans for the day, or later might have helped him to see that he was taking out his feelings on his sister and could have instructed him to *restrain* himself (6, p. 432).

Dollard and Miller believe that this kind of training in various situations would not have to be invoked very long before a child would get the hang of it and that such teaching masswise at elementary levels would prevent much that has to be done later by lengthy treatment. Both parents and elementary school teachers are admonished to train children to use their minds in solving emotional problems. The conviction is expressed that children with such training would then naturally have recourse as adults to self-study when they were faced with bothersome problems (6, p. 434).

This emphasis on training does not in any way negate the importance of all the influences in an environment that foster healthy personality development, such as affection, acceptance, and respect. It is the training within such an environment that will count toward good mental health. There are no simple, ready-made rules which can be formulated and applied in this work, but each leader needs to draw upon our storehouse of accumulated research and experience with intelligent discrimination at each step as to the readiness of members of a group for specific learnings and the boundaries beyond which there is need for special therapeutic assistance in addition to preventive or developmental guidance.

One of the most stimulating approaches to self-understanding is being made by Jersild, who has hurled a challenge to psychologists and educators in bold and inspiring terms. Some of his statements are quoted and summarized here (7): [2]

Every child is actually or potentially a child psychologist. From an early age, without being deliberate about it, he acquires ideas and attitudes about himself and others. These are woven into the pattern of his life. They may be true or false, healthy or morbid. Their development is left largely to chance. This is not as it should be, in my judgment. I propose that the study of child psychology, designed to promote understanding and acceptance of self and understanding of others, should be a planned feature of the education children receive from nursery school onward. . . .

There is one gloomy fact about children who now are growing up which underscores, as I see it, the need for such a program. A large proportion of children will move into adulthood troubled and unhappy about many things. Many will be afflicted by irrational fears which do not represent dangers in the external environment but unresolved problems within themselves. Many, as adults, will suffer from attitudes of hostility, vindictiveness, and defensiveness which are not a response to hostile forces in the outside world but repre-

[2] Reprinted by permission of the American Psychological Association, Inc., Washington, and the author.

sent attitudes carried over from unresolved childhood struggles. Many persons similarly will acquire persisting feelings of inferiority or other unhealthy attitudes regarding their personal worth which represent either an irrational estimate of themselves or a failure to accept themselves realistically as they are.

In numerous ways there is a vast carry-over of unhealthy attitudes regarding self and others from childhood and adolescence into adult life.

Is so much distress inevitable? I do not think we have to assume that it is. But I do not think the picture can be changed substantially if we simply try to extend the special services we now provide. These services are good, and need to be continued. But the answer cannot be found simply by offering more psychological counseling, psycho-analysis, or other forms of treatment of the kind now provided for severely disturbed people after they are already on the rocks. A bolder measure is needed for the benefit of the population at large. This measure, I maintain, must involve a vastly enhanced conception of the social functions of research in child psychology and of the role that child psychology might play in the education of children.

The general hypothesis underlying Jersild's proposal is that

. . . human beings, from an early age, have more capacity for learning to face and to understand and to deal constructively with the realities of life than we have hitherto assumed in our psychological theories or in our educational practices.

Each child is a student of human nature within the limits of his maturity level and what he has had an opportunity to learn. The home, the classroom, the playground, and other situations are psychological laboratories in which he is now a subject and now an observer. Child psychology will fully come into its own when it discovers the capacities children have for learning from these laboratories and explores the conditions under which these capacities can best be developed.

Jersild and his colleagues have secured written reports from nearly three thousand persons ranging from fourth grade through college as to what they liked and disliked about themselves. Some of the findings were reported in Chapter 3 as illustrations of problems. A significant feature of these written documents was the large proportion of appraisals of self in terms of social attitudes and relatedness to others that underscores the crucial impact of interpersonal relationships on the self. Jersild has held workshops with educators to study problems of education for self-understanding. Reports of these study groups offer no simple, easy solution. This is a service that penetrates every aspect of the school program as well as one that concerns direct teaching and group and individual guidance (8, 9).

In Chapter 3 we reviewed some of the ways in which teachers and counselors can increase their understandings of individuals in groups as a means of planning suitable group guidance activities. Here we shall consider some of the areas in which children can be helped to take a look at themselves.

Appraisal of interests

As in every aspect of personality, there are differing theories about the nature of interest. Most approaches to its measurement have involved the concept of feelings of liking or disliking. Miller (10, pp. 216–274, 329–399), in a thoughtful analysis of the nature of interests, has suggested that they are probably related to the developing values of the individual and to his concept of self, both of which may be deeper levels of the personality and significant for the understanding of interests. The trend of theories as to the sources of interests is toward the assumption that they are the product of the interaction of hereditary and environmental factors, and reflect the personality structure, needs, and drives of the individual (11). Thus, inherited potentials are likely to influence to what an individual gives attention, and an environment affording varied experiences is likely to foster interests that might otherwise never develop. There appears to be some relationship between abilities and interests, but one cannot be used to predict the other. In guidance work at any age, we are likely to move readily from the consideration of one to the other as we shall do here. We need, however, to avoid confusing these two facets of personality. Tyler's (11, pp. 62–75) study of children's interests, beginning in preschool and kindergarten, has shown many more likes than dislikes among children through the primary grades. Because of this, she found it necessary to differentiate on the basis of dislikes. An early differentiation of the sex role has been indicated with antisissy and antiwork attitudes prominent among the boys.

Jersild and his co-workers have used an "Interest Finder" in exploring the interests of children that contains the following items (12, p. 2):

My three wishes
What I'd like to learn more about in school
What I don't care to study about
What I like best in school
What I like best outside of school
What I like least at school
What I like least away from school
What I want to be or do when I grow up
The most interesting thing I have done at school in the last week or so
One of the places I especially like to go is _____
One of the happiest days in my life

Summaries of responses to such lists will contain many suggestions for valuable classroom activities and for discussions about experiences.

An important consideration for the elementary school teacher is the fact that interests may be *developed* as well as *discovered*. As a teacher observes indications of native bents in children, she has excellent opportunities in the elementary school program to encourage interest in activities related to these strengths and to foster attitudes of self-confidence and self-respect in children based on achievement in suitable activities. Pride in, and respect for, these achievements on the part of parents are likely to ensue.

Gary, for example, gives promise through his art work of latent talent in graphic arts and reveals a "green thumb" in caring for plants in the schoolroom or the school garden. His parents have ambitions for Gary as an architect, but he gives no evidence on tests or in achievement that he would be able to cope with the college training necessary to become an architect. His teachers have an opportunity gradually to foster positive interests in other levels of activity which might lead to landscape gardening, interior decoration, or various types of commercial art. Thus disappointment and an unhappy sense of failure may be prevented at a later stage when vocational decisions and plans must be made.

In attempting to foster suitable interests, the teacher needs to be alert to conditions that might block the expression or hinder the development of true abilities of children. Gary, for example, has a serious and progressive visual defect, which was not discovered and corrected with glasses until the end of the third grade. A problem for his teachers is that of discovering whether test data and schoolwork reveal his true mental ability or merely reflect his handicap. If general ability proves to be greater than he demonstrated earlier, the next step may be that of studying with parents and health specialists the possible effects of Gary's handicap on later plans for training. Should he, for example, plan extensive college training with its requirement of much reading, or should he emphasize the conservation of his vision through choice of activities which require less use of his eyes? Often this question cannot be answered decisively at an early age, but the fostering of many suitable interests and pride in possible achievements may lay the foundations for a happy and suitable compromise in vocational plans, if such compromise becomes necessary in adolescence or adulthood.

Childhood expressions of interest in various types of work may merely represent stages in maturing. These childhood choices or preferences have been referred to as "fantasy choices" (13), because a child may merely be expressing a desire to do what some adult does, or may have an immediate interest in some particular activity, such as that of the locomotive engineer or the bricklayer. The choice may have no relationship to the child's knowledge of his own abilities or of the external realities associated with the job or field of work. Most individuals are not ready for these considerations before the end of the elementary school period; even during adolescence choices are often tentative and not fully realistic in terms of occupational demands and opportunities.

However, these so-called "fantasy choices" may take on meaning when studied from the developmental point of view as part of the interest history of an individual. We do not know to what extent these childhood interests may be accidental, due to experiences; impulsive, due to unconscious emotional pressures; or actually the reactions of an individual with certain basic native patterns of ability which cause him to react more positively to some types of activities than others. Some interest biographies have suggested that there may be a developmental trend which is evidenced in the type of activities preferred, if not in the specific names of jobs (14). The noting and cumulative recording of expressed interests during the elementary school period is well worth the effort, not only for later study and analysis, but also for the immediate insights the records may yield about pupils. The same is true of expressed parent ambitions for children.

Work with parents at this level is likely to be both direct and indirect as far as parental awareness goes. Ambitions of parents for a child often stem from their own unrealized personal ambitions rather than from realistic knowledge about the child. Cooperative efforts of teachers and parents to study potentialities and needs of children can often be carried on more objectively at this early age than later when decisions about careers are pending. Positive efforts at the elementary level to discover and respect emerging patterns of interests and abilities may prevent the necessity of a negative approach later for both parents and children, when they must face realistically the demands and training requirements of occupations which may be unsuitable or unattainable. This work with parents is a two-way process which should yield mutually helpful information about children for both home and school. Where emotionally tinged ambitions of parents are involved, it must frequently be a subtle process. Group study with parents of some of the guidance implications of knowledge about children often helps to objectify problems related to unconscious motivations and to foster more emotionally mature attitudes on the part of parents.

Any pupils who leave school by the end of the elementary period will need assistance similar to that for adolescents in secondary school years, geared to the level of work they are likely to enter or reach. Plans for continued study in adulthood may be especially valuable for this group. With all pupils it is essential that the teacher and counselor be keenly aware of vocational-guidance objectives and plan carefully for their realization, even though they are incidental in the program and often not obvious to the pupils themselves.

Research has suggested that even junior high school is an exploratory period for vocational interests that may be highly tentative (see page 271), but problem inventories have indicated marked interest in future life work as early as the fourth grade (15). This suggests that some basic foundations in knowledge about self and the world of work should be laid at the elementary school level, whether the approach is direct or indirect, and whether expressed vocational interests are permanent or merely steppingstones along the way.

Patterns of abilities

The desirable approach to the appraisal of abilities at the elementary school level is usually informal, being related to skills, achievement, and behavior rather than to qualities and trends of personality. The urge toward the inward look at self does not normally manifest itself strongly until the adolescent period. In childhood it is especially important to develop self-confidence through emphasis on strengths in the various aspects of school activity. Usually weaknesses should be brought into the growing picture of self, only in relation to specific programs of improvement. Young children are probably much more aware of their abilities and disabilities than we have often assumed, and a simple, objective approach to their study that eventuates in definite things to do about them can be very satisfying.

Cooperation of teacher, parent, and pupil in the evaluation of achievement and progress in school provides one of the most natural methods of fostering wholesome self-knowledge throughout elementary school years. The system of reports to parents can be developed in a manner to facilitate this process. Report forms which include a breakdown of various skills in reading, arithmetic, work habits, health habits, citizenship, and all the many aspects of a modern school program can serve as a basis for both group and individual planning of objectives and of ways of measuring progress toward these objectives. Pupils can rate themselves on achievement, write letters to their parents along with those which may be sent by teachers, help to arrange parent-teacher conferences, and often participate in such conferences, to plan ways of overcoming specific difficulties or reaching optimum levels of achievement in areas of strengths.

Early developmental and health histories and pictures of present home life secured from parents form some of the essential foundations for understanding of children and are important, as preserved in personnel records, for interpretation of abilities, interests, and personality trends in adolescence and later years. Current anecdotal records by teachers from year to year, together with test data and achievement and health records, provide information necessary for any sound and reliable guidance services at the secondary school level.

The immediate value lies, of course, in the teacher insight into potentialities and problems of pupils for whom she can provide suitable experiences to meet needs. Guidance of pupil self-appraisal as suggested is one means which is a circular process bringing more insights back to the teacher. Fostering varieties of interests appropriate to developing abilities through both group and individual activities is another means.

Parent groups for mutual study of ways of helping children to grow wholesomely in self-understanding are perhaps more important than child groups at this stage in childhood. Attitudes of respect for all types of abilities and all types of work, if emphasized in these parent-teacher study groups, will lay foundations for real self-acceptance when the more direct approach to self-appraisal is made in adolescence. The problem of understanding human behavior, in self and others, provides many more direct approaches in group study and activity at the elementary school level than does the problem of self-appraisal of abilities and interests. Essential foundations must be laid, however, for the more direct approach in adolescence.

The whole gamut of human abilities would be included in any list of strengths and weaknesses that may be detected during elementary school years. Latent abilities may be evidenced in drawing, painting, clay modeling, music, rhythmics, playground games, storytelling, dramatics, construction work, fine, detailed handwork, writing of compositions, reading, arithmetic, research, thinking, and problem solving in science and social studies, and in all the varieties of human relationships present in an elementary school program.

The teacher does not need too many technical terms for abilities to describe and record observations helpfully. Among the general terms could be artistic, musical, mechanical, verbal, and number facility. Some of the more specific designations could relate to speed of reaction, muscle coordination, eye-hand coordination, manual and finger dexterity, appreciation of color and design, types of memory facility, observational attitudes, perceptual abilities, and reasoning power (judged in relation to mental age), practical judgment, ability to get along with others, leadership and followership in varieties of activities, physical energy and stamina, i.e., the pattern of energy level and expression, discrimination in hearing, in form, and spatial relationships, in touch, and in all the perceptual avenues.

Many of the characteristics mentioned above develop throughout childhood and adolescence, so that no final estimates of potential abilities can be made in early years, but significant clues as to strengths and weaknesses are more reliably evidenced in long-range records of behavior than in one test or other evidence at a particular time. The combination of both approaches to the study of abilities is ideal.

Evidences of apparent weaknesses in abilities in childhood should always be studied in relation to possible physical, health, or experiential handicaps. Impairment of sight or hearing, nutritional deficiencies, organic or other bodily deviations, and social or economic deprivations can serve to stunt the development or obscure the manifestation of native potentialities. Dogmatic judgments about pupils' abilities on the basis of current behavior or objective tests without reference to background history and present status may help to close doors to future opportunities.

A few brief case descriptions may serve to illustrate both the difficulties and challenges faced by teachers in fostering self-understanding and development through group activities.

Noel was frequently compared unfavorably in school with his twin sister Nancy, because he was so much slower in finishing his arithmetic assignments. His mother complained that he cried often because of his discouragement. Also, she pointed out that his reaction time was slower in everything than was Nancy's, but that he was usually much more accurate in his work. Test records indicated that he was much brighter than Nancy, and careful observation of his various activities verified the mother's judgment that he was both painstaking and accurate in his work. While his slow reaction time was often annoying in a class group, there were doubtless severe limits to the extent to which he could speed up without losing his admirable trait of accuracy. In this instance, it was important for the child to develop confidence about assets of industry and accuracy before being placed under pressure to speed up his efforts.

May had appeared to be slow and retarded throughout elementary school. Her family, wealthy and prominent in a small community, had sent her away to school eventually, because they were ashamed of her slow progress and awkward, reticent behavior in comparison with a very bright and vivacious younger sister. Ultimately, the private school asked the parents to withdraw her as no longer educable. At this point psychological study was initiated with a view to vocational guidance and adjustment. The process of study and therapy was long and arduous, but it revealed a potentially very bright and creative individual whose personal development had been blocked by emotional shocks and parental rejection at an early age, when two brothers were lost by illness and accident. The effect on May of the mother's temporary retirement from life, because of grief over the loss of her sons, was not obliterated by her mother's recovery in a few years. Her difficulties were even accentuated by the birth of a younger sister, who became the center of attention in the home.

The attempt through psychotherapy to tap May's creative abilities and release emotional inhibitions resulted eventually in her becoming a successful actress in a traveling troupe. How far she will go is problematical. But how many possibilities for tapping and releasing her potentialities were overlooked in childhood through ignorance of her background history and her inner attitudes and feelings toward herself and others!

Implications for School Guidance. A whole volume of case histories could reveal our many successes and our many failures in the schools to detect and foster talents, to discover handicaps, and to deal effectively with both. Carefully planned group activities might well have helped both the teachers and the individuals whose problems have been described to understand the difficulties or possibilities more fully and to plan what to do about them. Noel could have been helped to recognize and take pride in his special abilities, and could have outlined and worked on a plan to see how far he could go in speeding up his reaction time without sacrificing accuracy. The academically oriented private school that May attended failed to give her the opportunity, through creative and social activities, to release her inhibitions and to try out her artistic abilities. Her deep unconscious repressions may have required psychotherapy even at an early age, but the ease with which she responded to treatment in late adolescence suggests that much more might have been done earlier. Such services at the elementary school level and the transmission of basic information in personnel records for vocational guidance in high school and college are essential foundations for the development and conservation of our human resources—the greatest wealth of a democracy.

Appraisal of physical and health resources

The task of building wholesome attitudes toward oneself as a growing organism subsumes many problems in physical and mental hygiene. Because of the many physical ailments which children report (see pages 60 and 61) and the apparent justification of these complaints in clinical findings (16), an illustration will be included of an experimental program in which guidance in personal hygiene was coordinated with health instruction and medical examinations. In this investigation (17) conducted in a Chicago school, examinations by physicians and interviews with parents and children eventuated in planned health regimens for each child. Health instruction and activities in the classroom were interrelated with these individual health plans. The children in this experiment were compared with a control group who had the usual type of health services and instruction. At the end of a four-year period, the children in the experimental group were adjudged reliably superior in their health gains as measured by a series of checks on general physical condition, nutrition, firmness of muscle, posture, teeth, and the number of defects corrected. And interestingly enough, these children in the experimental group had also made greater gains than the control group in their records on tests of educational achievement.

We know full well that information about desirable practices in the health area, or in any other area, will not necessarily lead to the desired behavior. The next step beyond information about good health habits is that of examining their relevancy for a particular individual, since the needs of each individual are unique, because of differences in innate constitution, predispositions to disease, and possible handicaps resulting from previous illness or injury. The third step, then, is for each individual to create a tailor-made health regimen suited to his particular needs. And finally this tailor-made program must be translated into habitual behavior before it can have any significant effect on the individual's physical and mental health.

These last three steps require much understanding of the individual in his total milieu, understanding on the part of the teacher, the child, and the parents. However, the *techniques* of collecting, evaluating, and using the health information are pretty much the same for all individuals. Here is a place for planned group study with both children and parents that may lead to a really functioning health program that may actually affect human lives.

In the field of mental hygiene we have many suggestions as to guidance needs in such studies of children's fears as those of Jersild (12), which have indicated that children do not realize that something can be done about their fears and worries. Clinical studies, such as those of Gesell and Ilg, verify the succession of fears at different ages and suggest many common problems and worries which a skillful, understanding teacher can bring into the focus of casual, objective study and thus help to reduce emotional tensions inevitably associated with fear and worry.

Many of the personal- and social-adjustment problems of pupils can be approached through the group in various ways. Understanding of some of the problems of isolated or rejected children with handicaps or unusual characteristics can often be fostered indirectly through stories about such children. This approach has been widely used to increase general acceptance of racial and cultural differences and improve intercultural relationships. The method applies equally well to interpersonal differences with caution in not directing undesirable attention to already isolated children. A skillful teacher in the right school atmosphere can often enlist the cooperation of a group directly in helping a schoolmate.

The task of achieving personal independence relates not only to increased responsibility and self-direction in carrying through specific tasks but also to the widening sphere of activities in which children can make choices of activities both in and out of school. This widening of choices of activities presents the challenge to the school of providing opportunity for the exploring of a great variety of interests and of assisting children to discover and develop suitable interests that are not only of immediate value in personal growth but that may eventually be the foundations for vocational and avocational planning in adolescent years. Jersild reported (12, p. 81) that children did not evidence too deep an interest in radio, but rather appeared to be marking time in the hours spent with it for lack of anything better to do. How true is this of television? And are we fostering enough interests that may lead into creative expression throughout life? Also, considering the rather widespread concern shown from at least the fourth grade (see pages 60 and 69) about future lifework and the importance of deep and abiding interests for both vocational and avocational planning in adolescence, it may well be that much experimentation is needed to reveal what more can be accomplished through hobby clubs and various types of group guidance at the elementary school level to assist children to discover and develop more lasting interests and hobbies.

SELF-APPRAISAL AT ADOLESCENT AND ADULT LEVELS

With adolescence comes the interest in the inward look, and also the need for making decisions and plans for the future. This is the golden time for helping young people to start soundly on a direct approach to self-appraisal of assets, liabilities, and suitable interests, to the study of occupational life, and to the formulation of realistic educational and vocational plans. Since the task is lifelong in scope, each attack on the problem, group, or individual should embody several objectives:

1. The development of sound methods of self-appraisal that may serve the individual both immediately and beyond the years of formal education. This includes consumer enlightenment as to reliable guidance services so that wise choices of assistance may be made, if needed in adult years.

2. The assembling and synthesis of as comprehensive data as possible about self in the present, interpreted in the context of longitudinal data regarding past experiences, achievements, and development.

3. The formulation of tentative plans for the development and use of talents or assets, and for wise dealing with liabilities. Increasingly detailed information about occupational, educational, and social require-

ments, conditions, and trends is needed also, of course, to map out realistic life plans. This type of information is considered in succeeding chapters.

Examining the self-concept

A fairly unstructured approach to the study of self is often helpful at first in order to stimulate thinking about the complexity of the problem and help students gain a preliminary overview of what they *think* they are like. The author has always found a great deal of class interest in efforts to answer the question "What am I like?" Some recent investigations of this self-concept have been carried on with the so-called "W.A.Y. Technique," in which answers to the question "Who are you?" have been analyzed (18). Jersild's approach through open questions "What I like about myself," and "What I dislike about myself," has already been described (see pages 57 and 58).

Pictures of Self. In this initial over-all approach, the looking-glass concept of Charles Horton Cooley (19, p. 151) can provoke some valuable thinking and often release a good many tensions and anxieties about self. This approach might include written descriptions of:

1. What *I* think I am like
2. What I think *others* think I am like—my looking-glass self
3. What I think I *may* be like in the future

A comparison of these descriptions is likely to reveal a good many inconsistencies. A discussion of the varied causes of our common distortions of our self-images and of our looking-glass selves that we think we see mirrored in the looks and actions of others can, if handled tactfully, help to overcome many frustrating misconceptions. Then if the problem of harmonizing these is considered in relation to the possibilities of working toward what we wish to become, the door is opened for interesting exploration of our resources to be developed and used in the process.

A discrepancy between the self-concept and the objective realities of self as manifested to others is recognized as a comomn feature of maladjustment. A realistic concept of self and attitudes of self-acceptance, self-confidence, self-esteem, and self-respect are among the current concepts of positive mental health (20).

These goals of mental health can be achieved only as everyone who works with individuals holds every type of ability in high esteem, seeks to understand and respect every type of aspiration, and helps each person to feel an exciting challenge in planning and working for the realization of suitable ambitions. Some of the goals may seem unattainable, but, if realistic steppingstones are laid along the way and several paths kept open, self-appraisal and life planning need never be an unhappy and frustrating experience. Helping individuals to open new doors is better than trying to influence them to close others.

The well-recognized tendency for a person who feels inferior or negative toward himself to feel likewise toward others and to anticipate low esteem or appreciation by others appears to be reverified by studies of attitudes toward self and others (21, 22). One can be helped through guidance in objective observation of self to gain both a realistic and a positive attitude toward self, such as is embodied in the statement, "Know thyself; accept thyself; be thy best self."

Group Discussion of Self-findings. Until a group is truly acceptant of every member and has come to a realization of the inevitability of deviant problems in every personality, it is better not to discuss individual responses directly. However, tallies of areas and ways in which members have indicated discrepancies between self-concepts and mirrored images of self reflected from others will provide much material for thoughtful discussion that may clarify reasons for discrepancies and lead toward fuller self-understanding and self-improvement.

An Outline for a Personality Preview. A composition guided by questions such as those that follow [3] may provide a tangible introduction for fairly mature students to the problems of studying self. Some of the tests used later in the self-appraisal program are likely to provide checks on self-judgments made at this point and help to answer questions about which the individual is uncertain. These points have been formulated to cover in a nontechnical manner some of the trends in the organization of personality that are frequently inferred from various projective techniques of a clinical nature. Students who give indications of potentially serious maladjustments are likely to benefit from special clinical study as they proceed with self-appraisal. Discussion of points in this outline should, in the main, be kept within the boundaries of "normal" behavior. Case studies can be introduced helpfully to illustrate problems of adjustment in these areas, and to help the group to think and plan about ways to work toward improved adjustments. Instructions to students regarding the preparation of their self-appraisal compositions might be: "Jot down in your notebook illustrations of behavior related to the following questions before attempting to write a description of how you think you stand at present with respect to these matters."

1. *What are your ambitions and aspirations?* Do you have quite definite purposes that help to focus and direct your energies in work and play from day to day? Or are you drifting rather aimlessly without awareness of specific goals toward which you are striving? Do your present aspirations seem to be in harmony with potential abilities and aptitudes, your

[3] Adapted from M. E. Bennett, *College and Life,* 4th ed., McGraw-Hill Book Company, Inc., New York, 1952, pp. 273–274.

basic interests, and your over-all personality trends as you know them?

2. *How strong is your reality awareness?* Are your goals based on knowledge of your abilities and the world about you, or are they visionary and impracticable? Do you have a close and vital contact with your environment, or do you spend much of your time daydreaming instead of working and playing actively with others?

3. *What are you attitudes toward self and others?* Do you tend to feel inferior or superior to others? Do you respect both yourself and others and are you understanding of strengths and weaknesses in both? Do you try to be your own best self and recognize the same right for others? Are you essentially selfish and self-centered, or have you learned to share and cooperate happily with others? Are your feelings easily hurt? Are you sensitive to the feelings of others? Are you as interested in the welfare and happiness of others as you are in your own?

4. *What do you do about your emotions?* Do you tend to feel deeply and warmly about people and events, or are you usually somewhat cold, indifferent, or apathetic? Or where, approximately, would you place yourself between these two extremes? Do you have strong likes and dislikes, and what do you do about them? Are you able to express your feelings easily in ways that are acceptable to both yourself and others? Are you reserved and cautious about expressing your feelings and do you tend to bottle them up? Do you frequently have temper outbursts? Can you express your feelings naturally and spontaneously in ways appropriate to the situation and without being tactless or bizarre in your behavior? Do you sometimes have strong compulsions to do certain things without understanding why?

5. *What are your worries and tensions?* Do you often feel lonesome and uncertain as to whether others like you or love you? Or do you have a secure feeling of belonging to certain groups and of being accepted by them? Do you often feel depressed and unhappy, or are you fairly cheerful most of the time? Do you have swings of moods from happiness to unhappiness without much apparent cause for the changes? Do you have persistent fears, worries, or a sense of guilt or tension that you cannot explain or control? Are you preoccupied or worried about your body or your health? Are you able to face difficult or dangerous situations frankly with suitable concern and do something about them? Do you tend to be happy-go-lucky and avoid meeting difficult situations?

6. *How self-directive are you?* Can you direct your energies persistently in carrying through a plan of action, or do you give up easily when you meet difficulties or distractions? Are you rather stubborn and inflexible about changing your behavior or plans to meet new or changed situations? How readily can you adapt yourself to people and conditions without sacrificing basic essentials in your purposes and plans? How do you meet inevitable frustrations?

7. *Are you developing a serviceable life philosophy?* What are the
life values that you consider worth striving for? Are you using these as
criteria for choosing activities and friends and in formulating plans for
the future?

Informal appraisal through pupils' writings

Open Questions. This type of question, which calls for free responses
from students, offers good opportunities to tap feelings and thoughts
about many phases of self and life. A great variety of questions can be
used, such as "What I like about my home," "What I'd like to change
about my home," "What I like (and dislike) about myself," "What
makes me mad," "What worries me," "What are my three wishes?" A
group will need some warming-up discussion before writing on these
questions, and excellent rapport with the leader is important to elicit
meaningful replies. While they can open many doors to understanding
of individuals, they can be overused to the point where groups may
become wary of exposing their innermost thoughts and feelings (23,
pp. 98–119). While individual replies are always to be treated as confidential, reports of tallied items can often be discussed with profit by
a group to show common trends and problems in the area dealt with by
the question.

Sentence-completion Method. The open-end question, or sentence-
completion method, is a variation of the open question. It is closely
related to the word-association technique, but usually has a longer
stimulus and can be varied to tap great varieties of attitudes and trends
of thought and feeling. An informal comparison of sentence completions with autobiographical materials has been suggested as one promising method of checking the validity of each type of data (24, p. 298).
The sentence-completion method is well adapted to use with groups.
Sentence beginnings may be structured or relatively unstructured. That
is, they may begin with a specific suggestion such as "My most interesting experience during vacation was . . ."; or with an indefinite word
such as "Usually . . ." or "Now. . . ." Some beginnings may be phrased
in either the first or third person, such as "Mary . . . ," "John . . . ,"
"Mother . . . ," or "Father . . ." or "I wish . . . ," "I like . . . ," "I
dislike . . . ," "I feel happy (or unhappy) when. . . ."

Instructions may vary greatly. Sometimes they merely request the individual to complete the sentence and explain that any response is acceptable. Again, they may ask that subjects finish the sentences as quickly
as possible. Another approach is to encourage spontaneity by explaining
that each person will give different answers, and asking the subjects to
express their real feelings, to write down the first idea that comes to
mind.

The material supplied by these informal completions may be used in innumerable ways. Some research workers have attempted to group replies as showing (*a*) conflict and negative attitudes, (*b*) neutral attitudes, and (*c*) good adjustment and positive attitudes. Often the responses give valuable clues for interviewing, but caution is needed to avoid pushing a person beyond what he is ready to consider or reveal, since many unconscious attitudes may be tapped in the completions. The Rotter Incomplete Sentences Blank has been called a "vocational counselor's gold mine" with reference to responses to such stimulus words as "I wish . . . ," "I failed . . . ," "My greatest fear . . . ," "I want to know . . . " (25).

If tallied and classified responses are considered with a group, it is essential to avoid individual identifications, and also to avoid any suggestions of undesirable or unworthy attitudes which might accentuate feelings of guilt or shame. To understand but never to blame or ridicule is an ironclad rule with the use of this type of projective material.

Sentences which are structured to secure expressions of likes and dislikes, successes and failures, can be useful in approaching the question of interests, abilities, and aptitudes significant for self-appraisal looking toward educational and vocational planning.

A resourceful group leader will develop a variety of informal appraisal devices adapted to the needs and interests of a particular group. Among these could be diaries to reveal out-of-school activities and personal-social relationships, and forms for studying participation in school life (23). Autobiographies in various forms could be included in such a list (see pages 253 and 254); also great varieties of work sheets planned to guide students' thinking in analyzing problems, collecting pertinent materials, and arriving at plans of action. We might call these "things to do to find out."

More objective approaches to self-study

Rating Methods. Ratings are not as objective as standardized tests and inventories, but they serve a very useful purpose in group study. A composite of attempted lists of common human traits to be rated could include several thousand items. The problem for a class group is that of selecting a sizable list that will include characteristics significant for educational and vocational success and good personal adjustment. Surveys of characteristics employers consider important in jobs (26, 27), teachers in schoolwork, and mental hygienists for personal adjustment would provide an excellent project for class study (20).

From these lists simple rating scales could be formulated for individual use. To have any reliability, at least five to eight ratings should be secured by each individual from others who know him well. If rating scales are used as a part of student appraisal in a school, these may serve for class use; or scales used by business or industrial firms or by colleges as a part of the selection process for employees or prospective students may prove helpful.

Three different methods of rating are frequently used:

1. Judging an individual in relation to a group according to designated categories such as superior, average, or inferior, has proved more satisfactory for the over-all evaluation of performance in a given area than for specific traits.

2. Comparisons are sometimes used in which each person in a group is paired with every other person, and the name of the person adjudged to be superior in each pair with respect to the qualities or performance being rated is underlined. By counting the number of times each person's name is underlined, scores and ranks within the group can be obtained.

3. Another rating method aimed at eliminating emotional bias forces the rater to decide between series of alternative descriptive statements as applied to the individual being rated, instead of ranking him on specific traits.

In method 1 on rating scales for specific traits or characteristics, each point on the scale is frequently described in terms of observable behavior in order to eliminate subjective variations in judgment as to what constitutes superiority or inferiority in a given trait. Space is often provided for listing instances of behavior that support a judgment. The Personality Record (pages 248 and 249) is an example of a rating scale with behavior descriptions that is used in many schools.

Cronbach (1, pp. 518–519) has pointed out the value of comparing teacher and peer ratings, since they may involve different biases. The peer ratings may place weight on popularity and reputation, whereas adult ratings may be influenced by limited observations of initiative and other types of behavior.

Personality Inventories. Some of the earliest inventories with standardized norms were aimed at measuring such personality traits or trends as introversion-extroversion, dominance-submission, and self-sufficiency, or adjustment in areas such as home, social relationships, health, and emotional tendencies. The current trend is toward the statistical search for aspects of personality that are fairly independent of each other—in statistical terms, that do not correlate highly with each other, and that might be called independent factors in personality. At present there is little or no consensus as to either the number or the nature of factors that have been reliably identified, or as to what they should be called (1, pp. 464–505). None of these inventories should be used as an exact or final measure of an individual's personality. Usually they arouse interest in a group, and they may be used cautiously as a sort of mirror

PERSONALITY RECORD (CONFIDENTIAL)
(REVISED)

Room...........
Grade...........
Middle Name...........
First Name...........
Last Name...........

PERSONAL CHARACTERISTICS OF...........

School...........   Town or City...........   State...........

The following characterizations are descriptions of behavior. It is recommended that where possible the judgments of a number of the pupil's present teachers be indicated by the use of the following method or by checks:

Example: MOTIVATION

	Purposeless	Vacillating	Usually Purposeful	Effectively motivated	Highly motivated
		1 √	M (5) √√√√√		2 √√

M (5) indicates the most common or modal behavior of the pupil as shown by the agreement of five of the eight teachers reporting. The location of the numerals to the left and right indicates that one teacher considers the pupil *vacillating* and that two teachers consider him *highly motivated*. If preferred, the subject fields or other areas of relationship with the pupil may be used to replace the numerals.

1. MOTIVATION	Purposeless	Vacillating	Usually Purposeful	Effectively motivated	Highly motivated
2. INDUSTRY	Seldom works even under pressure	Needs constant pressure	Needs occasional prodding	Prepares assigned work regularly	Seeks additional work
3. INITIATIVE	Merely conforms	Seldom initiates	Frequently initiates	Consistently self-reliant	Actively creative
4. INFLUENCE AND LEADERSHIP	Negative	Co-operative but retiring	Sometimes in minor affairs	Contributing in important affairs	Judgment respected—makes things go
5. CONCERN FOR OTHERS	Self-centered	Indifferent	Somewhat socially concerned	Generally concerned	Deeply and actively concerned
6. RESPONSIBILITY	Unreliable	Somewhat dependable	Usually dependable	Conscientious	Assumes much responsibility
7. INTEGRITY	Not dependable	Questionable at times	Generally honest	Reliable, dependable	Consistently trustworthy
8. EMOTIONAL STABILITY	Hyperemotional	Excitable	Usually well-balanced	Well-balanced	Exceptionally stable
	Apathetic	Unresponsive			

Significant school activities and special interests or abilities. List membership and offices held in school activities:

Significant limitations (physical, social, mental):

Additional information which may be helpful, such as probable financial needs or work experience:

Principal's Comments and Recommendations

1. Specific statement concerning the applicant's fitness for acceptance by this college or employer:

2. Principal's estimate of applicant's future success, based on the purpose of this application.
☐ Little success ☐ May encounter some difficulty ☐ Average ☐ Above average ☐ Superior

3. Specific recommendation ☐ Recommended ☐ Not recommended for this college or position ☐ Prefer not to make recommendation

Date......... Signature......... Title.........

to reflect possibilities of which one may not be aware in subjective appraisal.

Some of these inventories were developed to aid in identifying the maladjusted or the mentally ill, and they contain items and use descriptive categories for traits that would be unsuitable for most guidance groups, particularly immature adolescents. In some regions it is necessary or desirable to secure permission of parents before such inventories are used.

The fact that some inventories can be faked by marking items that seem to describe socially acceptable behavior poses another problem. However, the climate of a group where the purpose of study is self-understanding can encourage honest responses. Thorough discussion of limitations as well as possibilities for self-knowledge should usually precede their use, though for those inventories that are intentionally camouflaged, the types of information that may be revealed to some degree in scores cannot be explained fully before administration without vitiating the results.

Another consideration that applies to all approaches to personality assessment is that of the stability of the characteristics being appraised. Cattell (28), in his intensive study of personality factors, seems to have found that some tend to persist over all ages, while others increase or decline with age. For some he finds indication of a strong influence of heredity or constitution, and for others a strong environmental influence. We should expect those that may have the strongest roots in hereditary potentials to be the most stable tendencies. Cattell has coined names for some of his factors to avoid confusion with varied meanings attached to commonly used terms, so that it is difficult to convey his ideas simply. His terms *cyclothymia* versus *schizothymia*, translated roughly as warm-heartedness, adaptability, adventurousness, and cooperativeness as contrasted at the opposite extreme with shyness, withdrawn quality, inflexibility, and oddness, appear from his statistical studies to have a large hereditary determinant. Dominance-submission appears to be about a 50-50 product of constitution and environmental influences. What he calls surgency-desurgency, the latter involving a form of generalized inhibition that may be related to early methods of punishment and repressive experiences, is considered to be largely a product of environment and tends to decline from adolescence to middle age. Cattell has urged that all researchers in the field of analysis of personality factors should pool their findings and develop a generally accepted list of trait or factor names. At present we must accept a large degree of vagueness and uncertainty with respect to objective methods of appraising personality.

ATTITUDES, OPINIONS, AND VALUE JUDGMENTS. Research in the measurement of attitudes and opinions has been carried on for many years, and some of the resulting scales would be of value in helping students develop insight into their tendencies with respect to the formulation of judgments and opinions in various aspects of life. Especially significant for vocational planning would be measures of importance attached to various life values such as economic, social-service, prestige, or philosophical (29, 10: pp. 369–394).

Appraisal of Interests. Super's (30, p. 377) classification of interests as *expressed, manifested, tested,* and *inventoried* is useful in the planning of their appraisal for an adolescent or adult group. Expressed interests of various sorts have probably been entered on personnel records at certain grade levels, and these, together with lists that pupils can prepare from memory or with the help of parents, may be useful in discovering interest trends. Even though expressed interests at succeeding ages may seem very different, an analysis of the activities involved might indicate some stable trends such as interest in people, ideas, or things, indoor or outdoor activity. This analysis may show up both stable and transitory interests, also some representing fantasy and others realism.

Informal interest questionnaires can be used to record likes and dislikes in subjects, extracurricular activities, reading, radio and television programs, wishes, work experiences, and vocational ambitions. A check list developed by one group (31) included items prepared by subject teachers, related to activities in their areas and arranged in random order to prevent a halo effect in judging likes and dislikes.

Manifested interests are those that are indicated by actual involvement in certain activities. Of course, the motives of an individual in engaging in a certain activity, even though entirely voluntary, must be understood before a specific interest is assumed. Does a boy or girl join a particular club because of liking for its activity or because of friends who are members?

Rothney and others (32, pp. 355–370) have developed a detailed activities report form. They suggest that counselors should prepare their own lists of items with local reference. Groups of students could readily assist in formulating such lists. Rothney's form includes an analysis section where items can be entered that appear to occupy a significant portion of a counselee's time, grouped under such headings as reading, sports, music, clubs, collecting, hobbies, animal care, domestic arts, and miscellaneous activities. Here again, adaptations to specific groups would be indicated.

For either expressed or manifested interests, Fryer (14, p. 370), in one of the first systematic treatments of research on interests, suggested a longitudinal approach in which a person would think carefully about experiences, pleasant and unpleasant, likes and dislikes, school, teachers, and friends at various periods in life, such as years of earliest recall, entering and last years of elementary school, junior and senior high school, college, beginning work experience, etc. These recollections could be organized in a chart under headings such as play, study, reading, religion, work and vocational interests, interest in people, and creative activities. The writer has used such a form with many high school and college groups (33, pp. 267–269).

All of the types of recall suggested for the study of expressed and manifested interests will be valuable material for the preparation of an autobiography dealing with many aspects of personal development (see pages 253 and 254).

Tests and inventories of interests are attempts at objective cross-section appraisal, usually of *vocational* interests. The tests infer interests from information or achievement, based on the assumption that an individual will acquire information about his areas of interest. Super and others (37, p. 379) found during World War II that an information test proved to be one of the most valid tests in the Air Force's selection and classification battery. Not many interest tests are available. The Michigan Vocabulary Test is one example.

Cronbach (1, pp. 406–419) has classified the most widely used interest inventories into three types as to theory of construction: The Strong Vocational Interest Blank has empirically developed scoring formulas that provide for comparison of one's interest pattern with that of successful people in a variety of vocations, mainly in professional, managerial, and technical fields. A new instrument, the Minnesota Vocational Interest Inventory, developed by Clark and co-workers, is similar but with keys chiefly for skilled trades (34). The original Kuder inventory was based on the organization of clusters of occupational interests, including within each cluster items of substantial correlation with each other. A later form has provided in addition some specific occupational scores similar to those of the Strong inventory. A third approach in the Lee-Thorpe Occupational Interest Inventory involves the selection of items based on an analysis of job descriptions, and scores are classified in six categories.

Super (30, p. 381) has compared the classifications of interest factors in all the various inventories and has suggested a synthesis of groupings as follows: scientific, social welfare, literary, material, system (clerical and computational), contact (persuasive, business, political), artistic, and musical.

Studies of the relationships of expressed and inventoried interests have indicated that they do not correlate closely enough to substitute one for the other. Each seems to give some additional and different information. It has been suggested that the use of both types of data can lead to more realistic self-appraisal than either one alone (34).

The Autobiography. Autobiographies have most often been used as a means of gaining information about developing interests and abilities for use in vocational planning. They can be equally helpful in studying general personality trends and the sources of personal difficulties or problems. The approach can be through creative writing, a systematic investigation of various phases of the life history, or a combination of both methods. Some guidelines are necessary to avoid superficiality and limited coverage, and good rapport between leader and group is essential to ensure the spontaneity and creativity that may reveal the real person. It has been suggested by several that an unstructured form is better when social-emotional aspects of personality are being appraised, and the structured form is more useful for educational and vocational planning (35, pp. 18–27). Rothney (36, 95–109) gives general instructions to students for both types. A detailed outline is provided for the structured form under three major headings: The present—What kind of person am I? The past—How did I get that way? The future—What do I hope to become? The instructions for the unstructured approach include the three questions with no outline.

Three other questions might guide the discussion: (*a*) what one starts with—his hereditary potentialities; (*b*) what has happened to one—all the environmental influences; and (*c*) how one has reacted to events and influences. The first question cannot, of course, yield categorical answers as to inherited potentialities, since we are at any time the resultant of the interaction of hereditary and environmental factors. Study of one's ancestors and present relatives may, however, offer valuable suggestions as to characteristics or talents to look for in one's self (33, pp. 215–240).

How one has reacted to all of the vicissitudes of living carries one into the inner recesses of personality, and the material dealing with these personal reactions to life should be treated with the utmost confidence and respect. If very disturbing emotions are uncovered and released, there may be the need for therapy in facing them and resolving conflicts.

The constructive aspect of this third question is the recognition that mastery of one's self and of life may reside in large part in the ability to control how he reacts to the past, to present conditions, and to future possibilities. One may or may not be able to control what happens to him, but there is always the possibility of controlling and directing his reactions and thereby mastering many situations that might otherwise mold his fate undesirably.

In preparing to write an autobiography, it is helpful to make jottings over several days of recollections of past events in the home, at school, with playmates, at work, in clubs or other groups, and when alone, noting happenings, emotional reactions, achievement and failures, and relationships with others. Discussion with parents and others may help to recall forgotten events.

After the autobiography is written, it is often helpful for vocational planning to go through it for the purpose of detecting and listing interests, evidences of abilities, and attitudes and behavior that might be significant for present self-improvement and later occupational adjustment.

If the autobiographies that are prepared by members of a class contain deeply significant personal information, it is not likely that they should be shared with other members of the group. The leader can provide helpful guidance through the presentation of hypothetical autobiographies for analysis and interpretation. He can include materials, carefully camouflaged, involving problems similar to those of some members of the group that might cause emotional conflict or tension because of difficulties or frustrations with respect to vocational or educational plans. Class discussions of possible causes of difficulties and ways to resolve them, and of the interpretation of events in the life of the hypothetical individual, may often yield insights to class members regarding their own problems and provide clues to constructive planning and action.

Biographical inventories have been used in business and industry and in the Air Force for selection purposes based on the assumption that one's past behavior is a good predictor of his future behavior. Super (37, pp. 35–38) has developed such forms for his Career Pattern Study and for selection purposes. Siegel (38) has developed a self-administering inventory for high school senior and college freshmen boys with multiple-choice items describing activities under such headings as social, religious, political, and heterosexual activities, literature, music and art, socioeconomic status, economic independence, social conformity, and lack of physical health.

As with expressed and inventoried interests, the written autobiography and the biographical inventory doubtless tap somewhat different facets of personality and supplement rather than duplicate each other.

Appraising Aptitudes and Abilities. There is no clear differentiation of these two terms in either research or practice. Theoretically, an aptitude may be a potential possibility of some sort, and an ability is a developed capacity to perform in some respect. Since potential aptitudes can only be inferred from observable or measurable performance or achievement, the term *abilities* is frequently used to include both aptitude and proficiency (10, p. 276; 30, pp. 61–62).

Another essential consideration in planning a group appraisal program is the fact that there is no complete consensus among research psychologists as to the number or kind of human abilities. The study of widespread efforts to discover "pure" abilities through factor analysis [4] has led Cronbach to conclude that the number of possible factors is inexhaustible, but that the important goal is to discover a dependable list of fairly important abilities (1, pp. 261–263).

We shall consider here some of the kinds of available objective, standardized tests, and also some more informal ways of appraising abilities. Chapter 5 has dealt more specifically with methods of planning and carrying out the testing program in an appraisal project with a group.

APPRAISING CHARACTERISTICS BY OBJECTIVE AND STANDARDIZED TESTS. We shall consider only a few of the major categories of ability tests from the viewpoint of student self-appraisal. The counselor or psychologist would invariably need more data for advising with students than would be made directly available to them through a group testing and guidance program. Other pertinent data should be interpreted to students when desirable as a means of questioning, verifying, or supplementing information gained through the group testing. "Desirable" should be interpreted as meaning whatever can help the individual to gain such an understanding of his probable potentialities that he can make realistic educational and vocational plans, and whatever he can use effectively and wholesomely in dealing with assets, liabilities, and adjustment problems.

GENERAL MENTAL ABILITY OR SCHOLASTIC APTITUDE TESTS. The term *intelligence* has been avoided, since there is much controversy as to its meaning and it would seem to serve no useful purpose in self-appraisal. The term *scholastic aptitude* can serve any necessary purpose in helping students to plan wisely with respect to training programs. When test results are stated in terms of percentile placements or standard scores on a normal probability curve, they provide the individual with the opportunity to see how he may compare with others in his ability to do scholastic work without classifying himself as bright, average, or inferior generally. When norms and critical scores for successful students in various training programs are available, an individual may be helped to discover what are his chances for success in various training fields that he may wish to consider.

When interpreting scholastic-aptitude scores to a group, emphasis should be placed upon the importance of implementing this basic ability by habits of industry, drive to accomplish, and social awareness and fa-

---

[4] This is a highly technical research method defined simply by Cronbach as "a systematic method for examining the meaning of a test by studying its correlations with other variables" (1, p. 247).

cility; also, upon the importance of the total pattern of abilities for success in any field of work. When scholastic aptitude is considered in relation to different types of work, it can usually be used best negatively to ascertain what occupational fields should *not* be entered because demands upon this ability would be too great on the one hand or too limited on the other hand to challenge fullest effort. Adult success in almost all fields requires many additional factors, which should all be assessed in the guidance process. Among these factors are social adjustment, emotional stability, and drive to accomplish.

No two general mental-ability or scholastic-aptitude tests measure exactly the same qualities in the same proportion, and no one test can be relied upon to give a thoroughly accurate picture of the individual's learning aptitude. This fact implies the need for more than one test of scholastic aptitude, and much supplementary data to verify or challenge results. Marks or scholastic records of students, and achievement tests, may serve helpfully as checks upon general ability tests, but factors such as reading disability, physical handicaps, or limited experience may affect these other types of information and render them all invalid as measures of potential ability.

This caution will be illustrated by a brief case history of an eleventh-grade boy, seventeen years old. Jack was in a guidance class with a teacher-counselor trained in music. On a series of interest, achievement, and aptitude tests administered to the group, he placed in the lowest quartile on all of them. He had shown some evidence of a reading disability, but it had not appeared serious enough to refer him to the reading laboratory for special help. Soon after the class members had made their individual profiles of test data, Jack stopped working, grew uncommunicative and morose. The teacher became concerned about him, tried to encourage him with praise, and eventually referred him to the psychologist, expressing fear that he might have suicidal intentions.

Psychological study revealed a person of very superior scholastic ability but with a deep sense of inadequacy, emotional immaturity, and a slow reaction time. The health history indicated hearing and visual difficulties, and a visual test showed very severe muscle imbalance which the oculist warned would serve as a barrier between his mind and books until corrected. A current health check yielded evidence of an endocrine imbalance and a severe vitamin deficiency. All his life, Jack had been called "slow" in comparison with brothers and sisters, but had succeeded in maintaining a fairly high scholastic average by dint of long and strenuous hours of study. He was bright enough to realize that something was wrong and to have ambitions for a professional career. His consistently low test data finally convinced him that he was "dumb" and that he should no longer strive to achieve. This classroom approach to self-appraisal by itself could have proved fatal to this boy's development, if an insightful teacher had not recognized that something was basically wrong in the situation.

MULTIFACTOR AND ACHIEVEMENT TESTS. The increased use of factor analysis has revealed much overlapping among factors sampled by tests of general mental ability, and of various aspects of educational aptitude and achievement. There are batteries of "differential-aptitude tests," of "educational-development tests," and of achievement in specific subject areas. Diagnostic and achievement tests in reading and other skill subjects are usually so designated, though a combination of these functions is claimed for some.

In 1957, Super (39–41), in summing up the present usability of existing multifactor tests, recommended only two for immediate guidance use: the Differential Aptitude Tests [5] for educational counseling, and the General Aptitude Test Battery [6] for some phases of vocational counseling. Some of the others were recommended as useful for research purposes, and counselors were urged to watch for further research that may bring other batteries into practical use as competitors or rivals of those already usable. Super points out that predictive research on the Differential Aptitude Tests indicates that it measures general academic ability to a large degree as well as some differential abilities for certain nonacademic subjects. He warns that much of the interpretation of the General Aptitude Test Battery has been based upon job analyses rather than actual validation for all the occupations for which patterns have been established.[7] Only continuous study of new research findings as they appear in professional literature can provide bases for wise selection and sound interpretation of any standardized tests. Locally developed norms are also important for many uses of tests. Further consideration of the use of test data with a group is included in Chapter 5.

General test batteries of educational achievement or educational development, of reading proficiency, and sometimes records of subject tests not included in general batteries, are likely to be available on the personnel records in most schools. These records, together with current

[5] By G. K. Bennett, H. G. Seashore, and A. G. Wesman, The Psychological Corporation. Names assigned to subtests in this DAT battery are abstract reasoning, space relations, mechanical reasoning, clerical speed and accuracy, and language usage—spelling and sentences (41).

[6] Published by the United States Employment Service (41). Names assigned to the subtests in this battery as in current use in 1956 are intelligence, verbal aptitude, numerical aptitude, spacial aptitude, form perception, clerical perception, motor coordination, finger dexterity, and manual dexterity (41).

[7] The GATB is administered through the local State Employment Offices except where special arrangements have been made with local school officials. Exchange of school and employment-office data is helpful in both vocational guidance and job placement.

achievement tests, provide valuable sources of self-knowledge. Results of all standardized tests should be studied in relation to school marks and other evidences of achievement, both in school and out-of-school activities; also in relation to interests, attitudes, motivation, and effort. Only thus can they have any reliable meaning as to potential abilities. If standardized commercial tests do not measure adequately the curriculum objectives in an institution or in certain subject areas, locally developed and normed tests may be more helpful in assessing some abilities.

VOCATIONAL APTITUDES. Except for individuals contemplating immediate entrance into specific jobs or highly specialized vocational-training courses, most vocational-aptitude tests are not likely to prove very meaningful in group guidance. Music or art tests, for example, may be both interesting and helpful in planning avocational pursuits, and of some value to those considering vocations in these areas. Studies of correlations between aptitude measures and occupational success have indicated that aptitude scores may be of little value in long-range prediction of occupational success (42, 43).

Miller (10, p. 316) concludes: "Tests of abilities may offer some assistance in making judgments of the immediate short-range variety, as to probable success in training for a specific job, but not much help for even short-range prediction of success on the job." Also he points out that for successive steps in training programs, from secondary school through college, previous achievement is the best single indicator (10, p. 309). Of course, tests and achievement are usually combined in selection criteria for advanced training. The batteries developed for admission to technical or professional schools are usually available only as a part of the selection and admission procedure. Understanding of the types of abilities and aptitudes required for courses in such schools can be used in assistance to individuals in acquiring the kind of information about themselves that will contribute to increased realism in formulating educational and vocational plans. There is a wide variety of tests of specific aptitudes or aptitude patterns such as artistic, musical, clerical, or mechanical that could provide helpful and interesting data.

No clear-cut boundaries can be drawn between educational and vocational aptitudes. Many of the abilities and aptitudes now measured in tests designed primarily for educational guidance are included in the characteristics listed for various occupations. We have already seen examples in the descriptions of the DAT and GATB (see page 257).

INFORMAL APPRAISAL OF ABILITIES. Every course and activity in an educational program affords opportunities to discover and appraise some assets and liabilities. All teachers can help in analyzing the abilities most tapped and utilized in their respective subjects. The writer once cooperated with committees of teachers in one school system who prepared lists of abilities and other personal characteristics important for various courses. These lists were duplicated for each department and thus were available in convenient form for study by pupils, teachers, and parents in relation to achievement and marks in courses.

Charts or work sheets can be developed to guide the student and instructor in estimating the degree to which the student's achievements are commensurate with his potential abilities. Evidence in descriptions or examples of specific achievements will serve to make these estimates more meaningful to both the teacher and the student.

Such a chart might have headings as follows:

EVALUATION CHART

| Abilities most needed in this course (or activity) | Ratings for each ability: weak; average; strong | | Illustrations supporting each rating |
	Student ratings	Instructor ratings	

The term *abilities* as used in the chart heading may well be interpreted broadly enough to include not only mental abilities and motor and mechanical skills and aptitudes, but the whole gamut of personal characteristics that are significant for successful work in each course or subject.

Lists of required abilities could profitably be developed cooperatively by instructor and class or activity group, or committee lists, such as those mentioned previously, could be examined critically and adapted to the particular class or activity. If each student kept his own chart in his notebook, he could be reminded of his self-appraisal problem frequently. With a general understanding that everyone has both strengths and weaknesses, this approach to self-knowledge can be genuinely wholesome in helping each student to accept his own pattern of abilities. It may also stimulate him to make the most of his strengths as well as the best of his weaknesses.

Notations from teachers to counselors regarding observed abilities or potentialities of students can provide a wealth of material to implement marks in courses and to serve as a rich background for interpretation of tests and other objective measures included in a self-appraisal unit. Each teacher or adviser has the splendid opportunity to inspire students by opening new vistas of opportunities. Here is a point where information should flow both ways between instructor and guidance worker, since an over-all view of a student's pattern of assets and liabilities may be more meaningful for the making of vocational plans than the strength of one or more abilities utilized in a course.

The values of this approach to self-appraisal through evaluation in exploratory courses in industrial arts, home economics, graphic arts, and music, and in specific vocational training, are quite obvious. It is likely to be equally valuable in all the various academic subjects such as science, mathematics, social studies, foreign language, and English, both for exploring abilities important in various professions and technical fields and for serving as partial checks upon the accuracy of test data on personnel records for intelligence or scholastic aptitude and differential aptitudes related to various subject areas. Problems of comparing certain types of abilities and other characteristics with the requirements of occupations and jobs are considered in Chapter 11.

Appraising Physical and Health Assets and Liabilities. Most modern schools and colleges keep health records that include a health history and reports of health examinations. These examinations in some schools are a bit routine in nature, but interpretations of all available health data should be used by students in their self-appraisal. From the writer's observation, this seldom happens.

Interpretations from doctors, nurses, physical-education teachers, and hygiene instructors, combined, should provide each person with reasonably good understanding of health and physical resources that can be used to plan a suitable regimen of living for the present and the future, and an educational and vocational career adapted to possible limitations and assets for work and other aspects of living.

Gaining a synthesized view

Patterns of personal characteristics are usually more significant for life planning than any one characteristic. Weakness in some phase of personality can fit into a total picture harmoniously and even be turned into an asset. On the other hand, some weakness such as procrastination, poor motivation, lack of effort, lack of persistence in the face of frustration, and lack of self-confidence can undermine achievement in spite of fine talents (44, 311–352; 45).

Individuals need guidance in learning (*a*) how to capitalize on assets in their planning, and (*b*) what to do about liabilities. Here the problems are often those of deciding how far to go in overcoming weaknesses before diminishing returns for efforts make the remedial process unwise, and how the liability may be fitted into a satisfactory program, when desirable limits of improvement have been reached. Too often, in our conscientious efforts to help students to achieve at their best levels, we overlook the need for their wholesome self-acceptance of patterns of ability, and an action program to make the *most* of their strengths and the *best* of their weaknesses. Interrelations of interests, abilities, value systems, personality traits, and the self-concepts are significant for any phase of life planning, and doubtless influence every choice and decision, whether consciously or not.

Interpretations of all the findings in a self-appraisal project and their applications in self-direction require the same types of understanding needed by the trained personnel worker. The group situation provides an opportunity for the leader to share some understandings of the limitations and possibilities inherent in the various kinds of subjective and objective, informal and standardized data at hand, of necessary gaps in knowledge about personality, of the limits of predictive techniques, and of the hunches and thought processes that enter into any diagnostic picture of an individual. Both art and science are needed in this process, and the attempt to explain it to immature students in a way that will help them synthesize and use their findings should cause any trained personnel worker to engage in a good bit of deep and honest introspection about how fully we can ever understand the varied facets of another human being. It is likely also to cause one to stress with a group the importance of developing skill in self-appraisal techniques that can be used throughout a lifetime.

We shall consider the use of self-knowledge in relation to each of the areas dealt with in succeeding chapters in this section, and more about methods of utilizing all phases of an educational program, as well as the direct approach in a guidance group.

REFERENCES CITED IN CHAPTER

1. Cronbach, Lee J.: *Essentials of Psychological Testing*, 2d ed., Harper & Row, Publishers, New York, 1960.
2. Carrel, Alexis: *Man the Unknown*, Harper & Brothers, New York, 1935.
3. Murphy, Gardner: *Human Potentialities*, Basic Books, Inc., Publishers, New York, 1958.
4. Jersild, Arthur T.: *When Teachers Face Themselves*, Bureau of Publications, Teachers College, Columbia University, New York, 1955.
5. Kubie, Lawrence S.: "The Psychiatrist Considers Curriculum Development," *Teachers College Record*, 50:241–246, January, 1949.
6. Dollard, John, and Neal E. Miller: *Personality and Psychotherapy: An Analysis in Terms of Learning, Thinking, and Culture*, McGraw-Hill Book Company, Inc., New York, 1950.
7. Jersild, Arthur T.: "Self-understanding in Childhood and Adolescence," *The American Psychologist*, 6:122–126, April, 1951.
8. Jersild, Arthur T.: *In Search of Self*, Bureau of Publications, Teachers College, Columbia University, New York, 1952.

9. Jersild, Arthur T., and associates: *Education for Self-understanding*, Bureau of Publications, Teachers College, Columbia University, New York, 1953.

10. Miller, Carroll H.: *Foundations of Guidance*, Harper & Row, Publishers, New York, 1961.

11. Layton, Wilbur L. (ed.): *The Strong Vocational Interest Blank, Research and Use*, Minnesota Studies in Student Personnel Work, no. 10, University of Minnesota Press, Minneapolis, 1960.

12. Jersild, Arthur T., and Ruth J. Tasch: *Children's Interests and What They Suggest for Education*, Bureau of Publications, Teachers College, Columbia University, New York, 1949.

13. Ginzberg, Eli, et al.: *Occupational Choice: An Approach to a General Theory*, Columbia University Press, New York, 1951.

14. Fryer, Douglas: *The Measurement of Interests*, Henry Holt and Company, Inc., New York, 1931.

15. Remmers, Herman H., and Robert H. Bauernfeind: *Examiners Manual for the SRA Junior Inventory, Form A*, Science Research Associates, Inc., Chicago, 1951.

16. Gesell, Arnold, and Frances L. Ilg: *The Child from Five to Ten*, Harper & Row, Publishers, New York, 1946.

17. Hardy, Martha C., and Carolyn H. Hoeffer: *Healthy Growth*, University of Chicago Press, Chicago, 1936.

18. Bugenthal, James F. T., and Seymour L. Zelen: "Investigation into the 'Self-concept'—The W.A.Y. Technique," *Journal of Personality*, 18:483–498, June, 1950.

19. Cooley, Charles Horton: *Human Nature and the Social Order*, Charles Scribner's Sons, New York, 1910.

20. Jahoda, Marie: *Current Concepts of Positive Mental Health*, Basic Books, Inc., Publishers, New York, 1958.

21. Strong, Donald J., and Daniel D. Feder: "Measurement of the Self Concept: A Critique of the Literature," *Journal of Counseling Psychology*, 8:170–178, summer, 1961.

22. Berger, Emanuel M.: "Relationships among Acceptance of Self, Acceptance of Others, and MMPI Scores," *Journal of Counseling Psychology*, 2:279–284, winter, 1955.

23. Taba, Hilda, et al.: *Diagnosing Human Relations Needs*, American Council on Education, Washington, 1951.

24. Anderson, Harold H., and Gladys L. Anderson (eds.): *An Introduction to Projective Techniques and Other Devices for Understanding the Dynamics of Human Behavior*, Prentice-Hall, Inc., Englewood Cliffs, N.J., 1951.

25. Hale, Peter P.: "The Rotter: A Vocational Counselor's Goldmine," *The Vocational Guidance Quarterly*, 9:119–123, winter, 1960–1961.

26. Worthy, James C.: *What Employers Want*, Life Adjustment Booklet, Science Research Associates, Inc., Chicago, 1950. (The bibliography in this booklet contains additional references on this question.)

27. Dickerson, Carl: "What Employers Look for in the College Graduate," *The Personnel and Guidance Journal*, 33:460–464, April, 1955.

28. Cattell, Raymond B.: "Foundations of Personality Measurement Theory in Multivariate Experiment," in Bernard M. Bass and Irwin A. Berg (eds.), *Objective Approaches to Personality Assessment*, D. Van Nostrand Company, Inc., Princeton, N.J., 1959, pp. 42–65.

29. Remmers, Herman H.: *Introduction to Opinion and Attitude Measurement*, Harper & Row, Publishers, New York, 1954.

30. Super, Donald E.: *Appraising Vocational Fitness by Means of Psychological Tests*, Harper & Row, Publishers, New York, 1949, pp. 376–480.

31. Smith, E. R., and R. W. Tyler: *Appraising and Recording Student Progress*, Harper & Row, Publishers, New York, 1942.

32. Rothney, John W. M., Paul J. Danielson, and Robert A. Heimann: *Measurement for Guidance*, Harper & Row, Publishers, New York, 1959, pp. 282–319, 353–370.

33. Bennett, Margaret E.: *College and Life: Problems in Self-discovery and Self-development*, 4th ed., McGraw-Hill Book Company, Inc., New York, 1952.

34. Christiansen, Harley D.: "Inventoried and Claimed Interests," *The Vocational Guidance Quarterly*, 9:128–130, winter, 1960–1961.
35. Cottle, William C., and N. M. Downie: *Procedures and Preparation for Counseling*, Prentice-Hall, Inc., Englewood Cliffs, N.J., 1960, pp. 224–256.
36. Rothney, John W. M.: *Guidance Practices and Results*, Harper & Row, Publishers, New York, 1958.
37. Super, Donald E.: "Theories and Assumptions Underlying Approaches to Personality Assessment," in Bernard M. Bass and Irwin A. Berg (eds.), *Objective Approaches to Personality Assessment*, D. Van Nostrand Company, Inc., Princeton, N.J., 1959, pp. 24–41.
38. Siegel, Laurence A.: "A Biographical Inventory for Students," *Journal of Applied Psychology*, 40:5–10, 122–126, 1956.
39. Super, Donald E.: "The Use of Multifactor Test Batteries in Guidance," *The Personnel and Guidance Journal*, 35:9–15, September, 1956.
40. Super, Donald E.: "The Multifactor Tests: Summing Up," *The Personnel and Guidance Journal*, 36:17–20, September, 1957.
41. "The Use of Multifactor Tests in Guidance," a reprint of articles on multifactor tests, *The Personnel and Guidance Journal*, 1956–1957.
42. Ghiselli, E. E.: *The Measurement of Occupational Aptitude*, Publications in Psychology, 8:101–216, University of California Press, Berkeley, 1955.
43. Thorndike, R. L., and Elizabeth Hagen: *Ten Thousand Careers*, John Wiley & Sons, Inc., New York, 1959.
44. Terman, Lewis M. (ed.): *The Gifted Child Grows Up: Twenty-five Years' Follow-up of a Superior Group*, Stanford University Press, Stanford, Calif., 1947.
45. Terman, Lewis M., and Melita H. Oden: *The Gifted Group at Mid-life: Thirty-five Years' Follow-up of the Superior Child*, Stanford University Press, Stanford, Calif., 1959.

ADDITIONAL REFERENCES

Cattell, Raymond B.: *Personality and Motivation Structure and Measurement*, Harcourt, Brace & World, Inc., New York, 1957.
Cohen, Dorothy H., and Virginia Stern: *Observing and Recording the Behavior of Young Children*, Bureau of Publications, Teachers College, Columbia University, New York, 1958.
Goldman, Leo: *Using Tests in Counseling*, Appleton-Century-Crofts, Inc., New York, 1961.
Gordon, Ira J.: *Children's Views of Themselves*, Association for Childhood Education, International, Washington, 1960.
Matteson, Ross W.: "Self-estimates of College Freshmen," *The Personnel and Guidance Journal*, 34:280–284, January, 1956.
Strang, Ruth: *The Adolescent Views Himself*, McGraw-Hill Book Company, Inc., New York, 1957.
Super, Donald E., and John O. Crites: *Appraising Vocational Fitness by Means of Psychological Tests*, rev. ed., Harper & Row, Publishers, New York, 1962.
Symposium: "Perceptions—Self and Others," *Journal of Counseling Psychology*, 5: 98–109, summer, 1958.

11 VOCATIONAL PLANNING

New vistas of understanding about vocational guidance have been opened up by research in the areas of human development and occupational life. The older approach of attempting to match human traits and job requirements as a means of helping persons to choose, enter, and adjust within an occupation is being transformed into the more complex task of helping individuals to plan how to integrate the evolving work aspects of life within their developing personalities in ways that will contribute to self-realization and to the welfare of society.

Super (1, p. 197) has defined this process as that "of helping a person to develop and accept an integrated and adequate picture of himself and of his role in the world of work, to test this concept against reality, and to convert it into a reality with satisfaction to himself and benefit to society."

More assistance is available from research and experience for the process of appraising aptitudes and other traits and attempting to predict their meaning for vocational planning than for the broader approach to vocational guidance. We have all too little tested truth and experience for this task as we view it today, but what we have has revealed the inadequacy of the older method alone, and the need for moving ahead on the newer front, incorporating what knowledge we have—which is more than any one person can master—into a service that must combine science, art, and our best insights about human life.

NEW PERSPECTIVES IN VOCATIONAL DEVELOPMENT

1. Both human personalities and the economic order are in process of continuous change and development. The tempo of change in work life is accelerating rapidly and requires understanding by individuals of the nature of trends in order to plan for future entrance or readjustment to changes, also flexibility in continuous adjustment and adaptation to changing conditions and work demands. Understanding is likewise needed regarding the nature of human growth and development and the meaning of this process in one's own life.

2. People differ in their patterns of potentialities and capacities for

work, but can qualify for a number of occupations, in some instances adapting jobs to their qualifications as well as adjusting to specific jobs.

3. Each occupation requires a characteristic pattern of abilities, interests, and other personal qualities, but tolerances are wide enough to allow some variation, and many of these characteristic patterns change with technological and other economic developments.

4. There are characteristic life stages through which each person tends to progress. These stages have been designated as those of growth, exploration, establishment, maintenance, and decline. The exploratory stage may be subdivided into fantasy, tentative, and realistic phases; and the establishment stage into trial and stable phases. There are variations among individuals with respect to the nature and tempo of development through these various stages.

5. Research indicates that the nature of the career pattern of an individual is influenced by parental and socioeconomic factors as well as his unique pattern of abilities, interests, and other personality characteristics.

6. Longitudinal research is being directed to the study of dimensions and stages of vocational maturity, the results of which may indicate the most helpful vocational guidance services at each stage.

7. The process of vocational development may be viewed as an integral aspect of the development of a self-concept which subsumes many facets of the personality and is intimately related to the envisaging of varied roles to be played in various life activities. This process of vocational development has been described as a compromise between individual and social factors, between self-concept and reality, but one that should contribute to the development and implementing of the self-concept.[1]

8. There are numerous theories as to the influences that enter into choices and decisions at various points in vocational development. There are, doubtless, multiple factors that influence a particular decision, some of which may be unrecognized by the individual, and some of which may be irrational in the light of available information about self and occupational life. One theory is that choices are made to meet personal needs.[2] Maslow's list of basic needs is frequently used in this approach to attempted understanding of influences affecting occupational decisions. This list includes physiological and safety needs, and needs for belongingness and love, importance, respect, self-esteem, independence,

[1] This statement and several others in this list have been adapted from Donald E. Super, "A Theory of Vocational Development," *The American Psychologist*, 8:185–190, May, 1953, and *The Psychology of Careers*, Harper & Row, Publishers, New York, 1957.

[2] Robert Hoppock supports this theory (2, pp. 74–112) and also summarizes various other theories that have been proposed.

information, understanding, beauty, and self-actualization (3, 4). The specific pattern of influences in a decision of a particular individual is likely to be unique as to the combination and relative weight of factors. Several long-range research projects are aimed at increasing our understanding of this decision making and the whole vocational development process (5).

9. Occupational planning for women involves special problems of relating homemaking and career. Sometimes homemaking becomes the lifetime career; again it is combined, as a double-track pattern, with work outside the home, either continuously or at varying times when the termination of child care, economic necessity, or other conditions prevail; and for some the work career is a single-track pattern as for men. These variations call for special approaches in guidance for girls and women. Zapoleon (6) has dealt ably and helpfully with these special problems of vocational guidance for women.

10. Work satisfactions and life satisfactions are closely interrelated with adequate utilization of abilities, interests, values, and other personal qualities in the work life, and the general way of life is in large degree determined by the type of work.

11. Vocational development is clearly a lifelong process, beginning in the home, extending through the periods of schooling and work life, and shifting into avocational development for some in the period beyond retirement.

12. Vocational guidance is a long-range process extending throughout the school life of the individual and beyond into work life when self-direction of vocational development does not prove adequate to meet new adjustment problems.

Volumes could be written to describe adequately the ramifications of these twelve brief statements regarding the new look in vocational guidance. However, this chapter must be limited to an overview of those phases of the services that can be dealt with most effectively in groups. The basic understanding of the total service, beyond this brief summary, must be assumed and recognized as essential.

First we shall consider some problems related to aspects of career planning, and then the possibilities for group work at various age levels.

PROBLEMS OF SELF-APPRAISAL

It would seem fairly simple to take a few aptitude tests, fill out a few interest and personality inventories and some rating scales, plot the results on a chart, and try to interpret a "personality profile." This is what has happened all too often as the method of self-appraisal in group-guidance units or courses. Our discussion in Chapter 10 has, we hope, indicated the inadequacies of this type of cross-section study, though this statement is not intended to criticize it as *one phase* of the process. The reader is referred to Chapter 10 to review the various aspects of a comprehensive, long-range appraisal program.

Less than a generation ago we would have looked chiefly for evidence of an aptitude and interest pattern that would suggest the suitability of considering certain occupations, and for the personality traits that would seem important for successful adjustment and achievement in these possible fields, and, in fact, in any type of work. We still look for these attributes, but as an integral part of a total functioning, developing personality with a unique pattern of physical and health assets and liabilities; of temperament trends; of needs; of attitudes, values, aspirations, and ambitions; of general mental ability; of socioeconomic status; and of life influences and experiences—all of which in their interrelationships may be predisposing the person to a given way of life into which his work role or roles must somehow find their place to further and enhance his self-realization and contributions to the life of which he is a part.

This is no simple, easy task for the counselor or for the counselee, but a challenging one. What we, as guidance workers, can do at any one point along the way is to keep doors open, open new vistas, feed in new information, help to interpret available long-range and current data, tentatively help to perfect techniques of self-exploration and planning, and assist individuals in resolving conflicts and making whatever choices and decisions are necessary at particular stages. Helping to avoid irreversible decisions at times is an important phase of the service.

As noted in Chapter 10, prognoses regarding the desirability of imminent steps ahead in training or work adjustment are more reliable than any judgments about success in a total career, but tentative maps of career patterns are essential to give meaning to each new step, even though the pattern changes and the paths shift in a new direction.

The purposes of the self-appraisal in vocational planning are several-fold:

1. To take a new and more comprehensive look at all available data about self, current and long-range, objective and subjective, in order to gain a new perspective on, and a new synthesis of, the self-concept. The term *synthesis* is generally used in the clinical connotation to refer to the process by which a psychologist may organize all data regarding a client in order to make a diagnosis of his problems. We are using the term here, as in Chapter 10, to refer to the process by which each person may organize and interpret data about self to gain a clearer self-understanding. Super (1, pp. 281–289) describes this process as a life-long learning experience in which available knowledge of ability, the

social view of one's human interrelationships, evaluation of experiences, and identifications with others are used in role-playing, internal or external, for reality testing.

2. To consider what one likes and dislikes in this self-concept; what one can change, if desired; and what one must accept, both happily and philosophically. This is a major problem of self-development and mental hygiene dealt with more fully in Chapter 6, but it is one important consideration in vocational planning.

3. To envisage the new picture of self in varying roles in the world of work. This can be done in imagination as one learns about all the possible work roles in our economic life. It has been done, presumably, over many years, but doubtless without a fully realistic understanding of the true nature of the various roles played in actual work. An accurate view can be gained only as one reads accurate and reliable information, visits establishments or sees films, hears descriptions by those in the work, or gains firsthand experience through part-time or full-time work.

To be realistic, this role-playing of self must be carried on also in a projected view into the future which portrays what a particular type of work may be like when one is ready to enter it and how one's self may have developed and changed by then. The same projection, though dimmer and more vague, should be attempted for successive stages in work life. Then the field of vision should broaden to encompass the total way of life within which each work role is to be played. What of residence, home and family life, economic status (such as security, income, and advancement), social and civic life, all types of human values, and work and life satisfactions?

Such attempted role-playing in imagination, or in dramatics within a group, will reveal some inconsistencies between reality and aspirations, and will require compromises between these two if the occupation is not discarded but kept within the list of possibilities.

One serious difficulty that will be encountered in attempted role-playing is the lack of available information that may depict many aspects of the probable way of life engendered by work in a particular occupation. We shall look at this difficulty in the next section.

4. To analyze the factors in the self most crucial for adjustment, success, and satisfaction in each type of work that passes the test of adequate compatibility with the self-concept. Some of these factors are ability to succeed in the training program required for entrance into the work; patterns of special abilities needed, such as in musical, artistic, mechanical, linguistic, or scientific areas; liking for particular situations, such as outdoor, indoor, working with people, things, or ideas; temperamental tendencies that might adapt one better to change, variety,

repetition, isolation, contact with people, authority, independence, uncertainty, or ambiguity; and physical and health resources that will meet the physical demands of jobs while allowing for a desirable conservation and use of these personal resources.

5. To consider desirable approaches to occupational decisions when opportunities are limited as to number or variety, or when no clear-cut vocational patterns have been discovered in the self-appraisal. The reasons for any of these possible limitations need careful study to avoid the overlooking of hidden factors or resources.

In the fast-developing technology it appears certain that the demand for unskilled labor will be reduced. This fact emphasizes the need for as much education as can be achieved by each person to develop flexibility, adaptability, and the fullest realization of potentialities. In the process, the late bloomer may discover untapped possibilities and shift easily into role-playing of specific possibilities.

For the individuals who seem destined for unskilled and somewhat undifferentiated jobs, perhaps the best question is, "What work that needs to be done can I do best?" Actually, that question should be asked seriously by every human being throughout the whole artificial hierarchy of jobs. If we can help to build up around this question the attitude that the real criterion of status in a job hierarchy in a democracy should be the extent to which an individual's inner resources are used effectively in doing to the best of his ability what needs to be done that he can do best, we can contribute to the self-respect, self-acceptance, and, without doubt, the increased value of our human resources.

6. To investigate environmental influence upon self—past and present —and plan ways of either utilizing or avoiding these influences in vocational development. This purpose is almost unlimited in its possibilities if all the various influences that impinge on our lives are considered. We shall limit consideration here to two factors, socioeconomic status and occupation of parent.

Innumerable studies have indicated that these are significant *determiners* of occupations entered by individuals (1, 3, 7–12). This seems like a fatalistic concept, out of harmony with democratic philosophy and individual variation and uniqueness. Accepting the proven influences of parental occupation and status (with many exceptions, of course, and with real advantages for some), what can guidance do to help offset the influences where they may hinder the discovery, development, and use of talents and thus limit our manpower resources and stifle self-actualization for many individuals?

Group study of these influences is one answer to the question. Another is both group and individual study of how the influences can be used to the best advantage when they are assets, and how they may be circumvented and avoided when they are liabilities. There is no dearth of biographical material that can be used with groups to inspire them to overcome disadvantages of socioeconomic status. Financial aid through scholarships can help many who possess suitable ability for lengthy training programs to continue in school, and information about such aid should be included in group study. Being exposed to the vast and varied opportunities in our economic world can challenge many who may have accepted certain limited opportunities passively as inevitable. Group work with parents may eliminate barriers from this source. All members of a school staff, and dedicated citizens in the community, as well as counselors, can exert influence through groups and individually to spark interest, ambition, and intelligent planning as to ways of moving into suitable avenues of vocational endeavor.

7. To appraise one's stage of vocational maturity. The term *vocational maturity*, denoting the stage of vocational development reached by an individual on the continuum from exploration to decline, is fairly new. Super (1, pp. 187–191) used this concept in his Career Pattern Study and formulated statements as to its dimensions for use in the longitudinal look at the vocational development of a group of boys.

Viewing adolescence as an exploratory stage, the dimensions of vocational maturity in this period were postulated as (a) concern with problems of vocational choice, (b) information and planning, (c) consistency of vocational preferences, (d) crystallization of traits and attitudes, and (e) wisdom of vocational preferences. Indices of these various stages were formulated and used to help in the study of the vocational development of boys in the career project.

The basic assumption concerning vocational maturity is that vocational behavior changes systematically with increasing age, becoming more goal-directed, more realistic, and more independent (13, 14). Crites (15) has examined various approaches to the appraisal of vocational maturity. One can compare an individual's behavior with typical behaviors of individuals at given age levels, or study it with reference to the criterion of developmental tasks to be expected at different life stages. The relative degree of vocational development can be measured by a Vocational Maturity Quotient, in which the estimated vocational life stage is divided by the chronological age, yielding a quotient similar to the IQ. Crites suggests developing measurement models based on expected characteristics of various age periods and the developmental tasks of each period, and then comparing an individual as to his stage of maturity with the appropriate age models. This is a research problem at present rather than a tested guidance procedure, but the research to date has provided helpful suggestions for attempting to adapt the guidance service to the needs of individuals at their respective stages of development.

Super (16) has recommended as a result of his longitudinal study, which is still continuing, that for the ninth-grade boys in his group the vocational-guidance problem was that of assistance in vocational exploration rather than in vocational choice or selection.

An interesting research reported by Hulslander (17) suggests that certain significant relationships may exist between growth-in-age units, including physical and other personality growth factors, and occupational interests of children. There is not yet enough evidence concerning this relationship to use specifically in guidance, but such studies should alert us to the importance of growth and developmental factors within the total personality and cause us to observe and cooperate with natural developmental processes and capitalize upon them rather than to impose artificial standards in the timing of guidance services that may prove ineffectual or even harmful before individuals have achieved the maturity needed to deal with certain aspects of vocational planning. Of course, as in reading and other educational fields, readiness may be stimulated naturally in many ways, not merely allowed to unfold without desirable nurture.

Some Problems of Providing
Occupational Information in Groups

Occupational information has been described by Hoppock (2, p. 6) as all kinds of information regarding any position, job, or occupation that is potentially useful to an individual in his vocational planning. Fine (18) has advised that adequate occupational information should include the following types of information: the structure of the world of work, how workers function and how trait information contributes to an understanding of such functioning, and job-worker situations as life behavior situations.

Our expanding concept of the nature of vocational planning has broadened our awareness of the kinds of information essential for it. When we consider work as an integral part of a total life plan, affecting many aspects of living, we realize the need for more information than that directly related to the work itself. To the extent that one's occupation affects other aspects of the life pattern, we need to help individuals use understanding of these occupational influences in making plans that are likely to lead to the kind of life desired.

Occupational materials now available do not readily provide all the desirable types of information. The counselor must be resourceful and well grounded in the understanding of reliable and varied resources to meet needs adequately. We shall examine a few of the problems related to this phase of vocational guidance.

1. *Helping Individuals to Understand the Complexity and the Tempo of Change in the Economic Order.* Change would seem to be the one certainty in life today. The influences of science and technology and the impact of other cultures upon our own are producing changes that are difficult to understand or to foresee clearly. Wrenn (19, pp. 4–5) has stated this problem succinctly as follows:

Projections into the future can be based upon analysis of present trends but these may be sharply modified by physical inventions and social innovations. The American society will be indirectly affected, for example, by discovery and innovation in world population control and food production but it will be changed even more profoundly if these innovations do not take place—and soon. Discoveries in energy production, weather modification, world communications, and outer space exploration will be startling but their occurrence is as certain as is their influence upon the lives of people in our society. Biological and social innovations are also certain to modify trends, such as the discovery of elements of man's ability to modify the evolution of man, new efficiencies in the process of learning, a swifter use of new knowledge before it becomes obsolete.

In summarizing some of the probably unprecedented changes in population composition, labor force, occupational shifts, and trends in our traditional economy and that of other nations, Wrenn (19, p. 6) comments that "occupational flexibility will be as important as suitable first choice." He further advises that "risks now may mean security later."

Our changing world presents an almost overwhelming challenge to the counselor or the group-guidance leader to keep abreast of changes as well as to help counselees to do so, and to develop proficiency in continuing to keep alert and informed as to possible new developments throughout the course of work life that may affect occupational adjustments. Wood (20) has summarized some of the apparent employment trends ahead and their significance for vocational planning. She points out that percentages of farm and unskilled labor occupations have declined steadily since 1910, skilled workers and service workers have held their own, and all other fields have increased. These trends point up the need for as much training as possible for each individual before completing formal schooling.

2. *The Need for New Types of Occupational Information.* The concept of vocation as an integral part of the self, influencing and being influenced by the total personality development, has highlighted the importance of the total environment in its impact on the work life of

the individual. Much of our occupational information is limited with respect to these broader implications. Occupational sociology has become a recognized field of research, and considerable material is available in books and journals regarding the sociological aspects of economic life (11, 12). However, this approach is not yet treated adequately in a good deal of the occupational-information literature. The same condition exists with respect to many psychological facets of work. Samler (21), in a critique of occupational information, points out these psychosocial limitations and makes a plea for attention to the *psychological man* (or woman) as well as the *economic man.*

Danskin (22, 23) has reviewed some of the studies of the sociological aspects of specific occupations and provided helpful bibliographical data for counselors. Recent books on occupational information and occupational bibliographies also give helpful references to this newer type of information (2, 24–26). The psychosocial approach is especially important in guidance because of the seeming determinism of socioeconomic influences in individual lives as indicated by research (1, 3, 28). Perhaps awareness through group study of the influences of family and socioeconomic status can help individuals to plan how to avoid some of them and become more self-determining in their life planning and working.

3. *Problems of Providing Reliable Occupational Information and Keeping It Up to Date.* Much printed material will contain some obsolete information by the time it is off the press. Continuous effort is needed to keep text, library, and file materials fairly current and accurate. Also, skill and training are required to appraise the accuracy and suitability of occupational literature—books, pamphlets, and articles.

Hoppock (2, pp. 35–44) has recommended five questions that should be asked about every source:

When? Copyright date may be one answer, though some kinds of information become obsolete more quickly than others.

Where? Note limitations as to geographical area covered.

Who? The professional status of the writer and reputation of the publisher are important.

Why? Some materials are prepared for recruitment instead of vocational guidance.

How? Is sound research behind the writing?

The comments on these five questions are merely suggestions which have many ramifications.

The Guidance Information Review Service Committee of the National Vocational Guidance Association (27) is giving a valuable service by rating current occupational materials. Revised bibliographies are issued frequently and are kept up to date by the continuous rating of new materials, lists of which are included quarterly in the *Vocational Guid-*

ance Quarterly published by the association. This committee has used as one of its standards for evaluating occupational literature an outline prepared by the Occupational Research Division of NVGA (29) together with a review form included in the Appendix of this book.[3] Both of these outlines would be helpful in evaluating any materials for which NVGA ratings are not available.

The sources of occupational-information materials and the filing and use of this information are not dealt with here except as they may relate to specific problems of group guidance. The reader is directed to references at the end of the chapter for technical guides (2, 24–26, 30).

4. *Utilizing All Available Resources for Occupational Information.* Members of an educational staff have valuable information at their disposal in professional journals in their respective fields and often in brochures issued by their professional organizations. Baer and Roeber (24, pp. 194–206) give a list of professional societies with their addresses.

Service clubs in most communities cooperate with the schools by giving talks, arranging plant visits for groups, and scheduling interviews with individuals. Some of these service clubs have vocational guidance as one of their general service policies. Schools often prepare rosters of citizens in the community who have volunteered for this type of service.

Science fairs have provided interesting and significant insights into the world of work, and such events are readily expanded beyond scientific fields. One such program was called a Job-O-Rama (31, 32). Parents can also be utilized to provide firsthand experiences with various jobs, especially for the younger students (33).

Television, both closed-circuit and commercial, has come into wide use as a source of information for both parents and students, and this medium requires well-planned group discussions, preferably before and after the programs, to realize optimum values (34, 35).

Assembly programs as well as class discussion are helpful media to utilize local talent—employers and former students, for example—and they can furnish helpful information about what employers want in workers as well as job conditions and requirements (36–38).

Career conferences appear to be changing in nature. There is a growing dissatisfaction with the one-shot conference scheduled perhaps once or twice a year. This attitude may be due in part to the fact that these conferences have often been relied on to carry the main burden of the occupational-information service instead of merely supplementing in-

---

[3] This form is included by courtesy of the present chairman of the Review Service Committee, Ward W. Leis, Division of Guidance and Counseling, Pasadena City Schools.

tensive group study and planned approaches that pervade the entire educational program (39, 40). One trend is to spread these conferences throughout the year, and sometimes they are combined with College Days or Nights. In San Diego County, California, schools and community organizations have planned series of Career Conferences scheduled on holidays and week ends. Groups in the community sponsor these, with school personnel serving in an advisory capacity (41).

Community occupational surveys yield valuable occupational information when a trained worker is available to plan, conduct, and evaluate the research in cooperation with interested citizens. Students, trained to participate in some phases of the information collection, can derive many benefits from their experiences (42).

There are many advantages of continuous, systematic cooperation between schools and community on the vocational-guidance program. Greater realism is brought into the service in the schools and there can be mutual influences on attitudes and understandings. A Jobs After Forty Committee in Pasadena, California, that has brought employers into active cooperation with the committee in serving the older workers, appears to be developing more favorable attitudes among the employers toward the hiring of the forty-plus worker, if one can judge from successive employer responses to surveys regarding opportunities for these workers in their establishments.

Information on opportunities in military service for vocational training and experience is highly important today. All of the Armed Forces provide informative bulletins that should be available to upper secondary school students. Student and teacher manuals for a unit entitled *Your Life Plans and the Armed Forces* have been prepared by a committee representing numerous professional organizations and the U.S. Office of Education (43–45).

5. *Making Information Readily Available to Students.* The solution of this problem varies from school to school and usually taxes the resourcefulness of the librarian and the guidance personnel. The filing system needs careful study to enable students to locate materials easily. Types of filing systems are described in great detail in books on occupational information (2, 24, 25). Browsing corners or rooms in counseling quarters and the library are aids for the utilization of waiting or leisure periods. Rooms where study groups meet should have some materials available, perhaps moved by some convenient method from room to room as needed.

6. *Providing Materials Suited to the Maturity Levels of Students.* The solution to this problem depends in large degree, of course, upon the producers of the materials. Among the criteria for selection purposes are conceptual and vocabulary level, illustrations, size of type, attractive-

ness of format, and nature of the material. Descriptions of industries and services, such as transportation, various aspects of manufacturing, health services, etc., usually fit into activity units at the elementary school level. Broad surveys of occupational fields are needed in exploratory periods,[4] and more specific materials on professions, trades, and specific jobs as students approach the time for tentative or more permanent decisions. Educational-information materials are needed also, in both the exploratory and planning periods, and these are considered in the next chapter. Some schools and numerous colleges prepare some of their own career materials to meet the specific needs of their student populations.

Biography and fiction with vocational implications and realistic portrayals of work are helpful resources at all levels, and bibliographies are available to assist in the selection of materials for various maturity levels (25, pp. 147–148). Feltman (46) found that an experimental group of eighth-grade girls changed their ratings of workers described in the fiction read, though few changed their choice of life work as a result of their reading. Films, filmstrips, and slides also make valuable contributions. Lists of audio-visual sources of information are included in most texts on occupational information (2, pp. 288–296; 24, p. 212; 25, pp. 157–158; 26), and some are included in the Appendix of this book.

7. *Providing Information That Can Be Readily Related to Self-knowledge.* Two illustrations of research aimed at facilitating guidance and/or placement are cited here.

The Minnesota Rating Scales (47) provide ratings for 432 occupations on seven abilities or aptitudes as these are required for each occupation in the combined judgments of raters: academic ability, mechanical ability, social intelligence, clerical ability, musical talent, artistic ability, and physical agility. While psychological research has not verified the existence or the possibility of measuring some of these so-called "aptitudes," such as social intelligence, the rating scale provides a rough and convenient estimate of some of the qualities or characteristics important for the occupations rated. Ratings range from "A" for the degree essential for professional, semiprofessional, and executive occupations, to "D" for semiskilled and unskilled occupations. The occupations are also grouped by levels of the seven characteristics rated and by similar patterns of these characteristics.

The United States Employment Service has developed estimates of trait requirements for 4,000 jobs that could prove helpful to individuals

---

[4] There is an excellent symposium on occupational information for junior high school youth in *The Personnel and Guidance Journal,* 38:115–127, October, 1960. Some of the issues dealt with in this symposium will be considered later in this chapter in relation to organization and techniques for vocational guidance in groups.

attempting to assess their work potentials for any of these or similar jobs (48, 49). Their estimates are deduced from ratings, based on definitions of these jobs in the *Dictionary of Occupational Titles*. These include time and level requirements for general and special vocational preparation; ratings on aptitudes in the GATB (see page 257, footnote); eye-hand-foot coordination and color discrimination; twelve traits of temperament such as would be involved in adjusting to variety and change, isolation, or performing under stress; ten interest factors; six physical capacities, with estimates ranging from sedentary to very heavy involvement of certain types of physical activity; and working conditions of seven types considered in relation to inside or outside, or both. Inspection of these tables of estimates would provide suggestions for some practical approaches to vocational assessment for those interested in the jobs thus rated or for those of a similar nature.

The occupational-information service has become a highly technical phase of vocational guidance, requiring specialized preparation. We have dealt here merely with a few of the problems pertinent for the group worker in planning and carrying out a vocational-guidance unit. Ginzberg (50) has emphasized how much these problems exceed the resources of any one counselor and how essential it is to elicit help from many sources. He describes the primary function of the counselor in this area as that of leader in focusing the assistance of parents, teachers, business, labor, government, and all who have specialized competence in various fields.

PROBLEMS OF ASSISTANCE IN VOCATIONAL CHOICE AND PLANNING

What factors enter into vocational choice? Many theories about these factors have been propounded as the result of research. We shall examine only a few. Roe (3, pp. 103–132) has summarized numerous studies, some of which indicate influences of family background and social inheritance. Hammond (51) identified four groups of motives that appeared to be related to the vocational choices of a group of college freshmen: a materialistic *economic-status need;* a competitive *personal-status need;* a technical or *structure need* involving a desire for system, definiteness, and security in detail in work; and a humanitarian *acceptance need* of service and belonging. Hoppock's (2, pp. 74–85) theory of needs as the determiners of occupational choice was noted earlier. His theory involves recognition that the relative weight of various needs and the complexity of patterns may differ among individuals. Super (52, pp. 11–15) and Tiedeman (52, pp. 15–21), who are engaged in research on the nature of vocational development, are both concerned with self-concept as it relates to the developing career pattern. One aspect of Super's study is that of clarifying stages in vocational maturity. Thus far his findings for the group of boys being studied indicate that at the ninth-grade level these boys are in an exploratory stage but are not yet ready to make decisive vocational choices (14, 53).

Tiedeman is searching for the sequence of decisions regarding school, work, and life in the developmental process, and he points out that some of the end decisions of one period become means at a later time. Ziller (54) has suggested that the degree of willingness of a person to take risks with respect to the future in making vocational choices may be one factor that enters into the decision-making process.

O'Hara and Tiedeman (55) found, in a study of vocational self-concepts of a group of adolescent boys of above-average scholastic aptitude, that there was increased congruence of self-estimates and test-estimates, interpreted as indicating increasing clarification of self-concepts, from grade 9 to grade 12, in four vocationally relevant areas: interests, work values, aptitudes, and general values. Congruence in the social-class area did not increase materially in these grades. Their data indicated that the primary differentiation of work values may have occurred before grade 9 (a possible implication as to the emphasis in vocational guidance in elementary school years). The development of general values seemed to progress through grades 9 and 10, an interest stage seemed to terminate by grade 10, an apparent secondary phase of work values proceeded through grade 12, and aptitude was relatively poorly perceived throughout the four grades, 9 to 12. The authors recognize that further research is needed before their conclusions are generalizable, but their findings offer suggestions for thoughtful consideration with respect to practice as well as for research.

Borow (52, p. 24) has characterized our current curricular and counseling practice concerning vocational choice and preparation as "largely based on a bizarre assortment of assumptions, folkways, intuitions, rule of thumb, and unconnected observations." He notes this condition as a reason for the need of continuing research in career development.

What can we do in practice? Awareness of gaps in our knowledge about vocational development is, of course, the fundamental safeguard. But we must go as far as we can in serving generations of youths and adults before our understandings are perfected—if they ever will be fully. Doubtless we shall always see new vistas of unexplored areas in the human personality. And William James sounded a wise caution in his comment that biographies were not likely to be written in advance of the events in human lives.

We need working hypotheses formulated on the basis of the understandings we have at any given time about vocational development. Here are a few suggestions:

1. Choices, decisions, and career plans are the resultant of many influences in human lives. The principle of multiple causation applies in vocational development as in other aspects of self. The many innate and environmental factors that determine choices and plans vary among individuals as to degree of influence, and their interaction results in unique patterns of influence.

2. The degree to which an individual can achieve self-determination and self-direction in his work life depends in part upon his understanding of these factors in his past and present life and his ability to foresee future trends. At any one time many influences are affecting his decisions without his conscious awareness of them.

3. Some of these influences may be inevitable and beyond human control except as compromises and adjustments are made. The decision as to the degree of inevitability may depend partly upon the improvement of guidance services that aid individuals in understanding and coping with them in the light of envisaged life goals. Guided group study of innate and environmental factors, combined with effective individual counseling, should contribute to wise decisions.

4. Research findings can be interpreted and applied helpfully only with reference to the populations studied and the nature of the guidance services provided for that population.

5. The improvement of guidance services involves improved quality of the guidance personnel and the total educational personnel, of parents, and of citizens generally. Our services at any point in time should be directed toward improvement in all these areas as a means of serving both present and future generations more adequately. All whom we serve at any time should be viewed as future members of some of these groups in our culture, and helped to see their future contributions to others as well as to make their personal choices and plans.

GROUP PROGRAMS FOR VOCATIONAL GUIDANCE

At the elementary school level

Elementary school teachers are providing a significant service in vocational guidance today through projects that bring children into vital contact with community life. Practically every social-studies unit in the elementary school curriculum affords many opportunities for developing understandings about the world of work and attitudes of respect and appreciation for all types of work that contribute to our comfort and well-being. Services to the home, in the community, products of various regions, world-wide transportation and exchange of commodities, historical development of different cultures, and all the various expressions of human life through these cultures are basic types of occupational information to be acquired throughout the elementary school period as a part of the understanding of human life (56, 57).

Many activities in the curriculum also afford opportunities for children to gain firsthand as well as vicarious experiences in some of the basic processes that enter into work life. These experiences are not, of course, tryout or self-exploratory as in the secondary school, but they serve as media through which children learn about the external world of people and things and develop attitudes toward work and workers which may persist long beyond childhood and may result in many suitable interests. Also, pupil and teacher evaluation of achievement in the great variety of activities provided in elementary school programs can yield insights for both as to potential talents. Cumulative records of these evaluations will be valuable as individuals reach choice points in educational and vocational planning.

There are indications in the professional literature that direct as well as indirect approaches to study of occupational life are being introduced into the elementary curriculum. Kaye (58) describes a unit in the fourth grade that combined study of occupations in general with the work of the pupils' fathers who participated in the study. Research, study, interviewing skills, critical thinking, and experience in preparing reports were listed among the learnings, together with improved attitudes toward work and more realism about future goals. All areas in the curriculum seemed to have been utilized in the study, and the report savors of a general enthusiasm on the part of parents and children as well as the teacher.

A report in 1959 of practices in elementary schools by Sinick and Hoppock (59) included fairly wide use of films and filmstrips, visits to business and industry, exhibits, units on occupations and personal requirements for job success, many types of special programs in assemblies, homerooms, and clubs, and some local surveys. In one survey, teachers expressed need for better occupational materials, less technical and more specific in nature, and adapted to the elementary school level (60).

Lifton (60) explored with classes of elementary school teachers the extent of their awareness of the interest of young children in the world of work and the degree to which they were helping children to gain a realistic picture of existing jobs. The results indicated a serious lack, both in teacher understandings and in suitable materials for children below the junior high school level. Lifton commented that several encyclopedias are including better materials on careers and vocations in revisions.

Attitudes of respect and appreciation for all types of useful work and workers should be developing in elementary school years as an integral part of the personality structure of a democratic citizen. There is a vast difference between the *propaganda* program for thought control in a totalitarian state and the *educational* program for personal development in a democratic order, but the latter should be planned as carefully and consciously as the former.

At the secondary, college, and adult levels

Organizing the Vocational-guidance Service to Utilize and Interrelate All Resources. Units or courses dealing with vocational planning are essential at strategic points when students need guidance in making vocational and educational plans, or in entering work. The work of the world is too vast to be crowded into a few weeks or months of study, and the objectives of this service cannot be realized in a brief span of time. Individuals need time to grow in awareness of all the ramifications of work in the world: its significance in group living; its possible meaning and influence in individual lives; the varieties of jobs and their requirements and working conditions; long-range occupational trends and their relationships to long-range vocational and educational planning; and the development of attitudes, work habits, and other personal characteristics important for the worker in a democratic social order. Also, the individual must develop skill in finding, evaluating, and using occupational information in his adjustments throughout life if he is to keep abreast of change. He must study the work life of his community first-hand, learn how to find jobs, to enter and progress in work, and to get along well with his associates. If all these learnings are achieved in a meaningful way, they must be timed to meet needs as the needs are anticipated. Of course, one aspect of the program should be that of helping to foster awareness at suitable times so that each individual will be ready to meet each new phase of his work life as he encounters it. Vocational guidance through groups in adult life and later maturity is a partial answer to this lifelong need. Careful planning is required to carry out this service, and every educator in the institution or system should be able to contribute to the program. The administrator is the most important key person, both in the organization of the plan and in the leadership that will inspire all members of the team.

A Planning Committee or Council. A trained, or training, personnel worker will usually be assigned responsibility for leadership in a committee or council to plan procedures and keep the program moving.[5]

---

[5] Since vocational guidance and vocational training are closely interrelated, an official in the vocational-training field will be a very important resource person and may even be a co-chairman in such a group. It is likely that committees of employers and union officials in the community will be members of committees established by those responsible for vocational training to cooperate in the planning of apprenticeship and other training programs to meet local labor-market demands.

No plan, however good, will *keep* moving ahead without the continuous catalyzing effect of evaluation and replanning.

Who should be represented on the council or committee? Certainly all the teaching departments and special services, such as health, student activities, student welfare, placement, the students themselves, and the parents' association. From the community there should be representatives of employers, unions, and strategic governmental, service, and welfare agencies. Local employment services should, of course, be represented. The pattern will vary with each community. The important point is that all groups in the school and community concerned with the occupational adjustment of citizens should participate in planning adequate services to future workers. There may well be committees within committees for special types of study and planning. Some of these may be primarily school planning groups. Somehow they should all be interrelated to assure a comprehensive service that will be functional in the lives of students and in the work life of the community.

SOME PROBLEMS TO BE STUDIED. 1. What is the occupational structure of the community? What jobs and services are needed in business, industry, transportation, and all phases of community life? What jobs are likely to be open to each new group of students as they leave school? What are the demands and rewards of these jobs? What new types of jobs may be in the offing? Which jobs may be suitable for the handicapped? For the older workers? For women who may enter and reenter work at different times in their lives?

An *occupational survey* for a community or region as a continuous process is required to provide adequate answers to such questions. This calls for trained leadership. Occupational mobility means that nationwide and world-wide occupational life must be studied, but the materials for this wider view will probably be selected by those responsible for the teaching about occupational life in the curriculum. Space does not permit detailed consideration of community-survey procedures. References describing various methods are included at the end of the chapter (24, 25, 30).

2. What are the work interests and resources of the students? The answers to this question will come in part from the school-wide appraisal of individuals. They will include data on socioeconomic background of the school population, age and general-ability range, health and physical assets and liabilities, interests, aptitudes, work experience, school achievement, work proficiencies and liabilities of students, and trends with respect to school-leaving and continued training beyond the level at which the survey is being made. Student questionnaires at intervals will help to keep information about interests and work plans up to date.

Employers in the community can supply valuable information on how well their employees are meeting their work needs and how the schools can help in the better preparation of oncoming employees and, perhaps, in further training of present employees. Follow-up studies of previous students can also bring realistic information about work to students that may help to guide and inspire them in their preparation for work.

This local information about work life, coupled with knowledge about the national and international scene, should help to bring students' vocational choices and plans more into line with the actual distribution of jobs. Of course, many factors, including the prestige value of jobs, remuneration, and the aspirations of parents and children represented in the self-concepts of individuals, are involved in vocational choices. Cooperative study of these factors by a committee such as is suggested might perhaps bring new opportunities to students and utilize more fully the potential work resources of all citizens.

Use of Community Resources in Vocational Guidance. The methods are legion, and some of the following are doubtless in operation in every school or school system adapted to the local community and school situation. Not all will be needed or desired in a particular community. A common tendency, however, is to exploit one or two of these methods and then to assume that somehow the job has been done, rather than to consider all the ways that are possible and desirable within the limits of time and energy that can be devoted to vocational guidance. A well-knit committee structure, including student members, with wide distribution of responsibility, will provide greater variety than is possible if the responsibility is centered solely in one person.

Another weakness of some programs stems from the assumption that these school-community contacts for students will turn the trick without systematic instruction. This outcome can no more be expected for occupational information than for English, social studies, or science. But the sytsematic instruction about occupational life is not likely to come alive without these contributing firsthand experiences for students, teachers, and counselors.

CAREER DAYS OR CONFERENCES. This method of bringing representatives of various fields of work into conferences with groups of interested students is used so widely that it scarcely needs description. If the Conference Day begins with an assembly, the suitable topic for the large group will depend partly upon what background the students already have through the school program. If they have already become familiar with the techniques of vocational planning and have had prior preparation in classes for using the conference experiences effectively, this assembly may be devoted to informative and inspiring talks on local employment trends, conditions, opportunities and demands in jobs, or on a wide variety of pertinent topics. Locally prepared films showing former students in current jobs usually arouse interest; panel discussions of employers and students, or planned or spontaneous skits dealing with application interviews, can open up fruitful questions. Any of these suggestions may be more suitable at other points in the total program. They are inserted merely to suggest variety.

In a well-planned Career Conference, speakers are likely to have received outlines or suggestions to guide them in their roles, and students will likewise have outlines, questions, or some forms to guide their participation and their later evaluations of the conference. The maturity of the students will help to determine whether speakers or discussion leaders deal with broad fields of work or more specific occupations. Reports of Career Day discussions cumulated from year to year often provide valuable instructional material to compare with information in books and pamphlets. Thus used, some of the tendencies of speakers to glamorize jobs or to exaggerate difficulties may be offset, and variations from the national picture in local jobs can be seen more clearly. In any plan it is important to provide for preconference preparation of students and postconference study of outcomes, if best values are to be extracted from the experience. Several Career Day programs throughout a school year provide wider contacts for more students than one elaborate program.

Some alert guidance leaders are using television or radio programs to supplement or replace the Career Day conferences. These have the advantage, if suitably timed, of bringing more parents into the thinking and planning process with their children. By themselves these programs may eliminate the very important firsthand contacts with adult workers that bring inspiration and challenge to youth; also, the opportunities to study their personalities and to glimpse what the jobs do to the workers.

Another variation of Career Day reported recently is that of students visiting the places of employment instead of meeting with representatives at school. Career Day provided each student with the opportunity to follow through for a day on a job and work as a regular employee. Prior individual arrangements between employer and student gave the latter information about hours, appropriate dress, and daily routine. Similar Career Weeks, when students have been assigned to the offices or places of business of volunteer leaders, have been sponsored by service clubs such as Altrusa International.

Still another variation is a Job Opportunities Forum, held in several evening sessions and providing opportunity for parents, students, administrative and guidance personnel, and employers to exchange information and think and plan together cooperatively on career problems of youth.

Only a few of the more recent variations are mentioned here. Books on the teaching of occupations are full of varieties of suggestions which need to be adapted to the student group and the community (2, 24, 25).

Some school systems have planned with community leaders for Education-Industry Days when teachers, counselors, and administrators visit industries and places of business and have opportunities to discuss problems of mutual interest with employers. This type of plan might well be combined with student visits in order that exchanges of experiences and observations might be continued in classrooms.

THE USE OF SERVICE CLUBS AND OTHER COMMUNITY ORGANIZATIONS. Altrusa International, the Business and Professional Women's Club, and Kiwanis International have had service programs of vocational guidance at some time or have projects in some phase of youth service. The American Association of University Women has an active program of scholarships, and the Sertoma International, a men's service club, has a major activity in the field of youth employment.

A roster of organization members who have volunteered for service is a very helpful tool in arranging lectures, informal talks, interviews, and plant visits. Members can also be very helpful in arranging for work experience for students. A committee of representatives from various organizations can be effective in enlisting cooperation of members and in helping to appraise the best services which each member can give. Organizations can become so interested in school projects that it is sometimes necessary to help guide their services into the most productive and educationally valuable channels. But they can greatly help teachers and counselors to become more realistic and vital in their school services.

In planning to utilize community groups, one should not overlook the churches or the recreation, health, and welfare groups. Youth programs in these agencies usually have important implications for the schools.

Dutch Aunt and Uncle programs, in which representatives of various types of work assume responsibility for friendly guidance of individual students interested in their respective occupations, can have far-reaching influences in young lives. Anyone who has read or heard expressions of appreciation by youths of this interest by admired adults in their prospective fields of work recognizes an inspiring challenge that extends far beyond the occupational information received.

LIAISON WITH LOCAL BRANCHES OF THE STATE EMPLOYMENT SERVICE. Schools which have their own placement offices may be concerned chiefly with local and state labor-market information and mutual study of common professional problems. Those schools which do not have their own placement service have developed a variety of relationships with the local branch of the governmental Employment Office. Some have maintained school representatives in the Employment Office to care for junior placements. In one school system a plan was developed to place teacher-counselors in the office for a semester in alternation in order to bring them into more realistic contact with job problems. There should be a highly valuable mutual exchange between the schools and the Employment Office of information about former students needing placement on the one hand, and of local labor-market information on the other hand. The Employment Offices also receive much valuable occupational information from state and national bureaus.

WORK EXPERIENCE, APPRENTICESHIPS, AND INTERNSHIPS. Part-time work experience of students during World War II broadened our vistas of the possibilities in this experience for realistic understanding by students of demands in the world of work while there was still time to prepare further for lifetime work. In times of employment slack, it is sometimes difficult to keep the door open for part-time student work, but cooperative planning with employers, coupled with adequate work orientation for students in groups at school, helps in this problem. Cooperative employer and school appraisal of student work when school credit is given for work experience provides valuable learning experiences for students. Opportunities to study and discuss work experience in groups tend to multiply the benefits for all involved in the group work.

When the work experience can be related to vocational interests of students, the greatest benefits are likely to accrue. The work-study programs at Antioch College, and the University of Cincinnati offer some of the best examples of this possibility at the college level. Projects in which high school or college students and their instructors cooperate with citizens to help solve local and regional economic problems, such as in the dust bowl area, are other examples of valuable work and citizenship experience.

Apprenticeship training and internships as a part of technical or professional training provide a high type of realistic experience. Terminal courses at the junior college or community college level offer especially good opportunities for internships. Apprenticeship training is quite closely controlled by law and union regulations, but the schools can cooperate by informing students about apprenticeship opportunities, and by helping to select the most promising candidates for such training. In one instance known to the author, a local apprenticeship committee asked for the services of the guidance department in the schools to help in the improvement of selection procedures for their apprentices, and a battery of tests, combined with long-range school records, was developed for this purpose.

EXHIBITS. Industrial and commercial firms are frequently eager to cooperate in the preparation of exhibits of new processes, equipment, and products. These can be arranged as late-afternoon or evening events open to the public and sponsored by school departments such as science, business, applied arts, and technology. Bulletin-board or library exhibits of photographs, posters, book jackets, etc., can also be a continuous source of interest and information and a challenge to vocational study and planning. Photographs of alumni at work have a wide appeal. Brochures describing job opportunities in an industry, a group of industries, or a community are appearing in increasing numbers.

PUBLICATIONS. Feature articles and columns in school or community journals and newspapers dealing with jobs or with problems of vocational planning and adjustment can help to keep student and parent interest high. Some schools have a policy of issuing attractive brochures describing types of work and showing their relationship to various educational offerings in the institution. Leaders and employers in the community can be used helpfully in the preparation of such materials, though at the college or university level contributions are likely to be drawn from a wider area.

OTHER COMMUNITY RESOURCES. Labor unions can supply much information regarding trades and labor needs. Libraries, city and county as well as school, can furnish lists of autobiographies, biographies, career fiction, and materials in specialized fields. They may assist in clipping career and business news from magazines and newspapers. Former students, dropouts and graduates can furnish much helpful vocational information through follow-up studies and through participation in various group programs. Allen, in the Providence, Rhode Island, schools, developed a plan many years ago whereby students, while still in school, were prepared to give information about their later work by using such data from former students in their own vocational study and thus learning how valuable it might be for succeeding groups of students. They were thus inspired to be helpful as citizens in later years.

How All Departments of a School May Contribute to the Vocational-guidance Service. Every field in the curriculum has its unique contributions to make. Exploration of possibilities in each field and cooperative planning as to ways of achieving desired results are essential if efforts are to be not merely incidental, hit-or-miss, and without aid to students in integrating their experiences. The following outline represents some tentative results of planning in one school system. These suggestions are general and are included here merely to challenge thought regarding the many possibilities.

Possibilities for Instruction in Occupational Opportunities and in Vocational Planning and Adjustment in Various Aspects of the Curriculum

I. History or social studies
   A. Social, economic, and political trends as they affect the vocational and avocational picture—as to opportunities, conditions, and human relationships
   B. Employer-employee relationships
   C. Trade unionism and labor problems
   D. Training in the evaluation of occupational-information materials as to authenticity, soundness, and comprehensiveness of data

II. The sciences
   A. Physical sciences
      1. Effects of technological developments on occupational trends and work conditions, and on avocational pursuits
      2. General vocational-information background of scientific nature
      3. Possibilities in term or special reports: Impact of Science on Human Activities
   B. Biological sciences
      1. General vocational-information background of scientific nature
      2. Interrelationships of physique, health, and hygiene with work and hobbies
      3. Relationship of physical assets and liabilities to vocational and avocational planning

III. Health education
   A. The hygiene of work and recreation
   B. Appraisal of individual health assets and liabilities in relation to vocational planning
   C. Planning of individual health regimen
   D. Health aspects of work efficiency and productivity

IV. English
   A. Philosophy of work as expressed in literature—personal and social values
   B. Work conditions as depicted in literature
   C. Study of workers as revealed in biographies
   D. Individual study of work interests and potentialities through writing of autobiographies

V. Orientation, vocational-planning, or personal-problems course
   A. Techniques of vocational planning and adjustment
   B. Survey of occupational trends, opportunities, and conditions from a more mature standpoint than formerly
   C. Self-appraisal of vocational and avocational potentialities utilizing testing and other appraisal methods, cumulated personnel data, etc.
   D. Intensive study of a few carefully selected vocational and avocational possibilities, or rechecking of previous vocational and avocational plans
   E. Problems of entering, adjusting, and progressing in work
   F. Projection of a training program, and of continued study of voca-

tional and avocational plans with counselor and in other courses as
suggested herein

VI. Industrial arts
    A. Exploration of interests and abilities
    B. Guidance in further study of occupational field through trade journals
    C. Trade unionism
    D. Trade ethics
    E. How to get a job
    F. Adjusting and making progress
    G. Vocational-course reports
    H. Vocational-data blanks
    I. Evaluation of work experience
    J. Industrial relations

VII. All other terminal courses, topics similar to those sketched above adapted
to the specific field

VIII. All other subject fields and courses
    A. Vocational and avocational implications of training in each field
    B. Appraisal of related interests and abilities
    C. Guidance in continued study of vocational trends, opportunities, and
conditions for those with suitable interests and abilities

IX. Other vocational and avocational guidance activities (extraclass)
    A. Vocational Conference Day
    B. Student vocational council
    C. Vocational library and browsing room
    D. Vocational-guidance column in school paper, and student-edited and
-published vocational-guidance magazine
    E. Interest clubs—exploration and development of vocational and avoca-
tional interests
    F. Assembly programs—planned to utilize community talent in inspira-
tional and informative talks; also, appropriate films and recordings—
the latter also used in various classes as preempted to avoid duplica-
tion

The following list of questions was proposed for study by one college
faculty in considering the contributions of each department to the occupational knowledge and vocational guidance of students:

1. Does each instructor show students the relationships of his area
of teaching to various careers and jobs?

2. To what extent can information about occupational conditions, requirements, and trends in related careers and jobs be woven into instruction?

3. Are students introduced at the appropriate times to technical or
professional journals in the areas of their vocational interests and encouraged to keep abreast of changing conditions?

4. Are we building attitudes of respect for all kinds of useful work
and helping students to place the stamp of highest approval on whatever
kinds of work are most suitable for the individual?

5. How can we organize a more systematic plan of developing a comprehensive, growing fund of information about occupations and workers, both local and world-wide, and make it readily available and attractive to students?

6. Can we intensify this program without departmental dangers of overselling of occupations to students who are better suited to other types of work?

7. Where in our educational program should we provide the opportunity for systematic instruction in vocational guidance and occupational adjustment?

How Courses and Units on Vocational Guidance Fit into the Plan. When the entire curriculum is organized to contribute to vocational guidance, specific units or courses are usually located at strategic points where students need to make vocational choices and formulate vocational plans as a basis for projecting training programs or for immediate entrance into employment. The ninth grade is frequently used for one course or unit providing an overview of occupations, an organized approach to self-appraisal, and guidance in formulating tentative vocational and educational plans. One reason for this placement is the need for the planning of college-preparatory training. The holding power of the school and the nature of the entire school population will tend to determine optimum placement of intensive study of occupational life, but this phase of guidance should have significant influences on the picture of dropouts, if it functions effectively in the lives of individuals, and it may require replacement in the curriculum at times.

The eleventh or twelfth year of senior high school and the freshman year of college are points at which the need for more intensive guidance in the study of a few occupational fields, for more searching self-appraisal, and for more specific plans is usually indicated. Sometimes the study of job finding and job adjustment is included at these points, and sometimes later when occupational adjustment is more imminent for the majority of students.

Ideally the opportunity to study problems of vocational planning and vocational adjustment would be available at different times to different students, but this flexibility is not easy to achieve in a curriculum organized for a large student population. A common-learnings or general-education type of curriculum can usually be adjusted to varying needs of students more easily than a curriculum of "subjects."

Organizing Courses or Units in Vocational Planning. Surveys of programs throughout the country reveal such a variety of practices that only a few generalizations seem feasible. Most of these surveys refer to the teaching of occupations, but reports of content of courses and units include a wide range of topics from self-appraisal and information about occupations to all the various problems of training, entering, and adjusting in work. One might hazard the following generalizations from available reports: There are at present more units on vocational guidance within subjects, such as social studies, than separate courses, but the latter seem to be increasing in number. Units in courses are more frequently offered in junior high school, and the separate courses are found more frequently in senior high school (61–63). At the college level, vocational-guidance units are often included in orientation programs, and special courses are increasingly provided throughout the college years for students who have problems of vocational planning.[6]

OBJECTIVES OF CAREER COURSES AND UNITS. Wright (61) secured ratings of the relative importance of listed objectives from teachers and guidance authorities. Among those objectives rated as most important were these: assistance to students in self-appraisal and in acquaintance with sound sources of occupational and educational information; the development of skill in using the information in making choices and in career planning; the development of wholesome attitudes toward work and service to society; techniques for seeking employment and for planning advancement on the job; and the development of avocational interests and understanding of their possible relation to vocations. Other objectives included understanding of the dangers of false guidance, and the encouragement of realism from the viewpoint of the distribution of workers in accordance with the needs of society.

TEACHING TECHNIQUES. These are as varied as the techniques in any course. The same ingenuity is required in career courses as elsewhere to plan suitable methods, but the opportunities for many firsthand experiences and for democratic teacher-pupil planning are probably greater than in most subjects.

Among the techniques reported through surveys are varieties of self-appraisal; use of audio-visual aids; visits to business and industry; speakers and interviews; career and other group conferences; laboratory study; group discussion, committee work and reports; work experience; practice in preparing letters of application; community job surveys; case conferences; and numerous types of dramatization, such as role-playing for practice in making interview appointments, applying for jobs, etc. (65). Both radio and television programs are widely used (see page 284).[7]

---

[6] Carter and Hoppock (64) reported in 1961 on 46 full-semester or quarter courses in colleges and universities with the large majority given full academic credit, and units in 44 other courses.

[7] An interesting year-long radio series called "What's My Future?" in Hawaii resulted from cooperation of the Department of Public Instruction, the Hawaii Employers' Council, the Hawaiian Branch of the American Personnel and Guidance Association, and other organizations. A survey indicated that 20,000 students, grades

The case conference, long used for many purposes in group guidance (66), has been subjected to research by Hewer (67) in connection with a course in Choosing Your Vocation at the University of Minnesota. After background understanding about vocational planning had been laid in the regular class, small experimental groups met in which each student was the object of a case study. His data were presented anonymously for group discussion as to suitability of vocational plans. The control group received individual counseling. No differences were found between the experimental and control groups with respect to certainty of and satisfaction with vocational choices, or as to realism of choices. For the latter, there was not a high level of agreement among the judges. Hewer comments that continued exploration is needed both with and without class background to find methods of meeting increasing needs for counseling with larger student populations. Examples of brief case descriptions developed in secondary schools to improve thinking and problem solving related to vocational planning are included in the Appendix. DuBato (68) has described experiences with the case-conference technique in high school where the student himself presents his case for discussion.

HELPING INDIVIDUALS MAKE DECISIONS. When we were approaching this problem primarily from the viewpoint of matching job requirements with worker qualifications, there were no easy solutions. It has long been recognized that any individual can match himself fairly well against several jobs, and many jobs can be adapted within limits to somewhat varying patterns of individuals. Also, the value system of the person has always been in the picture—the relative values he attaches to material rewards, independence, recognition, prestige, service, or any of the attributes that characterize his desired way of life. Emphasis on the self-concept and on all the possible unconscious and irrational motives that may enter into choices complicates the helping process materially. Likewise, the rapid shifts in the labor market, due to technological developments, complicate the question of what constitutes a realistic career plan.

Comparisons of recent and earlier studies of realism in vocational choice have suggested that there may be greater realism than formerly, judged from the standards of the occupational structure and of individual fitness for chosen work. In one study it was reported that the students clearly distinguish between aspirations and actual plans (69). In another, some 95 per cent of the group were adjudged realistic in their plans in not overshooting their intelligence level, though 37 per cent were adjudged to have undershot their possibilities, and they might

---

9 through 12, had listened to the programs during school hours and others had listened to tapes later (59).

represent wasted manpower (70). We have much to learn about true and wise realism of career planning in our economic world of the present and the future.

Schutz and Blocher (71) made a study to test Bordin's (72) theory that vocational preferences are related to occupational stereotypes accepted as self-descriptions. They compared the expressed vocational preferences of a group of high school boys with their choices, as most self-descriptive, of short character sketches designed to correspond to major occupational groups into which their preferences were fitted. They found a significantly consistent relation between the vocational preferences and the self-descriptive choices. They caution against any generalized conclusions from the study, and present it as a stimulus to further research, emphasizing also the need for students to gain more accurate knowledge of workers in different occupations. These researchers have also presented tentative findings suggesting a relationship between a person's level of occupational choice and aspirations and his evaluation of himself, his feeling of personal worth and his satisfaction with himself—a theory propounded by Holland (74).

These possible relationships are introduced here as ideas worthy of inspection by fairly mature individuals who are in the process of making career choices and plans, in order to help them to bring as many influences as possible into the conscious level. They may have minor significance for some, but the complexity of factors influencing decisions should be recognized to achieve any real self-determination. Most theories regarding vocational choice today recognize that the total personality is involved, and that presumably the more knowledge one has of self and the world of work the wiser his decisions may be.

Who Should Teach the Course or Unit? Some of the earliest examples of the teaching of occupations and vocational planning were in English classes. This work is now more frequently included in social-science, block-time, general-education, or special guidance courses. Lowenstein and Hoppock (75) reported that their survey of the teaching of occupations in 1952 showed for the first time that the majority of the schools from which they received replies had occupations classes taught by counselors rather than regular teachers. These reports were from schools recommended by college-counselor trainers as doing a superior job of presenting occupational information to their students through the medium of a class in occupations. The authors of the survey comment: "Apparently, school administrators are taking cognizance of the fact that perfunctory workbook units forced upon harassed ninth year civics teachers seldom make for a worth-while course in occupations."

A description of the guidance program in the Warwick, Rhode Island, Public Schools (76) places responsibility upon grade counselors for teaching, through classroom groups, those desirable educational, occupational, and social-living knowledges which are not included in the teaching of other departments. Classroom teachers are responsible for occupational information as part of the subject being studied—to give the student an idea of the ways in which the course is related to vocational life. Grade counselors meet with their counselees in groups for two periods per week. Where this plan for using counselors is not yet feasible, there should be extremely close cooperation between teachers and counselors in planning the program and in coordinating the teaching and individual conferences related to career decisions.

In 1961 Carter and Hoppock (64) reported that college courses in careers were taught by a variety of personnel including directors of placement, deans, student personnel workers, department chairmen, and members of the instructional staff.

The increased recognition of vocational guidance as essential to national defense, evidences of the greater efficiency of interrelating individual and group guidance, and rising standards for preparation and certification of counselors will undoubtedly bring more of the group services in vocational guidance into the functions of the trained counselor. The new organization, Academy of Teachers of Occupations, may, in the meantime, raise the level of service in the teaching of occupations.

EVALUATION OF GROUP APPROACHES

Much of the early research on the teaching of occupations related to measurement of the amount of information acquired and the percentages of students who expressed vocational choices. More recently there have been attempts to evaluate the quality of thinking that entered into choices (see page 278), and the wisdom and realism of these choices. Also, as we have noted earlier in this chapter, research has been aimed at discovering some of the factors that enter into the process of decision making.

Another trend is that of using long-range criteria rather than more immediate or intermediate outcomes. Cuony (77) made a follow-up study five years after an experimental group of high school seniors had taken a course in job finding and orientation. Compared with an equated control group, the experimental group were better satisfied with their jobs, had experienced less unemployment, and had earned more money. Lowenstein (78) in a follow-up in college of students from a twelfth-year "Career Opportunities" course, judged that the course had probably enabled them to make better adjustments in the freshman year than members of a control group who had not taken the high school course.

In the 1959–1960 report on research in the teaching of occupations,

Sinick and Hoppock (79) comment that many evaluative studies are utilizing opinions of students, teachers, and guidance specialists, and that experimental evidence, though highly regarded, is still low on the total poll of researches in this field.

SUMMARY

The new trend in vocational guidance is that of helping individuals to means of self-realization through useful work. This search requires much knowledge of self and of the complex world of work, and techniques of directing continuous growth and readjustment in a swiftly changing technological world.

Vocational-guidance service requires highly specialized training on the part of personnel workers for both group and individual counseling, the coordination of all pertinent services in an educational program, and the utilization of all community resources.

Research has contributed to our understanding of the nature of the processes involved in vocational planning and adjustment, and has demonstrated many of the values of vocational guidance through groups, but much continuous experimental research is needed to improve and expand these services.

REFERENCES CITED IN CHAPTER

1. Super, Donald E.: *The Psychology of Careers: An Introduction to Vocational Development,* Harper & Row, Publishers, New York, 1957.
2. Hoppock, Robert: *Occupational Information, Where to Get It and How to Use It in Counseling and Teaching,* McGraw-Hill Book Company, Inc., New York, 1957, pp. 74–112.
3. Roe, Anne: *Psychology of Occupations,* John Wiley & Sons, Inc., New York, 1956.
4. Masloe, A. H.: *Motivation and Personality,* Harper & Row, Publishers, New York, 1954.
5. Super, Donald, David V. Tiedeman, and Henry Borow: "Vocation Development, a Symposium," *The Personnel and Guidance Journal,* 40:11–25, September, 1961.
6. Zapoleon, Marguerite Wykoff: *Occupational Planning for Women,* Harper & Row, Publishers, New York, 1961.
7. Davidson, P. E., and H. D. Anderson: *Occupational Mobility in an American Community,* Stanford University Press, Stanford, Calif., 1937.
8. Hollingshead, A. B.: *Elmtown's Youth,* John Wiley & Sons, Inc., New York, 1940.
9. Berdie, Ralph F.: "Why Don't They Go to College?" *The Personnel and Guidance Journal,* 31:352–356, 1953.
10. Allen, P. J.: "Childhood Backgrounds and Success in a Profession," *American Journal of Sociology,* 20:186–190, 1955.
11. Caplow, Theodore: *The Sociology of Work,* University of Minnesota Press, Minneapolis, 1954.
12. Thomas, Lawrence G.: *The Occupational Structure and Education,* Prentice-Hall, Inc., Englewood Cliffs, N.J., 1956.
13. Super, Donald E.: "Dimensions and Measurement of Vocational Maturity," *Teachers College Record,* 57:151–163, 1955.

14. Super, Donald E., and Phoebe L. Overstreet: *The Vocational Maturity of Ninth Grade Boys*, Bureau of Publications, Teachers College, Columbia University, New York, 1960.
15. Crites, John O.: "A Model for the Measurement of Vocational Maturity," *Journal of Counseling Psychology*, 8:255–259, fall, 1961.
16. Super, Donald E.: "The Critical Ninth Grade: Vocational Choice or Vocational Exploration," *The Personnel and Guidance Journal*, 39:106–109, October, 1960.
17. Hulslander, S. C.: "Aspects of Physical Growth and Evaluation of Occupational Interests," *The Personnel and Guidance Journal*, 36:610–615, May, 1958.
18. Fine, Sidney A.: "What Is Occupational Information?" *The Personnel and Guidance Journal*, 33:504–508, May, 1955.
19. Wrenn, C. Gilbert: *The Counselor in a Changing World: A Preliminary Report of the Project on Guidance in American Schools*, American Personnel and Guidance Association, Washington, 1961.
20. Wood, Helen: "The Manpower Future—Its Challenges for Vocational Guidance," *The Personnel and Guidance Journal*, 38:300–304, December, 1959.
21. Samler, Joseph: "Psycho-social Aspects of Work: A Critique of Occupational Information," *The Personnel and Guidance Journal*, 39:458–465, February, 1961.
22. Danskin, David G.: "Occupational Sociology in Occupational Exploration," *The Personnel and Guidance Journal*, 34:134–136, November, 1955.
23. Danskin, David G.: "Studies on the Sociological Aspects of Specific Occupations," *The Personnel and Guidance Journal*, 36:104–111, October, 1957.
24. Baer, Max F., and Edward C. Roeber: *Occupational Information*, rev. ed., Science Research Associates, Inc., Chicago, 1958.
25. Norris, Willa, Franklin R. Zeran, and Raymond Hatch: *The Information Service, Occupational, Educational, Social*, Rand McNally & Company, Chicago, 1960.
26. Forrester, Gertrude: *Occupational Literature: An Annotated Bibliography*, 3d ed., The H. W. Wilson Company, New York, 1958.
27. Guidance Information Review Service Committee, National Vocational Guidance Association: *NVGA Bibliography of Current Occupational Literature*, The National Vocational Guidance Association, a division of the American Personnel and Guidance Association, Washington, 1959 revision.
28. Friend, F. G., and E. A. Haggard: "Work Adjustment in Relation to Family Background," *Applied Psychology Monographs*, 16, Stanford University Press, Stanford, Calif., 1948.
29. Publication Committee, Occupational Research Division, NVGA: "The Basic Outline for the Study of an Occupation," *Occupations, The Vocational Guidance Journal*, 28:320–322, February, 1950.
30. Shartle, Carroll L.: *Occupational Information, Its Development and Application*, rev. ed., Prentice-Hall, Inc., Englewood Cliffs, N.J., 1959.
31. Musselman, D. L., and L. A. Willig: "The Science Fair, a Vocational Guidance Opportunity," *The Vocational Guidance Quarterly*, 9:153–156, spring, 1961.
32. Parker, Herbert S.: "Ever Hear of a Job-O-Rama?" *The Vocational Guidance Quarterly*, 7:11–13, autumn, 1958.
33. Boyd, Gertrude A.: "Parents and Teachers Team Up to Give Prevocational Guidance," *The Vocational Guidance Quarterly*, 6:12–14, autumn, 1957.
34. Beachley, Catherine: "Careers via Closed-circuit Television," *The Vocational Guidance Quarterly*, 7:67–70, winter, 1958–1959.
35. Tarbet, Donald G.: "Guidance by TV," *The Personnel and Guidance Journal*, 33:145–147, November, 1954.
36. Dickinson, Carl: "What Employers Look for in the College Graduate," *The Personnel and Guidance Journal*, 33:460–464, April, 1955.
37. Forte, James J.: "What Business Expects of the High School Graduate," *The Vocational Guidance Quarterly*, 6:103–104, winter, 1957–1958.
38. Andrews, Margaret E.: "Employers Speak Up on Attitudes of Young Workers," *The Vocational Guidance Quarterly*, 4:54–56, winter, 1955–1956.
39. Roskin, Ronald: "Career Day," *The Personnel and Guidance Journal*, 36:501–502, March, 1958.

40. Rubinfeld, William A.: "Weekly Group Conferences on Careers," *The Personnel and Guidance Journal,* 33:223–225, December, 1954.
41. Brundage, Erven, and Stanley D. Frank: "The Career Conference Concept in San Diego County," *The Personnel and Guidance Journal,* 40:174–176, October, 1961.
42. Leis, Ward W.: "Pasadena's Occupational Survey Features Segments and Cycles," *The Vocational Guidance Quarterly,* 4:110–112, spring, 1956.
43. Teacher's Handbook for *Your Life Plans and the Armed Forces* (prepared under the direction of the Defense Committee, North Central Association of Secondary Schools and Colleges), American Council on Education, Washington, 1955.
44. *Your Life Plans and the Armed Forces* (prepared under the direction of the Defense Committee, North Central Association of Secondary Schools and Colleges), American Council on Education, Washington, 1955.
45. Ohlsen, Merle M., and Arthur E. Smith: "Educational-Vocational Planning in Terms of Military Service," *The Personnel and Guidance Journal,* 34:366–368, February, 1956.
46. Sacopulos, Eugenia: "Vocational Guidance through Fact and Fiction," *The Personnel and Guidance Journal,* 39:670–671, April, 1961.
47. Paterson, Donald G., C. d'A. Gerken, and Milton E. Hahn: *Revised Minnesota Occupational Rating Scale,* Minnesota Studies in Student Personnel Work, no. 2, University of Minnesota Press, Minneapolis, 1953.
48. Fine, Sidney A., and Carl A. Heinz: "The Estimates of Worker Trait Requirements for 4,000 Jobs," *The Personnel and Guidance Journal,* 36:168–174, November, 1957.
49. "Estimates of Worker Trait Requirements for 4,000 Jobs as Defined in the *Dictionary of Occupational Titles,*" U.S. Department of Labor, 1956.
50. Ginzberg, Eli: "Guidance—Limited or Unlimited," *The Personnel and Guidance Journal,* 38:707–712, May, 1960.
51. Hammond, Marjorie: "Motives Related to Vocational Choices of College Freshmen," *Journal of Counseling Psychology,* 3:257–261, winter, 1956.
52. Super, Donald E., David V. Tiedeman, and Henry Borow: "Vocational Development, a Symposium," *The Personnel and Guidance Journal,* 40:11–25, September, 1961.
53. Super, Donald E.: "The Critical Ninth Grade: Vocational Choice or Vocational Exploration," *The Personnel and Guidance Journal,* 39:106–109, October, 1960.
54. Ziller, Robert C.: "Vocational Choice and Utility for Risk," *Journal of Counseling Psychology,* 4:61–64, spring, 1957.
55. O'Hara, Robert P., and David V. Tiedeman: "Vocational Self Concept in Adolescence," *Journal of Counseling Psychology,* 6:292–301, winter, 1959.
56. Grell, Lewis A.: "How Much Occupational Information in the Elementary School?" *The Vocational Guidance Quarterly,* 9:48–59, autumn, 1960.
57. National Society for the Study of Education: *Social Studies in the Elementary School,* Fifty-sixth Yearbook of the National Society of Education, University of Chicago Press, Chicago, 1957, part 2.
58. Kaye, Janet: "Fourth Grades Meet Up with Occupations," *The Vocational Guidance Quarterly,* 8:150–152, spring, 1960.
59. Sinick, Daniel, and Robert Hoppock: "Research on the Teaching of Occupations, 1956–1958," *The Personnel and Guidance Journal,* 38:150–155, October, 1959.
60. Lifton, Walter M.: "Vocational Guidance in the Elementary School," *The Vocational Guidance Quarterly,* 8:79–81, winter, 1959.
61. Wright, Ralph E.: "Teaching Occupational Information in Illinois," *The Personnel and Guidance Journal,* 35:30–33, September, 1956.
62. Sinick, Daniel, and Robert Hoppock: "Research by States on the Teaching of Occupations," *The Personnel and Guidance Journal,* 39:218–219, November, 1960.
63. Foster, Charles R., and James Dungan: "Occupational Information: State by State," *The Vocational Guidance Quarterly,* 8:227–234, summer, 1960.

64. Carter, Edward M., and Robert Hoppock: "College Courses in Careers," *The Personnel and Guidance Journal*, 39:373–375, January, 1961.
65. Henderson, Harold L.: "Occupational Information through Assignment, Small Group Discussion, Role Playing," *The Vocational Guidance Quarterly*, 3:44–46, winter, 1954–1955.
66. Allen, Richard D., et al.: *Common Problems in Group Guidance*, The Inor Publishing Company, New York, 1933.
67. Hewer, Vivian H.: "Group Counseling, Individual Counseling, and a College Class in Vocations," *The Personnel and Guidance Journal*, 37:660–665, May, 1959.
68. DuBato, George S.: "Case Conference on Occupations," *The Vocational Guidance Quarterly*, 7:257–259, summer, 1959.
69. Stephenson, Richard M.: "Realism of Vocational Choice: A Critique and an Example," *The Personnel and Guidance Journal*, 35:482–488, April, 1957.
70. Lockwood, William V.: "Realism of Vocational Preference," *The Personnel and Guidance Journal*, 37:98–106, October, 1958.
71. Schutz, Richard A., and Donald H. Blocher: "Self-concepts and Stereotypes of Vocational Preferences," *The Vocational Guidance Quarterly*, 8:241–244, summer, 1960.
72. Bordin, E. S.: "A Theory of Vocational Interest as Dynamic Phenomena," *Educational and Psychological Measurement*, 3:49–65, 1943.
73. Schutz, Edward A., and Donald H. Blocher: "Self-satisfaction and Level of Occupational Choice," *The Personnel and Guidance Journal*, 39:595–598, March, 1961.
74. Holland, J. L.: "A Theory of Vocational Choice," *Journal of Counseling Psychology*, 6:35–44, 1959.
75. Lowenstein, Norman, and Robert Hoppock: "The Teaching of Occupations in 1952," *The Personnel and Guidance Journal*, 31:441–444, April, 1953.
76. Warwick School Department, *Organization and Administration of Guidance, for Grades VII through XII*, Curric. Pub. no. 1, Warwick, R.I., January, 1954. Also, *Can We Leave Counseling to Chance?* by C. S. Taylor, Nov. 12, 1957. (Both mimeographed.)
77. Cuony, E. R., and Robert Hoppock: "Job Course Pays Off Again," *The Personnel and Guidance Journal*, 36:116–117, October, 1957.
78. Lowenstein, Norman, and Robert Hoppock: "High School Occupations Course Helps Students Adjust to College," *The Personnel and Guidance Journal*, 34:21–23, September, 1955.
79. Sinick, Daniel, and Robert Hoppock: "Research on the Teaching of Occupations," *The Personnel and Guidance Journal*, 40:164–168, October, 1961.

ADDITIONAL REFERENCES

Darley, John, and Theda Hagenah: *Vocational Interest Measurement*, University of Minnesota Press, Minneapolis, 1955.
Fryer, Douglas: *The Measurement of Interests*, Henry Holt and Company, Inc., New York, 1931.
Herzberg, Frederick, et al.: *The Motivation to Work*, John Wiley & Sons, Inc., New York, 1959.
Lurie, Walter A., et al.: "An Intensive Vocational Counseling Program for Slow Learners in High School," *The Personnel and Guidance Journal*, 39:21–29, September, 1960.
Occupational Outlook Handbook, 1961 edition, U.S. Bureau of Labor Statistics, 1961.
Schloerb, L. J.: *School Subjects and Careers*, Science Research Associates, Inc., Chicago, 1950.
Segel, David, et al.: *An Approach to Individual Analysis in Educational and Vocational Guidance*, U.S. Office of Education Bulletin 1959, no. 1, 1959.
Super, Donald E., and John O. Crites: *Appraising Vocational Fitness by Means of Psychological Tests*, rev. ed., Harper & Row, Publishers, New York, 1962.

Tenneson, W. Wesley, et al.: *The Teacher's Role in Career Development,* Minnesota State Department of Education, St. Paul, 1960.

For sources of occupational information see:

Baer, Max F., and Edward C. Roeber: *Occupational Information,* rev. ed., Science Research Associates, Inc., Chicago, 1958.

Forrester, Gertrude: *Occupational Literature: An Annotated Bibliography,* 3d ed., The H. W. Wilson Company, New York, 1958.

Hoppock, Robert: *Occupational Information,* McGraw-Hill Book Company, Inc., New York, 1957.

Norris, Willa, Franklin R. Zeran, and Raymond N. Hatch: *The Information Service in Guidance, Occupational, Educational, Social,* Rand McNally & Company, Chicago, 1961.

NVGA Bibliography of Current Occupational Literature, 1959 revision, National Vocational Guidance Association, a division of the American Personnel and Guidance Association, Washington, 1959.

Shartle, Carroll L.: *Occupational Information, Its Development and Application,* rev. ed., Prentice-Hall, Inc., Englewood Cliffs, N.J., 1959.

For student texts, see list in bibliography for Chapter 12.

12 EDUCATIONAL PLANNING

This area of planning involves all of the other areas in group guidance, since educational experiences should contribute to the realization of goals in all phases of living, both in the present and the future. There are both private and public aspects of educational planning, since education is provided in a free society to serve both individual and public interests. Each person should be aware of all of these purposes in planning his own program and make choices in the light of all of his life goals insofar as he is aware of them. One important consideration is that of the tempo of change in his world that means preparation for continuous readaptation as new conditions develop. Other considerations are the increasing demand for higher degrees of skill and understanding in a technological world, and the increasing importance of interpersonal relationships in a world of concentrated populations and intensified intercommunication.

The background of understanding cannot be achieved in a few brief interviews, and, even if it could be, there would be a tragic waste of counselor time in the repetition needed merely to impart information, without reference to the attitudes, appreciations, and convictions that must be a part of any citizen's understanding of the values of education.

LIMITATIONS OF THE PROGRAMMING INTERVIEW

Counselors, teacher-counselors, or advisers in many educational institutions spend incredible numbers of hours, often splintered into ten-, fifteen-, or twenty-minute interviews, helping students make out programs. Then, at the beginning of a new term, they spend additional weary hours, perhaps splintered into two-, five-, or ten-minute interviews, changing many of the programs they made during the previous term.

There can be no doubt that programming interviews serve many useful purposes. Through them the counselor becomes better acquainted with the student. If parents participate in the initial programming conference, the encounter is usually enlightening to both the counselor and the parents. Often, in the course of such an interview, other problems of the student come to light which might not otherwise be recognized, and in many cases a friendly relationship between counselor and student is established, which may open the door to confidences and the possibility of helpful personal guidance. Finally, the programming interview serves the basic function of preventing students from choosing the wrong courses and thereby losing time in their training programs.

Offsetting these advantages, it must be conceded realistically that, because of the large number of counselees who must be served in most educational institutions, most programming conferences are so brief that they allow no real opportunity for learning experiences for most students. There is rarely time for pursuing any other question than "What shall I or must I take?"

LEARNINGS ESSENTIAL FOR SOUND EDUCATIONAL PLANNING

First we shall consider some of the learnings essential for intelligent planning of educational programs, and then some of the ways in which group experiences may contribute to these learnings and may also lay foundations for more effective individual counseling.

The term *learnings* is used here to include understanding of self, of conditions and demands in the environment, of the nature and purposes of varied types of educational opportunities, and of the meaning of education for the individual.

Self-knowledge important for educational planning

Points listed here are brief restatements of learnings dealt with in previous chapters and brief previews of learnings treated by the next three chapters. Any approach to a real-life problem has ramifications in many areas and can never be treated in isolation or with all pertinent information at hand. Educational planning is always a spiral process with new vistas on the horizon and new information available at each stage of development.

1. Growing understanding of self, including potentialities for all aspects of living—work, home, citizenship, social, religious, recreational, and esthetic. This self-knowledge includes patterns of abilities and aptitudes, interests and aspirations, and character and personality trends, all of which should enter into the developing self-concept and a realistic and idealistic view of a life pattern.

2. Sound methods of growing in self-knowledge and self-awareness.

3. Ways of developing personal value standards and life philosophy as they relate to a total way of life.

4. Sound methods of developing vocational, avocational, and total

life plans congruent with the self-concept, growing life values and understanding of environmental demands.

5. Ways of developing and improving personality requirements for effective work and all interpersonal relationships.

Understanding of environmental demands

1. Knowledge about the world of work in terms of patterns of work, and the related work conditions, hazards, opportunities, demands and requirements, remuneration, human relationships, and social values.

2. Understanding and use of reliable sources of information about occupational life and about trends and changes in the labor market.

3. Learning to make choices and adjustments compatible with knowledge of self and work opportunities.

4. Knowledge of requirements for effective home living and parenthood, citizenship, and all social, recreational, religious, and other personal pursuits of a well-balanced, satisfying life.

5. Understanding of the requirements and rewards of education carried to the optimum point of returns for each individual. While monetary rewards may not be the most significant returns from education, every teen-ager should be aware of estimates released by the U.S. Department of Labor, the U.S. Office of Education, and the U.S. Department of Defense to the effect that a high school graduate tends to earn $64,000 more in a lifetime than a high school dropout, and that a college degree may add $100,000 to lifetime earnings.

6. Formulating an educational and training program to prepare for work and all other aspects of living. Personal and financial resources to carry through this program are, of course, considerations that enter into the making of plans. Then comes the choice of preparatory work in high school, if this is involved in the plan, the selection of a training institution beyond high school or of terminal vocational training in high school, and eventually the selection of specific courses in the program and perhaps suitable work experience or internship.

Understanding of the purposes of education in a democracy

Each institution is likely to have its list of objectives for its total educational program and also for each department, subject, or activity area, and for specific courses and activities. In addition, there are numerous statements of national goals for American education that have doubtless influenced the formulation or reformulation of goals in each institution.

Perhaps no other area in group guidance is more important than this one: to help all individuals to understand why they have the privilege of educational opportunities, whether compulsory or voluntary, and what these opportunities should mean to them and to their country. For this reason we are considering it in some detail.

This is a guidance objective at all levels. In the elementary school the approach may be informal, at least until entrance to the secondary school level looms ahead. But at all levels there should be planned group study and discussion aimed at the growing awareness of why a democratic society establishes, maintains, and ever improves educational opportunities for all citizens, what these opportunities mean both to the individual and to society, how each individual can utilize these opportunities to the fullest extent, and what each citizen's responsibilities are in return for this privilege through suitable services to his world in helping to improve the way of life for all as well as enhancing his own life.

At the secondary school, college, and adult levels this guidance objective will be achieved through individual and group study and individual applications in the planning of educational programs to meet individual needs and aspirations as a future worker, homemaker, and citizen. This is frequently a part of orientation programs.

The study of guidance objectives could begin with consideration of educational aims such as those stated by the Educational Policies Commission in 1938 and in succeeding reports (1–3). The broad aims seem to be timeless: self-realization, democratic human relationships, economic efficiency, and civic responsibility. Their interpretations in terms of the nature of educational programs change inevitably with changing times. Some of their meanings for the sixties have been interpreted, with urgency in these fateful times, by the President's Commission on National Goals (4) and the Rockefeller Panel Reports on *Prospects for America* (5). Every citizen should be informed regarding the interpretations of the meaning and purposes of education in America as stated in these reports, and plan how he can realize these objectives most fully in his formal schooling and in continuing education throughout life.

Only a few of the points stressed in these reports can be summarized here:

1. The education of all individuals is essential to the preservation and improvement of our free society.

2. A major purpose of education is to foster the optimum individual fulfillment of every citizen. This purpose is based on recognition of the uniqueness of each individual, the dignity and sacredness of each human being, the right of each to opportunities to develop his unique potentialities to the utmost, and his responsibility to take advantage of these

opportunities, and to use his talents wisely in individual and social living. Here is evidence of the awareness that our human resources are our greatest wealth as a nation.

Equality of opportunity does not imply the same quantity or type of education for all, since each individual differs in his educational needs, but it does mean the pursuit of excellence for all in terms of unique potentialities.

3. Some phases of education are fundamental for the preparation of citizens to perform their functions as free, rational, responsible persons; as leaders and followers in a democratic way of life where new dangers and new challenges are ever appearing; as homemakers, workers, and consumers of leisure time and the ever-increasing wealth of material resources.

For the sixties, at least, these fundamentals include increased breadth and depth of understanding about our physical, biological, and social world; about the implications of the vastly accelerated tempo of change due to technological developments; about the ideals and moral implications for every citizen of our American heritage and culture, and our obligations within the world culture. Included in these fundamentals are the basic skills of reading, writing, and all forms of communication, mathematics, physical and social sciences, foreign languages, at least for many, and those experiences that foster self-knowledge, self-development, self-discipline, problem solving and creative thinking, and all of the habits, attitudes, commitments, value systems, and qualities of character essential for citizenship in a free, open, democratic society.

4. Vocational preparation no longer means for anyone *merely* specific training for a specific job or profession. More training and skill are required increasingly for every type of work, and the demand for unskilled labor is steadily decreasing. But the basic essentials for any kind of work are grounded in understanding of fundamental principles and the ability to keep abreast of new developments and to adapt continuously to changing conditions of work as technological changes occur.

5. Human talent of every kind is needed for creative innovations in all aspects of life to improve conditions, to perfect democratic processes, and to protect and safeguard our free society in a world in which its existence is threatened by totalitarian forces.

Both government and private agencies are providing opportunities through scholarships, fellowships, and loans to enable those who may be limited financially to continue their education to an optimum point with reference to their potentialities. Guidance services, and in fact the entire educational service, has the responsibility of sparking the desire of each person to take advantage of these opportunities for optimum self-fulfillment. This is an especially important service for potential dropouts and for those who are not planning training programs consonant with their abilities.

6. It is each person's privilege and responsibility to develop a system of values that will enable him as a member of a free society to make choices and plans and take advantage of educational opportunities that may result in his fullest self-realization and his best contributions to human life.[1]

The development of understanding of these opportunities and responsibilities within the American educational system is not solely a responsibility of the guidance service. All staff members—teachers in every subject field and leaders in the extracurriculum or allied activities —have responsibilities for interpreting the values inherent in their phases of the program and for assisting individuals to realize these values as fully as possible. The guidance service, through both group and individual counseling, has the opportunity to help individuals to gain an overview of their educational opportunities and responsibilities, to appraise their talents and full potentialities, and to plan how to develop and use them. Some will need special assistance in overcoming blocks to the full utilization of their educational opportunities.

SOME GENERAL CONSIDERATIONS IN PLANNING GROUP SERVICES IN EDUCATIONAL GUIDANCE

Obviously, all the learnings mentioned cannot be achieved in a few interviews, important as they are, or in one brief unit of instruction. Many depend on personality development as well as planned study over many years. Some general problems of counselor planning for these learnings and for those considered in the rest of this chapter are (*a*) What are suitable age or grade-level expectancies for each type of learning? (*b*) How may the program be adapted to varying maturity patterns and needs of individuals? (*c*) When and how is counseling to be coordinated and integrated with the group procedures?

Following are some of the specific questions related to the planning of group services in educational guidance at a particular level.

1. What foundations have already been laid in the orientation program, in special group-guidance units or courses, in every subject area, in meetings with parents, and in interviews with students and parents? Orientation programs usually include some consideration of the purposes

---

[1] Adapted and summarized from the following references by permission of the publishers: John W. Gardner, "National Goals in Education," in *Goals for Americans*, the Report of the President's Commission on National Goals, by the American Assembly, Columbia University, 1960, Prentice-Hall, Inc., publisher; and *Prospect for America*, by Rockefeller Brothers Fund, Inc., Doubleday & Company, Inc., publisher.

of education and the opportunities within the particular institution. Most teachers help their students to see the purposes and values of their subjects, and this is increasingly a service of the leaders of activities as they have become a more fully recognized part of the entire educational program. Self-appraisal and vocational planning have usually been included in units or courses by the ninth- or tenth-grade level, and personal-social problems and life values are usually given some attention at various points.

A review and reconsideration of all of these factors, adapted to the maturity level of the individuals, is usually desirable before attention is given to questions of immediate choices of subjects and activities and long-range program planning. The nature of earlier services in all the areas mentioned will, of course, help to determine the emphasis in an education-planning unit, together with the immediate decision requirements of students.

2. Is new information needed for self-appraisal to be added to that already available? When this is the case it may be desirable to plan several types of group experiences. Fairly large groups could often be used to provide understanding about tests if they are to be used, to administer the tests, and to interpret group norms and the general aspects of individual applications of test results. Smaller groups and individual conferences are more valuable—and safer—for studying individual profiles of test results and interpreting their possible meanings for decisions and plans. Local norms and probability estimates are often more significant than national norms in this process.

3. Is new occupational and educational information needed before wise decisions and plans can be made? If the educational-planning unit is a part of a vocational-guidance unit or course, this need may have been met already. If review and new information are indicated, this may be the time to introduce some of the career, college, and technical-school conferences, movies, assemblies, visits and interviews with employers and other workers in the community; to study the results of community surveys and of work and training opportunities, and to plan new reading and research projects for individuals. Career-curricular conferences in which both vocational and educational information are provided are being introduced increasingly. A counselor will, of course, plan to have an adequate supply of catalogues and bulletins for all institutions that may provide advanced educational and training opportunities for any students.

4. What are the major criteria that individuals should be trained to use in the choice of electives and majors, and the formulation of long-range plans? These will merely be listed here, since every counselor,

doubtless, keeps them ever in mind and recognizes their importance.

a. Meeting requirements for graduation.

b. Meeting requirements for vocational training.

c. Keeping doors open as fully as possible for changes in plans as new conditions emerge or new interests develop.

d. Planning a program that will capitalize on the full range of personal potentialities.

e. Preparing for the full range of life goals and values.

f. For most women, planning to prepare for the double role of homemaker and creative individual in work or other pursuits.

g. For the especially gifted academically, planning for enrichment, acceleration, or for advanced study of a college level while still in high school, if the possibility is available.

h. For those with very special talents of any nature, planning to utilize them to the fullest extent, but with clear awareness of the wide range of life activities in self-fulfillment for which education offers preparation.

i. For all, preparation to contribute to the improvement of life for mankind as well as for self-fulfillment. This criterion has been added hopefully, since the present emphasis appears to be placed by most students upon self-centered, personal goals. Perhaps some guided study of the interrelationships of social and personal welfare may help to shift this balance a bit. It may even be that our emphasis in educational goals on individual development has helped to produce the emphasis on private satisfactions in living rather than public service. There are, of course, other factors involved, some of which may have influenced our educational objectives.

5. What techniques and guidance materials are helpful in the program planning? Here are a few suggestions:

a. Students can be taught in groups to read and interpret school bulletins or catalogues for themselves. To facilitate such learnings, devices such as quiz sheets or panel discussions have proved to be useful.

b. Study and discussion of general college or technical-school entrance requirements can be carried on with interested groups. This will eliminate the many repetitions of the same material through a series of personal interviews. One exposure to this information will not necessarily answer all the questions or serve all the needs of every member of the group, but this is a problem that recurs in all phases of learning. However, two or three repetitions addressed to the entire group seem preferable to several hundred repetitions in individual interviews. Often a discussion of pertinent questions can lead to greater awareness of the reasons (or lack of good reasons) for some of these requirements.

Mimeographed bulletins, revised when necessary, can become a helpful part of students' notes for such study.

c. Beyond the group study of these general requirements, students can be subdivided into smaller groups for the exploration of the varying requirements of different colleges, universities, or technical and other special schools. Each student should participate in several of these subgroups in order to obtain perspective on the educational outlook.

d. Duplicated or printed work sheets can be developed which will help guide students in collecting, organizing, and using data for educational planning as readily as for vocational planning. Usually such data are included in vocational-guidance manuals or workbooks, since the kinds of information needed for both objectives are interrelated.

e. Arrangements can be made for small groups of students to visit classes in subjects which they contemplate taking, or for an eleventh-grade student, for example, to come in and talk with a group of eighth-grade students about a particular course. Similarly, tours through colleges or technical schools can be planned for groups of students who expect to enroll in a specific institution.[2]

f. The participation of parents in programming has often proved to be sound and constructive. Part of this can be done through parent study groups, bulletins for parent study, and local radio or television programs.

g. Slides, films, and other audio-visual aids can help students to visualize opportunities in advanced courses or in new educational levels ahead.

h. Group discussions can be planned to deal with a variety of problems related to the use of all the foregoing types of information pertinent to educational planning. These discussions can clarify understanding of requirements and of elective opportunities, and foster a sense of challenge and excitement about the new experiences ahead.

Effective use of the counseling interview

With a background of group study of programming problems, the counseling interview can be used to consider special and unique problems of individuals that cannot be resolved through the group work. Both counselor and counselee will have a common background of understanding that will enable them to consider significant questions without the wasted effort of repetitious consideration of matters that can be taught and learned readily in groups. This shift in the utilization of counselors' time can be effected without depriving students of any vital service. It could result in more time available for significant

[2] See also description of college summer clinics, pp. 189 and 199.

counseling that is essential and should be expanded rather than contracted.

Through a judicious combination of learning in groups and learning in interviews, students can gain power in one phase of self-direction that should carry over into lifelong planning of learning.

Routine aspects of programming

The actual checking of programs which have been mapped out by students, to verify their fulfillment of requirements, can in large measure be done by the students themselves, with the aid of check lists and questionnaires. Or this checking can be done with parental assistance, with parents asked to sign their names to the proposed programs as evidence of their cooperative effort. Beyond this point the job can be done by competent clerks or secretaries. It should not require the time of counselors whose skill and training might better be applied to more challenging problems.

The writer is fully aware of the fact that all of the above suggestions and others are embodied in many educational-guidance programs all over this country. However, years of experience and observation have led to the conclusion that traditional "programming" practices are especially resistant to change in many educational institutions; and since some of these practices seem to involve a woeful waste of professional counseling skills, the need for re-examining all of them has been emphasized in this discussion.

SOME SPECIAL PROBLEMS IN EDUCATIONAL GUIDANCE

Salvaging the dropouts

Our manpower policies have led us to conclude that every person who withdraws from school before he has achieved his optimal education is a wasted resource in our national economy. This policy has led to an intensification of guidance services to potential dropouts, who can usually be identified at an early age by many factors such as educational status relative to age, attendance, health, learning rate, reading ability, participation in school activities, interest in school work, and general adjustment.

The Holding Power Project in New York State secondary schools is an example of an intensified guidance and curricular program in which specially trained counselors and teachers identified the potentially vulnerable pupils and worked intensively with both them and their parents in an effort to prevent their withdrawal before graduation. Marked reduction in the dropout rate in New York State has been reported (6, 7).

Enough evidence is now available regarding the fate of early school leavers to provide a thoughtful challenge to those who are contemplating withdrawal, and to those with high academic potential who may not be adequately motivated to continue their education beyond high school. The findings also present a severe challenge to the schools to provide educational experiences better suited to the needs and interests of many potential dropouts.

Studies by the Bureau of Labor Statistics, U.S. Department of Labor, and other governmental bureaus have yielded excellent information to use in group guidance (8, 9). Wolfbein has reported that dropouts secured more unskilled jobs, received lower wages, and experienced a much higher rate of unemployment than did high school graduates. The boy dropouts, for example, averaged three times as much unemployment in regions surveyed as the boy graduates. We have already noted the decrease in percentage of unskilled workers in the labor force and the relationship between life income and level of education. All of these facts should be faced squarely by all teen-agers in their educational planning, and they should be thoroughly informed about all types of available training in vocational and technical schools, in apprenticeship, and on-the-job training programs as well as in colleges.

Wolfbein's report has many implications for schools as well as teen-agers. Among them are the need for an earlier start on vocational guidance for many, educational experiences better adapted to individual needs and interests, and for some a combined work-school program with the work ideally related to the individual's interests and career plans (10).

Identifying and guiding the gifted and talented

Since Sputnik, more attention has been directed, fortunately, to the discovery and cultivation of talent and giftedness. There is difference of opinion as to what the term *gifted* implies. A study, by Getsel and Jackson (11, pp. 1–18) suggests that this term may not always apply only to the academically talented. Their study of *creativity* interpreted the word as meaning the aptitude for achieving new meanings having social value, and differentiated a *high*-IQ and a so-called *high-creative* group in several respects. According to their measuring instruments, they found the high-IQ group to be more *convergent*, i.e., conforming more to conventional standards, and the high-creative group to be more *divergent*, with a rich and available fantasy life. Both groups were equal in performance on standardized achievement tests, but the creative group had a markedly lower average IQ. They evidenced more humor, playfulness, and unusual responses on tests than did the high-IQ group. Teachers' responses on a test indicated that they preferred to have children in their classes with the qualities evidenced by the high-IQ group. This group aspired to qualities for themselves similar to those rated by teachers as predictive of success, whereas the high-creative group favored personal qualities which had no relationship to those they believed made for adult success, and which were in some ways the reverse of those they believed their teachers favored. The authors of this study make a plea for a multidimensional approach to the study of giftedness.

Our talent search has emphasized the identification of the academically talented, and the prevailing practice seems to be to start with screening by means of group mental tests. It is the writer's judgment that we are likely to miss many of those we are seeking by this process. During a ten-year period of psychological service at the college level, when individual tests were used exclusively, comparisons of these results with those from group tests on cumulative records yielded differences ranging from 20 to 60 points in IQ in nearly half of the individuals tested, and most of these differences were in the upward direction. Discovered causes of these discrepancies were multiple. Among them were reading disabilities, lack of motivation in taking the group tests, visual and other handicaps, and probably some faulty test administration and clerical errors. It would seem wise to start the talent search on a broad basis of many types of records and observations if we expect to locate most of our academically talented youths.

Many of them crowd the ranks of the underachievers, and many fail to reach their optimum educational levels because of poor study habits, poor scholarship, lack of incentives, lack of self-confidence, financial limitations, and other conditions. Most of these obstacles might, perhaps, be eliminated if they were discovered early enough and direct attacks through group study and counseling were intensified. These students have unusual power to think clearly and creatively if they are helped to come to grips with all the facts. Group-guidance services should be provided for this purpose.

We shall hope for more leads and insights for their guidance through the results of Project Talent (11, pp. 67–83) and other current and future researches along many lines already recognized as essential (12, pp. 69–80), as well as through our intensified services for the gifted (13). We shall be considering many of their problems as well as those of their academically less favored peers in several of the topics that follow.

Motivating the low achiever

The upsurge of interest in the low achiever is in large part a reflection of our concern for the maximum development of all of our human resources, especially manifested in our search for the talented who swell the ranks of the underachievers.

A comparison by Pierce and Bowman (11, pp. 36–66) of high- and low-achievement boys and girls in the top 30 per cent in intellectual ability in their high school yielded some marked differences, especially among the boys in motivation patterns. High-achieving boys scored higher than low-achieving boys on the unconscious need for achievement as measured by a projective test. Measures of strength of educational motivation and adjustment favored the high-achieving students, who also gave evidence of higher values attached to concepts of school, work, imagination, and competition. The education and cultural expectations of parents of high achievers were higher than those of the other group, and more students were first-born or only children. Studies have shown also that underachievers tend to display more hostility and to perceive themselves less favorably than achievers. For boys, many of these differences appear frequently in the primary grades; for girls a bit later, usually.

We know too little as yet about all the factors that enter into motivation. However, research has strongly indicated that the low achievers can be identified early in the elementary school years and that this is the time to start guidance services to remedy difficulties. Both research workers and practitioners are urging that greater attention be given in connection with the study of achievement to a variety of factors such as interest, attitudes, critical thinking, self-understanding of factors involved, problem solving, value standards, appreciations, emotional and social adjustment, and personal adaptability.

The causal patterns of low achievement will doubtless vary with each individual, but we are now alerted to some of the factors to look for. A U.S. Office of Education bulletin (14) on guidance for the underachieving superior student reviews problems and current practices and suggests some possible causes of underachievement: lack of motivation in the home, peer groups, school, and the prevailing social culture. Some bright youngsters may prefer peer acceptance to scholastic excellence. Some seem actually to lack confidence in their ability. How many have slipped effortlessly through early school years without developing skills and character traits needed for advanced work? How many find no challenge or worthwhile meaning in the school offerings? The writer has encountered these factors frequently.

In both elementary and secondary school years we might well help individuals to study the problem directly in groups in light of what evidence we have as to possible causes. Numerous efforts have been made through small therapeutic groups such as were described in Chapter 6, but reported results have not been conclusive as to the adequacy of this approach alone. We should, doubtless, make a concerted attack on many fronts, direct and indirect, with emphasis on both emotional therapy and intellectual understanding, not overlooking needed changes in the curriculum and the possibility of incentives and inspiration derived from the deep, personal interest of an adult, either counselor or teacher. Group study of the problem with parents is another promising approach.

A pilot study of group counseling with underachieving seventh-grade boys who were demonstrating acting-out behavior has led to a two-year project with a Federal grant under the direction of the Board of Cooperative Educational Services, Bedford Hills, New York (15). Cohn (16), who conducted the pilot study, provided opportunity for these boys to explore their feelings and attitudes. The discussions dealt first with the curriculum and revealed (as interpreted by the leader) more interest in manipulative than verbal skills, considerable hostility toward some teachers, a need for more understanding and consideration of the students' feelings, a basic desire to like their teachers, and sensitivity about their own intellectual capacity. Peer group and leader became objects of hostility at times, and the setting of limits was necessary, as is usual in such a group.

The twenty-week period allowed was considered inadequate, but outcomes were sufficiently positive to move into the two-year project, which will also include group discussions with teachers to improve their techniques with underachievers. Among outcomes reported for the pilot group were greater awareness by the boys of need for remedial help, increased sensitivity to others, and improved attitudes toward school. Recommendations included improved teacher attitudes toward underachievers, more opportunities created for success, avoidance of situations where underachievers are "labeled," and their inclusion in group projects outside their chosen cliques.

Guiding the mentally and physically handicapped

Those with extreme handicaps in special classes will usually carry on their group guidance with their special teachers in cooperation with counselor or psychologist, and, at the appropriate age, with a counselor from the State Rehabilitation Service. The vocational and educational guidance for these groups is a specialized service that requires the assistance of those with special training. Employment records of the handicapped show that, rightly placed, with reference to their assets, they can make very satisfactory work adjustments and often exceed the records of nonhandicapped with comparable assets. The educational guidance for living, aside from the work aspect, need not depart too widely from that for all others (17, 18).

Guiding the emotionally disturbed

This service was stressed in Chapter 6 in the treatment of group counseling. One approach is that of placement in special classes where regular education and special services may be combined. An important step in planning for guidance and education of the emotionally disturbed is, of course, the discovery of causes and special needs (19). This is as complicated as the whole child-study question. Only two approaches to diagnosis and treatment will be mentioned here. Tobias (20) has reported medical findings showing significant relationships between emotional disturbances of children and youth and delayed maturation as measured by wrist x-ray, cerebral dysrhythmia, subnormal blood calcium and blood sugar, and high cholesterol. On the other hand, Harvey (21) and many others have produced abnormalities in the growth potential and behavior of animals by subjecting them to protracted stress. The psychiatrist Spotnitz (22) has suggested that the very complicated body chemistry might be more adequately controlled by a healthy emotional state than by the administration of man-made drugs.

These points of view carry our thinking around in a circle. Perhaps one way we can help to break through the circle is to offer all possible encouragement to the emotionally disturbed person in as stressless an environment as can be provided, together with opportunity for awareness of acceptance, respect, and real human interest from another person, no matter what limitations may be needed on overt behavior. Medical services may likewise help to break the circle. Perhaps the poet Robert Browning gave us a deep insight when he wrote, "Nor soul helps flesh now more than flesh helps soul."

Motivation for college or other training beyond high school

We have already considered some of the factors in our culture that emphasize the need for guidance efforts directed at motivation and planning to achieve optimum education—rising standards of preparation for work, lack of incentives stemming from some home and cultural backgrounds, our national objectives for the cultivation of talent, and our educational objective of self-actualization for every individual. Rising standards for admission to institutions of higher education have added another impelling reason for beginning the program of motivation early enough to prevent the closing of doors to potentially qualified individuals because of poor scholastic records and inadequate background of academic requirements. Many schools are beginning programs of group and individual study of college values and requirements in the ninth or tenth grade and are also including parents in the study.

Since not all high school students can or should enter college or university, it is important to include all types of training beyond high school, as well as some terminal vocational training in high school, in this study where groups are heterogeneous in composition. The same caution applies here as in vocational guidance—to foster an attitude of respect for all types of training and recognition that status should be related to training suited to one's best potentialities rather than to college per se. Grouping on the basis of types of training institutions is doubtless desirable, after the total scope of opportunities has been envisaged, both for economy of effort and efficiency. A timetable for varying types of approach is important to the counselor and group leader (23).

Guidance in Choosing a College or Technical School. This problem and the next one are of such widespread interest today, and so much has been written on both questions, that it seems needless to write more. Some of the most significant questions for group study as a foundation for individual decisions are outlined here, and a selected list of references is included in the chapter bibliography. References in this field need to be updated continually by the counselor.

1. Should I go to college or is some other type of advanced training more suitable for me?

Self-appraisal and vocational planning are essential background for this question, but tentative decisions may be necessary before vocational plans have fully matured. Some initial questions are: What are the values of a college education? What are the relative values of liberal education leading toward depth and breadth of understanding of life, the possible effect on life income of a college degree, and the foundations for professional training? Are my interests and abilities congruent with general college requirements and values?

2. What colleges or universities are likely to be available to me? Here enter such questions as scholarship and course requirements, costs, possible means of financing costs, geographical location, desirability of junior or city colleges for the first two years.

3. What criteria should I apply in choosing among those colleges that may be available? Among these are the following: accreditation; variety and strength of offerings in fields of interest; library and laboratory facilities; nature of student body as to size, coeducation or non-coeducation, cosmopolitan make-up, etc.; location and living facilities; social, recreational, athletic, and cultural opportunities; military training; work-study programs; availability of part-time jobs if needed; types of financial aid through scholarships, loans, etc.; placement services; and suitability of preparation for advanced training if contemplated.

There are many more possible criteria, such as the achievement records of graduates, but those listed above are basic.

Much the same criteria would apply for those choosing graduate professional schools, but with more emphasis upon standards and reputation relative to a particular profession, possibilities for fellowships, and significant placement contacts.

4. What are the various types of technical schools or other advanced training facilities available to me?

Here it is important to develop a sense of high privilege, perhaps even glamour to the limits of reality, to prevent this question from meaning a choice second-best to college for those not suited for college. Information about all varieties of technical schools, apprenticeship opportunities, on-the-job training, work-study programs, and reliable correspondence schools should be available.

All this means a wide collection of college and school bulletins and brochures readily available for study, in addition to general references on educational information. Several of these general references include evaluation forms to aid students in collecting pertinent information, and many schools develop their own duplicated forms.[3]

Guidance in Getting into College or Other Advanced Training Institution. The pressure of increased numbers applying for admission to colleges and universities has caused much anxiety to students and parents. Group study with both parents and students of the following questions is important to meet this situation.

What are the prevailing policies of colleges in choosing applicants for admission? These policies vary among institutions, but the following points are good general guides:

1. Evidence of sound scholarship with high rank in class in relation to ability. This question of rank in relation to ability has been added for two reasons: the range and level of scholastic ability of students vary greatly among institutions, so that one who should go to college can probably find a suitable place; colleges are greatly interested in finding students who are living up to their ability, not just those who are very superior. This attitude applies also to those with superior aptitude, since the serious underachievers have not usually proved to be good scholastic risks.

2. The pattern of high school subjects is important. This holds not only for general requirements but also for the relationship to students' interests and educational and vocational plans. The very superior stu-

---

[3] A sample form is included in Norris, Zeran, and Hatch, *The Information Service in Guidance*, Rand McNally & Company, Chicago, 1961, pp. 202–205, reproduced from the Teacher's Supplement for Mahoney and Engle, *Points for Decision*, Harcourt, Brace & World, Inc., New York, 1957.

dents who have avoided honors and advanced placement courses may find this matter questioned from the viewpoint of their real interest and motivation for college work.

3. Achievement on college board examinations is one important factor in the admissions picture, but this record is always studied in relation to all other factors with recognition of possible errors and reliability limits. Special types of preparation for these examinations are not likely to be as significant as consistent, conscientious study throughout high school.

4. Leadership and participation in school activities are important, everything else being equal, in choosing among candidates, but they are not now being given the same emphasis as formerly. The kind of contribution made by a student, indicating his social and citizenship values, is more important than number of activities. Students who must carry part-time jobs and are therefore limited as to activity participation are not likely to be handicapped if other factors are satisfactory.

5. Recommendations from the counselor or principal indicating admirable qualities of personality and citizenship are most valuable.

What are the most helpful kinds of preparation for admission to a desired college?

1. Choosing a college suitable for one's abilities and interests rather than on the basis of prestige or parental desire.

2. Choosing wisely as to the educational program in high school.

3. Developing effective study and learning habits and maintaining a consistently good scholarship record throughout the high school years.

4. Selecting school activities wisely and participating effectively in a desirable number.

5. Developing good interpersonal relationships and citizenship in the school life. This will redound to increased self-realization that will be reflected in important personal qualities.

6. Visits to colleges by student and parents, perhaps during vacation and desirably by appointment, are highly approved by most colleges.

7. Summer college clinics conducted by numerous colleges and universities (see pages 189 and 199) have proved very helpful to many high school students in making suitable decisions and plans.

8. Applications for scholarships and loans should usually be on the basis of need, considering the total family finances.

9. The use of the College Admissions Center of the Association of College Admissions Counselors for handling applications may prove very convenient to some, since this service helps in the selection of institutions where applications are likely to be successful.[4]

[4] A record, *Getting into College Today*, produced by the national Association of College Admissions Counselors, Record Division, in conjunction with Guidance Asso-

Planning the Financing of College or Other Special Training. A major concern in public policy today is the fact that many talented youths do not continue their education beyond high school because of financial limitations and the increased cost of college education. The American School Counselor Association (24) estimated these costs to range from $900 to $2,400 per year varying with the type of institution.

Since public policy now includes the assumption of both national need and individual right for college training of those qualified to benefit from it, the sources of financial aid have pyramided to the point where few should be deprived of college for financial reasons alone. These sources include government and private scholarships and loans, remission of fees and tuition, employment opportunities for students, installment financing by commercial organizations, and installment plans for tuition fees by some colleges and universities.

All students should be informed about these varied possibilities at an early stage in their high school careers, including requirements as to scholarship standards and a variety of other specifications and ways and time for making applications. Only thus can they be helped to meet requirements if and when they need the financial assistance. One important consideration for group study is that of the relative desirability of the various types of financial assistance. This may vary with the individual. A complete up-to-date set of materials providing information about financial aids of all sorts is, of course, an essential for this service. Some references are listed in the chapter bibliography, but current publications must be added continually.

Helping students choose extracurricular activities

The extracurriculum has acquired stature as a vital part of the total educational program with values highly important for individual development. This recognition of its importance has led to the frequent use of the terms *cocurriculum* or *allied activities* to avoid the connotation of frills or extras. However, in spite of this increased valuation, a large percentage of students in schools and colleges do not participate in extracurricular activities and, at the other extreme, some students overparticipate. A study at Southern Illinois University (25) showed that as enrollments increased, the percentage of the total population holding leadership responsibilities decreased.

Reich (26) who tapped student opinion on college social life on 71 campuses in 34 states, found wide differences of opinion as to the degree of student interest in organized activities. She did not interpret her find-

ciates, Pleasantville, N.Y., would be of interest to a parent or student group studying this question. The College Admissions Center is located at 610 Church Street, Evanston, Ill.

ings as supporting fully the claim of Wise (27) that student interest in this area has steadily dwindled, but both writers suggest that students may be selecting activities for more personal than traditional reasons and that rising academic standards may be shifting more of student time to studies.

A survey of pupil opinions on high school guidance programs (28) brought a response from 65 per cent that they belonged to student organizations in which they were not interested, chiefly because of friends or faculty encouragement. Approximately half reported that they had not participated as much as desired in the school activities program.

In some secondary schools, participation is encouraged by providing periods within the school day for club and other activity-group meetings, and is controlled as to degree of participation by a point system or other means of limiting amount of activity. Poor scholarship has been one traditional way of excluding students from participation in some extracurricular activities, but there is a growing awareness that this may prevent many from needed and valuable experiences, and that these may in turn act as incentives that will often improve academic achievement.

There has seldom been as much guidance provided for the choice of extracurricular activities as for subjects and courses in the curriculum. If extracurricular activities have the values ascribed to them in our educational philosophy, this would seem to be a serious lack in educational guidance. The purposes of guidance would be to encourage wise selection of activities, limit unwise participation, and help students to achieve a good balance. To be effective, this guidance should be closely interrelated with the adult leadership of the activities, involving exchanges of information about student aptitudes, interests, and special needs in the interpersonal area and about the nature of student participation and achievement. The participation and achievement phase will be considered in Chapter 14. Here we are concerned with what assistance can be provided through groups in the selection of activities.

Informing Students about the Purposes and Values of Group Activities. Group activities of all sorts, whether social, recreational, interest groups, athletics, or service groups, help the student to identify and develop his own skills, to use these skills to advance a group goal, to become aware of the interaction of people in a group situation, to learn to make his own best contribution within the structure of a group undertaking. Over and above all these specific values, he learns to understand and value himself and others.

Many of the attitudes which are developed and the techniques which are perfected in the course of student group activities are pertinent to the individual for the rest of his life. These activities form a miniature testing ground, in which the student acquires experience in the sort of situations he will later encounter in the business and professional community, as a member of a family group, and in social, political, and civic situations. The sensitivity to the needs and rights of others, the habit of cooperation, the willingness to assume leadership and the response to good leadership, the adherence to accepted rules of procedure—all these by-products of good group activities for students may carry over profitably into later life. Krumboltz (29) has concluded from his review of research on this question that much more objective evaluation is needed of the claimed values of extracurricular activities. Doubtless much research is needed, also, to indicate ways of improving their values.

Many of the activities may lead into recreational and leisure-time pursuits in adult life, and this forward look is important in deciding as to the relative values of many sports and special-interest opportunities in the extracurriculum. Also, the possibility of avocations leading into vocations in our shifting world of work should not be overlooked.

Informing Students about Specific Extracurricular Opportunities. This service is generally provided for freshman students as a part of their orientation program. Student manuals and other publications, student counselors, talks by students and faculty members, and various social events usually provide students with a considerable amount of information about their extracurricular opportunities. Should this service be continued beyond the freshman stage as in the curriculum?

Helping Students to Choose, Enter, and Plan Democratic Participation in Suitable Activities. This step is not so easy and, judging by the extent of student participation in activities, is not so well accomplished in most educational institutions. Fairly satisfactory achievement of this goal for all students depends upon at least three conditions: (*a*) a student culture which is so democratically oriented and so cohesive that all students are as fully expected to play a part in the extracurriculum as are members of a family in the home life; (*b*) as much guidance to individuals in choosing their extracurricular activities as in their curricular programs; (*c*) guidance in learning good democratic leadership and followership and any of the social skills essential for good personal interrelationships, and in evaluating the outcomes of experiences in the extracurriculum.

Bases of Choice of Activities. Choices of activities by students do not necessarily need to be governed by special abilities and interests as in vocational selection. At times students may wish to strengthen weaknesses or develop new interests rather than to capitalize upon strengths. A perspective on a lifelong plan that takes into account the changing interests and activities of adult and later years is important to achieve while still young.

Factors that enter into students' educational choices

Research has not shed much light on this question. There is evidence, however, to suggest that these problems of educational choice are as complicated as those of vocational choice, involving many factors in differing patterns of relationship for various individuals. It seems clear that "knowledge of ability plus interest equals choice" is not the equation that describes the process of choice for most students.

Cass and Tiedeman (30) have studied the question of the election of a high school curriculum with a group of students in a Maine high school. In their conclusions they express the conviction that curriculum choices appear to evidence reflections of the self consistent with the self-theory in vocational development. Their data suggest the importance of the sex role, family income, concepts developed in the elementary school, and interests. Aptitudes appeared to figure but little in educational choices. It will be recalled that studies of vocational development reported in Chapter 11 (see page 278) likewise showed little awareness of aptitude among high school boys. The authors comment that "youth still ignore potential because their information, progress, experience and resulting orientations do not permit its consideration" (30, p. 544). Also, they point out that testing and informing students and financing their education will not alone accomplish the will of the government to cultivate our talent resources.

Perhaps the findings in this research, which could doubtless be duplicated in many other high schools, suggest what might be done through group study at crucial choice points of all the factors that could and do enter into curricular choices, and what may be really important factors in these choices when students' perspectives reach far enough into the future. This may be one of the essential learnings for real self-direction. This statement does not imply that we should tell students what the factors should be, but merely that they should become aware of what factors *may* be influencing their choices, consciously or unconsciously, and thus be helped to make themselves more open to more of their experiences and bring more of self-determination into their lives. Is this not the major purpose of guidance in all areas of living?

SUMMARY

Emphasis has been placed upon the broad spectrum of learnings related to educational opportunities and requirements essential for sound educational planning and for the full realization of all the values inherent in educational experiences. Possibilities have been explored for the use of group services to provide opportunities for these learnings, to guide sound thinking and problem solving with respect to educational plans, and to lay basic foundations for the most effective use of counseling interviews. Possibilities for common learnings that will free the interview for concentration on the unique needs of individuals have been considered.

Special problems of educational guidance have been examined for the following groups: dropouts, the gifted and talented, the underachievers, the mentally and physically handicapped, the emotionally disturbed, the college-bound, and those planning advanced technical or other special types of training.

Problems of guidance for the choice of extracurricular activities and curriculum offerings have been examined, primarily from the viewpoint of factors that should enter into these choices.

REFERENCES CITED IN CHAPTER

1. Educational Policies Commission: *The Purposes of Education in American Democracy*, National Education Association and the American Association of School Administrators, Washington, 1938.
2. Educational Policies Commission: *Education for All American Youth*, National Education Association and the American Association of School Administrators, Washington, 1944.
3. Educational Policies Commission: *Manpower and Education*, National Education Association and the American Association of School Administrators, Washington, 1956.
4. President's Commission on National Goals: *Goals for Americans: Programs for Action in the Sixties*, Prentice-Hall, Inc., Englewood Cliffs, N.J., 1960.
5. The Rockefeller Panel Reports: *Prospects for America: The Problems and Opportunities Confronting American Democracy—in Foreign Policy, in Military Preparedness, in Education, in Social and Economic Affairs*, Doubleday & Company, Inc., New York, 1961.
6. Munson, Harold L.: "School Dropouts Greatly Reduced," Bulletin to the Schools, State Education Department, Albany, N.Y., 1956.
7. *Holding Power Project Bulletins* 1 and 2, September, 1955, 1956, Bureau of Guidance, Division of Pupil Personnel Services, The University of the State of New York, State Education Department, Albany. (Mimeographed.)
8. Wolfbein, Seymour L.: "Transition from School to Work: A Study of the School Leaver," *The Personnel and Guidance Journal*, 38:98–105, October, 1959.
9. *Transition from School to Work*, Subcommittee on Transition from School to Work of the Interdepartmental Committee on Children and Youth and the U.S. Office of Education, 1957.
10. Crocker, Mary, and Marvin Powell: "Too Little and Too Late," *The Vocational Guidance Quarterly*, 9:266–267, summer, 1961.
11. *The Gifted Student Research Projects Concerning Elementary and Secondary School Students*, U.S. Office of Education, 1960.
12. Anderson, Kenneth E. (ed.): *Research on the Academically Talented Student*, National Education Association, in cooperation with the American Educational Research Association, the American Psychological Association, and the Association for Supervision and Curriculum Development, Washington, 1961.
13. Drews, Elizabeth M. (ed.): *Guidance for the Academically Talented Student*, National Education Association and the American Personnel and Guidance Association, Washington, 1961.

14. Miller, Leonard M. (ed.): *Guidance for the Underachiever with Superior Ability,* U.S. Office of Education, 1961.
15. Dunsmoor, C. C.: *The Effects of Group Counseling on School Adjustment of Under-achieving Junior High School Boys Who Demonstrate Acting-out Behavior,* Board of Cooperative Educational Services, Bedford Hills, N.Y., June 28, 1961.
16. Cohn, Benjamin: *A School Report on Group Counseling,* Board of Cooperative Educational Services, Bedford Hills, N.Y., June, 1961.
17. U.S. Department of Health, Education and Welfare: *Preparation of Mentally Retarded Youth for Gainful Employment:* a study sponsored jointly by the U.S. Office of Education, the U.S. Office of Vocational Rehabilitation, and the Project on Technical Planning of the American Association on Mental Deficiency, Bulletin 1959, no. 28, 1959.
18. Mackie, Romaine P., and Frances P. Connor: *Teachers of Crippled Children and Teachers of Children with Special Health Problems,* a report based on findings from the study, *Qualifications and Preparation of Teachers of Exceptional Children,* U.S. Office of Education Bulletin 1960, no. 21, 1960.
19. Bower, Eli: *Early Identification of the Emotionally Handicapped Child in School,* Charles C Thomas, Publisher, Springfield, Ill., 1960.
20. Tobias, Milton: *Some Physiological Correlates of Emotionality,* Research and Guidance Association in conjunction with the Los Angeles County Superintendent of Schools Office, Division of Research and Guidance, Los Angeles, 1960.
21. Harvey, Herman: *Reaction and Résumé,* California Educational Research and Guidance Association in conjunction with the Los Angeles County Superintendent of Schools Office, Division of Research and Guidance, Los Angeles, 1960.
22. Spotnitz, Hyman: *The Couch and the Circle,* Alfred A. Knopf, Inc., New York, 1961.
23. Morris, Glyn: *Using a Timetable in Educational Guidance,* Department of Rural Education, National Education Association, Washington, 1961.
24. American School Counselor Association: *How about College?* The Association, a division of the American Personnel and Guidance Association, Washington, 1959.
25. Greenleaf, Elizabeth A.: "Student Leadership in a Program of Co-curricular Activities," *The Personnel and Guidance Journal,* 35:293–297, January, 1957.
26. Reich, Helen: "A Survey of Student Opinion of Campus Social Life," *The Journal of College Student Personnel,* 3:11–16, December, 1961.
27. Wise, Max: *They Came for the Best of Reasons,* American Council on Education, Washington, 1958.
28. Gibson, Robert L.: "Pupil Opinion of High School Guidance Programs," *The Personnel and Guidance Journal,* 40:453–457, January, 1962.
29. Krumboltz, John D.: "The Relation of Extracurricular Participation to Leadership Criteria," *The Personnel and Guidance Journal,* 35:307–314, January, 1957.
30. Cass, John C., and David V. Tiedeman: "Vocational Development and the Election of a High School Curriculum," *The Personnel and Guidance Journal,* 38:538–545, March, 1960.

ADDITIONAL REFERENCES

Boroff, David: *Campus, U.S.A.,* Harper & Row, Publishers, New York, 1961.
Community Resources—in the Guidance Program, College of Education, Bureau of Research and Service, Michigan State University, East Lansing, Mich., 1956.
Dyer, Henry: "The Need for Do-it-yourself Prediction in High School Guidance," *The Personnel and Guidance Journal,* 36:162–167, November, 1957.
Gardner, John W.: *Excellence—Can We Be Equal and Excellent Too?* Harper Colophon Books, Harper & Row, Publishers, New York, 1962.
Hanna, Geneva R., and Mariana K. McAllister: *Books, Young People, and Reading Guidance,* Harper & Row, Publishers, New York, 1960.

Hays, Donald G., and John W. M. Rothney: "Educational Decision-making by Superior Secondary-school Students and Their Parents," *The Personnel and Guidance Journal,* 40:26–30, November, 1961.

Kilzer, Louis R., Harold H. Stephenson, and H. Orville Nordberg: *Allied Activities in the Secondary School,* Harper & Row, Publishers, New York, 1956.

Matteson, Ross W.: "Educational Experience, Academic Interests, and Curriculum Choices," *The Personnel and Guidance Journal,* 39:717–720, May, 1961.

Miller, Franklin A., James H. Moyer, and Robert B. Patrick: *Planning Student Activities,* Prentice-Hall, Inc., Englewood Cliffs, N.J., 1956.

Schulim, Joseph: "Experimenting with a Career-curricular Conference," *The Personnel and Guidance Journal,* 38:222–225, November, 1959.

Shaw, Merville C., et al.: "The Self-concept of Bright Under-achieving High School Students as Revealed by an Adjective Check List," *The Personnel and Guidance Journal,* 39:193–196, November, 1960.

Strang, Ruth: *Group Work in Education,* Harper & Row, Publishers, New York, 1958.

Some references on advanced training

(These references become outdated quickly, so they must be kept updated.)

Babbidge, Homer D., Jr.: *Student Financial Aid,* American College Personnel Association, a division of American Personnel and Guidance Association, Washington, 1960.

Bowles, Frank H.: *How to Get into College,* E. P. Dutton & Co., Inc., New York, 1959.

Brownstein, Samuel C.: *College Bound,* Barron's Educational Series, Great Neck, N.Y., 1959.

Burkel, Christian E., and associates: *College Blue Book,* Harcourt, Brace & World, Inc., New York (latest edition).

Cohen, Nathan M.: *Vocational Training Directory of the United States,* Nathan M. Cohen, Washington, 1958.

College Admissions Data Service, Educational Research Corporation, Cambridge, Mass. (Bulletins, Handbook, and Guidance Counselor's Desk Calendar).

Directory of Technical Institute Courses; National Council of Technical Institutes, Washington, 1959.

Dunsmoor, C. C.: *Choosing a College,* Board of Cooperative Educational Services, Katonah, N.Y., 1958.

Feingold, S. Norman: *Scholarships, Fellowships and Loans,* Bellman Publishing Company, Cambridge, Mass., 1962, vol. 4.

Fine, Benjamin: *How to Be Accepted by the College of Your Choice,* Channel Press, Inc., Great Neck, N.Y., 1957.

Hodnett, Edward: *Which College for You?* Harper & Row, Publishers, New York, 1960.

Home Study Blue Book, National Home Study Council, Washington, 1959.

How to Visit Colleges, National Vocational Guidance Association, Washington, 1954.

Irwin, Mary (ed.): *American Colleges and Universities,* American Council on Education, Washington, 1960.

Kempfer, Homer: *How to Choose a Correspondence School,* Bellman Publishing Company, Cambridge, Mass., 1959.

Kursh, Harry: *Apprenticeships in America: A Guide to Golden Opportunities in Industry for Students, Parents, Teachers, Guidance Counselors, and Leaders in Education, Labor, and Industry,* W. W. Norton & Company, Inc., New York, 1958.

Lovejoy, Clarence E.: *Lovejoy's College Guide,* enlarged, 6th ed., Simon and Schuster, Inc., New York, 1961–1962.

Mattingly, Richard C.: *Scholarships and Fellowships, a Selected Bibliography,* U.S. Office of Education Bulletin 1957, no. 7, 1957.

National Science Foundation: *Information on Science Scholarships and Student Loans,* Washington, June, 1960.

Norris, Willa, et al.: *The Information Service in Guidance,* Rand McNally & Company, Chicago, 1960, pp. 532–535.

Sargent, Porter: *Junior Colleges and Specialized Schools and Colleges,* Porter Sargent Publications, Boston, 1959.

Shosteck, Robert: *The College Finder,* B'nai B'rith Vocational Service, Washington, 1955.

U.S. Department of Labor, Bureau of Apprenticeships: *Apprentice Training—An Investment in Manpower,* 1957.

Why Finish High School? American Personnel and Guidance Association, Washington.

Wilson, Eugene S., and Charles A. Bucher: *College Ahead!* rev. ed., Harcourt, Brace & World, Inc., New York, 1961.

Some examples of text and reference materials for students

Bailard, Virginia, and Ruth Strang: *Ways to Improve Your Personality,* McGraw-Hill Book Company, Inc., New York, 1951.

Beery, Mary: *Manners Made Easy,* McGraw-Hill Book Company, Inc., New York, 1954.

Beery, Mary: *Young Teens Talk It Over,* Whittlesey House (McGraw-Hill Book Company, Inc.), New York, 1957.

Bellman Pamphlet Series, Bellman Publishing Company, Cambridge, Mass.

Bennett, M. E.: *College and Life: Problems in Self-discovery and Self-direction,* 4th ed., McGraw-Hill Book Company, Inc., New York, 1952.

Billet, Roy O., and J. Wendell Yeo: *Growing Up,* D. C. Heath and Company, Boston, 1958.

Borow, Henry, and Robert V. Lindsey: *Vocational Planning for College Students,* Prentice-Hall, Inc., Englewood Cliffs, N.J., 1959.

Brewer, John M., and Edward Landy: *Occupations Today,* Ginn & Company, Boston, 1956.

Byrn, Delmond K.: *Express Yourself Vocationally,* National Vocational Guidance Association, Washington, 1960.

Cribbin, James J., et al.: *Insight Series: It's Your Education; It's Your Personality; It's Your Life; It's Your Future,* Harcourt, Brace & World, Inc., New York.

Duvall, Evelyn: *Facts of Life and Love for Teen-agers,* Association Press, New York, 1956.

Duvall, Evelyn: *Family Living,* The Macmillan Company, New York, 1957.

Fedder, Ruth: *You, the Person You Want to Be,* Whittlesey House (McGraw-Hill Book Company, Inc.), New York, 1957.

Glanz, Edward C., and Ernest B. Walston: *An Introduction to Personal Adjustment,* Allyn and Bacon, Inc., Englewood Cliffs, N.J., 1958.

Greenleaf, Walter James: *Occupations and Careers,* McGraw-Hill Book Company, Inc., New York, 1955.

Hanna, Laverne: *Facing Life's Problems,* Rand McNally & Company, Chicago, 1956.

Hatch, Raymond N., Morgan D. Parmenter, and Buford Stefflre: *The Opportunity Series—Planning Your School Life; Planning Your Life's Work; Planning Your Future,* McKnight & McKnight Publishing Company, Bloomington, Ill., 1962.

Jenkins, Gladys Gardner, W. W. Bauer, and Helen S. Schacter: *Teen-agers: Health and Personal Development Text for All Teen-agers; With Special Interest for 14, 15, 16 Year-olds,* Scott, Foresman and Company, Chicago, 1954.

Katz, Martin R.: *You—Today and Tomorrow,* 3d ed., Cooperative Test Division, Educational Testing Service, Princeton, N.J., 1959.

Landis, Judson T., and Mary G. Landis: *Building Your Life,* Prentice-Hall, Inc., Englewood Cliffs, N.J., 1959.

McKinney, Fred: *Psychology of Personal Adjustment,* John Wiley & Sons, Inc., New York, 1960.

Mahoney, Harold J., and T. L. Engle: *Points for Decision,* Harcourt, Brace & World, Inc., New York, 1957.

Murray, Lois Smith: *Effective Living: An Interdisciplinary Approach,* Harper & Row, Publishers, New York, 1960.

Neugarten, Bernice L., et al.: *About Growing Up: Our School Life: Being Teenagers: Discovering Myself: Planning My Future: Toward Adult Living,* National Forum Foundation, Chicago, 1957.

Randolph, Pixley, et al.: *You and Your Life,* Houghton Mifflin Company, Boston, 1956.

SRA Guidance Series Booklets for Junior High School and High School, Science Research Associates, Inc., Chicago.

Stephenson, Margaret, and Ruth L. Millet: *Good Manners, the Magic Key,* McKnight & McKnight Publishing Company, Bloomington, Ill., 1959.

Teen-age Guidance Series, Keystone Education Press, New York.

Zapoleon, Marguerite: *The College Girl Looks Ahead: To Her Career Opportunities,* Harper & Row, Publishers, New York, 1956.

See also lists of student references in Chapters 8 and 9 bibliographies, and sources of references on occupational information in Chapter 11 bibliography.

13 PERSONALITY AND INTERPERSONAL RELATIONSHIPS —APPROACHES

Some implications of guidance in personality and interpersonal relationships

The title for this chapter was chosen for a specific purpose. A few decades ago books on personality development were rolling off the presses. The treatment of this subject ranged from superficial emphasis on appearance and manners to more profound considerations of mental, emotional, and spiritual aspects. Courses and units on personality with similar ranges of treatment appeared in educational programs. More recently other materials have been pyramiding on human relationships, culture patterns, social classes, group dynamics, role-playing, sociometric and other techniques for studying and working with groups. Units and courses on human relations have been introduced into the curriculum in many places, sociometric and role-playing techniques are being widely used, and "group dynamics" has become a popular term as well as a focus of highly active and intensive research.

Both these trends, emphasizing the individual and the group respectively, should complement each other helpfully, but it appears instead at times that the educational pendulum might be swinging from one to the other. When varieties of new techniques are introduced so widely and rapidly, it is well to question whether they are being kept in the context of their philosophical origins and used to serve their best purposes or are becoming bags of new tricks for bored or jaded educators. Innovations have a way of becoming passing fads if they are not thoroughly grounded in our educational philosophy and used thoughtfully as means of attaining well-understood goals. The new trends are too vitally important to democracy and human welfare to be regarded as fads.

One may well ask what the study of personality and interpersonal relationships will contribute to our American dream of a democratic way of life. Will personality study lead toward an exaggerated drive to excel or toward the development and use of one's own unique pattern of talents? Will the emphasis on human relationships lead toward the manipulation of groups for selfish ends or toward empathy and respect for all human beings and improved ways of applying the golden rule in a democratic order? Are we always "playing roles" in life, or can we learn to *live* as integrating personalities with our fellow beings? These questions lead to another: Will the years ahead see a closer union in educational practice of these two trends, which will recognize that personality and interpersonal relationships are two aspects of the same thing and that neither can be dealt with in isolation, that personalities mature through desirable interpersonal relationships, and that no human relationships are more stable or democratic than the personalities that create them?

One affirmative answer to this question is being evidenced in the increasing numbers of research reports and treatises on personality *in* interpersonal relationships. Psychology, sociology, and anthropology are joining forces. This trend is clearly stated in the following paragraph (1, p. 78): [1]

In a sense, and paradoxical as it may sound, the strenuous attempt to follow through the study of social groups with the aid of some such concept as that of interpersonal relations in the field of social psychology leaves the investigator in the position where social psychology as commonly understood today disappears and in its place there is established some type of personality study in which the integrations of individuals in a variety of interpersonal situations are frankly recognized as the unit of study. Whether this reorientated discipline is termed social psychology, psychiatry or socio-psychiatry seems almost a matter of indifference—although psychiatry, because of popular and semantic associations with the abnormal and the mentally disordered might not, on a balance, be as good a terminological expression as the more neutrally toned term, social psychology. The point, however, is not to argue about a name or a definition. It is rather to suggest that the concept of interpersonal relations enables us to take the individual out of the private preserve of statistician or laboratory expert and by putting him back in a social situation to enlist the services of psychiatrist, anthropologist, sociologist and social psychologist for a better rounded and all embracing study of man-in-situation.

The objectives are twofold: helping to build healthier personalities and to foster more democratic human relations; but the approaches to these objectives are merging.

Medical services to the physically ill have led to increased understanding and application of preventive physical hygiene. Likewise, psychiatric and psychological study of the mentally ill has led to much understanding of ways of preventing personal maladjustment and fostering healthy personalities. We have not made as much progress in the field of preventive and positive mental hygiene as in the field of physical hygiene. There is much evidence that the two areas are closely interrelated and that wholesome personality development is as dependent upon whole-

[1] Reprinted from *A Study of Interpersonal Relations,* Patrick Mullahy (ed.), by permission of Hermitage House, Inc., New York.

some interpersonal relationships as physical health is upon sanitation. Maslow (2) has said that people who are happy, hopeful, and optimistic are simply more resistant to disease; they just live longer. The Committee on Preventive Psychiatry of the Group for the Advancement of Psychiatry (3) has recognized the important part that schools can play in the development of positive mental health by the promotion of certain programs in elementary and secondary schools. Some of these are described in Chapter 14.

Some implications for group guidance of research and experience in the field of personality

Even with the delimitations emphasized in this topic, it is a difficult one to discuss, both because of the extensiveness of research on the one hand and the many areas which research has not yet fully explored on the other hand. However, a few major concepts that have emerged through both research and experience can be identified as particularly pertinent to guidance.

1. Sources of personality. Guidance can help the individual understand the nature of both the biological and the social influences which have interacted in shaping his personality, so that he can move realistically toward self-knowledge and intelligent self-direction of his life as he approaches adulthood.

2. Nature of personality development. An understanding of the conflicting claims upon the self which are made by inner drives and by external pressures can provide the individual with insight concerning problems of growing up and facilitate his learning to make choices and to maintain satisfying and effective adjustments throughout life.

3. Human likenesses and variations. Both the awareness that many needs and problems are common to all of us and the acceptance of the validity of individual variations from the common pattern can be utilized in guidance to foster self-understanding and self-realization.

4. Self-awareness. Harmonizing the concepts which the individual has of himself with the impact he makes on others and bringing these two factors into realistic focus are essential steps in setting attainable goals— a major function of guidance in personality development.

5. Awareness of others. Clinical and research studies which suggest the progression of our attitude toward self and others from a dependent, self-centered to an interdependent, group-centered relationship point up guidance implications for orienting young people to mature living based on reciprocal respect and acceptance.

6. Emotional development. The vast body of findings from anthropology and psychology about the positive and negative effects of deeply seated emotions on the development of attitudes toward oneself and

others should be utilized in guiding individuals toward self-evaluation and self-acceptance.

7. Learning self-direction. What we know about the changes which life imposes on the individual and about the skills in problem solving which can aid him in restructuring aspects of his life to meet these changes can be incorporated into the guidance process to help the individual learn self-direction and self-development.

8. Group relationships. Research in the dynamics of group life is yielding a tremendous amount of information about effective ways in which groups can conduct their activities in moving toward accepted goals, and in which individuals can best perform their various roles within groups. Since the self-realizing individual must learn not only to come to terms with himself but also with a wide range of group relationships, this area is directly linked to the guidance process.

9. Standards of conduct. Our American culture imposes on the individual a constantly shifting standard of behavior, from early childhood training in accordance with parental standards to emphasis in adolescence on peer group standards to the infinitely complex standards of adult life. The concept of self-learning as a lifelong process should be stressed through guidance, so that the individual is always prepared to adapt to new cultural demands through creating new patterns of living congruent with his life goals.

10. Values and choices. No more crucial type of learning can be provided for growing citizens in a democracy than that which fosters creative, responsible thinking about the formulation of life values and the choice of activities which support those values.

The above overview of types of learning involved in personality development and interpersonal relationships might, because of its brevity, be thought of as a "jet-plane view." Its chief purpose is to highlight those types and varieties of learnings essential for every individual if our educational goals of intelligent self-direction, social efficiency, and responsible citizenship in a dynamic culture are achieved. Responsible citizenship has been included here because of our growing recognition that political as well as social and economic processes are the product of the participating personalities. We cannot hope to improve government without improvement of the personalities of citizens and their chosen leaders.

Learning needs in personality development and interpersonal relationships

To what extent are we meeting the learning needs of children and youth in these areas? This is a question for which there can, of course, be no generalized answer, since programs vary so much from school to school and teacher to teacher. Also, evaluation of the outcomes of either direct or indirect approaches is difficult in areas of such complexity and subtlety as personality and human relationships. A logical question to ask is to what extent curricular or extracurricular programs make any specific provisions for learning experiences of the sort needed to under-stand self and others, and to develop skill in self-direction and social relationships. Obviously, these are basic goals, both implicit and explicit, for any modern program.

One phase of these questions is to what extent it is merely *assumed* that desired outcomes in some of the areas under consideration will result from a sufficiently rich and varied program. The other phase is to what extent these outcomes are planned for through direct, purposeful learning, or through other learnings which it is assumed will indirectly yield them. For example, will an individual learn all he needs to know about himself through the study of literature and the biological and social sciences, through testing out his interests and abilities in various subject fields, and through a few counseling interviews? Will he develop adequate knowledge of others and acquire social skills and the ability to continue his learning in these areas beyond school years through these same studies and through opportunity to work and play with others in democratically organized classes and school activities? Certainly no one would question that all the above experiences are basic essentials as preparation for democratic citizenship. The critical question is whether they are enough.

One way to approach the answer is to check learnings provided for in a given school curriculum against learnings considered as essential by authorities in personality development and interpersonal relation-ships. We might initiate a rather superficial investigation into this ques-tion by attempting to check usual types of school units and courses against the following list of criteria of ego structure, or ego strength, presented by Kluckhohn and Murray in a symposium on personality (4, pp. 24–26).[2]

Some of the criteria of ego structure, or ego strength, are the following:
A. Perception and apperception.
    1. *External objectivity:* the ability to perceive actions and events without distortion, to analyse and interpret them realistically, to predict the behavior of others.
    2. *Internal objectivity:* the capacity for self-detachment and self-analysis; insight into one's own motives, evaluations, and emotional reactions; also, the entertainment of a goal of personal development and accom-plishment which is suited to one's own circumstances and capacities.

[2] Clyde Kluckhohn et al., *Personality in Nature, Society, and Culture,* reprinted by permission of the publisher, Alfred A. Knopf, Inc., New York.

3. *Long apperceptive span:* the habit of making causal connections between events that are not temporally contiguous in experience; the ability to foresee broad or distant consequences of one's actions (time-binding power or long time-perspective).

B. Intellection.

4. *Concentration, directionality:* the ability to apply one's mind to an assigned or selected topic, to direct one's thoughts along a chosen path, to persist when bored, to inhibit day-dreaming.

5. *Conjunctivity of thought and speech:* the ability to think, speak, and write clearly, coherently, and logically, to inhibit irrelevant ideas.

6. *Referentiality of thought and speech:* the habit of using concepts and words which refer to real things, events, and experiences; the absence of vague, undefined, essentially meaningless terms and expressions.

C. Conation.

7. *Will-power:* the ability to do what one resolves to do and is capable of doing, to persist in the face of difficulties, to complete a prescribed or elected course of action; also, to re-strive after failure (counteraction).

8. *Conjunctivity of action:* the ability to schedule and organize one's activities, to make a plan and follow it, to live an ordered life.

9. *Resolution of conflicts:* the ability to choose between alternative courses of action. The absence of protracted periods of hesitation, indecision, vacillation, or perplexity.

10. *Selection of impulses:* the power to repress temporarily, inhibit, or modify unacceptable emotions or tendencies, to resist "temptations"; also, the habit of selecting and expressing, without qualms or conflict, impulses which are intrinsically enjoyable or extrinsically rewarding; absence of disturbing worries or anxieties.

11. *Selection of social pressures and influences:* the ability to choose among the demands, claims, enticements, and suggestions that are made by other people, to comply with those that are acceptable and reject those that are not; especially the power to resist intolerable coercions from society, but to submit if there is no way out; power "to will the obligatory."

12. *Initiative and self-sufficiency:* the ability to decide for oneself and act without waiting to be stimulated, urged, or encouraged. The habit of trusting one's own nature, of having reasonable confidence in one's own decisions (self-reliance). Also, the ability to stand alone, to do and finish things alone, without help; to endure solitude and to tolerate misfortune without appealing for sympathy; absence of marked dependence on others.

13. *Responsibility for collective action:* the willingness and ability to take responsibility and effectively organize and direct the behaviors of others; the experience of feeling secure in a position of authority, rather than being threatened, worried, and on the defensive.

14. *Adherence to resolutions and agreements:* the disposition and ability to abide by long-term decisions and commitments, to keep a promise or pledge.

15. *Absence of pathological symptoms:* freedom from incapacitating neurotic or psychotic symptoms.

This outline of individual needs should be balanced by one dealing with criteria of the strengths of group structures. We considered the other half of the picture in Chapter 4.

As to prevailing emphases and to outcomes in school programs, those of us who can view education from the inside would doubtless assign the highest rank to the points under "*B*. Intellection" in this outline. Present trends seem to place increased emphasis on these intellectual aspects. However, the mental-health approach does not discount the importance of intellectual competence or practical efficiency. Samler (5), in reviewing some of the experimental programs directed at positive mental-health outcomes, comments upon the recognition of heavy investment in knowledge and understanding of subject matter as well as of the growing human personality, and also the recognition that the fully functioning person is productive and skillful as well as emotionally healthful. Efforts to include in the objectives of the curriculum many of the other items in the outline can be traced through the various programs over several decades of orientation, group guidance, homerooms, applied psychology, core, general education, and life-adjustment education. They are implicit in the emphases upon human relations and upon democratic procedures in curricular and extracurricular programs in modern education.

If all educational institutions could be rated upon the extent to which the fostering of all these criteria of ego strength is included, not only in stated objectives of the programs but also in planned opportunities for learning experiences, they would doubtless form a continuum from those which give negligible attention to most of them, other than those under "Intellection," to those which give considerable emphasis to all of them. But if the curve of distribution were skewed, in which direction would the greater incidence of practice lie?

With all the emphasis today upon cooperative research in the sciences related to human life, there is little question regarding the trend in the future—provided we discover soon enough how to avoid the use of atomic power for destructive purposes. But the research findings about human life must be interpreted in their applications to education and incorporated more fully into textbooks and reference materials for various age and ability levels, before schools generally can move out rapidly into these relatively new fields of educational endeavor.

The author can recall vividly the exciting efforts that were made in the early twenties with high school and college students to interpret history and other social sciences in the light of the psychology, sociology, anthropology, and biographical literature of that period. It was a rewarding task from the viewpoint of the interest of students, but the many frustrations due to paucity of suitable materials led, in at least one instance, to a shift into the personnel field where firsthand study of the individual yielded more specifically satisfying results. Like many other personnel workers, the author continued to experiment with a group approach aimed at the learnings which could not be achieved in interviews alone, and which were not provided for elsewhere in the curriculum.

Today, this type of job analysis is more complicated than formerly because of the expansion of aims and content in the entire curriculum. For many educational institutions the questions now are where the learnings should be placed and who should be responsible for directing them. Always, in guidance, there is the question of how they should be related to counseling in order that uniquely individual aspects can be cared for adequately.

Making This Job Analysis. In view of the broad aims of education today, there is a clear directive for cooperative study of the task by all who teach and guide and by all who plan and administer the curriculum. *Curriculum* is here used to cover extracurricular activities as well as teaching and counseling. Interlocking school and system-wide councils or committees for continuous study of this phase of the program would seem to be as important as those which are frequently formed for the study and planning of vocational guidance. Such councils would have the responsibility of stimulating thinking by all professional personnel as to what their respective contributions are to optimum personal development and human relationships within the school or system. There is no good reason why this study should not be directed to the school staff as well as the students. Personality development is a lifelong process, and good human relationships and satisfying living are as important to this process in adulthood as in earlier years. Actually, they are prerequisites for the staff if they are to work for these same objectives in the lives of children and youth.

Before each staff member can formulate his contributions, it is important to think through the question of what learnings can be achieved through direct study and which are by-products, as it were, of wholesome living. The answer to this question is not the same for all age levels nor for all individuals of a given age. "Teachable moments" are especially important to recognize and utilize in the area of personality, provided we have met our obligations to immature individuals by preparing them sufficiently for new experiences so that unwholesomely traumatic effects of failure or difficulties are avoided.

An analysis of the ever-widening sphere of choices and responsibilities of children and youth will reveal topics and problems for study and the suitable placement of such study as well as the types of experiences through which indirect learnings are anticipated. Inventories of youth problems and worries yield important data for planning, as do also the interviews and informal conferences of counselors and teachers. This is one area in the curriculum where the pupils or students, themselves, can help plan the areas and problems to be studied. Invariably they do this with alacrity. They need leadership and guidance with respect to reliable sources of information and suitable learning techniques, but in a permissive and democratic climate, interest is not likely to lag when they have the opportunity with their peers to come to grips with vital problems of living and growing from day to day. With increased maturity these vital problems include increasingly long-range goals with respect to self-development, self-direction, and adjustments with others.

It has already been mentioned that curriculum study must be continuous in these areas which touch so intimately the current lives of youth. This same need prevails in all other areas, but the evidences of outmoded content are not so quickly and strikingly obvious in some of the more traditional and accepted fields as they are here. The approaches and organization must be ever readapted as cultural changes bring new life styles and new choices and new adjustments into the picture. Technological developments are accelerating the tempo of change to the point where assistance in adaptation to new conditions of life may be needed quite as much as guidance for living in the present. It has been questioned how much change human beings can take with equanimity (6).

Studies of the growth needs, or "developmental tasks," and adjustment problems of individuals at various stages in their lives have shown continuity in the emergence of many common life patterns. But these common patterns vary as to tempo and emphasis not only among individuals but in response to social change. There is a continuous interaction here of many forces that necessitates our keeping ever attuned to the voices of the present. Listening to children and youth as we work with them helps us to keep thus attuned. But we need also to keep the voices of the past and the future within our range, if we help each new generation to interpret the present as a transition to the future. Only thus can we change tempo or transpose key as we move into the unknown ahead.

Approaches through the curriculum

How is the curriculum to be utilized in the study of personality and interpersonal relationships? What are the goals? For all education we can state them as (a) optimum development and use by all individuals of their unique patterns of potentialities; (b) skill and finesse in democratic, satisfying human relationships; (c) improved ways of living for all individuals and groups within our social order and improved relationships with other groups throughout the world. For guidance we can state these goals as (a) increased understanding of self, and reciprocally of others, and the development of sound techniques of self-appraisal; (b) skill in making wise and satisfying choices and adjustments at each stage of development; (c) sufficient insight into types of maladjustment to recognize them in oneself, to deal with them effectively, or to secure appropriate assistance in making improved adjustments.

What is the content? The content, to be drawn upon as needed, comprises all that we know through research and experience about personality development and interpersonal relationships. And that includes the experience of the leader and the group. It is an open question whether present practice does not frequently place too great emphasis upon the latter. In our efforts to avoid authoritarian methods and to create a permissive, nondirective climate, we often stop where we should merely begin in the use of content. Unless some of the pertinent store of accumulated research and human experience is brought to bear upon problems which pupils study, they may be taught merely to rearrange their prejudices instead of moving forward in creative problem solving.

One task of the skillful group leader is to recognize when members of a group need to draw upon information and experience beyond their present ken and utilize it in their problem solving. When a group is in need of new light on a problem, they welcome the opportunity to search for it. One of the responsibilities of a leader is to help a group to broaden and deepen their perspectives and to reach out for new understandings. The skill comes in stimulating this eagerness for new perspectives from within the group rather than trying to impose it from without.

Often new perspectives result from a reinterpretation of knowledge and experience already acquired and their use in new combinations. This ability to use previous learnings in new situations is one of the most valuable skills for lifelong growth in a dynamic culture. Whenever a group can draw upon what they have learned in physical, biological, or social sciences, English, mathematics, the fine or applied arts, their school and out-of-school activities to shed some light on a problem, they are developing an important self-directive skill. The same holds true for every experience within special subjects or activities which throws some new light on their understanding of self and others and of problems of social living.

Cooperation of teachers from every field in the curriculum in supplying information needed in the study of various problems is an essential aspect of this type of study. Such cooperation will have reciprocal effects in enlivening and vitalizing teaching in every area, since it will inevitably keep teachers more alert to the implications for guidance and for living in their respective fields of teaching.

There seem to be some indications that increased emphasis upon immediate problems of national defense and of services to the mentally ill may be obscuring the long-range problem of preventing maladjustment and of developing all of our human resources. The Joint Commission on Mental Illness and Health, authorized by Congress in 1955 and reporting its recommendations for action for mental health in 1960 (7), emphasized detection by teachers of potential problems of pupils, but suggested no positive program of instruction or guidance in the schools, other than adding some guidance psychologists to school staffs. Awareness is expressed that "the educational system stands in a unique position to condition the mental well-being of future generations for the good" (7, p. 131). There is an implicit assumption in the brief section on the school as a mental-health resource that the preoccupation with scientific education will spread to re-emphasis upon instruction in all traditional subject areas.

Roe (8), in her presidential address to the American Psychological Association in 1958, sounded warnings regarding the dangers of overlooking man's need for conscious awareness of himself and of the world around him. This need she calls "Man's Forgotten Weapon," now essential in choosing the direction of his social evolution. She comments:

If we are ever to raise a generation of aware and confident people, we must deliberately start in infancy to help them to become freely aware of themselves, and of what it is to be a human; to be able to accept and control and enjoy their emotions, their thoughts, and their bodies; to be able to tolerate their own and other people's problems (8, p. 265).

Roe makes it clear that she is not suggesting the introduction of psychology instruction in each grade, but rather an examination of ways in which self-awareness can be encouraged within the present framework. As an example she asks why children's readers could not include stories directly relating to problems common and important to them, such as the arrival of a young sibling in the home.

Examples of this type of program may be found in a challenging project in guidance through literature in Placer County schools, California. At the elementary school level, stories chosen to reflect group or personal situations and read to the children precipitate discussions in which there is "sharing of common problems, release of tensions, and development of healthy attitudes toward others through critical thinking." This leads into other areas of personal and school problems and into related reading. In high school, all forms of literature are utilized, including novels and biography that expand vocational perspectives. Much in-service professional study and the development of an annotated bibliography are reported as aspects of the project.[3]

Roe continued her warning of the dangers of neglecting human and social values in the schools in an address to the National Vocational Guidance Association in 1960. She commented that something about our present cultural situation is producing more disturbed people who need therapeutic services than can possibly be cared for individually. Proficiency in language skills and all the skills needed in interacting with people and the nonpersonal environment are recognized as vital, but as means, not as ends in themselves. Self-perception needed for making choices, and general competency in living and in mastering human problems, were emphasized as vital if humanity is to survive. Observing that our knowledge of technology seems to have outstripped our knowledge of ourselves, that it is easier to toy with nuclear forces than to come to grips with human problems, Roe adds:

It may be true that our species has not the effective adaptive range to meet this challenge and that it *will* be replaced by some more adaptable species as so many other species have been replaced in the long history of life on this planet. Only man will care. And unless he cares enough he will not survive (9, p. 198).

SUMMARY

Personality and interpersonal relationships are inseparable. Personalities mature through desirable interpersonal relationships, and no human relationships are more stable or democratic than the personalities that create them.

All of the sciences dealing with human life make contributions to our understanding of ourselves and others. Research in these fields and human experience provide many implications for guidance of individuals with respect to learnings needed for self-awareness and self-direction. An entire school program contributes to these learnings but the guidance service has special responsibilities.

The lag in knowledge and its applications for effective living, as compared with developments in the material environment, seems to be creating more problems of human maladjustment than can be cared for individually. One important task for group guidance is to help close this gap by assisting individuals to acquire the awareness of self and others necessary for competency in living and mastery of human problems.

[3] Reported by Julia Gonsalves, Office of the Placer County Superintendent of Schools, Auburn, Calif.

REFERENCES CITED IN CHAPTER

1. Mullahy, Patrick (ed.): *A Study of Interpersonal Relations: New Contributions to Psychiatry*, Hermitage House, Inc., New York, 1949.
2. Maslow, Abraham H.: "Some Frontier Problems in Psychological Health," in *Personality Theory and Counseling Practice*, papers presented at the First Annual Conference on *Theory and Counseling Practice*, University of Florida, Gainesville, Fla., Jan. 5–7, 1961.
3. Committee on Preventive Psychiatry of the Group for the Advancement of Psychiatry: *Promotion of Mental Health in the Primary and Secondary Schools: An Evaluation of Four Projects*, Report no. 18, Topeka, Kans., January, 1951.
4. Kluckhohn, Clyde, et al. (eds.): *Personality in Nature, Society and Culture*, Alfred A. Knopf, Inc., New York, 1953.
5. Samler, Joseph: "Basic Approaches to Mental Health: An Attempt at Synthesis," *The Personnel and Guidance Journal*, 37:638–643, May, 1959.
6. Samler, Joseph: "Basic Approaches to Mental Health: An Introduction," *The Personnel and Guidance Journal*, 37:26–31, September, 1958.
7. Joint Commission on Mental Illness and Health: *Action for Mental Health*, Basic Books, Inc., Publishers, New York, 1961.
8. Roe, Anne: "Man's Forgotten Weapon," *The American Psychologist*, 14:261–266, June, 1959.
9. Roe, Anne: "High Hopes," *The Vocational Guidance Quarterly*, 8:195–201, summer, 1960.

14 PERSONALITY AND INTERPERSONAL RELATIONSHIPS— AREAS AND PROGRAMS

This area of group guidance could subsume most of human life. It is too comprehensive for any adequate coverage of even major topics in one chapter. We shall consider briefly only a few crucial aspects that relate in varying degrees to guidance at different age levels.

TECHNIQUES IN THE AREA OF PERSONALITY AND INTERPERSONAL RELATIONSHIPS

Some of the common human problems at various age levels revealed by a variety of methods ranging from free response to clinical study were summarized in Chapter 3. Many of these problems were in the areas under consideration here.

A leader may find it expedient to use both free responses and check lists in introducing group study in this area as suggested in Chapter 3, and will also find it helpful to use all of the other approaches to understanding group members suggested in that chapter. The presentation of camouflaged case studies may be desirable at the start if a group is not yet sufficiently cohesive for members to introduce their own problems. Another approach would be through generally recognized school problems of interpersonal relationships; and still another would be an organized study of personality and ramifications in interpersonal relationships if the group is mature enough to benefit from this more academic approach. Whatever the method, the objectives should be kept in mind by both leader and group members of increased understanding of self and others, and of ways of dealing with problems and working to achieve more mature and effective personal-social adjustments.

Most of the techniques considered in Chapter 5 are applicable to some phase of activity in this area. One caution is entered here. This is an area requiring special training, experience, and insight into the possibilities for traumatic as well as beneficial experiences in the study of emotionally tinged problems. The leader must be alert to note emotional disturbances that may require individual counseling or even clinical services. One technique often helpful in this area is to encourage students to write freely about their personal insights and their feelings during the study and to share with the leader in conferences any reactions that bother them especially.

SOME CRUCIAL ASPECTS OF PERSONAL-SOCIAL ADJUSTMENT

Most of the areas dealt with in this chapter have implications in the area of mental health. Some of the current thinking about the nature of mental health is summarized in Chapter 6 (see pages 145 to 147). A review of these concepts may prove helpful in planning activities related to aspects of personal-social adjustment.

Accepting self and others

What is true of most guidance services is especially true here—acceptance of self and others cannot be taught or learned in a few simple lessons. Our self-concepts are probably so infused with emotionally tinged attitudes that changes will require experiencing that involves both intellectual and emotional realms of the personality.

The pervasive climate of an entire educational institution will help to determine the possibilities for an accepting attitude by both staff and students. All teachers as well as group leaders make their contributions through attitudes of acceptance and respect for all individuals, through recognition of achievement that fosters wholesome pride and ego strength, and through environmental manipulation and remedial help when needed that will facilitate desirable status for all. Gillham (1) has provided many illustrations of how insightful teachers can unobtrusively utilize varieties of school situations to achieve these results. Children can readily catch the spirit and cooperate in the undertaking.

Careful study and observation of a pupil who seems to be an isolate or reject in a group is almost certain to reveal some asset that can be utilized in group activity to call forth recognition and respect. Jim, for example, was unpopular with his fifth-grade classmates. He teased and annoyed them in various ways and was rarely chosen on any playground team. He was becoming sullen and uncooperative in the classroom. Discussion with his mother about his problems revealed that he had a muscular difficulty which prevented facile use of his legs and impaired his skill in active games. This difficulty was being studied by a physician. It did not affect his manual and finger dexterity, and he was spending much time at home drawing cartoons and writing plays. The teacher began to bring him into dramatics more actively, both in writing and performing, and asked him to display some of his cartoons as well as to draw new ones for special occasions. As Jim won respect and acceptance in his class for his unique contributions, the teasing and annoying behavior stopped. Also, his playmates became more tolerant of his awkwardness in games and found places for him more often on teams. His play skills improved gradually through special instruction by an after-school playground director.

Direct approaches through learning are also essential. In self-appraisal, for example, one will learn about human variation in all sorts of characteristics, and the inevitability of strengths and weaknesses in everyone. Of course, parents, teachers, and counselors had better accept and apply these facts themselves if they are to help children and adolescents to do so, and to guide them in planning how to make the *most* of their strong points and the *best* of their weaker ones.

Environmental conditions that seem beyond the control of an individual frequently contribute to his sense of inferiority. Also, lack of understanding and appreciation by peers of the nature and influence of environments foreign to their experience may prevent acceptance and status of some individuals within groups. Here both learning and first-hand experiencing are important. This has been a function of our human-relations programs for minority groups for many years, and it needs to be expanded to serve all individuals who may not be accepted readily for some reason within the peer culture.

Those individuals who seem caught irrevocably in an undesirable environment can often be helped by fuller understanding of causal factors that may lead to greater acceptance of home and family, and by learning how to deal with undesirable influences that cannot be avoided. Recognizing that how one *reacts* to life experiences is more important than what *happens* to one can result in a very important step toward positive mental health and wholesome personal development. Thom and Johnston (2) made a significant study many years ago of the home environments of children adjudged to be very well adjusted. While the majority came from homes and neighborhoods rated as good or excellent, one of the significant findings was the number of adverse factors in the lives of some: extreme deprivation in many necessities as well as all luxuries, parental conflicts and rejection, faulty discipline, race discrimination, unfavorable neighborhood influences, or severe physical or mental handicaps. Here was tangible evidence that adverse surroundings need not prove destructive to an individual if he has developed the adaptability to cope with them effectively. This type of learning is important to everyone for self-mastery, since no one seems to avoid some type of situation that may be warping in the course of a lifetime.

Olson (3) has emphasized that a strong tendency exists throughout nature for the self-selection of those factors in the environment appropriate to the needs of the plant, animal, or human being; that a person may work creatively for the conditions that advance his well-being. He applies this theory to education. Perhaps through guidance we can help individuals to develop skill in applying it in all aspects of living.

Parent-child relationships

Many studies of parent-child relationships have indicated the importance of parental influence in personality development and social adjustment, but several surveys of the problems of children and adolescents have not always placed these home and family problems high on the list as to percentage of incidence (see pages 60 to 67).

Schutz (4) investigated the pattern or structure underlying responses of 500 girls in grades 10 and 11 on 156 items of the Billett-Starr Youth Problems Inventory, Senior Level (5) and extracted three clusters of problems which he designated as general personal anxiety and insecurity, tension concerning relations with others, and difficulty in getting along with parents.

It is doubtless significant that five of twelve problems, among the 441 items in the Billett-Starr inventory (5), rated as urgent by a jury of twelve specialists in the personnel field, were in the area of home and family life.[1] Among items in this area marked by 20 per cent or more of the norm group were: "My *brother sister* is always causing me trouble"; "My *father mother* is always criticizing (blaming) (nagging) me"; "I'm afraid to tell my *father mother* when I've done something wrong." Two interesting responses that tend to offset these negative ones are the following: "My *father mother* has to work too hard" (marked by one-fourth to one-third of the norm group), and "I'd like to be more helpful to my parents" (the most frequently marked item in the home and family life area).[2]

There is quite general recognition that adolescents normally have dif-

---

[1] The problems rated as urgent by the jury (5, p. 16) are:
I have "spells" when I can't hear or see anything
I have a bad reputation to live down
My *father mother* accuses me of very bad things that aren't true (approximately 10 per cent of a norm group marked this)
I'm happy at home (more girls than boys marked this)
I'm often afraid to go home
I dislike my *father mother* very much
I'm thinking of leaving home
I dislike school so much I can hardly stand it
I sometimes think of killing myself
I feel I'm not wanted
Everyone is against me
I think someone is after me to hurt me

[2] Appreciation is expressed to Harcourt, Brace & World, Inc., for permission to quote from the Billett-Starr Manual, and to Blythe C. Mitchell, in their Test Department, for supplying helpful materials.

ficulty in making the adjustment toward adult status and that they will experience considerable tension during this period in relationships with parents. In a study of conflicts between adolescents and their mothers Block (6) secured responses from several hundred junior and senior high school students to a fifty-item check list of complaints. Girls checked a larger number of complaints than boys, and the largest percentages of grievances of both sexes included matters pertaining to manners, habits, appearance, school marks, use of money and the car, educational and vocational choices, unfavorable comparisons with siblings, choice of friends, dating, parties, and nagging about little things.

Hackett (7) initiated a Purdue Opinion Poll with the hypothesis that the feelings existing between children and parents might have greater weight in promoting satisfactory adjustment than the more objectively apparent relationships. In testing this hypothesis, he first investigated the *felt conflicts* of a nationwide sample of adolescents based on felt differences in their own and parent's attitudes. Then, with a selected group, he had adolescents fill out questionnaires regarding their own attitudes and what they thought were their parents' attitudes on a variety of issues. He reversed the process with their parents to discover the degree of empathy of parents and children. Among the conclusions from the resulting data were the following.

The *actual* differences in attitudes of parents and children were fewer than the *felt* differences. Adolescents felt greater conflict with parents on issues of relationship with their peers than on those concerned with family relationships. A high degree of felt conflict was evidenced also over disciplinary measures. Older students showed greater felt conflict with parents than did the younger ones. There was also a high degree of agreement shown on many issues.

Boys tended to be less in agreement with the attitude of parents than did the girls. There was a tendency for greater actual difference to exist in attitudes of children and their parents on issues concerned with social customs and moral conduct. Adolescents seem to feel more deeply involved emotionally with mothers than with fathers, and to feel that mothers are more likely to wish to exercise control over them and to be less willing than fathers to admit lack of understanding of or interest in their children. The study suggested that parents seem to estimate the attitudes of the children better than the children estimate parental attitudes, i.e., that parents are able to empathize with children more than children are with parents.[3]

These are only a few of the findings indicated by the study, but they suggest the need for assistance to both children and parents in understanding parental attitudes and problems related to this period of matur-

[3] Summarized by permission of H. H. Remmers, Purdue University.

ing toward adulthood as well as those of the adolescent. Greater actual understanding could probably eliminate many of the tensions and help both parents and children to gain perspectives and develop more cooperative measures in coping with the inevitable problems of growing up.

The writer has had the interesting experience of receiving requests from both children and parents for cooperative study of problems. Sometimes this study has been carried on in separate groups with both parents and children suggesting to each other what problems should be considered. Sometimes they have met jointly to study their mutual problems. The outcome in either situation is likely to be deeper understanding and a more cooperative approach to the solution of problems.

Mahler and Caldwell (8) report an adaptation of the Adlerian group technique in an experiment where a group of parents listen to children's discussion of problems and then the reverse situation occurs with children observing the parents' discussion.

Dating, courtship, and marriage

In Chapter 3 (see pages 65 and 66), it was noted that adults view marriage and parenthood as two of the three greatest sources of happiness or unhappiness, the other being work providing economic security. While the majority of the sampled population did not spontaneously mention family relationships as a source of distress, the over-all findings showed that they were frequently a cause of worry and concern. The divorce rate, of course, attests to considerable maladjustment in this area. Courses and units in family relations in college and high school have resulted from recognized need of preparation for marriage and parenthood. In colleges and universities, where the trend is for a large percentage of the student population to be married, marital counseling has become one of the major professional services of personnel workers (9–11). This is one area where much group therapy is being carried on by psychiatrists and psychologists for the general population, and this technique could serve an important function both for premarital and marital problems in higher education.

Among adolescents, dating and courtship are topics of deep interest, and the wise guidance of group discussions of these basic concerns of youth is of inestimable value.

As with the study of the total peer culture, cooperative, democratic planning is of extreme value. Adolescents are never lacking in suggestions on what they wish to understand better and what assistance they desire from peers and accepting adults who can help them examine standards and practices and reach well-considered conclusions on the best ways to achieve desired values and satisfactions. Preaching is, of course, beyond the pale, but youths will welcome the broader and deeper insights that are implicit in scientific research and human experience and, at appropriate times and in judicious manner, the ideas and values held by adults. This question of sharing of values in guidance will be considered in more detail in Chapter 15. The adult guide must somehow steer between the Scylla of imposition and the Charybdis of irresponsibility, and if he steers a wise course his guidance is usually welcomed sincerely, especially in this field of dating where youth gropes with few well-established standards.

Etiquette is always a subject of live interest in the dating period, and it can be used as a bridge to the consideration of basic courtesy and concern for the happiness and welfare of others. Active participation at any age in the study and formulation of the rules of etiquette in games, and every aspect of home, school, and community living can help to build attitudes and standards of conduct that may give meaning to all of the social amenities in interpersonal relationships. Opportunities for this group guidance occur in homerooms, classrooms, special guidance groups, and every phase of school activities and government.

Franklin and Remmers (12) conducted one of the Purdue Opinion Panels in 1961 on youth's attitudes towards courtship and marriage that provided a comparison with a similar poll in 1950. The results will furnish interesting data for study by adolescents. Only a few of the findings can be summarized here.[4]

As to dating etiquette, the authors found that more teen-agers now believe that a kiss on the first date is all right. Fewer believe that girls should be as free as boys in asking for dates or that girls should share the expense of dates. More teen-agers now appear to get most of their sex instruction from reading or a friend of their own age.

There was considerable shift in the ranking of traits desirable in a future mate. The seven traits judged "very desirable" by at least four out of five teen-agers in 1961 are as follows: is dependable, can be trusted; is considerate of me and others; takes pride in personal appearance and manners; shows affection; acts own age, is not childish; desires normal family life with children; has a pleasant disposition.

Boys and girls differed somewhat in their attitudes on numerous items in the questionnaire, and sex differences usually show up in group discussions—one advantage of including both sexes in these discussion groups.

There is a wealth of material available for group study on all phases of dating, courtship, and marriage, and some references are included in the chapter bibliography. Students never seem at a loss to suggest

---

[4] Summarized by permission of H. H. Remmers, Purdue University.

the problems they wish to study in this area under the leadership that they accept.[5]

Guidance with respect to peer culture

If one can judge from available studies of peer culture, this is one of the most potent influences in the lives of children and adolescents, particularly the latter. The tendency of adults has been to respect this culture as the private world of youth that should not be invaded except where gangs or other groups come afoul of the law and require control in the interest of public welfare. This statement is not made without awareness of all the projects aimed at creating wholesome environments for recreation. However, with some exceptions and some general controls, it would seem that the values, the status system, the mores and customs regulating interpersonal relationships have usually been pretty much left to youth without adult guidance. An assumption has been that they are learning democratic ways of living.

Several studies of adolescent culture (14–17) indicate that the status system within this peer culture may be far from democratic. It may exert a warping influence upon personalities, both for those who fail to qualify for membership in groups and for those who do qualify by standards external to their own personalities that may emphasize *feeling superior* rather than *being superior* (18). Of course, this is not a condition entirely absent from adult society, but if we are concerned, in guidance and in all of education, with optimum personality development, we can scarcely overlook this vital influence of the peer culture. There would seem to be no good reason why youths should not examine, understand, and work to improve their culture in the interests of all, as well as that of adult society and our form of government. Such study is likely to evoke more intrinsic interest than the traditional history and civics, and may build a bridge to a more realistic approach to the study of their future adult citizenship.

The leader for this peer-group study would require a special kind of empathy to provide effective guidance. Reports from both high school and college levels indicate that student-teacher relationships are deteriorating, that teachers are becoming isolated symbols of academic learning and grades, and that other values and standards derive primarily from the peer group (13, 19, 20). Has this always been so, or have we been napping while it happened? And what can we do about it if we wish to strive for the achievement of our guidance objectives for all youths and for the future of our free world?

[5] The September, 1961, issues of *Life* magazine carried an interesting series of articles on courtship and marriage, reporting ideas of marriage counselors.

Here is one picture of adolescent society developed out of rather intensive investigation of students in several high schools, in varying socioeconomic environments. Coleman and his collaborators (13) found that popularity and membership in "the leading crowd" were based upon status systems that included varying emphases in different communities upon family position, money, residence in the right neighborhood, expensive clothes, athletic prowess, good looks, car, and good grades. But good grades and intelligence were only minority responses in the schools as entrees to the leading crowd and were always combined with other factors. The scholarship factor was a stronger influence in one city than in any of the others. Generally, among the boys the brilliant, studious nonathlete ranked lowest on a continuum for popularity.

Coleman suggests two types of solutions to the problem of the adolescent living more and more in a world of his own: (a) that the family take over more responsibility at an earlier age to prevent some of the precocious sophistication; (b) that education reverse the strategy, taking the adolescent society as it is, and providing opportunity for responsibilities that will eliminate passive roles leading to irresponsibility. He suggests many types of intergroup competition and a novel use of modern games of strategy in which adolescents would face decisions on finances, careers, political situations, and a wide variety of difficult problems such as they will encounter as adults. These suggestions are aimed at capturing and directing adolescent energy.

Is there a third possibility? One basic assumption underlying group guidance is that individuals will be helped to understand as fully as possible all the factors that may influence their choices and decisions, thereby gaining greater power of self-determination. Can we not do more than we have in the past in helping them to understand the forces operating in their peer culture, challenging creative thinking about the relative values of all these forces, and active planning to create the kind of world that will be most meaningful, both in the present and the future?

A poll of teen-agers' attitudes toward teen-age culture by Franklin, Maier, and Remmers (21) suggests that adolescents are critical of many aspects of the gang or the group in spite of their reliance upon it for approval and status. There are indications in their replies of a desire for freedom from too great reliance on the group and for autonomy to make up their own minds. This would seem to be a hopeful gleam through the clouds of pessimism hovering over the "other-directed" and "organization" men of our times. Perhaps it could light the way to more significant influences through group study. We have tackled the problem of intergroup relations directly and vigorously with respect to minority groups, and there may be quite as urgent a need to tackle the problem of influences of peer culture on all of its members. This question will be raised again in the next chapter on values.

EXAMPLES OF PROGRAMS IN HUMAN RELATIONS

The University of Iowa project

Significant work is being done by Ralph H. Ojemann and his colleagues at the University of Iowa (22, 23) in developing insights through a group approach. Ojemann is concerned with pointing up the differences between the "surface" approach and the dynamic or causal approach in understanding human behavior. In developing an understanding of the relationships between *what* people do and *why* they do it, his primary targets were teachers and parents. Do they handle the behavior problems of children in terms of overt acts, or are they equipped to handle them in terms of the deeper motivations?

With this problem as the springboard, Ojemann went a step further and started to explore the question of developing in children an understanding of their peers—and ultimately an understanding of themselves.

The aim of his work is to introduce children to the idea that people do not behave as they do "just because"—that there are reasons underlying human behavior. By encouraging children to observe how their friends and playmates behave and to try to grasp some of the reasons for this behavior, children are exposed to two premises that are basic to the development of insight: *motivation* and *multiple causation*. They begin to understand the *why* behind individual behavior and to grasp the idea that a number of different factors can "add up" in causing a pattern of behavior. From this understanding begins to emerge a change in the child's system of values—a broad-spectrum set of values in place of the polarity of "right" and "wrong."

It is the belief of Ojemann and his colleagues that once children are habituated to examining behavior in terms of motivation, they can begin to apply these newly acquired insights in their own interpersonal relationships, and ultimately use them in handling their own problems.

It is evident that to develop this type of understanding through a classroom approach calls for extremely unorthodox handling of standard content. Ojemann's work, which is still being developed experimentally, has involved a relatively cautious and conservative handling of his premise. Rather than an outright introduction of courses in human relations, he has sought to emphasize the human-relations aspects of material in existing curricula. In other words, wherever classroom material involves human behavior, he has suggested ways in which the material can be re-examined so that the motivation behind that behavior is brought to the attention of the students.

For example, in an existing course in Civics, he suggests that a study of crime might include not only a review of the organization and function of the police force, the role of the courts, methods of apprehending criminals, and structure of the penal system, but that it be augmented to include an understanding of motivation in the causes of crime and in the outlook for rehabilitation. This approach can lead directly into the study of causes and prevention of juvenile delinquency problems (24). It could also tie in with the question of discipline, self-control, and self-direction.

Specifically, Ojemann has proposed ways of inserting the human-relations approach in the curriculum throughout the elementary and secondary systems. This approach is now being used in several pilot schools, where the results are being carefully watched and analyzed for further implications.

In these pilot schools, the material at the preschool and primary grades is limited to plays, skits, and stories through which behavior patterns at the child's level are dealt with and talked about; a manual for teachers which helps them understand and handle classroom and playground situations at a motivational level; some rewriting of reading selections to emphasize human relations.

For the fourth, fifth, and sixth grades, special readings have been prepared which will lead children to examine how other children behave. In addition, through participation in room councils, children are encouraged to apply the dynamic approach to their own actual problems. At the seventh-grade level, in studying civics, students analyze community problems in terms of underlying human behavior. By the time the student reaches the eighth grade, he is ready consciously to apply what he has learned about the causes of human behavior. He is asked to examine his own experiences at school, at home, and in his relationships with others, and to make plans for himself in terms of what he now knows about himself, his pattern of handling problems, his relationships to others. In addition, the home-economics course at the eighth-grade level provides an opportunity for an exploration of the subject of family relationships.

In the ninth and tenth grades, as students are taught world history and the history of major social institutions, this material is presented not only in terms of overt events but in terms of how these developments responded to major human needs.

In the eleventh grade, within the framework of the study of conservation of human resources, students approach the entire problem of mental hygiene, illuminated now by what they already know about the dynamics of strain and tension in the human personality.

Finally, in the twelfth grade, as students examine modern social problems, they are equipped to approach the problems of courtship, preparation for marriage and parenthood in terms of what has become a habitual analysis and understanding of human behavior.

Comparisons of experimental and control groups yielded significant differences in favor of the experimental groups in causal orientation with respect to interpretation of behavior and in changes from authoritarian to democratic attitudes (23).

The Delaware, Maryland project

This mental-hygiene project, undertaken through the medium of human-relations classes, has been widely publicized, so that only a brief description of the work will be given here. H. Edmund Bullis, who has directed the Delaware project, reports its beginnings in a program of group discussions for shy and recessive children under the auspices of the Canadian Committee for Mental Hygiene. The Delaware State Society for Mental Hygiene has sponsored the Delaware project through its executive director, Bullis.[6]

Classes in human relations were first introduced into the seventh and eighth grades in the Delaware schools, using lesson plans (25)[7] that included stories or playlets involving emotional problems to be used as starters for class discussion of numerous topics such as The Importance of Friends; Getting Along with Others; Relationships with Brothers and Sisters; Problems of a New Pupil in School; Advantages and Disadvantages of Being Timid and Shy; How Punishment Affects Us; Frustrations and Conflict; Necessity for Self-discipline; Emotional Problems That May Lead to Delinquency; Results of Continual Failure on Personality Development; Setting Goals in Line with Capacity and Opportunity (26). Films and recordings of radio dramatizations have been used at times as stimulus material for discussions, though the time element here has been reported as a problem in limiting discussion, which was judged to be the most significant aspect of the program.

In attempts to evaluate outcomes of the human-relations classes, decided changes have been reported in the point of view of some teachers as a result of their conducting the discussion lessons and changes in the social acceptance and social status in their groups of very shy children.

[6] Leaders in this early project were William Line, of the University of Toronto, J. D. M. Griffith, of the Canadian Committee for Mental Hygiene, and Stan Watson, principal of the Essex School of Toronto.

[7] Courses have been developed for grades 6 through 9, but one of the teachers' manuals, *Human Relations in the Classroom, Kindergarten through Twelfth Grade*, stars lesson outlines recommended especially for lower grades.

Training courses and manuals for teachers have been included in the services for developing and spreading experimentation in this area of human relations.

The Forest Hill Village human-relations classes [8]

These classes were part of an extensive mental-hygiene program in a small suburban community in Canada. Seeley (27) has described the project, which comprised an incredible number of facets, ranging from a more or less traditional clinic for disturbed children to preparation of specially selected educators for special mental-health work in schools, one phase of which was conduct of the "human-relations classes" as a means of promoting positive mental health. The program carried over into participation in school policy, community public affairs, parental education, and a referral service for adults. Only a few aspects related to group approaches in guidance can be summarized here, and a brief summary is certain to lose some of the enthusiasm and inspiration communicated in the description from which it is drawn.

A few essential foundations for the human-relations classes were (a) specially selected teachers exposed to a special training experience; (b) training oriented toward teaching, but with thorough exposure to clinical practice, understanding of the "venture into promotion of positive mental health," and opportunity to "work through emotionally" the experiences presented (to the point of psychotherapy in a few cases); (c) access to the psychiatric clinic for any child who, on the basis of preexisting disturbance, might become more deeply disturbed as a result of experience in the classes.

Experimental classes were organized from grade 4 to grade 12 in Forest Hill Village, and down to grade 1 elsewhere. The classes were composed of "normal" children in everyday classrooms. Matched controls were selected for each child in the experimental group, and certain types of test, inventory, and rating data for both experimental and control children were secured initially for later evaluations.

The classes, which met one hour a week, provided for free discussion of anything the children wished to talk about. There was no dearth of topics for discussion. The role of the leader was chiefly that of listening, making only rare interventions to clarify statements or summarizing to dispel confusion. No approval or disapproval of acts reported or statements made was shown—with the exception of one leader who had accepted the idea of the program intellectually but was unable to cope with the situation emotionally, and inevitably revealed his reactions in

[8] Summarized by permission of the journal editor and the author, John R. Seeley, who helpfully edited the description.

facial expression. The report described the method as "nondirective, unstructured, and group-determined."

Two illustrations are given by Seeley of the sequence of topics that developed in a couple of groups. One started with the topic of bombs and moved eventually into a discussion of "things we fear." The mention of fear of being on the stage led to discussing the criticisms adults were believed to make of children's behavior, and the expectations they seemed to have, and ultimately to a decision by the children to request a session with a particular teacher to share their feelings and learn what she really expected. This was interpreted as a set toward reality testing and action instead of worry.

In another group, talk of punishment led into the topic of adolescent relation to authority, and into the question "To whom can you tell what truths?" Thence it led to Jewish-Gentile relations, and to a realistic finale on problems of reforming the world—or one's own corner of it.

These glimpses of a six-to-nine-month program can only hint at some of the possibilities, but anyone who has experienced these free discussions would not be surprised (as were some of the uninitiated observers) at the emotional depth, intellectual grasp, and ethical concerns of these children.

In reporting outcomes, Seeley frankly admits that evaluation "by naked eye" was more convincing than the measured results, but these were not inconsiderable as reported for grades 6 and 10. Differential gains for the experimental group over the control group on the battery of personality measures were statistically reliable in varying degrees, and the check on school achievement for grade 10 classes showed (as a bonus) differential gains over the controls in school marks, despite loss of time in regular classes. Out of five scholarships awarded on the basis of competitive examinations by an outside body in the graduating year, four were won by members of this group, although they represented only a fifth of the graduating population.

Courses on personality and interpersonal relationships

These courses are legion and have a great variety of titles—Social Living, Senior Problems, Personal and Social Problems, Mental Hygiene, and Psychology of Personality—to cite only a few. Core, general-education, and life-adjustment programs include numerous units or topics within these areas. Most of these courses have an organized body of content for systematic study and use psychologically oriented texts and reference materials, though accounts of methods used would indicate that applications of the study to personal and group problems are an integral part of the work in most of them.

The workshop group on Education for Self-understanding, mentioned earlier,[9] expressed the view that, while (28, p. 38)

. . . courses that included attention to personal problems, human relations, and social adjustment should be taught in lower grades, . . . not until the eleventh or twelfth grades should psychology be taught as such. Such a course should include academic subject matter but should also emphasize personal implications.

With respect to psychology as mental hygiene, the report states (28, pp. 5–6):

It is possible to try to teach psychology in such a way that students are encouraged to face and try to solve issues in their personal lives. The closer teaching comes to a forthright approach to the deep-seated feelings and problems of students, the more important and profound its psychological content will be, even though the student is not required at the moment to learn technical terms or master psychological theories in the abstract. There is no psychological subject matter more important than the feelings and emotions of human beings.

Good teaching of psychological principles does not mean, however, that generalizations and abstractions should be discarded. Conceptualization must be an integral part of well-rounded learning, whether it is academic or designed to have a personal impact. One does not learn by simply taking part in an emotional revel. Mere expression of emotion as such, unconnected with any struggle to grow or effort to learn, probably has little, if any, educational value. While teaching psychology purely as an academic subject may have little or no value from the point of view of the emotional welfare of the learner, teaching that arouses emotion but offers no opportunity to learn from the feelings aroused may be not only valueless but very harmful.

GUIDANCE THROUGH THE EXTRACURRICULUM

Here we shall consider the extracurriculum as an integral part of the total educational program and deal only with group approaches to the guidance of students through their experiences in extraclass activities. In Chapter 12 the question of guiding students into activities was examined. Here the question is that of values in personal-social development that may accrue to individuals through participation in activities.

Fostering a democratic extracurriculum through the group approach

One of the major responsibilities of the administrator and various group leaders is that of fostering a democratic peer culture, in which the student-body government, all the various living, athletic, and special-

[9] Reprinted by permission of Bureau of Publications, Teachers College, Columbia University, New York.

interest groups and clubs, and the class and general social activities will provide opportunity for participation of all students in activities suited to their interests and their needs for personal development. This means a peer culture in which democratic leadership and followership can flourish and in which there is widespread opportunity for tryout and learning in both types of roles by all students in some capacity without the stigma and traumatic effects of failure that might ensue from some unwise choices of roles in adult life.

Before a situation of this kind can become a reality, the students themselves must be thoroughly aware of these purposes of the extra-curriculum and cooperate in its development. Reports of student groups that have come to grips with this problem indicate that they can envisage democratic possibilities with enthusiasm. But continuing reports of limited participation in school and college activities by large percentages of student populations, and the continued preponderance of leadership in the hands of a minority in many groups, suggest that students need much skillful assistance in moving toward democratic goals in their peer cultures. Here is a problem that may well enlist the co-operative efforts of students and psychologists and various social scientists in a school faculty as well as administrators and personnel workers. Learning in this area which actually eventuates in greater democratization of a school culture can well have profound reverberations in life beyond the school.

Discussions in committees or councils representing the student body and the faculty are helpful in spearheading progress toward greater democracy, but they need to be followed up by opportunity for every student to think about the problem and to plan what part he can play in the movement. In a high school, suitable opportunities may be afforded through homerooms, special guidance classes, or the social studies. This topic can be a very realistic challenge to applied thinking and actual practice in courses where social and political problems are being studied. In college, the living groups and orientation or other guidance courses can suitably bear part of the responsibility for "action research." A social science, psychology, or education club could have real live issues for study in this area. Administrators, personnel workers, and faculty members can bring knowledge and experience into such study, and the relatively sheltered environment of an educational institution provides the freedom for experimentation that can never be duplicated in adult life.

Adolescents are particularly susceptible to an appeal for the welfare and concern of others and can be inspired as at no other age to undertake a project that looks toward service in the interest of opportunities and fair play for all. Of course, the service motive must be linked with plenty of fun and organized freedom as well as study and work, if it really functions.

Many schools have carried through on an extensive study program for reorganizing student government or the extracurriculum. Too often these programs have petered out after the reorganization. There is no substitute for continuous study and vigilance with respect to the functioning of democracy. Also, this group vigilance needs to be supported by guidance of individuals in making choices of activities and in learning to participate well.

School Government. This is a term coming into use in some schools and colleges to replace the term *student government.* There have been many criticisms by students and adult leaders about the tendency in some institutions to give authority to students in name only or to limit student control to what has been termed the *dirty work* that administrators and faculty preferred not to do, such as policing halls and cafeteria, and keeping the grounds clean. Administrative veto has often undermined any authority ostensibly conferred on student governing groups.

The term *school government* would seem to represent a realistic approach to a democratic school environment recognizing (*a*) legal responsibilities of administrators; (*b*) guidance functions of counselors, teachers, and group leaders; (*c*) the need for participation of all members of a school community in a truly democratic government.

Where these concepts have been applied, students have been brought into participation in nearly every phase of planning and execution of policy in administration, curriculum, extracurriculum, personnel, and various school regulations; in some matters with voting privileges, and even majority membership on committees; and in other matters with opportunity for consultation. In these ways student influence can be exerted in all phases of the school life, with the likelihood that student needs will be met more fully, and on some questions students may have the deciding vote, but with opportunity of sharing views cooperatively with the faculty. One student (29) commented in a report of faculty-student cooperation in developing the campus social structure, "What an exciting way to learn!" A student report on similar developments throughout the country emphasized educational values for students and their emerging *responsibilities* rather than *rights* in college government (30). These reports seem to reveal real democracy in action. There has been widespread study by administrators of the methods and degrees of involving student and faculty in policy making. In one symposium in 1959 (31–33) the trend of thinking seemed to be that students' contributions had been so substantive that the profitable question is not whether but how best they should be involved.

Developments in this area are occurring from elementary school through higher education (34). To the extent that they result in the fuller understanding and meeting of individual needs, they are contributing significantly to the guidance service as well as to democratic citizenship.

The Role of the Adult Leader. Current concepts of leadership were reviewed in Chapter 4 (see pages 88 to 93). Here they will be considered in relation to the question of how the adult leader can exercise his functions in ways to help students derive the greatest value through their group activities. These functions will vary, depending on the program of the specific group and its place within the total extracurricular program of the school, but some functions and qualifications are common to all adult leaders working with student groups.

The leader should have a sound understanding of the working of group dynamics, and some facility in the techniques of group work. Through these techniques, he can prevent a group from being "taken over" by a few dominant members, at the expense of successful participation by all the members. He can guide the group purposefully forward, rather than permit it to squander its efforts aimlessly. But in performing the role, he must be sure he is *guiding*, not *propelling*. He can send up warning flags, but it must be left to the group to recognize the need to rechart its path.

If the group activity is focused around a specific skill or interest, the adult leader should be prepared to serve, in a measure, as an expert. He should be familiar with the background in the field, have some proficiency in it himself, be able to help students perfect their own skills in the field, and know what the resources are for students who wish to pursue an interest intensively.

He must be prepared to function as moderator between the conflicting interests and conflicting personalities which inevitably manifest themselves in a group. This will involve an ability to assess the emotional needs of each student, and to have insight into problems which might be only obliquely expressed through group situations. He must adroitly balance one student's needs against another's, so that all members of the group emerge from the experience with the rewarding sense of having succeeded as members of the group. He may encounter a situation in which a student is recognizably in a group which does not best meet his needs, and he should help the student find a more suitable activity and attach himself to it. All this should be accomplished without the students' feeling that they are being manipulated. Rather, the adult leader should help the student identify his own problems and should guide him in evolving solutions.

The personal endowments of the adult leader cannot be completely dissociated from his performance of these exacting roles. It is obvious that he must have the personal qualities which inspire and stimulate students; he must be patient and understanding; he must have integrity and humility. But skilled leadership rarely rests on personal attributes alone. The leader must know how to foster democratic leadership and followership within his group.

The Development of Student Leadership. For the student, one of the most rewarding consequences of group activities is the realization of his abilities to function as a leader, and the enjoyment of status which derives from this role. Self-confidence, a sense of accomplishment and service, growing skill in human relations, and the gratifying awareness that he has earned the approval of his peers—these are some of the constructive by-products of student leadership.

It is the responsibility of the adult leader to see that these rewarding experiences of leadership are widely distributed among members of the group. Except for the nominal leadership roles of group chairman or president, most leadership functions can deftly be rotated among the membership. This process of rotation is not prompted solely by a drive to "share the glory"; it involves a very realistic conservation of human resources. As the situation within the group shifts, and the work to be done varies, the leadership requirements for the situation also vary, and the student who can best meet those requirements should be encouraged to assume leadership responsibility.

Some students are highly verbal and spontaneously assume leadership when a problem is being talked out. Others have a flair for "making arrangements" and can best take over when plans need to be carried out. Some are most proficient in dealings with others and should be encouraged to assume responsibility for representing the group with outsiders—faculty, members of the community, other student groups.

The selection of student leaders should not be the function of the adult adviser; this should be done democratically by the students themselves. But the adult leader can help the group recognize the specific areas in which individual members can function as leaders, and can encourage the less assertive student who has never thought of himself as the leader type to avail himself of situations in which he can develop leadership traits.

The adult leader should also provide constant counsel for student leaders, so that the experience develops their self-understanding and augments their insight into themselves and others. This counsel should embrace the questions of the effects of leadership action on others in the group; the contribution of the leader in advancing the group goals; facility in handling differences within the group; skill in bringing out members who are not sufficiently aggressive; use of leadership qualities in molding the group into a cohesive unit.

A concomitant of constructive student leadership is the concept of student followership. If the adult leader is helping the group make good use of all its potentialities, he will develop among the members an understanding of the responsibilities of followership. These involve a realization that to be a follower is not a passive role; that follower responsibilities include keeping the group in balance, helping to carry out the program adopted by the majority, accepting and performing assignments which advance the group goals, and in some instances developing the techniques for presenting a minority point of view. The followership role, too, offers rewards for the student, in service performed and in learning to work as part of an organization. But under a sound program, no student is permanently pegged as either a leader or a follower.

Guidance of individuals through extracurricular activity

The same principles and procedures used in vocational and curricular guidance apply to extracurricular guidance: (a) self-appraisal; (b) acquisition of information about opportunities; (c) choices of activities; (d) entrance and participation; (e) adjustment through remedial help when needed; (f) evaluation of experiences; (g) replanning and new choices when the need is indicated.

Appraisal of Individuals. Leaders of activities, like subject teachers, have excellent opportunities for firsthand observation of individuals, and under especially favorable circumstances for seeing the whole personality in action. Such observations should be shared with a guidance worker and become a part of the student's personnel record. Leaders also have excellent opportunities in informal groups and situations to help students appraise themselves in various respects and plan how to solve some of their problems or better utilize their possibilities.

Group Conferences. With skilled leadership, informal-discussion groups in various clubs or housing units can go far toward helping students to face and resolve many personal conflicts or worries and, also, group problems of interrelationships—dating problems, love affairs, marriage, home relationships, friends, etiquette, social facility, shyness, appearance, grooming, health, morals, religion and philosophy, intercultural relationships—the list is endless if students get the opportunity for understanding and democratic guidance. A caution in these situations is not to get beyond one's depth and to recognize when some individuals need the specific assistance of a trained counselor, psychologist, physician, or psychiatrist.

What Wise (35) has urged for the achievement of educational objectives in college residences could apply in degree to almost any activity group other than purely social. He has suggested organized discussion groups, forums, panels, and speeches devoted to current campus and public issues, with both student and faculty leadership and participation, that would stimulate critical and creative thinking, and provide practice in intellectual conversation about topics of interest.

Remedial Assistance. Many students will need assistance on some phase of group participation in order to enter easily and successfully into chosen activities. Appearance, dress, grooming, etiquette, social or athletic skills, undesirable mannerisms, shyness, unsocial or antagonizing behavior are frequent difficulties. Guidance classes or homerooms can provide group study of the more common problems, but laboratories or special remedial groups have been found helpful in some institutions for those with special needs.

The strong interest in facing these problems and the spirit of mutual helpfulness that can be engendered were well illustrated in a group of high school freshmen. This group of several hundred students—a situation that should never exist—were meeting in an orientation class during the last period of the day on a hot Friday afternoon. They had been studying that week about school customs, traditions, rules, and etiquette. Etiquette had been examined from the viewpoint of courtesy and consideration for others, as well as adherence to form, but they wished to check themselves on social conventions, and had been given an etiquette test. They insisted on staying beyond the hour to correct the test, because they did not wish to wait until Monday to know all the answers. Doubtless week-end dates were in the offing. As correct answers were read, a girl near the front raised her hand and said, "You must have read the wrong answer to question 7." This question dealt with the eating of hot soup. Thoughtlessly, the leader asked, "Which answer did you think was right?" To which she replied, "Blow gently on it in the spoon," and added, "What else could you do?" It took only a quick glance at the group to check the imminent explosion of laughter, and instantly a boy spoke up with a snicker, "I got the one on the olive pits wrong!"

Discipline. Policies for handling discipline in a democratically organized school life require the application of guidance principles to protect the needs of individuals. It has been clearly demonstrated by experience that no faculty can be as effective as the combined efforts of student body and faculty in the formulation and enforcement of regulations for school conduct in classes, halls, school grounds, and at athletic and social events. Group study of school regulations, not only in the interests of an informed citizenry but also of continual improvement of regulations, is an obvious necessity that is not always kept at the point of highest efficiency. Research in group dynamics has shown that individuals are more likely to carry out group decisions which they have helped to make than their own individual decisions (see Chapter 4). No administrator needs proof that group decisions are more readily enforced than administrative fiat.

The disciplining of individuals who fail to conform to regulations presents a different problem. Here, there is frequent need of individual study by trained personnel workers to ascertain the reasons for the behavior and best means of helping the individual to improve it. Group study by students of the various combinations of causes of poor school citizenship and unacceptable behavior may serve as one preventive measure and may help students in their leadership functions in the student body. But the differentiation between discipline problems that can be handled by students and those that require psychological study needs to be defined carefully.

Evaluation of group activities

This evaluation by members of groups, both as to group progress and individual contributions, is an essential means of assuring progress toward the realization of goals. Both discussion and simple forms can be used in this process. It presupposes that a group has formulated purposes for itself and has mapped out plans for activities in harmony with these purposes. An evaluation form will usually invite comments from members regarding meetings, other activities, leadership, and member participation, and suggestions for improvements and new plans. The tallied data can provide excellent material for good discussions and for planning ahead (36).

An evolving extracurriculum

As counselors work with students on their problems of choosing and participating in activities and making long-range plans, they obtain knowledge of unmet needs which should be shared with the person in charge of the extracurriculum. Students and faculty members should likewise share their ideas either directly or through whatever committee or council is responsible for the planning of the ongoing program. In this way the extracurriculum can be kept flexible and responsive to the ever-changing picture of student needs for self-development and self-direction through creative activity in a democratic social life.

<h3 style="text-align:center">SUMMARY</h3>

Learnings in the areas of personality and interpersonal relationships subsume most of human life. Many of the problems of living which vitally concern individuals are in the personal-social area. One of the crucial aspects of personal-social adjustment is that of mental health. Other crucial areas relate to problems of accepting self and others; parent-child relationships; dating, courtship, and marriage; and living within the peer culture.

Various examples have been cited of programs to increase understanding of and wholesome adaptation within human relationships. Guidance through the extracurriculum has been considered as one important aspect of human relationships within the school environment.

REFERENCES CITED IN CHAPTER

1. Gillham, Helen L.: *Helping Children Accept Themselves and Others,* Bureau of Publications, Teachers College, Columbia University, New York, 1959.
2. Thom, D. A., and F. S. Johnston: "Environmental Factors and Their Relation to Social Adjustment: A Study of a Group of Well-adjusted Children," *Mental Hygiene,* 23:379–413, 1939.
3. Olson, Willard C.: "Developmental Theory in Education," in Dale B. Harris (ed.), *The Concept of Development: An Issue in the Study of Human Behavior,* University of Minnesota Press, Minneapolis, 1957.
4. Schutz, Richard E.: "Patterns of Personal Problems of Adolescent Girls," *The Journal of Educational Psychology,* 49:1–5, 1958.
5. Billett, Roy O., and Irving S. Starr: *Manual, Billett-Starr Youth Problems Inventory, Junior and Senior Levels,* Harcourt, Brace & World, Inc., New York, 1961.
6. Block, Virginia L.: "Conflicts of Adolescents with Their Parents," *Journal of Abnormal and Social Psychology,* 32:193–206, 1937.
7. Hackett, Clarence G.: *Use of an Opinion-polling Technique in a Study of Parent-Child Relationships,* Studies in Higher Education, No. 75, Purdue University, Division of Educational Reference, Lafayette, Ind., June, 1960.
8. Mahler, Clarence A., and Edson Caldwell: *Group Counseling in Secondary Schools,* Science Research Associates, Inc., Chicago, 1961.
9. Luckey, Eleanor B.: "Implications for Marriage Counseling of Self Perceptions and Spouse Perception," *Journal of Counseling Psychology,* 7:3–9, spring, 1960.
10. Romano, Robert L.: "The Use of Interpersonal System of Diagnosis in Marital Counseling," *Journal of Counseling Psychology,* 2:10–19, spring, 1960.
11. "Marriage Counseling and Counselors: A Symposium," *Journal of Counseling Psychology,* 5:24–38, spring, 1958.
12. Franklin, R. D., and H. H. Remmers: *Youth's Attitudes toward Courtship and Marriage,* Report of Poll 62 of the Purdue Opinion Panel Division of Educational Reference, Purdue University, Lafayette, Ind., April, 1961.
13. Coleman, James S., John W. C. Johnstone, and Kurt Jonassohn: *The Adolescent Society: The Social Life of the Teenager and Its Impact on Education,* The Free Press of Glencoe, a Division of the Crowell-Collier Publishing Co., New York, 1961.
14. Taba, Hilda: *School Culture,* American Council on Education, Washington, 1955.
15. Gordon, Calvin W.: *The Social System of the High School,* The Free Press of Glencoe, a Division of the Crowell-Collier Publishing Co., New York, 1957.
16. Hollingshead, A. B.: *Elmtown's Youth,* John Wiley & Sons, Inc., New York, 1949.
17. Laughlin, Frances: *The Peer Status of Sixth and Seventh Grade Children,* Bureau of Publications, Teachers College, Columbia University, New York, 1954.
18. Dodge, Raymond, and Eugen Kahn: *The Craving for Superiority,* Yale University Press, New Haven, Conn., 1931.
19. Carpenter, Marjorie (ed.): *The Larger Learning: Teaching Values to College Students,* William C. Brown Company, Publishers, Dubuque, Iowa, 1960.

20. Eddy, Edward D., Jr.: *The College Influence on Student Character,* American Council on Education, Washington, 1959.
21. Franklin, R. D., M. H. Maier, and H. H. Remmers: *Teenagers' Attitudes toward Teenage Culture,* Report on Poll No. 55 of the Purdue Opinion Panel, Division of Educational Reference, Purdue University, Lafayette, Ind., May, 1959. (Mimeographed.)
22. Morgan, Mildred L., and Ralph H. Ojemann: "The Effect of a Learning Program Designed to Assist Youth in an Understanding of Behavior and Its Development," *Child Development,* 13:181–194, September, 1942.
23. Ojemann, Ralph H.: "The Human Relations Program at the State University of Iowa," *The Personnel and Guidance Journal,* 37:198–206, November, 1958.
24. Kvaraceus, William C.: *Juvenile Delinquency: What Research Says to the Teachers,* Department of Classroom Teachers, American Educational Research Association of the National Education Association, Washington, 1958.
25. Bullis, H. Edmund, and Emily O'Malley: *Human Relations in the Classroom, Kindergarten–Twelfth Grade,* Hambleton Printing and Publishing Company, Wilmington, Del., 1944.
26. Tarumianz, M. A., and H. Edmund Bullis: "The Human Relations Class: A Preventive Mental Hygiene Program for Schools," *Understanding the Child,* 13:7, October, 1944.
27. Seeley, John R.: "The Forest Hill Village 'Human Relations Classes,'" *The Personnel and Guidance Journal,* 37:424–434, February, 1959.
28. Jersild, Arthur T., and associates: *Education for Self-understanding,* Bureau of Publications, Teachers College, Columbia University, New York, 1953.
29. Berman, Deborah: "Evolving Patterns of Social Control at Brandeis University," *The Journal of Educational Sociology,* 28:353–359, April, 1955.
30. Freidson, Eliot (ed.): *Student Government, Student Leadership, and the American College,* United States National Student Association, Philadelphia, 1955.
31. Gould, Samuel B.: "Faculty and Student Participation in Administration," Fourteenth National Conference on Higher Education, Association for Higher Education, Chicago, Mar. 2, 1959. (Mimeographed.)
32. Lunn, Harry H., Jr.: "To What Extent Can Administration Involve Faculty and Student Participation, and Still Be Efficient?" Fourteenth National Conference on Higher Education, Association for Higher Education, Chicago, Mar. 2, 1959. (Mimeographed.)
33. Lunn, Harry H., Jr.: *The Student's Role in College Policy-making,* American Council on Education, Washington, 1957.
34. Gaynor, Alta I.: "Student Councils in Selected Elementary Schools," *The Personnel and Guidance Journal,* 35:249–250, December, 1956.
35. Williamson, E. G., and Max Wise: "Symposium: Residence Halls in Higher Education," *The Personnel and Guidance Journal,* 36:392–401, February, 1958.
36. Lippitt, Gordon L., and Warren H. Schmidt: *My Group and I: A Manual for Those Who Belong to Associations, Including Tested Techniques for Making Their Groups More Valuable to Themselves and to Their Members,* Educators' Washington Dispatch, an Arthur C. Croft Publication, Washington, 1952.

ADDITIONAL REFERENCES

Bloch, Herbert A., and Arthur Niederhoffer: *The Gang: A Study in Adolescent Behavior,* Philosophical Library, Inc., New York, 1958.
Brunelle, Peggy: "Exploring Skills of Family Life at School: Sociodrama with Fourth Grade Group," *Group Psychotherapy,* 6:227–255, 1954.
Byrd, Oliver E.: *Family Life Source Book,* Stanford University Press, Stanford, Calif., 1956.
Coffield, Kenneth E., and T. L. Engle: "High School Psychology: A History and Some Observations," *The American Psychologist,* 15:350–352, June, 1960.

Collins, A. E.: "Guidance through Human Relations Classes," *The School Guidance Worker*, 14:12–16, May, 1959.

Davis, Donald A.: "Effect of Group Guidance and Individual Counseling on Citizenship Behavior," *The Personnel and Guidance Journal*, 38:142–145, October, 1959.

Detjen, Ervin W., and Mary Ford Detjen: *Elementary School Guidance*, 2d ed., McGraw-Hill Book Company, Inc., New York, 1963.

Kelley, Janet: *Guidance and Curriculum*, rev. ed., Prentice-Hall, Inc., Englewood Cliffs, N.J., 1956.

Klopp, Gordon: *College Student Government; A Guide to Student Participation in College Administration as a Democratic Privilege and a Laboratory for Citizenship*, Harper & Row, Publishers, New York, 1960.

McKinney, Fred: *Teaching Personal Adjustment: An Instructor's Manual*, John Wiley & Sons, Inc., New York, 1960.

Pullen, C. H. W.: *Building Citizenship*, Allyn and Bacon, Inc., Englewood Cliffs, N.J., 1958.

Spoerl, Dorothy T. (ed.): *Tensions Our Children Live With: Stories for Discussion*, The Beacon Press, Boston, 1959.

Wills, Clarice Dechent, and William H. Stegman: *Living in the Primary Grades: A Handbook for Teachers of First, Second, and Third Grades*, Follett Publishing Co., Chicago, 1957.

For student source materials see lists in bibliographies for Chapters 8 and 12.

15 LIFE VALUES AND PHILOSOPHY

The discussion of this topic is intentionally neither erudite from the philosophical viewpoint, nor thoroughly documented, but a rather extensive list of references is included in the chapter bibliography. Questions will be raised for which no conclusive answers are available, but which pose problems to be studied in each new generation. This is an area that has evoked renewed interest, research, and consideration in recent times, particularly from the viewpoint of the preservation and improvement of our way of life. Mark Twain's facetious comment on the weather can scarcely apply except for the matter of general interest, since there has been increased effort for several decades to improve moral, spiritual, and character education. Each person or each project appears to have a slightly different orientation and approach to this vital issue. An attempt to survey present trends reminds one of the words of St. Paul, "There are, it may be, so many kinds of voices in the world, and none of them is without signification." [1]

One reason for these many voices is doubtless the fact that values are intensely personal and develop through experience, but to the extent one identifies with a group there are inevitably many common values that operate, often unconsciously, in the lives of members of a group. For some, there are both conscious and unconscious motives that cause them to repudiate many group values, and others accept them uncritically, often, perhaps, in response to an urge for security and belongingness, or merely because they have never been stimulated to examine what life may mean to them. Nothing would seem more fundamental in our guidance efforts to foster self-knowledge and power of self-direction than assistance to individuals in seeking, at suitable maturity levels, for insight with respect to the various influences, past and present, that are operating to determine the values that enter into choices and decisions in every aspect of living. This insight, leading into the development of a growing life philosophy, is the central factor in any real self-determination.

[1] I Corinthians 14:10.

Problems of Guidance with Respect to Values

For many years, the writer (in this chapter, I should like often to depart from the usual professional etiquette of the use of the impersonal third person and communicate directly person to person, hoping that readers will respond likewise with the question "What do *I* think or believe about this matter?") has read and read, and experimented much with groups and individuals in attempting to help them examine the sources of their convictions or lack of them, and develop techniques of assessing and using values consciously in making decisions.

Should we share our values with counselees in this guidance process?

This question has been discussed widely, in recent years, in the professional literature (1–6). I feel strongly with Samler (7, p. 38) in his comment that "a congress of psychologists determining by vote whatever values should be, scares the daylight out of me," and certainly the attempted imposition of the values and beliefs of any one person may be still more dangerous. On the other hand, I have questioned for many years the theory that a counselor should never communicate any of his beliefs or convictions to a counselee, but merely help him to discover and develop his own. One reason for this questioning is the probability that we *do* communicate our attitudes and convictions in one way or another despite efforts to avoid doing so. Whenever a group or an individual asks for my opinion on a controversial issue, my usual practice is to answer their request as honestly as possible with both certainties and uncertainties, but always with the caution that no one may see the whole truth and that each person has the responsibility of reaching his own conclusions on the basis of all facts and understandings available to him. (Of course, at times, group action must result from acceptance of group decision.) Sometimes, when there has been no request, I have deemed it important, as a group leader, to explain some of my convictions to warn a group against any subtle influence on their deliberations that might stem unintentionally from my point of view. If I feel that a certain attitude should be inculcated in the interest of group welfare, for a specific group or generally for our culture, I want a group, usually, to know what's happening to them. Only thus can such influences carry over effectively into varied life situations in a changing culture.

I confess to certain reservations on this point related to the maturity and the ability level of individuals. Without doubt, a certain amount of conditioning is important for very young children who have not yet developed power of critical thinking. Also, I am inclined to agree somewhat with a delightful writer of the decade of the twenties, who urged that the happy moron should be led down the church aisle in the best Victorian tradition. Perhaps the value of this attitude depends on the extent to which any individual must face up to conditions beyond his potential power to grapple with them, and I suppose all of us become involved in some such situations at times.

What are some of the basic considerations in developing values and a life philosophy?

The question of what is truth about life has never had an answer that satisfies everyone, and probably never will. It is a continuous quest for every thinking human being. Lignon (8), during years of experimentation in developing a character education program, has formulated a belief in what he calls the "infinity principle." If I understand it aright, this means to him that research will continually reveal new aspects of truth that may lead to an ever expanding concept of life meanings and the emergence of ever finer and better concepts of human potentialities for the good life with no final answers and no ultimate limitations.

A good many, in this generation as well as previous ones, have expressed the pessimistic conviction that moral standards and behavior are deteriorating, and that as the old saying goes, "Youth is going to the dogs." We hear much about the increase of delinquency and crime in the adolescent years, and no one could deny the seriousness of the situation. However, Brinton (9), who has made an intensive study of the history of Western morals from ancient civilizations in the Near East to the present, counters the pessimistic view that moral conditions are worsening with a positive attitude toward improvements. He admits that the record shows no moral progress comparable to our material progress, but he finds evidence that over two centuries there has been a decrease in the violence and uncertainties of daily living and an expanded consciousness of the dignity of man and of social values in human life. He finds many constants in the history of Western morals, e.g., honesty, loyalty, kindness, self-control, industry, and cooperativeness as virtues; and lying, treachery, cruelty, self-indulgence, laziness, uncontrolled aggressiveness, and selfishness as vices—with many in-group limitations, yet a strong note of universalism (9, pp. 416–417).

Some anthropological studies of different cultures have tended to stress the relativity of ethical standards, while others have indicated the existence of many universal trends, at least in their implications for in-groups. The sociologist Charles Horton Cooley interpreted the trend of human history as exemplifying a gradual enlargement of social consciousness. Doubtless we would all agree that there are still vast realms to conquer in this respect.

The English anthropologist Rivers made a fascinating observation in his study over a period of many years of head-hunting tribes in New Guinea. In his first visit, he found vigorous, zestful people in the various tribes, vitally interested in their communal life. On his return years later, he found this same condition of vigor and zest in some tribes and an extreme apathy and lack of vigor in others. In these latter groups, he noted that an individual who became ill would frequently die quickly for no apparent good reason. Comparing the two types of situations, he discovered that the more vigorous, zestful tribes had either retained their ancient head-hunting expeditions or had adopted Christianity and were living by its tenets. The others had neither. Head-hunting had originally been the center of interest in the life of a tribe, with general participation in the lengthy preparations leading up to the head-hunting expeditions and in celebrations following the return of the hunters. They had found nothing to replace their lost traditions.

One of the greatest current concerns of modern philosophers, educators, and other students of our national life has been the apparent apathy of youth—and many adults—regarding not only moral problems but public issues generally. Can we find a possible parallel here between our culture and some of the New Guinea tribes? Have we fully retained the convictions about the principles upon which our nation was founded, the appreciation of the values inherent in our culture, and awareness of the continuous, wholehearted effort needed to maintain and improve it? Or have we lapsed somewhat into a complacent acceptance? Still another question: Have we grown so large and impersonal as a nation that enthusiastic personal involvement in our way of life has become difficult to achieve? There are many other pertinent questions on this issue of apathy, some of which will be raised under another topic.

Returning to the question of how we develop values, we should doubtless face up to the claim of some philosophers in the field of ethics that there are no moral *standards;* there are only moral *decisions* based on understanding of specific situations and of the consequences of varied decisions leading to conduct. This idea brings us directly into the question of guidance to assist individuals in making decisons. The case method described in Chapter 5 (see pages 121 to 124) illustrates one approach, with a group, whereby situations that are never fully duplicated are analyzed with a view to developing skill in coping with each new situation as it is met in life through consideration of the possible consequences of alternative courses of action. Out of such experiences in living may develop not only techniques but growing convictions regarding life values and meanings. As these values become established within the personality, there is less need for struggle and conflict in making choices. Then the problem may be that of keeping the value system open to gain new and enriched meanings through ever new experiences.

One of the great opportunities in group guidance lies in the area that Festinger (10) has called cognitive dissonance. By this he means difficulties encountered in "fitting together" beliefs, attitudes, and understandings. Everyone today is likely to experience a good deal of this dissonance because of our cosmopolitan culture. Students are especially vulnerable as they explore various fields of knowledge and work and play with associates from many cultural *milieus*. Festinger concluded from his study that an individual will either try to reduce dissonance or avoid situations that increase it. The guidance group is an ideal place to examine various points of view and seeming conflicts in knowledge, experience, and beliefs. Through this process one may be helped to develop skill in organizing one's life philosophy, learning to live with many uncertainties, and keeping the way open for the assimilation of new experiences and new meanings.

What are some of the values that have developed through human experience?

The word *values* is used here to connote personal judgments of truth, worth, or excellence with no intention of conforming to any philosophical theory of values. We have already touched upon several types of values under the previous questions.

Among these are *truth values*. How to discover truths and use them in thinking and living is an age-old question. Some have depended on direct mystical revelations, while others have set store by the scientific method of observation, thought, and verification. These seemingly different approaches may merely be operating in different levels or areas of life. There are many scientists as well as mystics (and some are both) who envisage man as both a biological and spiritual being with the foundations of universal brotherhood in both realms. Some view the course of human life as stages of biological, mental, and spiritual development with individual differences of tempo and nature of growth in each realm. Recognition of the spiritual nature of all beings is certainly a helpful approach to that essential in guidance of full acceptance of every person regardless of other obvious manifestations that may tend to repel.

Moral values are held by some to be inherent in universal principles of right and wrong. Others view them as an outgrowth of human experience in achieving types of human relationships that foster the highest welfare of both society and the individual. The golden rule can doubtless be cited as exemplifying one value cherished by both groups. Some believe in the doctrine of original sin that requires discipline and expiation; others, that human nature is basically good but is distorted through unwholesome experiences. Rogers (11) has expressed faith in the essential wisdom of the human organism to choose those values which redound to both individual and social welfare. He sees problems stemming from the child's attempted introjection of the values of those upon whom he must depend for love and esteem, and true moral growth toward a commonality of value directions occurring in a climate of freedom for a continuous valuing process. Piaget (12) reports, from his study of moral judgments of children, a shift from conduct based upon the external demands of rules to a moral code based upon internal standards of right and wrong. He observed growth in increased ability to judge others upon bases of circumstances, motives, and intentions rather than inflexible standards.

The question has been raised by several (13, 14) in recent times as to whether the Freudian concept of the imposed superego and the many-faceted causal study of behavior has not tended to eliminate personal responsibility in conduct and remove controls essential for both the individual and the group. The concept of sin as a cause of maladjustment and the desirability of a sense of guilt resulting from really bad behavior are receiving consideration today, coupled, of course, with questions of wholesome ways of dealing with the awareness of guilt. Personal responsibility for the consequences of personally determined behavior keyed to the maturity level of the individual is being recognized as important for positive mental health.

This concept implies, however, the need for guidance in learning how to evaluate all kinds of situations, how to think through to the possible consequences of different courses of action, and how to deal responsibly with the consequences. This learning cannot be achieved by preaching or merely by reading. Group guidance, using "teachable moments" incidentally, or planned group study throughout the years of formal schooling is one of the major resources for this learning.

Beauty values or *aesthetics, ideal values,* expressed through *religion,* and *values pertaining to the understanding and appreciation of reality* are all aspects of a comprehensive life philosophy. Education, considered in all its aspects, should be contributing to all of these phases of a growing life philosophy. The legal separation of church and state in our nation has, without doubt, limited the possibilities for any direct study of religion. There is growing awareness, however, of both the need and the possibilities for study of the nature and significance of the major religions in world culture. Many institutions of higher learning, especially, have introduced courses in comparative religion, and religious groups are included in extracurricular activities in both public schools and colleges and universities. No one can counsel adolescents without awareness of the deep need of many for assistance in thinking through problems of religious conflict and development. These problems can become a vital part of group work also, without infringing on the legal proscription of specific religious teaching.

What does research indicate about current life values?

Many surveys of the moral attitudes of adolescents and college youth have indicated that their views tend to be strongly traditional and conventional, but with considerable tolerance for diversity in standards and points of view. Comparisons with parental viewpoints have shown much similarity (15, 16).

Surveys of the attitudes of college students, especially, have indicated that the great majority have a basic faith in a Divine God or a Supreme Being, and a strongly felt need for religious or philosophical guides to provide orientation and meaning in their lives. Goldsen and others (17), in their interpretations of findings in the Cornell Values Study, comment that these expressed religious values seem to be only weakly engaged in the opinions, attitudes, and behavior reported in other spheres of life. They raise an unanswered question as to the impact and relevance of educational experiences in this area.

Getzels (18) has interpreted findings in several studies at the secondary school level as indicating changes in secular values in four areas: from the work-success ethic to sociability; from future-time to present-time orientation; from personal independence to group conformity; and from moral commitment to moral relativism. He found little change in what he termed sacred values, among which he included democracy, individualism, equality, and human perfectibility.

Peck, Havighurst, and associates (19) have presented both pessimistic and optimistic views of the possibilities for character development through education from interpretation of intensive case studies of thirty-four children and their parents. Some of the less encouraging findings for their subjects were strong evidence of the determining influence on a child's character of parental character, attitudes, and mode of discipline; indication that school influences seemed less to shape character than to sharpen contrasts through punishment and rewards.

The investigators grouped their subjects into five character levels: the *amoral*, who had remained at the infancy level of self-centeredness where others meant only the satisfaction of their whims; the *expedient*, arrested at the early childhood level, who used people for their own ends and conformed primarily for selfish purposes; the *conforming* and the *irrational-conscientious*, arrested at the level of later childhood, the first conforming to external standards, and the second to internal but rigid standards that were not open to rational considerations; and the *rational-altruistic,* who had achieved adolescent or adult levels, with internalized standards open to rational consideration of new experiences, with real interest in the welfare of others, and able to adapt their ethical standards intelligently to the changing vicissitudes of living. These brief descriptions do not cover adequately all of the personality dynamics involved in the investigators' concepts. Another pessimistic finding was that not more than a fourth of their subjects could be classified in the *rational-altruistic* group on the basis of their appraisal data, and the estimate was made that this percentage has probably always applied to the population at large.

Among the optimistic views presented were the following: character seems to be *learned* more than inherited (19, p. 179); many therapists have proved that it is possible to *teach* children to have dramatically improved personality and character, though the process is slow; the ethical principles and behavior of the *rational-altruistic* individuals seem to be universally desired and respected by others.

The recommendations of the investigators are too numerous to summarize here and are worthy of careful study. Only a few will be considered in relation to possibilities in group guidance. The personal interest and influence of an emotionally and socially mature guidance leader can be of inestimable value in providing a sense of sincere acceptance, respect, and love for the immature character, and a motivation for growing into a more mature behavior pattern. The power of the peer group can be drawn upon more effectively in both curricular and extracurricular activities. An attitude of acceptance within a peer group that can be fostered through group guidance may help to break through the arrested development and open the way for further growth. Study and critical thinking about the dynamics of human development and behavior and opportunities to experience wholesome group relationships emotionally as well as intellectually may help to prepare for improved parenthood and therefore improved character in the next generation as well as to improved ethical standards, inner controls, and self-direction toward more socialized and happier living in the present.[2]

These are some of the fundamental threads of purpose throughout the whole fabric of group guidance. It is an exciting question to ponder whether we might extend that estimated 25 per cent of rational altruists in the population by well-planned, well-executed guidance services aimed at improved awareness of possible life values, consciously developed personal values, and rational choices of behavior based on understanding of relevant factors in each new situation. Some of the

[2] Summarized with permission of: Robert F. Peck, Robert J. Havighurst, and associates, *The Psychology of Character Development,* John Wiley & Sons, Inc., New York, 1960.

programs described in Chapter 14 (see pages 349 to 354) are pertinent to this goal.

One type of learning described by Tyler (20) in the White House Conference reports as particularly appropriate and essential for the schools relates to the re-examination and interpretation of experience. Tyler describes this approach thus:

Our basic ethical values are commonly involved in the daily experiences of youth. Questions of justice, fairness, goodness arise again and again on the playground, in the marketplace, and elsewhere. It is not likely, however, that sheer contact with these ideas will be enough to help the individual youth to develop values that are clearly enough understood and effectively utilized. The school can provide opportunity from time to time to recall these experiences, to examine them, and seek to interpret them, thus clarifying the meaning of values as well as helping youth to appreciate them more adequately. In the realm of ethical values this type of responsibility will be shared by the home, the Church, and youth organizations, but in the realm of esthetic values it is probably true that only the school is likely to provide the opportunity systematically (20, pp. 79–80).

Only through education can people learn to make wise economic choices as well as wise choices in the personal, social, and political fields (20, p. 73).

One is reminded of Aristotle's statement, "Through education I learn to do by choice what other men do by the constraint of fear."

How May Group Guidance Contribute to the Development of Values?

The place of "character education"

Research and experience have demonstrated that knowing what is right or wrong does not necessarily lead to socially approved behavior. Habitual ways of behaving that have been firmly established through early training will carry one a long way, but not necessarily in the right direction for every type of desirable behavior in a complex and changing culture. Under severe stress the habit may break down and leave no inner resources for developing a new and perhaps better mode of behavior. Or if a habit persists under severe stress, the individual himself may break—a victim of forces within and without which he does not understand and therefore cannot control.

James X may serve as a classical example of what may happen under these circumstances. James was referred to the psychologist because of insolent behavior with teachers whenever any authority was implied or invoked with reference to him. Study revealed an exceedingly immature person, emotionally, brought up under strict authoritarian control by his father who would brook no questioning of his orders. James was now rebelling against any authority or any person who to him symbolized authority. He was thoroughly unhappy and maladjusted and had decided that communism was the only form of government under which he could live and keep to his "principles" of independence. It took a long period of therapy before he began to recognize his immaturity and the bases of his resistance to authority. He still does not see the inconsistencies between his overweaning desire for independence and his adherence to communistic theories.

James, who is a college student, seems to be trying honestly to study how to grow up emotionally, but he has as yet developed no resources within himself to establish mutually satisfying relationships with others. He was so thoroughly imbued with the authoritarian pattern in his childhood that he can conceive of no other pattern to use with others. He feels that he is losing ground intellectually—the only field in which he has felt superior to others.

The ego strengths, listed in the Kluckhohn and Murray outline on pages 331 to 333, include the essentials for a strong character—that of one who understands the forces within his personality and those of others, has learned to resolve conflicts, to control and direct impulses, has developed standards of value to guide his conduct, and has acquired the will power and persistence, the sense of responsibility, and the dependability to carry through on self-determined plans of action. These are certainly qualities of a strong character. However, a strong character can be socially desirable or undesirable and, if the latter, can be more dangerous than a weak one.

Only the strong character of one who has thoroughly identified his interests with the interests of all other fellow human beings and has learned to enjoy cooperating with others in the pursuit of mutually desirable and satisfying goals can be a socially strong character. This type of character and citizenship will entail sacrifice of numerous individual satisfactions, but the sacrifice will not be viewed with regret, since it will result from a choice between lesser and greater satisfactions and loyalties. This is the essence of a mature personality. Parents, educators, and all who guide youth should themselves be mature if they are to provide the environment, the experiences, and the examples to foster this maturity.

Are the objectives of character education better achieved through direct or indirect methods? This question has been debated for centuries with apparently no conclusive answers. When character is thought of as the core of a personality, the answer to the question would obviously seem to be "Both." Certainly no one will learn to cooperate unselfishly with others by precept or merely by reading and talking about the process. He must feel what the cooperation is like in his firsthand experience. Many of our school activities and our "socialized" classrooms provide opportunities for learning cooperation in and with groups. Just what one learns, from the viewpoint of character, in competitive situations should doubtless be the subject of a good deal more study than has been made to date, if we are thinking and planning in terms of better democracy in the future.

No one seems ever to have improved upon the golden rule as a *precept* to guide conduct, but there appears to be a good deal of improvement needed in its application everywhere, in homes, schools, social and work groups, and between nations. To follow it one must learn to love and respect one's neighbor as oneself. Beyond this love and consideration of others, one must understand self and others sufficiently well to know how one would like to be treated if one were the other fellow with his unique personality and in his particular situation. Neither unselfish love nor understanding can grow in a personality suffused with fears, anxieties, and sense of guilt that have never been faced, and torn by conflicts which have never been resolved. Trial-and-error methods of learning in our interpersonal relationships are too costly when we have so much accumulated knowledge about why human beings think, feel, and act as they do.

Individuals at all ages show eagerness to understand themselves and others at their levels of maturity. As our critical and appreciative powers develop, we may resent being told the moral of a human situation as much as the moral of a fable, story, or a work of art. But freedom to explore these moral implications with one's peers and with guidance of a leader who can help the group to bring their heritage of knowledge and human experience to bear on a problem offers untold opportunities for character development, provided there are also opportunities to apply their findings in actual living. We not only learn what we live, but must also live what we learn, if we are to build upon past human experience.

Homerooms, guidance classes, and all subjects that deal with some phase of life—and what one does not?—afford opportunities for significant growth in character of an understanding sort that can be used with intelligence and fine sentiment in ever-new situations. One of our tasks as educators and guides is to plan—and much more often with pupils— for these opportunities, be they direct or indirect, incidental or intentional, instead of leaving them to chance. With a plan in hand, we are better prepared to take full advantage also of all those "teachable moments" which cannot be foreseen.

The direct study of life values

Questions of perennial interest to both high school and college students are "What do I now think I want of life?" "What am I likely to value most ten or twenty years hence?" "What are the ways that I may best be able to realize these values?" "What are my present sources of happiness?" "What are they likely to be as an adult?"

The writer has asked these questions many times of groups of students. The tallied responses to the first question by a group of eleventh-grade students, which are included here, are quite characteristic of the trends for other secondary school students. In fact, lists for college students and adults seem not to vary too much from this pattern.

Life values listed by students	Per cent listing each life value
A happy home life	81
Success in a suitable or desired vocation	66
Sufficient income for comfort	53
Friendships	44
Happiness	38
Sufficient education to enjoy the finer things in life	31
Service to others	22
Recognition by others	16
Amusement (parties, excitement, etc.)	13
Travel	13
Wealth	9

Concerns of adolescents about social relationships, vocational plans, and success in school are clearly related to these types of aspirations for later life.

Some comparisons by adolescents of their estimated sources of happiness with those estimated by adults (21, 22) have indicated slight shifts in emphasis from ephemeral to more stable interests in adult life, such as home, friends, work, and nature, though these estimates of sources of happiness have never seemed to vary too widely from desired life values in groups considering these questions thoughtfully. There has always seemed to be a gain in perspective with re-evaluation of present aspirations when the long view ahead has been attempted. Material wealth is rarely given a high rating as a desired life value or source of happiness except as it contributes to security and comfort—not as a source of luxury or a possession per se. These types of values expressed by students in group discussions do not seem to verify the accusations of many that prevailing values in this country are superficial and immature as compared with those of youths in other cultures (23).

However, the findings in many surveys (17, 24–26) point to a certain self-centeredness with emphasis on private rather than public interests that amounts almost to apathy with respect to many political and social issues. Some of the suggestions and experiments for citizenship training and character education have been directed toward the overcoming of this apathy through active involvement of students in real-life issues.

Involvement of students in service and citizenship projects

The trend toward large student bodies has created a situation in which a real community life is difficult to achieve. Some of the newer school buildings have been planned to provide for small units within the large institution, and this same trend is apparent in some of the newer housing units in colleges.

McNasser and Patterson (27) have proposed an experiment for civic education at the high school level that would allow for a small student-faculty community during a summer session, in which students help to plan the all-day program and engage actively in the work of the school community as well as in class and individual study and recreation. Some talented adults from the community would participate in instruction and a panel of leaders in community life would cooperate with groups of the students in work-assignment programs in community institutions. These summer "villages" would be cumulative over several years and would be aimed at providing adolescents with a sense of shared social responsibility and a reality base for self-imagery in relation to civic life relationships.

If one can judge from reports in professional literature, there were more projects involving students actively in community life in the decades of the thirties and forties than now. Perhaps the current stress on intellectual aspects of education has tended to close some of these avenues into the community life.

Hartford's (28) description of the "Kentucky Movement" to incorporate moral values into the entire educational program provides some inspiring examples of democratic cooperation of faculty, students, and community in planning and developing a way of life based on growing moral and spiritual values inherent in our cultural traditions. Workshops at the University of Kentucky initiated a five-year pilot study in one school, and other colleges cooperated in these workshops as new schools were added to the experiment. These groups studied the question of how school may become a laboratory in which the normal experiences of social living are subjected to analysis, appraisal, and experimental testing; how pupils may be helped to identify values and develop them into controls of conduct, by making choices regarding alternative outcomes of behavior in varieties of school situations and carrying commitments through to action. The program was planned to involve the total school community—curriculum, individual and group counseling, sports, recreation, and all social activities.

In the various schools faculty and students cooperated in developing standards with respect to courtesy, responsibility, and all the interpersonal relationships of school citizenship. Both teachers and pupils developed codes of ethics. One procedure reported was to use behavior episodes or incidents to analyze relationships involved, identify values, and plan steps to realize best values. Parents and other members of the community were brought into some projects, and pupils volunteered for community services.

These brief statements are barely touching the surface of a few of the many projects reported. A few of the outcomes as evaluated by students and faculty at various times are the following: Over a five-year period in one school, disciplinary cases practically disappeared. According to the report, new students quickly learned from the older ones "how we do things around here." The school had its best record ever in the matter of dropouts. Rules were rarely invoked, and when they were, it was often at the suggestion of the student council. Marked increase in teacher-pupil cooperation was reported—a significant development in light of the supposedly growing distance today between student and faculty cultures. Is this an example of how youths can be guided in studying and improving their peer culture?

One pupil evaluation yielded the following results: received better grades, 57 per cent; made more friends, 84 per cent; cooperated better, 60 per cent; appreciated things more, 65 per cent; developed more interests, 68 per cent; read more good books, 62 per cent.

All this suggests an educator's heaven! Reading the report revived memories of senior civics students in a large high school, who had become deeply involved in democratic planning that reached out beyond academic study into service in their school community, into cooperation with junior high school students in their citizenship projects, and into many city projects. One day's experience with a substitute using formal teaching methods led to the complaint that she interfered with their work! Later experiences on their own proved them capable of responsible action. Apparent evidence that academic achievement was not slighted came from an instructor of a required social-science course that many entered at the nearby university, who reported on their unusual interest and background in the field of study.

Any educator who has worked in this cooperative type of program knows how much more time, energy, and planning are required than in formal academic teaching, and also how great the satisfactions are in watching the growth in both social responsibility and academic excellence. Should we perhaps ask ourselves whether the student apathy noted so widely with respect to public issues and civic values may be in part shared by adults, and perhaps reflected to some extent in youths?

Do adults as well as youths tend to feel somewhat inadequate about ways of contributing to civic values in our complex civilization? Perhaps we need to examine our own attitudes, enthusiasms, and life values in order to help guide youths with theirs. Should we ask ourselves how deeply we care about the values that seem to give meaning to life for us, and how fully we affirm our faiths in a manner of living that strikes responsive chords in others' lives?

References Cited in Chapter

1. Lowe, C. Marshall: "Value Orientations—an Ethical Dilemma," *The American Psychologist*, 14:687–693, November, 1959.
2. Mowrer, O. Hobart: "Some Philosophical Problems in Psychological Counseling," *Journal of Counseling Psychology*, 4:103–112, summer, 1957.
3. Symposium: "Religious Factors and Values in Counseling," *Journal of Counseling Psychology*, 6:255–274, winter, 1959.
4. Patterson, C. H.: "The Place of Values in Counseling and Psychotherapy," *Journal of Counseling Psychology*, 5:216–223, fall, 1958.
5. Williamson, E. G.: "Value Orientation in Counseling," *The Personnel and Guidance Journal*, 36:520–528, 1958.
6. Wrenn, C. Gilbert: "The Ethics of Counseling," *Educational and Psychological Measurement*, 12:161–177, 1952.
7. Samler, Joseph: "Change in Values: A Goal in Counseling," *Journal of Counseling Psychology*, 7:32–39, spring, 1960.
8. Lignon, Ernest M.: *Dimensions of Character*, The Macmillan Company, New York, 1956.
9. Brinton, Crane: *A History of Western Morals*, Harcourt, Brace & World, Inc., 1959.
10. Festinger, Leon: *A Theory of Cognitive Dissonance*, Harper & Row, Publishers, New York, 1957.
11. Rogers, Carl: *On Becoming a Person*, Houghton Mifflin Company, Boston, 1961.
12. Piaget, Jean: *The Moral Judgment of the Child*, The Free Press of Glencoe, a division of the Crowell-Collier Publishing Co., New York, 1949.
13. Shoben, Edward Joseph, Jr.: "Personal Responsibility, Determinism, and the Burden of Understanding," *The Personnel and Guidance Journal*, 39:342–348, January, 1961.
14. Symposium: "The Role of the Concept of Sin in Psychotherapy," *Journal of Counseling Psychology*, 7:185–201, fall, 1960.
15. Remmers, H. H., and D. H. Radler: *The American Teenager*, The Bobbs-Merrill Company, Inc., Indianapolis, 1957.
16. Siegel, Laurence, et al.: "Expressed Standards of Behavior of High School Students, Teachers, and Parents," *The Personnel and Guidance Journal*, 34:261–267, January, 1956.
17. Goldsen, Rose K., et al.: *What College Students Think*, D. Van Nostrand Company, Inc., Princeton, N.J., 1960.
18. Getzels, Jacob W.: "The Problem of Values, Value Change, and Personal Identity in Education, Some Recent Studies," in Paul Halverson (ed.), *Frontiers of Secondary Education*, IV, Syracuse University Press, Syracuse, N.Y., 1960, pp. 26–37.
19. Peck, Robert F., Robert J. Havighurst, and associates: *The Psychology of Character Development*, John Wiley & Sons, Inc., New York, 1960.
20. Tyler, Ralph W.: "Educational Objectives," in Eli Ginzberg (ed.), *White House Conference Reports: The Nation's Children, Development and Education*, Columbia University Press, New York, 1960, vol. 2, pp. 70–90.

21. Watson, Goodwin: "Happiness among Adult Students of Education," *The Journal of Educational Psychology,* 21:79–109, 1930.
22. Gurin, Gerald, Joseph Veroff, and Sheila Feld: *Americans View Their Mental Health: A Nationwide Interview Survey,* Basic Books, Inc., Publishers, New York, 1960.
23. Gillespie, James M., and Gordon W. Allport: *Youth's Outlook on the Future,* Random House, Inc., New York, 1955.
24. Jacob, Philip E.: *Changing Values in College,* Harper & Row, Publishers, New York, 1957.
25. Eddy, Edward D., Jr., Mary Louise Parkhurst, and James S. Yakovakis: *The College Influence on Student Character,* American Council on Education, Washington, 1959.
26. Carpenter, Marjorie (ed.): *The Larger Learning: Teaching Values to College Students,* William C. Brown Company, Publishers, Dubuque, Iowa, 1960.
27. McNasser, Donald: "New Designs for Civic Education in the High School," in Franklin Patterson and others, *The Adolescent Citizen,* The Free Press of Glencoe, a Division of the Crowell-Collier Publishing Co., New York, 1960.
28. Hartford, Ellis Ford: *Moral Values in Public Education: Lessons from the Kentucky Experience,* Harper & Row, Publishers, New York, 1958.

ADDITIONAL REFERENCES

Allport, Gordon: *Becoming,* Yale University Press, New Haven, Conn., 1955.
Argyle, Michael A.: *Religious Behavior,* The Free Press of Glencoe, a Division of the Crowell-Collier Publishing Co., New York, 1959.
Benezet, Louis T.: "Guidance in Moral and Spiritual Values," in Hardee, Melvene Draheim (eds.), *Counseling and Guidance in General Education,* Harcourt, Brace & World, Inc., New York, 1955.
Clark, Walter Houston: *The Psychology of Religion: An Introduction to Religious Experience and Behavior,* The Macmillan Company, New York, 1958.
Dukes, William F.: "Psychological Studies of Values," *Psychological Bulletin,* 52: 24–50, January, 1955.
Earle, Howard: "Teen Codes of Conduct Score for Youth Decency," *The International Altrusan,* 39:11–15, March, 1962.
Edwards, H. W.: "Life Values as Fifth Graders See Them," *Instructor,* 63:81, 1957.
Everett, Millard Spencer: *Ideals of Life: An Introduction to Ethics and the Humanities,* John Wiley & Sons, Inc., New York, 1954.
Feifel, Herman (Chairman): "Symposium on Relationships between Religion and Mental Health," *The American Psychologist,* 13:565–579, October, 1958.
Hobbs, Nicholas: "Science and Ethical Behavior," *The American Psychologist,* 14: 217–225, May, 1959.
Huxley, Julian: *New Bottles for New Wine,* Harper & Row, Publishers, New York, 1957.
Kemp, C. Gratton: "Changes in Pattern of Personal Values," *Religious Education,* 56:63–69, January–February, 1961.
Langer, Susanne K.: *Philosophy in a New Key: A Study in the Symbolism of Reason, Rite, and Art,* 4th ed., Harvard University Press, Cambridge, Mass., 1960.
McGreal, Ian: *The Art of Making Choices,* Southern Methodist University Press, Dallas, 1953.
Maslow, Abraham H.: *New Knowledge in Human Values,* Harper & Row, Publishers, New York, 1959.
Montague, Ashley: "Helping Children Develop Moral Values," *Better Living Booklet,* Science Research Associates, Inc., Chicago, 1953.
Montague, M. F.: *The Direction of Human Development: Biological and Social Bases,* Harper & Row, Publishers, New York, 1955.
Perkins, Theodore F.: "Research Relating to the Problem of Values," *California Journal of Elementary Education,* 23:223–224, May, 1955.

Perry, Ralph Barton: *Realms of Value: A Critique of Human Civilization,* Harvard University Press, Cambridge, Mass., 1954.

Phillips, Dorothy Berkeley, et al. (eds.): *The Choice Is Always Ours: An Anthology of the Religious Way,* rev. ed., Harper & Row, Publishers, New York, 1960.

Redl, Fritz, and David Wineman: *Controls from Within,* The Free Press of Glencoe, a Division of the Crowell-Collier Publishing Co., New York, 1952.

Sheviakov, George V., and Fritz Redl: *Discipline for Today's Children and Youth,* new revision by Sybil K. Richardson, Association for Supervision and Curriculum Development, a department of the National Education Association, Washington, 1956.

Tournier, Paul: *The Meaning of Persons,* Harper & Row, Publishers, New York, 1957.

Underhill, Evelyn: Mysticism: *A Study in the Nature and Development of Man's Spiritual Consciousness,* Meridian Books (by arrangement with E. P. Dutton & Co., Inc.), New York, 1955.

APPENDIX

APPENDIX

SELF-DESCRIPTIVE Q-SORT STATEMENTS OF TRENDS OF GROUP MEMBERS [1]

Dependency Statements

Inclined to go along with the dominant mood of the group
Preferred to proceed along established lines
Annoyed when the actions of the leader were not what he expected
Inclined to follow the suggestions of the leader
Liked to appear in a good light in relation to group leaders
Comfortable when the leaders were active and directive
Expected the leaders to take major responsibility for planning group activities
Tended to defend the leaders when they were attacked by others
Inclined to follow the suggestions of another group member
Inclined to direct his comments to the leaders rather than to group members

Counterdependency Statements

Wanted to assume active leadership himself
Tended to express negative feelings about the leader
Tended to maintain himself in a focal position during discussions
Enjoyed counterposing himself to the leaders
Tended to look to other members to back up his position
Tended to suggest alternative action to that proposed by the leader
Tried to lead others against the leader
Inclined to assume a directive role in the group
Felt competitive toward individuals who attempted to dominate the group
Concerned with maintaining a high status in the group

Pairing Statements

Inclined to extend group friendships outside the group
Liked to keep the group discussion on a personal level
Inclined to bring intimate material to the group
Would have preferred a smaller, more intimate group
Wanted to be a member of a clique
Attached to one or two particular members
Wanted to know some of the other members of the group intimately
Liked to make side comments to one other member
Felt that social relations were maintained on too formal a level
Enjoyed personal interchanges with one or two particular members

[1] Reprinted from *Emotional Dynamics and Group Culture*, by Dorothy Stock and Herbert A. Thelen, no. 2 of the Research Training Series, National Training Laboratories, Division of Adult Education Service, National Education Association of the United States, Washington. New York University Press, New York, 1958, pp. 274–275, by permission of the publisher and the authors.

Counterpairing Statements

Felt that social relationships were too intimate

Resistive against breaking up into smaller subgroups

Detached in manner

Preferred discussing issues in intellectual rather than personal terms

Disinclined to make personal comments about other members

Disinclined to form special friendships

Oriented toward the group as a whole rather than toward particular members

Embarrassed when other members make personal comments about him

Unresponsive to gestures of friendship

Tended to discourage personal discussion between two other group members

Fight Statements

Ready to take sides in an argument

Tended to express annoyance toward other members of the group

Tended to become sarcastic when annoyed

Subtle in attacking others

Tended to start arguments

Critical of other members

Impulsive in expressing negative feelings

Prolonged or intensified arguments

Eager to respond to attack by counterattack

Tended to sidetrack the group from its goals

Flight Statements

Uncomfortable when negative feelings were expressed in the group

Reluctant to come to meetings

Didn't like to express negative or critical opinions

Inclined to mediate arguments

Preferred to remain neutral when several members of the group were arguing

Tried to avoid being drawn into an argument

Inclined to make light of ill feeling expressed

When attacked felt uncomfortable and remained silent

Uneasy during group disharmony

Tried not to show his true feelings

A CHECK LIST FOR APPRAISING A SECONDARY SCHOOL GUIDANCE PROGRAM [1]

Consider each item carefully. Then check it in the appropriate column: (1) Our program is strong in this respect. (2) Our program is fair in this respect but needs improvement. (3) Our program is very weak in this respect.

Administrative aspects of the program	Strong (1)	Fair (2)	Weak (3)
1. Does the administration provide adequate leadership in developing the guidance program?..............			
2. Are the resources of the faculty utilized by delegating appropriate guidance duties to various members?....			
3. Is the support of the community enlisted in the development of the guidance program through contacts with organizations which influence public opinion and might serve as resource groups?....................			
4. Are staff members encouraged to increase their understanding and competency through in-service training in guidance and other means?....................			
5. Does each counselor have a private office for counseling and the necessary facilities, clerical help, telephone service, etc., for carrying on his duties?............			
6. Is a reasonable counselor-student ratio maintained or being developed as new staff members are employed?.			
7. Does every student have opportunity for a periodic interview with a counselor and for further interviews as needed?.....................................			
8. Is the practice avoided of assigning to counselors duties which may be detrimental to their professional relationships with students?....................			

[1] From Donald E. Kitch and William H. McCreary, "Improving Guidance in Secondary Schools," *Bulletin of the California State Department of Education*, vol. 19, no. 8, December, 1950. Reprinted by permission of the authors.

Administrative aspects of the program (*Continued*)	Strong (1)	Fair (2)	Weak (3)
9. Are the needs of the guidance program specifically considered in making up the school budget?.........			
10. Has a qualified person been given direct responsibility for the operation of the guidance program?..........			
11. Has a guidance committee been established to serve as an advisory and coordinating body in matters involving guidance policies and practices?............			
12. Have members of the guidance staff worked out together a satisfactory statement of their respective functions and responsibilities?....................			
13. Have classroom teachers been adequately oriented to their roles in the guidance program?................			
14. Has effective liaison been established between the school guidance program and referral sources in the community, including any services provided by county or city school departments?................			
15. Have good working relationships been established between the guidance staff and staff members working in the areas of health, child welfare and attendance, special education, and related fields?................			
Orientation aspects of the program			
1. Does the school have a planned, regularly conducted program of orientation activities for new classes coming from feeder schools?.......................			
2. Does the school have such a program for students who transfer in at the beginning of or during the year?.....			
3. Have students, teachers, counselors, administrators, and parents been consulted in the planning of the program?....................................			
4. Is the program planned in terms of the transfer problems that students are likely to consider important rather than altogether in terms of what the teachers and administrators consider important?............			

Orientation aspects of the program (*Continued*)	Strong (1)	Fair (2)	Weak (3)
5. Have representatives of the sending schools, the county- or city-office guidance staff, and other interested parties been involved in planning the orientation activities?...................................			
6. Does the orientation program provide for the following:			
a. Conferences with parents?.........................			
b. The preparation, use, and transfer of cumulative records on all new students?.....................			
c. Planned visits to sending schools by staff members?.			
d. Recognition of incoming students with special learning problems?...........................			
e. Visits to the new campus by prospective students?..			
f. Student handbooks or other devices for giving new students information concerning the school and its program?...................................			
g. Activities to provide new students with an opportunity to get acquainted with each other and with students who have been in the school before?.....			
7. Are the orientation activities a part of a planned program of coordinating the educational philosophies, the teaching practices, the curriculum content, and the guidance services of the sending and receiving schools?.....................................			
Group-guidance aspects of the program			
1. Does the school have a planned program of group-guidance activities in connection with a homeroom system, a basic-course program, required courses, or special classes of a guidance nature?...............			
2. Is the group-guidance program planned to provide needed learning experiences for all students?.........			

Group-guidance aspects of the program (*Continued*)	Strong (1)	Fair (2)	Weak (3)
3. Are studies of the adjustment problems important to students made periodically to help develop the content of group-guidance activities?.................			
4. Are the units included in group guidance placed on grade levels appropriate to the physical, social, and emotional maturation of students?................			
5. Are group-guidance activities planned in such a way as to prepare students for making decisions that they are expected to make in connection with their school programs?.......................................			
6. Are the following topics covered by one or more units included in the curriculum as a part of the group-guidance program:			
a. Orientation to the school?......................			
b. Effective study habits and use of the library?.....			
c. Self-appraisal and self-understanding?...........			
d. Education and occupational planning?...........			
e. Effective human relationships?.................			
f. Applying for a job?...........................			
g. Use of leisure time?...........................			
h. Good mental and physical health practices?.......			
7. Do teachers of group-guidance activities generally have the personal traits and training necessary to effective teaching in this area?....................			
8. Are group-guidance teachers provided with necessary materials and teaching aids?.......................			
9. Is a planned program of in-service training carried on for group-guidance teachers?....................			

Group-guidance aspects of the program (*Continued*)	Strong (1)	Fair (2)	Weak (3)
10. Are special activities such as Career Conferences, College Days, Work Days, and special assemblies carried on at appropriate intervals as a part of the group-guidance program?................................			
11. Is the cocurricular program of the school used as a part of the group-guidance program?..............			
The information service			
1. Does the school maintain an adequate collection of school and college catalogues and other types of information about educational and training opportunities?..			
2. Does the collection cover opportunities such as junior colleges, vocational and trade schools, adult and evening schools, and apprenticeship programs?..........			
3. Does the school have a collection of books, pamphlets, and other materials on a wide range of occupations, which is kept up to date?........................			
4. Is the collection of occupational information easily available to counselors, teachers, and students?......			
5. Are the educational- and occupational-information materials used in connection with planned group activities which enable all students to become familiar with them and their uses?........................			
6. Are members of the school staff assigned specific responsibilities for keeping the materials up to date and in usable condition?............................			
7. Do the teachers regularly provide their classes with occupational information related to their respective subject-matter fields?............................			
8. Are individual students assisted to work out their educational-vocational plans through interviews with a trained counselor?................................			

Guidance-curriculum relationships	Strong (1)	Fair (2)	Weak (3)
1. Are studies made of the problems that young people feel to be important to them? Is this information used in the development of learning activities based upon such problems?.............................			
2. Is the guidance staff expected to analyze, organize, and present to the staff data on the individual characteristics of students for the purpose of assisting in the evaluation and improvement of the school's curriculum?...........			
3. Are students who would benefit by special curricular adaptations to individual handicaps or special abilities identified and reported to the staff?............			
4. Do teachers plan the content of their courses and their classroom activities with regard for available information concerning the problems, interests, and abilities of students?............................			
5. Is information concerning former students and their experiences after leaving the school collected and used in evaluating the curriculum?.....................			
6. Have units or courses been added to the curriculum recently as a result of studies of student characteristics and needs?...............................			
7. Have units or courses been dropped from the curriculum as the result of such studies?...............			
8. Have changes been made in the curriculum as the result of studies of the community?...............			
9. Does the curriculum provide an opportunity for students to make progress toward their individual goals and objectives?.................................			
10. Have the administrative, curricular, and instructional practices of the school been examined from the standpoint of good mental-health practices?.............			

REVIEW FORM: OCCUPATIONAL LITERATURE ACCORDING TO NVGA STANDARDS [1]

Occ. File No. _____

A. GENERAL PUBLICATION DATA

Coding _____

1. Title_____
2. Author(s)_____
3. Publisher_____Address_____
4. Date of Publication_____5. Number of pages_____Price_____

B. CONTENTS

Evaluation of the contents. Check the most appropriate description for each content item: D.N.A.—does not apply; A—adequate; I—inadequate; O—omitted.

D.N.A.	A	I	O	Content Items
_____	_____	_____	_____	History of the occupation
_____	_____	_____	_____	Duties and nature of the work
_____	_____	_____	_____	Need for workers—trends and outlook
_____	_____	_____	_____	Qualifications
_____	_____	_____	_____	Preparation—general education, special training, experience
_____	_____	_____	_____	Methods of entering and advancement
_____	_____	_____	_____	Related occupations
_____	_____	_____	_____	Earnings—wage range, other benefits
_____	_____	_____	_____	Working conditions, hours, hazards
_____	_____	_____	_____	Typical places of employment
_____	_____	_____	_____	Advantages and disadvantages
_____	_____	_____	_____	Sources of additional information
_____	_____	_____	_____	Scope of information presented (local, state, national)

C. STYLE AND FORMAT

1. Evaluation of the style and format. Check the most appropriate description: D.N.A.—does not apply, S—satisfactory, U—unsatisfactory, O—omitted.

[1] Courtesy of Ward W. Leis, Chairman, Guidance Information Review Service Committee, NVGA.

D.N.A.   *S*   *U*   *O*

————	————	————	————	Clear and concise
————	————	————	————	Interesting
————	————	————	————	Vocabulary adapted to intended readers
————	————	————	————	Pictorial illustrations
————	————	————	————	Charts, graphs, tables (properly titled and interpreted)
————	————	————	————	Table of contents or index
————	————	————	————	Cover color and design
————	————	————	————	Suggested readings

2. Type of binding. Check those that apply:

————thin paper cover   ————spiral binding
————heavy paper cover   ————ordinary cloth binding
————does not apply   ————other (specify)

3. Type of format. Check one:

————sheet   ————book
————sheets stapled   ————booklet
————leaflet   ————pamphlet

D. CLASSIFICATION AND LISTING

1. Type of publication. Check one:

A——Career fiction   I——Occupational or industrial descrip-
B——Biography   tion
C——Occupational monograph   J——Recruitment literature
D——Occupational brief   K——Poster or chart
E——Occupational abstract   L——Article or reprint
F——Occupational guide   M——Community survey, economic re-
G——Job series   port, job analysis
H——Business & industrial des-   N——Other (specify)————————
     criptive literature

2. Recommendation for listing. Check one:

1——Highly recommended
2——Recommended
3——Useful
4——Not recommended

3. Coding (as it is to appear when listed)————————————————————

4. Comments on and/or opinions of publication:

Reviewed by————————————————————
Date————————————————————

PROBLEMS IN VOCATIONAL PLANNING [1] (EXCERPTS)

Directions to students: On the basis of the information given, check the appropriate blanks and write in the numbers of the reasons (listed at the end of each exercise) which seem to support your choices.

Costume Designer
Fashion Illustrator
Buyer

Helen is an attractive high school girl, sixteen years old. She has a flair for clothes and would like to choose some occupation in the field of fashion. Although she is not good at sewing, she can select clothes which are very attractive and stylish without paying much for them. Her friends like to have her go with them on shopping trips to help them choose clothes which are stylish and yet practical. Helen has worked in a clothing store during summer vacation and has found that she likes sales work and has real ability in it. Helen's favorite subjects this year are bookkeeping and window display. She thought she would like her course in fashion illustration but has found she has little ability in sketching. Helen's aunt is a costume designer with a large clothing company.

The *costume designer* designs dresses, coats, etc., either sketching or draping the costume as she pictures it. She must be both creative and practical. She should know materials and should have had experience in both pattern drafting and sewing.

Advisable_____ Not Advisable_____ Reasons_____

The *fashion illustrator* sketches the latest fashions for magazines and newspapers.

Advisable_____ Not Advisable_____ Reasons_____

The *buyer* in a women's clothing store chooses and buys costumes from wholesalers. Very frequently a buyer is in charge of her department—the proper display of goods, the pricing of goods, keeping records, and general management. A buyer must understand people and their tastes. She must be practical as well as creative. A girl who wishes to be a buyer must usually begin as a salesgirl.

Advisable_____ Not Advisable_____ Reasons_____

[1] From California Guidance Bulletin no. 3 (revised) January, 1952, California State Department of Education, Bureau of Occupational Information and Guidance, Sacramento, Calif. Reprinted by permission of Donald E. Kitch, chief of the bureau. These materials are adapted from tests prepared by Georgia Sachs Adams.

Reasons:

1. Helen's aunt is a costume designer.
2. Helen selects her own clothes well.
3. She likes sales work.
4. She is interested in the field of fashion.
5. Her friends like to have her advice in selecting their clothes.
6. Window display is one of her favorite subjects.
7. Helen is not good at sketching.
8. She has what is known as style sense.
9. Helen has liked her course in bookkeeping.
10. She has real ability in sales work.
11. She is practical and considers the cost of different garments.
12. She is not good at sewing.

Secretary
Bookkeeper
Dictaphone Operator

Susan is interested in office work and has been taking a commercial course in high school. She has made good grades in bookkeeping and is good at operating calculators and other office machines. She also liked the typing courses very much and is a rapid typist. Although she has had two full years of shorthand, she cannot take dictation rapidly and still has difficulty in transcribing her notes. English has been one of Susan's favorite subjects. She can spell, punctuate, paragraph, and set up letters nicely on the page. Susan does not like to meet people because her nearsightedness makes thick glasses necessary. Susan sees quite well with her glasses but has to avoid too much strain on her eyes. Her hearing is unusually good.

One of the chief duties of a *secretary* is to take down in shorthand the letters, speeches, etc., of her employer, then to transcribe her notes. A secretary usually makes many personal contacts with many different kinds of people.

Advisable————— Not Advisable————— Reasons—————

A bookkeeper works with figures all day, recording purchases, sales, and other dealings in record books, preparing financial statements, etc. So much close work, often under electric light, is likely to cause eyestrain. Since bookkeeping machines are being used so much today, the demand for bookkeepers is likely to decrease.

Advisable————— Not Advisable————— Reasons—————

The demand for good *dictaphone operators* is increasing. When a dictaphone is used, the employer records letters, speeches, etc., on records, and the dictaphone operator plays the records on her transcribing machine and types what she hears. A dictaphone operator must be able to type rapidly and to spell, punctuate, and paragraph correctly.

Advisable————— Not Advisable————— Reasons—————

Reasons:
1. Susan has made good grades in bookkeeping.
2. She is a rapid typist.
3. She cannot take dictation or transcribe her notes rapidly.
4. She can spell, punctuate, and paragraph correctly.
5. She does not like to meet people.
6. Susan must avoid eyestrain.
7. Her hearing is unusually good.
8. She is good at operating calculators and other office machines.
9. Susan is interested in office work.
10. She can set up materials nicely on the page.
11. The demand for good dictaphone operators is increasing.
12. The demand for bookkeepers is decreasing.

Fireman
Fire-protection Engineer
Fire Inspector

Bob is one of the most popular boys in the junior class. He is husky, energetic, and active in athletics, public speaking, and school politics. His best grades are in public speaking, physics, and chemistry; in other subjects he is just average. Tests indicate that Bob is capable of making better grades. He is not too interested in routine classroom work. He likes laboratory work better. The counselor gave Bob a vocational interest test on which he scored highest in the persuasive or business contact area. On a mechanical aptitude test which measures ability to visualize geometric forms, his score was slightly above average.

A year ago his home burned, and Bob was impressed by the way the fire inspector determined the cause of the fire. Bob made friends with the inspector and has since accompanied him at every opportunity. Bob's parents have suggested that he plan to attend the university and study engineering as his older brother did. Because of the expense of the fire, they could not pay more than half of his college expenses. There is a junior college in town, which Bob could attend at little cost. Some technical work is offered there. Bob had a job as a file clerk last summer but did not like the inside, routine work.

A *fireman* must be at least twenty-one years of age, have physical strength and ability, have knowledge of the use and maintenance of fire-fighting equipment, and be dependable, calm, and unafraid in emergencies. Though not required, college training improves one's chances of advancement. Jobs at good pay are open in many fire departments. Promotion depends on merit, years of service, and the passing of qualifying examinations. Applicants must pass a civil service examination.

Advisable————— Not Advisable————— Reasons—————

A *fire-protection engineer* is a college graduate in engineering. His duties are concerned with the planned prevention and control of fire. His knowledge must cover a wide range of technical matters such as water supply and pressure; pipe, valve, and pump sizes and capacities; the design, arrangement, installation, and maintenance of automatic sprinkler and alarm controls; heating, ventilating, and light systems; fire resistance of various building materials; and construction methods. If he has not had basic training or experience in fire fighting, he will need to acquire this knowledge on the job and through study and the aid of his superiors.

Advisable_____ Not Advisable_____ Reasons_____

A *fire inspector* detects and eliminates fire hazards. He inspects fire-protection equipment and reports unsafe conditions or practices to the fire marshal, along with suggestions for their elimination. He may be assigned to determine the cause of a fire or to detect evidence of arson, to address public meetings, and to instruct classes in fire safety. Inspectors are employed in municipal and industrial fire departments and by insurance companies. They usually come up from the ranks of the fire department, having shown aptitude and interest in this type of work.

Advisable_____ Not Advisable_____ Reasons_____

Reasons:
1. With above-average intelligence Bob probably can succeed in college.
2. He can speak effectively before a group.
3. His scholastic work in high school was above average.
4. He seems to have a strong interest in the field of fire protection.
5. A fire-protection engineer needs a degree in engineering.
6. There is a junior college in his home town which offers some technical training.
7. If he attended the university, he would have to work part time to make expenses.
8. His achievement in mathematics was above average but not superior.
9. Bob has slightly above-average ability in visualizing spatial relationships.
10. His best grades have been in public speaking, chemistry, and mathematics.
11. His strongest measured interest is in the persuasive or business contact area.
12. Bob is a husky, athletic boy.
13. His parents would like to see him take an engineering course in college.
14. Bob's older brother is a successful engineer.

Economics Teacher
Bookkeeper
Statistician

A shy, rather retiring lad, Arden is an orphan, living with an aunt. His father left him an endowment that will see him through four years of college. Although he is very cooperative and will work behind the scenes on school projects when asked, he does not care to mix with the other fellows; yet he has a few close friends. Once in a while other fellows will ask him for help in arithmetic. He is usually asked to assist the student-body treasurer because, while he is never elected to the office, he is so systematic and conscientious that he keeps the books in "apple pie" order. He has made a rather impressive record in mathematics, algebra, geometry, and bookkeeping, getting almost straight "A's." He is also interested in civics, social science, and history. Although he gets good grades in other subjects, he doesn't show particular interest in them. He is an all-round good student and likes to read and study. His reading of the metropolitan newspaper is not confined to the funnies. He reads *Time* regularly. His teachers all agree that he has an analytical mind. He is greatly interested in economics.

An *economics teacher* in a high school or college instructs students in the theory and principles of this subject and the application of economic laws to contemporary problems of production, distribution, and consumption. He should like and understand young people and be socially competent. He must be able to present the subject matter in a clear, stimulating manner and enjoy group discussion. An M.A. or Ph.D. degree is required.

Advisable————— Not Advisable————— Reasons—————————

A *bookkeeper* keeps a complete and systematic set of records of all business transactions of an establishment. In a large firm he may work on a single section or phase of the records. He must be methodical, accurate, conscientious, and must like routine work. High ability in theoretical mathematics is not required. The high school graduate may secure adequate training for a beginning job in one to two years in a business school or junior college and advance to higher responsibilities as he gains experience.

Advisable————— Not Advisable————— Reasons—————————

A *statistician* at the professional level is a college graduate with a major in mathematics, economics, or other field of application, plus training in statistical theory and techniques. Mathematical aptitude, accuracy, ability to analyze and draw sound conclusions from masses of data, vision, and initiative characterize the successful statistician. Good jobs at good pay are open, for the present demand for these workers far exceeds the supply.

Advisable————— Not Advisable————— Reasons—————————

Reasons:
1. Arden is financially able to attend college for four years.
2. He has made high grades in bookkeeping and kept the school books.
3. He has demonstrated an aptitude for mathematics.
4. He is systematic, careful, and conscientious.
5. He is shy, rather retiring, not a "good mixer."
6. He is very cooperative and willing to help other students when asked.
7. He has an analytical mind.
8. He likes to read and study and is an all-round good student.
9. He is interested in social science, history, and current events.
10. He does not take much part in school activities.
11. His present interest is in the field of economics.
12. The field of statistics offers many opportunities.

PASADENA PUPIL JUDGMENT TEST [1] (EXCERPTS)

Directions to pupil: This is a test of how well you understand people. In each problem, you will read information about a boy or girl, you will choose one of the four reasons which you think may best explain that boy's or girl's behavior, and you will choose one of the four ways you think may be most helpful for handling the situation.

1. Mary is fifteen years old, the youngest of three children. She likes to read novels and go to motion pictures, and is always trying to imitate the heroine of some book or movie in her voice and manner. She seldom talks with other boys and girls or goes to the class parties. She does her homework well, often doing more than is required. However, she often fails to answer in class when the teacher calls on her, because she is daydreaming.

    a. Perhaps *one* of the chief reasons why Mary acts the way she does is that:
    1. She is lazy and finds it easier to dream than to listen to her teachers.
    2. She does not know how to concentrate.
    3. She has not found satisfaction in her regular daily life.
    4. She reads too much.
    5. She is not interested in schoolwork.

    b. Which *one* of the following procedures would help Mary the most?
    1. She should be helped to realize that she will never get any place by dreaming.
    2. She should be taught how to concentrate.
    3. She should be encouraged to imitate someone who is very worthwhile.
    4. She should be helped to make friends and develop many interests.
    5. She should not be allowed to read so much.

2. Don is an eighth-grade boy, fourteen years old. His father died when he was young, and Don has lived with his widowed mother and her parents. Don is always making funny remarks or doing clownish tricks in class and in the halls. Although he is not disliked by the boys and girls, he is never chosen as a leader in any group, and his friends seldom follow his suggestions as to what to do or where to go. The boys tease him and call him "Stubby" because he is small for his age. Don really likes his studies and does his homework well. However, during study period, he is often poking or pinching students seated near him, whispering, or writing amusing notes. Don's mother says he is just like his father, who always acted the clown.

    a. Perhaps *one* of the chief reasons why Don acts the way he does is that:
    1. He is trying to get even with the boys who tease him.
    2. He has inherited his father's disposition.

[1] Reprinted by permission of Georgia Sachs Adams. These are adaptations, as to form, of items in a previous test prepared by Harold C. Hand and the author for an evaluation study.

    3. He has found no better ways of gaining attention.

    4. He is just naturally mischievous.

    5. He is not interested in his schoolwork.

b. Which *one* of the following procedures would help Don the most?

    1. He should be kept after school whenever he disturbs the class.

    2. He should be helped to understand that he is making himself ridiculous.

    3. The other boys should not be allowed to tease him.

    4. His schoolwork should be made more interesting.

    5. He should be helped to develop some skill or interest through which he could win approval.

3. Kathryn has a disagreeable disposition. She does not take criticism well, is jealous of the other girls, and always has "a chip on her shoulder." She thinks the junior high school boys have poor manners and that the girls are snobbish. Her favorite pastime is reading. Although she seldom recites in class, she does her homework well and receives good grades. She is tall for her age and rather unattractive. Kathryn is a strong, husky girl. At home she helps with the younger children and the housework. She makes her own clothes and dresses neatly.

    a. Perhaps *one* of the chief reasons why Kathryn acts the way she does is that:

    1. She does not like boys and girls of her own age.

    2. Most of the junior high school girls are snobbish.

    3. Kathryn feels sensitive about her appearance.

    4. She is such a student and "bookworm" that she does not care whether others like her or not.

    5. Her ill temper is probably caused by poor health.

    b. Which *one* of the following procedures would help Kathryn the most?

    1. She should be helped to realize that her disposition is making her unpopular.

    2. Her classmates should treat her as rudely as she treats them.

    3. She should receive medical care.

    4. She should be left out of social affairs until her attitude improves.

    5. She should be helped to develop a pleasing personality.

4. Betty is a beautiful auburn-haired girl of sixteen. She is usually friendly and enthusiastic. She has the lead in the class play this year and has been outstanding in dramatics since she was in elementary school. Several times during rehearsals Betty has had a fit of temper because she could not have her own way. Her older brother says that since she was a small child she has often thrown herself on the davenport or the floor screaming when not allowed to do as she pleased. Betty's mother feels that she is the only one who understands Betty and her dramatic temperament. "Betty is strong-willed just like her grandfather," says the mother, "and the only way to handle her is to let her have what she wants."

    a. Perhaps *one* of the chief reasons why Betty acts the way she does is that:

    1. No one but her mother really understands her.

    2. Betty has a dramatic temperament.

    3. She has found no other way of gaining attention.

      4. She has inherited her grandfather's strong will.

      5. She has found an effective way of getting what she wants.

   b. Which *one* of the following procedures would help Betty the most?

      1. Everyone should try to avoid arousing Betty's temper.

      2. Betty should be disregarded when she has a fit of temper.

      3. Her friends should be helped to understand Betty's dramatic temperament so that they will make allowances for her.

      4. Betty should be allowed to have her own way in order not to break her will.

      5. The lead in the class play should be taken away from her.

5. Chester, an eighth-grade boy, is smaller than most boys his age. Although he likes sports, he is not able to run so fast or throw so far as the other boys in his physical education class. He still plays with the elementary school boys in his neighborhood, usually serving as pitcher in their ball games. He is usually seen with boys much younger than himself. Chester is not disliked by the boys and girls of his own grade level, but they often tease him about his size.

   a. Perhaps *one* of the chief reasons Chester acts the way he does is that:

      1. He is poor in athletics.

      2. He has not been in junior high school long enough to get acquainted.

      3. He feels inferior to boys his own age.

      4. He likes to serve as pitcher in baseball games.

      5. He does not like to be teased.

   b. Which *one* of the following procedures would help Chester the most?

      1. The younger boys should refuse to play with Chester.

      2. Chester should be given special practice in running and throwing.

      3. He should not be allowed to play with younger children.

      4. He should be helped to find activities in which he can succeed among boys and girls his own age.

      5. The older boys should be asked to stop teasing him.

6. Many of the boys do not like Tom because he always tries to "run the show." If some problem is being discussed in a class or club meeting, Tom tries to hold the floor too long and urge that his ideas be accepted. When he first came to junior high school, he was elected chairman of his homeroom. Most of the boys and girls felt he was too bossy, and the teacher had to remind him several times that other pupils should have a chance to make suggestions. Tom's friends say that he is very different at home. His father gives all the orders there and punishes any of the children who do not obey instantly. Tom does just as he is told without asking any questions.

   a. Perhaps *one* of the chief reasons Tom acts the way he does is that:

      1. His election as homeroom chairman "went to his head."

      2. The fact that he has no rights at home makes him want to boss everyone at school.

      3. Tom feels superior to other boys and girls.

      4. He has probably inherited his father's "bossy" disposition.

      5. He is naturally a good leader.

   b. Which *one* of the following procedures would help Tom the most?

      1. His friends should show him what it feels like to be bossed around.

2. He should be helped to understand why he likes to boss and "run the show."
3. He should be recognized as a promising young leader.
4. The teacher should punish him as his father does.
5. He should be helped to realize that he is becoming very unpopular.

7. Louise is fifteen years old, a good student in school and usually a member of the school honor society. She plays a good game of tennis or badminton. Many of her friends do not like to play with her, however, because she is such a poor loser. In fact if she loses two sets of tennis in a row, she will often refuse to play any more. She enjoys checkers, chess and many other games so long as she is winning. She likes to serve on school committees if she can be chairman. Louise is the only girl in the family but has four brothers who are several years older than she. Every member of the family is very fond of "little sister" as they call her and likes to see her win. Since the father is successful and all the boys are working, they are able to give Louise almost anything she likes in clothes, parties, and special trips.

a. Perhaps *one* of the chief reasons Louise acts the way she does is that:
1. Losing upsets her for she feels she has not done her best.
2. She wants to live up to her family's hopes for her.
3. Her love of sports and interest in games make her prize success in them.
4. She is used to having everything the way she wants it.
5. She has more ambition and will power than the average person.

b. Which *one* of the following procedures would help Louise the most?
1. Since success is so important to Louise, she should play with friends who are not as good in sports as she is.
2. Louise should be helped to realize that she is disliked for being a poor sport.
3. She should be encouraged in her desire to win in everything she does.
4. Louise's family should be helped to realize that they should be less indulgent with her.
5. She should be helped to improve her playing of tennis, checkers, and other games, so that she can win more frequently.

A BIBLIOGRAPHY OF VISUAL AIDS

The following motion pictures are recommended for illustrating and supplementing various concepts treated in this book. While the bibliography is reasonably inclusive, no attempt has been made to list all films bearing on the subject. Readers, if interested in locating additional films, including new releases, should consult the following references:

Motion Pictures on Child Life, Children's Bureau, U.S. Department of Health, Education, and Welfare, Washington 25, D.C.

Psychological Cinema Register. Pennsylvania State University, University Park, Pa.

Reviews of Medical Motion Pictures, American Medical Association, Chicago, Ill.

Film Reference Guide for Medicine and Allied Sciences, Public Health Service, U.S. Department of Health, Education, and Welfare, Atlanta, Ga.

All the motion pictures in the following bibliography are 16-mm films. Unless otherwise indicated, they are sound and black and white films; color and/or silent films are so identified. The running time of each film is given in minutes (min). The primary source and the date of production immediately follows the title of each film. Abbreviations used for the names of distributors are defined in the list of sources at the end of the bibliography.

The films are listed and described under three general headings descriptive of the character of the films and the nature of the audiences for whom they are intended, namely:

Part I. Professional films for professional personnel
Part II. Technique films for counselors and related guidance specialists
Part III. Practical films for students

PART I. Professional films for professional personnel

An Approach to Understanding Dynamics (VA, 1950, 34 min). Depicts an interview between a patient and a psychiatrist, analyzes the dynamics of the interview, and explains the patient's reactions to certain experiences and the meaning of these reactions to the psychiatrist.

Clinical Types of Mental Deficiency (Minn U, 1957, 40 min). Demonstrates, through performance testing, classification of mental deficients into morons, imbeciles, and idiots. Describes the eight major pathological groups of mental deficiency, using typical cases to illustrate each type.

404

Embryology of Human Behavior (IFB, 1951, 28 min, color). Describes the development of eye-hand coordination, beginning with intrauterine growth of the anatomic structure of eyes, hands, and central nervous system; shows the development of eye grasp, hand grasp, and prehension; illustrates the concept of reciprocal interweaving and the child's conquest of gravity; and demonstrates the rationale of clinical tests of child development. Produced by the Association of American Medical Colleges.

Hypnotic Behavior (Assn, 1949, 24 min). Demonstrates the induction of hypnotic trance, eye and arm catalepsy, abnormal sensory illusions, trance awakening, posthypnotic amnesia, and posthypnotic suggestion.

Mental Mechanisms (McGraw-Hill, 1947–1954). Five films, produced by the National Film Board of Canada, portraying case studies of adults with mental illnesses and tracing the causes of these illnesses, by means of dramatized flashbacks, to experiences in their childhood and youth. Produced for group therapy to be used under psychiatric leadership. The individual films are:

> *Breakdown* (40 min). Story of a young woman's schizophrenic breakdown, treatment, and recovery in a modern mental hospital.
>
> *Feeling of Hostility* (27 min). Reenactment of a case history demonstrating the importance of hostility in molding the character and shaping the life experiences of a girl from early childhood to adulthood.
>
> *Feeling of Rejection* (23 min). Case history of a neurotic young woman suffering from headaches and physical fatigue, and an explanation, through scenes of her early life, of the psychosomatic reasons for her physical ills.
>
> *Feelings of Depression* (30 min). Case history of a man in his early thirties who suffers periods of great despondency, and an explanation, through scenes of his early life, of the psychological reasons for his condition.
>
> *Overdependency* (32 min). Case study of a young man who has been crippled mentally and emotionally by overdependency upon his mother, sister, and wife.

Mental Symptoms (McGraw-Hill, 1952). Series of nine films demonstrating manifestations of various mental disorders. Showings restricted to professional personnel. Titles are:

> *Depressive States: I* (12 min)
> *Depressive States: II* (11 min)
> *Folie a Deux* (15 min)
> *Manic State* (15 min)
> *Organic Reaction–Senile Type* (10 min)
> *Paranoid Conditions* (13 min)
> *Schizophrenia: Hebephrenic Type* (13 min)
> *Schizophrenia: Catatonic Type* (12 min)
> *Schizophrenia: Simple Type Deteriorated* (11 min)

Stress and the Adaptation Syndrome (Pfizer, 1956, 35 min, color). Presents the concept of stress as developed by Dr. Hans Selye by recapitulating his original experiments and interpretation of them which led to the recognition of nonspecific biological stress. Demonstrates the stages of the general adaptation syndrome (alarm reaction, resistance, exhaustion) in a rat. Illustrates by animation the endocrine mechanism of stress.

PART II. Technique films for counselors and related guidance specialists

Administration of Projective Tests (PSU, 1951, 19 min). Burgess Meredith acts as subject to demonstrate a variety of standard projective tests (excluding Rorschach) such as TAT, Szondi, sentence completion, etc.

Age of Turmoil (McGraw-Hill, 1953, 20 min). Portrays early adolescence, ages thirteen to fifteen, and the behavior characteristics of giggling, noisiness, criticisms of school, daydreaming, and seemingly useless activities. Gives examples of different personality types and of various parent-child situations.

Angry Boy (IFB, 1951, 33 min). Portrays a boy caught stealing and his sympathetic treatment at a child-guidance clinic. Demonstrates the effect of unconscious motivation on the behavior of both children and adults.

Children's Fantasies (McGraw-Hill, 1956, 21 min). Explains how a child's fantasies develop and their effect upon the behavior and growth of children.

Client-centered Therapy. Part 1: A First Interview (PSU, 1952, 31 min). A documentary record of an initial interview between a psychologist and a female graduate student perturbed by social isolation.

Client-centered Therapy. Part 2: Therapy in Process; the 32nd Interview (PSU, 1952, 30 min). Presents an essentially continuous record of an interview between a psychologist and a middle-aged married woman troubled by her relationships with her husband and daughter.

Common Fallacies about Group Differences (McGraw-Hill, 1957, 15 min). Analyzes seven common notions about races, heredity, and group differences in the light of known scientific evidence, and shows how each one is fallacious.

Conflict (McGraw-Hill, 1956, 18 min). Dramatizes four basic types of conflict in problem situations familiar to college students as illustrated with rats under laboratory-controlled situations.

Counseling Adolescents (McGraw-Hill, 1955). Series of three films designed for use in training counselors. Titles and running times are:

    A Counselor's Day (11 min)
    Diagnosis and Planning Adjustments in Counseling (18 min)
    Using Analytical Tools (14 min)

Counseling—Its Tools and Techniques (Mahnke, 1948, 22 min). Portrays a counselor interviewing a high school student; illustrates his preparation for the interview, establishment of proper relationships, identification and analysis of problem, planning a course of action, and followup to the interview.

Development of Individual Differences (McGraw-Hill, 1957, 13 min). Points out that no two individuals are alike and that differences result from both heredity and environment. Reviews and illustrates what is known and generally accepted about the relative influence of those two factors.

Emotional Health (McGraw-Hill, 1948, 20 min). Shows that emotional upsets are common among people of college age; explains that if a disturbance of this kind is prolonged, a need for professional counsel and care is indicated; and demonstrates the basic techniques of psychiatric treatment.

Experimental Studies in Social Climates of Groups (Iowa U, 1940, rev. 1953, 31 min). Shows the behavior of groups of boys organized in clubs run on democratic principles, as an autocracy, and as a laissez-faire group. Shows responses when groups are changed from one type to another.

Facing Reality (McGraw-Hill, 1954, 12 min). Illustrates and explains some common defense mechanisms—rationalization, projection, negativism—and some typical escape mechanisms such as daydreaming, identification, suppression, and malingering.

Fears of Children (IFB, 1951, 30 min). Dramatizes some of the emotional problems of a five-year-old boy, his fears of the dark, of being alone, of new situations. Explains that these fears are common to children of his age and are accentuated when parents become either unduly protective or overly severe.

Giving the Rorschach Test: Klopfer Method (PSU, 1951, 9 min, color). After introductory remarks, gives a brief outline presentation of the Klopfer method with a single subject. Employs actual Rorschach cards.

Group Discussion (McGraw-Hill, 1954, 10 min). Illustrates the various check points in group discussion, the basic types of group discussions, and the responsibilities of the leader.

He Acts His Age (McGraw-Hill, 1951, 13 min, color or black and white). An over-all picture of a child's emotional, physical, and psychological growth from one to fifteen years of age.

Importance of Goals (McGraw-Hill, 1950, 10 min). Illustrates through the case study of a thirteen-year-old that education is essentially a process of attaining meaningful goals.

In Time of Trouble (McGraw-Hill, 1954, 14 min). Portrays the family minister counseling a young married couple and helping them understand the reasons for their disagreements and ways in which satisfactory adjustments can be made.

Individual Differences (McGraw-Hill, 1950, 23 min). Case study of a shy, slow child who is different from his classmates and his older brother. Points out the need to recognize differences among individuals.

It Takes All Kinds (McGraw-Hill, 1950, 20 min). Portrays a series of young couples reacting to tense situations, relates their reactions to their possibilities for marriage success or failure, and emphasizes the point that marriage partners should be carefully chosen.

Judging Emotional Behavior (CW Films, 1953, 20 min). Motion picture test designed to measure the sensitivity of individuals to the emotions of others. Ten sequences are shown in which two people react as if certain events described by a narrator were happening to them.

Meaning of Adolescence (McGraw-Hill, 1953, 16 min). An overview of the social, emotional, mental, and physical changes which occur in the adolescent between childhood and adulthood.

Our Invisible Committees (NEA, 1951, 25 min). Explores the point of view that one of the important obstacles to group thought and decision making is the conflict of social pressures which operate within individuals during a meeting. Presents a case study of such a group.

Sibling Relations and Personality (McGraw-Hill, 1956, 22 min). Demonstrates relationships that a child has with his brothers and sisters throughout the developmental years and explains their importance in the shaping of personalities.

Sibling Rivalries and Parents (McGraw-Hill, 1956, 11 min). Describes the reasons for rivalry among brothers and sisters, its various manifestations, and methods of coping with the resultant frictions.

Social-Sex Attitudes in Adolescence (McGraw-Hill, 1953, 22 min). Portrays a boy and a girl taken through their entire adolescent experience, their early sex education, awareness of the opposite sex, dating, finding common interests, falling in love, and marrying.

A Technique for Measuring Minimal Social Behavior (VA, 1957, 12 min, color). Demonstrates the administration and scoring of a test designed to measure the minimal social behavior of severely withdrawn psychiatric patients.

Testing Intelligence with Stanford-Binet (Ind U, 1950, 18 min). Gives an overview of the types of items on an intelligence test and the method of administering the test.

Unconscious Motivation (Assn, 1949, 38 min). Film record of hypnosis of two subjects during which an experimental neurotic conflict is produced, allowed to manifest itself in the posthypnotic state, and then relieved by aiding the subjects to recall the implanted traumatic material through the interpretation of manifest dream signals and free association to modified psychological projective tests.

When Should I Marry? (McGraw-Hill, 1958, 19 min). A minister advises a young couple, eager to marry, by describing the experiences of two other couples who married at an early age.

PART III. Practical films for students

Basic Study Skills (Cor, n.d.). Twenty-one films, each 11 min, color or black and white, with the following self-explanatory titles:

> *Building an Outline*
> *Developing Imagination*
> *Do Better on Your Examinations*
> *Find the Information*
> *Homework: Studying on Your Own*
> *How to Concentrate*
> *How to Develop Interest*
> *How to Judge Authorities*
> *How to Judge Facts*

> *How to Observe*
> *How to Prepare a Class Report*
> *How to Read a Book*
> *How to Remember*
> *How to Study*
> *How to Think*
> *How to Write Your Term Paper*
> *How We Learn*
> *Improve Your Study Habits*
> *Know Your Library*
> *Learning from Class Discussion*
> *Look It Up!*

Habit Patterns (McGraw-Hill, 1954, 15 min). Portrays, by contrasting two adolescent girls, the effects of disorderly habits on personality and social life.

Personality and Emotions (EBF, 1955, 13 min). Designed for high school and college audiences studying personality development and mental health. Gives an overview of the development of emotions leading toward the achievement of emotional maturity.

Successful Scholarship (McGraw-Hill, 1954, 11 min). Describes a schedule of good study procedures and routines following a plan-place-method technique, and illustrates the techniques through a portrayal of experiences of an average college student.

Understand Your Emotions (Cor, 1950, 14 min). Demonstrates various aspects of the psychology of emotional behavior, and discusses emotional responses, their physiological accompaniments, and the conditioning of emotions.

Main sources of listed films

Assn–Association Films, Inc., 347 Madison Ave., New York 17, N.Y.

Cor–Coronet Instructional Films, 65 E. South Water St., Chicago 1, Ill.

CW Films–Churchill-Wexler Film Productions, 801 N. Seward St., Los Angeles 38, Calif.

EBF–Encyclopaedia Britannica Films, Wilmette, Ill.

IFB–International Film Bureau, Inc., 332 S. Michigan Ave., Chicago 4, Ill.

Ind U–Indiana University, Bloomington, Ind.

Iowa U–State University of Iowa, Iowa City, Iowa.

Mahnke–Carl Mahnke Productions, 215 E. 3d St., Des Moines, Iowa.

McGraw-Hill–McGraw-Hill Book Company, Inc., Text-Film Dept., 330 W. 42d St., New York 36, N.Y.

Minn U–University of Minnesota, Minneapolis, Minn.

NEA–National Education Association, 1201 16th St., N.W., Washington 6, D.C.

Pfizer–Pfizer Laboratories, Film Library, 630 Flushing Ave., Brooklyn 6, N.Y.

PSU–Pennsylvania State University, University Park, Pa.

VA–Veterans Administration, Washington 25, D.C.

NAME INDEX

Adams, Georgia S., 25, 48, 395n., 400n.
Albrecht, Ruth, 74
Allen, P. J., 295
Allen, Richard D., 40, 75, 121, 122, 298
Allport, Gordon W., 380
Anderson, H. D., 295
Anderson, Harold H., 222
Anderson, Kenneth E., 322
Andrews, Margaret E., 296
Apostal, Robert, 25
Arbuckle, Dugald S., 25, 175, 198, 201
Argyle, Michael A., 380
Armstrong, William H., 223
Arnold, Dwight L., 174
Asch, S. E., 95
Atreya, B. L., 201
Austin, Alexander W., 160
Ausubel, David P., 75, 145n., 161

Babbidge, Homer D., Jr., 324
Bach, George R., 121n., 149, 151, 161
Baer, Max F., 274, 296, 299
Bailard, Virginia, 325
Bales, Robert F., 113, 134
Ballin, Marian R., 48
Balser, Benjamin H., 161
Barbe, Walter B., 134
Barker, J. Cecil, 222
Barr, John, 175
Bartlett, Sir Frederic, 223
Bass, Bernard M., 74, 95, 223
Bath, John A., 75
Bauer, W. W., 325
Bauernfeind, Robert H., 74, 262
Beachley, Catherine, 296
Beery, Mary, 325
Benezet, Louis T., 380
Benne, Kenneth D., 134
Bennett, Edith, 95
Bennett, G. K., 275n.
Bennett, M. E., 25, 48, 201, 222–223, 243n., 262, 325
Bentley, Edward, 222
Berdie, Ralph F., 67n., 295
Berenda, Ruth W., 95
Berg, C. C., 201
Berg, Irwin A., 74, 223
Berger, Emanuel M., 262
Berman, Deborah, 363
Biber, Barbara, 169–170, 175
Billet, Roy O., 325, 362
Bingham, Alma, 134
Bion, W. R., 83, 149, 161
Bird, Dorothy, 62, 63, 74

Blackwood, Paul E., 223
Blaine, Graham B., Jr., 75
Blake, Walter S., 202, 222, 223
Blecha, Edward J., 184, 186–187, 200
Bloch, Herbert A., 363
Blocher, Donald H., 293, 298
Block, Virginia Lee, 344, 362
Bloom, Benjamin S., 134
Boltz, Joseph K., 134
Bonner, Hubert, 96
Bonney, Merle E., 161
Bookman, Gladys, 48
Bordin, E. S., 293, 298
Borgatta, Edgar F., 135
Boroff, David, 323
Borow, Henry, 17, 25, 48, 171–172, 175, 278, 297
Bossing, Nelson L., 48
Botel, Morton, 223
Bower, Eli, 323
Bowles, Frank H., 324
Bowman, Fred Q., 200
Boyd, Gertrude A., 296
Brammer, Lawrence M., 25, 200
Brewer, John M., 325
Brinton, Crane, 367, 379
Broder, Lois J., 134
Broedel, John, 161
Browning, Robert, 314
Brownstein, Samuel C., 324
Brundage, Erven, 297
Brunelle, Peggy, 363
Buchanan, Daniel C., 201
Bucher, Charles A., 325
Bugenthal, James F. T., 262
Bullis, H. Edmund, 351, 363
Burgess, E. W., 63
Burkel, Christian E., 324
Burton, William Henry, 223
Busaker, William E., 200
Butler, John, 95
Byrd, Oliver E., 363
Byrn, Delmond K., 325

Caldwell, Edson, 135, 162, 345, 362
Caplan, Stanley W., 15, 25, 157
Caplow, Theodore, 295
Carpenter, Marjorie, 362, 380
Carrel, Alexis, 225, 261
Carter, Edward M., 291n., 294, 298
Cartwright, Dorwin, 80, 94
Cass, John C., 321, 323
Casteel, John L., 48
Castore, George F., 123, 134
Cattell, Raymond, 250, 262, 263
Cavan, Ruth S., 63, 74

Chandler, John Roscoe, 201, 223
Chapman, A. L., 58, 74
Christiansen, Harley D., 263
Cieslak, Edward C., 201
Clark, Walter Houston, 380
Cleary, Florence D., 135
Coe, George A., 33n.
Coffield, Kenneth E., 363
Cohen, Dorothy H., 263
Cohen, Nathan M., 324
Cohn, Benjamin, 161, 313, 323
Cole, Luella, 223
Coleman, James S., 348, 362
Coleman, William, 175
Collins, A. E., 364
Combs, Arthur W., 99, 100, 133
Connor, Frances P., 323
Cooley, Charles Horton, 242, 262, 367
Copeland, Theodore H., Jr., 48, 192, 198, 200
Corman, Bernard R., 214, 222
Corsini, Raymond J., 29, 47, 139, 144, 160, 161
Costar, James W., 175
Cottingham, Harold F., 25, 175
Cottle, William C., 263
Cowley, W. H., 25
Cribben, James J., 325
Crites, John O., 135, 263, 270, 296, 298
Crocker, Mary, 222
Cronbach, Lee J., 247, 252, 255n., 261
Crutchfield, Richard S., 95
Cuony, E. R., 289, 294

Daane, Calvin J., 201
Dailey, Charles A., 74
D'Amico, Louis A., 85, 95
Danielson, Paul J., 262
Danskin, David G., 273, 296
Darley, John, 298
Davidson, P. E., 295
Davis, Donald A., 364
Davis, Ruth G., 161
Deese, James, 223
De Gabriel, Eugene, 201
De Haan, Robert F., 75
Detjen, Ervin W., 135, 201, 364
Detjen, Mary F., 135, 201, 364
Deutsch, Morton, 94, 95
Dickinson, Carl, 262, 296
Dodge, Raymond, 362
Doermann, Henry J., 37
Dollard, John, 207, 222, 230, 231, 261, 295
Donham, Wallace Brett, 123, 134
Downie, N. M., 263

411

SUBJECT INDEX